For Isabelle, Alexander, Joe and Abigail

Contents

List of figures and tables

Figures

Tables

List of contributors

Tony Addy, head of international education, Diaconia University of Applied Sciences, Finland
tony.addy@diak.fin

Janki Andharia, professor, Tata Institute of Social Sciences, India
andharia@tiss.edu

Gaby Atfield, research associate, Institute for Employment Research, University of Warwick, UK
g.j.atfield@warwick.ac.uk

Patricia Bell, research associate, Evangelische Hochschule, University of Applied Sciences, Darmstadt, Germany
bell@efh–darmstadt.de

Heather Blakey, researcher, International Centre for Participation Studies, University of Bradford, UK
h.blakey2@student.bradford.ac.uk

Kavita Brahmbhatt, consultant, Regional Support Hub, Office of the United Nations High Commissioner for Refugees
kibiriti@hotmail.com

Lisa Brophy, director of research, Mind Australia and senior research fellow, Centre for Population Health, Policy and Economics, University of Melbourne
lbrophy@mindaustralia.org.au lbrophy@unimelb.edu.au

Philip Brown, research fellow, Salford Housing and Urban Studies Unit, University of Salford, UK
p.brown@salford.ac.uk

Liam Buckley, consumer consultant, St Vincent's Mental Health, Melbourne, Australia
liam.buckley@svhm.org.au

Stephanie Burns, PhD student, Centre for Research in Political Psychology and School of Education, Queen's University Belfast, Northern Ireland, UK
sburns08@qub.ac.uk

Jim Campbell, director, Centre for Lifelong Learning and Community Engagement, Goldsmiths, University of London, UK
j.campbell@gold.ac.uk

Jenifer Cartland, research associate professor, Northwestern University Medical School, and director, Child Health Data Lab. Children's Memorial Research Center, USA
jcartland@childrensmemorial.org

Bagele Chilisa, professor of research and evaluation methodologies, Department of Educational Foundations, University of Botswana
chilisab@mopipi.ub.bw

Rapelang Chilisa, lecturer in psychology, Department of Psychology, Faculty of Social Sciences, University of Botswana
rapelang.chilisa@mopipi.ub.bw

Andrew Clark, lecturer, School of English, Sociology, Politics and Contemporary History, University of Salford, UK
a.clark@salford.ac.uk

Nadine Cocks, consumer consultant, Mind Australia
ncocks@mindaustralia.org.au

Martin Daly, service user consultant, Belfast Health and Social Care Trust, Northern Ireland, UK
martin.p.daly@belfast.hscni.net

Gavin Davidson, lecturer in social work, Queen's University Belfast, Northern Ireland, UK
gavin.davidson@qub.ac.uk

Lisa Goodson, lecturer, Institute of Applied Social Studies, University of Birmingham, UK
l.j.goodson@bham.ac.uk

Aitor Gómez, lecturer, Department of Education, Universitat Rovira i Virgili, Spain
aitor.gomez@urv.cat

Hameed Hakimi, independent research consultant, UK
hameed_hakimi@yahoo.com

Kieran Halloran, group operations manager, Packaged Services, Mind Australia
khalloran@mindaustralia.org.au

Neeta Hardikar, founder member and executive director, Area Networking and Development Initiatives, India
neeta.hardikar@gmail.com

Moira Harper, carer advocate, CAUSE, Northern Ireland, UK
moira@cause.org.uk

Caroline Holland, research fellow, Faculty of Health and Social Care, Open University, UK
c.a.holland@open.ac.uk

Patricia Jones, research associate, Third Sector Research Centre, University of Birmingham, UK
pajok222@yahoo.co.uk

Ricky Joseph, research fellow, Institute of Applied Social Studies, University of Birmingham, UK
r.joseph@bham.ac.uk

Sakari Kainulainen, director of research, Diaconia University of Applied Sciences, Finland
sakari.kainulainen@diak.fin

Damien Kavanagh, student social worker, Queen's University Belfast, Northern Ireland, UK
dkavanagh02@qub.ac.uk

Barbara Kawulich, associate professor, Educational Innovation Department, University of West Georgia, USA
bkawulic@westga.edu

Louise Kilburn, community activist, Bradford, UK
louisekilburn@live.co.uk

Katarzyna Koterba, doctoral researcher, School of Social Work, University of Central Lancashire, UK
k.koterba@hotmail.com

Jayne Lewis, project officer, Mental Health Service Development Unit, St Vincent's Mental Health, Australia
jayne.lewis@svhm.org.au

Melinda Madew, lecturer, University of Applied Sciences, Ludwigsburg, Germany
madew@gmx.de

Rosemary Mann, research fellow, McCaughey Centre, University of Melbourne, Australia
rmann@unimelb.edu.au

Terri Mannarini, associate professor of social psychology, University of Salento, Italy
terrimannarini@hotmail.com

Maryann Mason, associate director, Child Health Data Lab, Children's Memorial Hospital, USA
mmason@childrensmemorial.org

Claire McCartan, research assistant, Institute of Child Care Research, Queen's University Belfast, Northern Ireland, UK
c.j.mccartan@qub.ac.uk

E.-J. Milne, research fellow, School of Applied Social Sciences, University of Stirling, UK
elisabeth.milne@stir.ac.uk

Pat Niner, honorary senior lecturer and foundation fellow, Centre for Urban and Regional Studies, University of Birmingham, UK
p.m.niner@bham.ac.uk

Ann-Marie O'Brien, project manager, Women's Mental Health, Royal Ottowa Health Care Group and School of Social Work, Carleton University, Canada
aobrien@rohcg.on.ca

Tamra Ogletree, associate professor, Collaborative Support and Intervention Department, University of West Georgia, USA
togletre@westga.edu

Therese O'Toole, lecturer, School of Sociology, Politics and International Studies, University of Bristol, UK
therese.otoole@bristol.ac.uk

Melissa Petrakis, senior research fellow, St Vincent's Mental Health, Melbourne, and lecturer, Department of Social Work, Monash University, Australia
melissa.petrakis@svhm.org.au

Jenny Phillimore, senior lecturer, Institute of Applied Social Studies, University of Birmingham, UK
j.a.phillimore@bham.ac.uk

Holly Ruch-Ross, researcher, Child Health Data Lab, Children's Memorial Hospital, USA
hruchross@aol.com

Dirk Schubotz, young life and times director, ARK, School of Education, Queen's University Belfast, Northern Ireland, UK
d.schubotz@qub.ac.uk

Karen Schwartz, associate professor, School of Social Work, Carleton University, Canada
karen_schwartz@carleton.ca

Matthew Scott, consumer consultant, St Vincent's Mental Health, Australia
matthew.scott@svhm.org.au

Lisa Scullion, research fellow, Salford Housing and Urban Studies Unit, University of Salford, UK
l.scullion@salford.ac.uk

Terese Sordé Marti, professor of sociology, Immigration and Ethnic Minorities Studies Group, Universitat Autonoma de Barcelona, Spain
teresa.sorde@uab.cat

Michael Stylianou, consumer consultant, Mind Australia
mstylianou@mindaustralia.org.au

Bogusia Temple, professor of health and social care research, School of Social Work, University of Central Lancashire, UK
btemple1@uclan.ac.uk

Adje van de Sande, associate professor, School of Social Work, Carleton University, Canada
adje_vandesande@carleton.ac.ca

Maretha Visser, professor, Department of Psychology, University of Pretoria, South Africa
maretha.visser@up.ac.za

Richard Ward, project worker, Ageing and Mental Health, University of Manchester, UK
richard.ward@manchester.ac.uk

Deborah Warr, senior research fellow, McCaughey Centre, University of Melbourne, Australia
djwarr@unimelb.edu.au

Richard Williams, PhD student, Swimburne Institute for Social Research, Australia
richardwilliams@groupwise.swin.edu.au

Acknowledgements

The inspiration for this book has come from many different places and people. The beginning of our journey into community research started when we evaluated a Single Regeneration Budget (SRB)-funded young offenders programme some ten years ago and realised that the only way we would find out what young offenders really thought of the training programmes they were on and what type of interventions could reduce reoffending rates would be to encourage them to work together to explore their own experiences. From this beginning a new way of working emerged, which we honed over many years until we were able to develop a programme that was accredited at a range of different levels. Over this time some 80 or so people from different backgrounds including young homeless people, small-community group leaders and new migrants have participated in our programmes and undertaken research into a number of issues such as mental health, homelessness, unemployment and community cohesion. Throughout this period we have learned so much from those individuals, both in terms of pedagogical skills and experiential knowledge. We are profoundly grateful to them and the organisations that sponsored these research programmes including the Joseph Rowntree Foundation, HACT, Barrow Cadbury Trust, Progress GB funded by the European Refugee Fund and the Digbeth Trust. In particular we thank Emma Stone, Dipali Chandra, Heather Petch, Devan Kanthasamy for their support, advice and guidance, and their willingness to take what some might consider as a risk.

We are eternally grateful to Ann Bolstridge, our loyal supportive friend and colleague, whose contribution has been invaluable. Without her support the process would have been much less manageable and less enjoyable. We should also thank other colleagues who have worked with us over the years in developing our approach, particularly Deborah Hennessy, Ricky Joseph, Pat Jones, Helen Thompson and Jayne Thornhill. We have stayed in touch with many community researchers. They have continued to contribute to research projects and have become both professional colleagues and friends. We thank them for their ongoing support.

Throughout the life of this project we have faced a number of personal challenges, the best of which has been the arrival of Isabelle and Alexander Goodson-Thabet. We are grateful to our friends and family for their continued support both with these challenges and with the writing of the book.

Part One

Theoretical and methodological issues

One

Community research: opportunities and challenges

Lisa Goodson and Jenny Phillimore

Introduction

The contributions in this book, and the level of international interest sparked by our original call for chapters, are testimony to a growing research movement interested in community research. In recent years, academics as well as practitioners, research funders and evaluation commissioners have realised that those traditionally viewed as research objects possess skills, knowledge and expertise that can enable them to make a wide range of valuable contributions to research projects. Engaging members of different communities to research social life, problems or processes within their own communities can bring new dimensions and perspectives to research questions and can bring insider knowledge about social life within communities rarely reached by 'outside' researchers (see Goodson and Phillimore, 2010). In this book we use the term 'community research' to distinguish the approach from other more familiar and more widely documented practices such as community-based participatory research (CBPR) or community-based research (CBR): whereby research is conducted as an equal partnership and community members are involved in all aspects of the research process (see Minkler and Wallerstain, 2003, 2008; Strand et al, 2003; Israel et al, 2005), participatory action research (PAR) or simply action research (AR): where through the participation of community members, projects are concerned with collectively improving the quality of their community or the area concerned and may be ideologically or politically motivated (see Reason and Bradbury, 2001; Stringer, 2007). Each of these approaches aims to empower community members. This book is not about empowering communities per se, although empowerment may be implicit or even explicit in some community research projects. This book is about how to involve communities in the production of knowledge.

While community research has been employed by both academics and practitioners in a number of fields, such as education, health and social care, housing, psychology and community development, there is a dearth of systematically collected knowledge and reflective accounts about the

3

approach, including its implementation and impact. This book helps to bridge a gap in knowledge by considering both theoretical and practical issues, from a range of different perspectives and disciplines, with a view to stimulating thinking about how methodological advancements can be made in the field of community research. As well as being of practical help to those wishing to adopt a community research approach, we hope that this book will encourage thinking about the epistemological, ontological and methodological questions and challenges relating to community research.

Community research and social science

A range of different terms have been used to refer to methodologies that aim to draw on 'local', 'emic' or 'insider' knowledge through the involvement of community members, including 'action', 'participatory' and 'empowerment' research to, more recently, the use of the term 'community' research, which encompasses 'peer', 'citizen' and 'user' research practice. In this edited collection, community research is defined as the practice of engaging community members as co-researchers to research issues within their own communities with a view to accessing community specific knowledge. We recognise, however, that communities are not necessarily bound by spatial proximities or localised interpersonal relationships, but can also exist beyond geographical locations as communities of shared interest or common experience.

The community research approach ultimately involves collaboration between professional social researchers, funding agencies and the group or organisation being researched, to utilise 'community-based knowledge' to create new knowledge for the purpose of deepening our understanding or building theory about a particular community or issue, or to stimulate action-oriented outcomes and policy change. The community research process can sometimes involve a period of training to prepare community members (general citizens, service users) to work alongside professional researchers, be they academics, consultants or practitioners, in all, or part, of the research process. Unlike traditional research in which researchers generate research themes and interpret findings, but similar to some of the participatory or action research approaches outlined above, community research often involves community members in shaping research agendas, owning the research process and reaching collaborative conclusions (see Goodson and Phillimore, 2010).

Arnstein (1969) argues that equipping communities with the skills to have some control in the development of their own knowledge base and some control and power to bring about change can improve the quality of their own lives. For her, this approach is at the highest level of achievement on the ladder of participation, which ranges from manipulation and non-participation on the bottom rung through to citizen control and power at the top. Participation is a nebulous concept and can mean different things to different people. A review of the participation literature (Brodie et al, 2009), which explored the range of participation activities people engage in, identified three categories of participation. The first is public or 'vertical participation', whereby individuals engage with the state, democratic structure and institutions, such as getting involved in government consultations, for example. The second is social or 'horizontal participation', which refers to the activities in which individuals engage collectively, such as being a member of a community group. The third is individual or 'everyday politics', which refers to the choices individuals make on a day-to-day basis which are statements about the type of society in which they wish to live, such as buying fair trade goods, signing petitions or supporting a worthy cause.

The contributions in this book illustrate the diversity, different interests and contexts in which community can, and is, used. Contributions range from discussions of fully participatory and action-oriented research projects (see Gomez et al, this volume) to more traditional research approaches that involve members of the community as data collectors (see Brown et al, this volume). The rationale for including a diverse range of projects is to enable the exploration of theoretical, methodological and practical issues and to illuminate the challenges, as well as the strengths and weaknesses associated with different community research approaches. Although all projects share common ground in involving communities in the research process in some way, the extent to which communities have power or control over the research process differs markedly. Different types of community research projects can be represented on a continuum, illustrated in Figure 1.1, according to the breadth and depth of community involvement, the stage at which community members become involved and the level of power and autonomy community members have over the research process. Furthermore, the projects vary in the extent to which they aim to promote action to resolve social problems or inequalities. While participatory approaches, aiming to improve the lives of individuals through empowering communities or improve their capacity to facilitate change, have been argued to be the most desirable way to conduct research (Greenwood and Levin, 1998), we need to acknowledge that in reality this is not always the way projects play out in practice for a whole range of different reasons. Even those projects that start with the best of intentions may be constrained by factors such as the overall project aim (often defined by the project funder/sponsor) and duration of projects, research budgets, interests of different actors, and lack of resources.

The chapters in this book demonstrate a variety of different models of community research, with varying levels of involvement, empowerment, participation and impact on people, policy and practice. The activities and

Figure 1.1 The relationship between community researchers' level of involvement and power and control

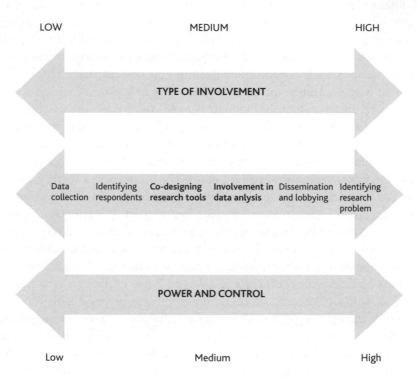

actions involved in community research projects can straddle one, or all three, types of participation outlined in Brodie et al's (2009) model. Type of participation is influenced by the focus of projects; the way they are managed and the level of community researcher involvement in shaping the research agenda; their role in the interpretation of research findings; the extent to which they are involved in 'action'-type lobbying or change-seeking activities and individual progression onto other projects, work or training. The chapters in this book demonstrate that models of community research can be conceived of as 'joint endeavours' wherein community and professional researchers come together in a bid to access local or insider knowledge.

The concept of 'local knowledge' has been a preoccupation of scholars from different disciplines for many years, including Anthropology (see Geertz, 1973, 1983), Sociology (see Berger and Luckman, 1966) and Planning (see Arnstein, 1969). In the 1960s and 1970s planning scholars (Gans, 1968; Arnstein, 1969; Kramer, 1969; Gilbert and Eaton, 1970; Pivan and Cloward, 1977) sought to oppose models that relied on technical planners making decisions on behalf of local residents, without taking account of local knowledge. Around the same time the works of Freire

(1972) in developmental education and his seminal piece, Pedagogy of the Oppressed, expressed the importance of dialogue and practice that, rather than involving individuals to act on each other, entailed them working with one another. His preoccupation with the production of dialogue not only adds to knowledge but makes a difference to, and is situated in, the lived experience of participants and opened up new ways of working within educational practices which has since traversed disciplinary boundaries. Geertz's work on local knowledge (1983) and his earlier arguments focusing on 'thick description' (1973) led to what has become known as 'the interpretive turn', which refers to the 'turn[ing] from trying to explain social phenomena by weaving them into grand textures of cause and effect to trying to explain them by placing them in local frames of awareness' (Geertz, 1983: 6). The works of Berger and Luckman (1966) and those engaged in feminist standpoint theory (see Haraway, 1988; Alcoff and Potter, 1993) further strengthen the belief that social realities relate to personal experience and as such are 'situated' rather than universalised. Thinking about 'local knowledge' as situational and developing out of lived experiences, places it in a phenomenological context as a legitimate and valuable source of knowledge (Yanow, 2004).

Community research aims to bring together both local and experiential knowledge to form what we refer to in this book as 'community' knowledge. From a methodological point of view community research has its roots in 'participatory', 'action' and 'empowerment' research (Fals-Borda and Rahman, 1991; Tolley and Bentley, 1996; Kemmis and McTaggart, 2000; Reason and Bradbury, 2001; Coghlan and Brannick, 2007; Stringer, 2007; McIntyre, 2008). Community research cannot be defined by a single approach, but rather an approach that can cross-cut a number of methods with the overall intention of helping communities and those who work with them to gain better understanding of social life, problems or processes with a view to advancing theory or bringing change or benefits for the community. Community research can have similar objectives to participatory action research in seeking change or improvements relating to a particular practice or policy.

A fundamental difference between community research and participatory action research concerns the position of the research, which leads to a slight departure of the two approaches on epistemological grounds relating to the way in which knowledge is acquired. In participatory action research projects practitioners and facilitators usually have a strong foundation in the field, but are not necessarily part of the community under research, while for community research projects a fundamental requirement is that community researchers belong to, or at least share common ground with the intended participants. A significant difference between mainstream (positivist) and participatory research methodologies relates to the position of power in the research process (Cornwall and Jewkes, 1995). Research located within the participatory paradigm challenges traditional positivist notions of research, whereby research is considered the exclusive domain of 'objective' scientists (Denzin and Lincoln, 2005; Silverman, 2005). Like other interpretative approaches such as action research and some feminist methodologies (see Alcoff and Potter, 1993), which have emerged following concerns about the politics of research, community research problematises control and power within the research process, especially between the researcher and the researched, and the extent to which community researchers have control over the research process depends on their level of involvement at different stages (see Figure 1.1).

In social research the ability to tap into 'community' knowledge requires a methodology that enables familiarity and understanding of the particulars of the local/community situation to emerge through tapping into the rich understanding held by people in particular contexts. These understandings become known as a result of their interactions and experiences with other people, programmes, operations or objects (Yanow, 2004). Community research represents a clear move away from top down research, in the type of knowledge and data which it aims to produce. It adopts the standpoint that community members are 'experts' within their field of experience or as Gramsci has argued 'organic intellectuals' (1971), people who utilise their local knowledge from life experience to address changes and problems in society. Involving community researchers in all aspects of the research process means projects are more likely to succeed methodologically; from initial recruitment of community researchers, to the quality of data collected, retention rates and the satisfaction level of community researchers themselves (see Barnes et al, 2000; Kemshall and Littlechild, 2000; Gonsalves, 2005); and gain access to authentic community knowledge.

In their Handbook of Qualitative Research, Denzin and Lincoln (2005) categorise the history of research in the 20th century and beyond into eight phases. Community research and participatory research have a similar heritage that can be traced back to both phenomenology and postmodernism. While in theory community research can take much of its epistemological and ontological base from earlier phenomenology, in practice the use of community research methodologies have not become visible until more recently in what Denzin and Lincoln (2005) refer to as the fifth moment of research, or the postmodern period, which emerged in the early 1990s. It is not until this moment that reference is made to action, participatory and activist-oriented research. Denzin and Lincoln regard this moment somewhat as an experimental period whereby researchers attempt new ways of representing the 'Other' (see Fine et al, 2005).

In the sixth moment or post-experimental enquiry, which relates to the period from 1995 to 2000, 'new excitements' in research were being discovered by the interpretative community. Some of these were concerned with co-constructed representations, a method that has progressed in community research projects as will be seen later in this book. The seventh and eighth moments, or the methodologically contested periods, emerged in the early years of the new millennium and continue to the present day. These moments are not necessarily created out of cutting edge research, as Denzin and Lincoln point out 'we are clearly not implying a progress narrative with our history' (2005: 20) but instead research that recognises that gender, class, race and ethnicity make it a multi-cultural process. This process requires new approaches, such as community research, to be developed as legitimate and respected lines of enquiry which are capable of capturing and making sense of increasing levels of diversity experienced in communities as we enter an era of superdiversity (Vertovec, 2008).

Community research, policy evaluation and the policy process

While shifts in social science have led to increased acceptance of participatory methodologies, similar trends have been mirrored in the policy evaluation process. These moves can be identified in the growing body of literature concerned with the changing nature of the policy process. Those changes have had some influence on government attitudes to policy evaluation and the increased investment in commissioned evaluations (such as those involved in the Sure Start programme in the UK as well as European programmes such as the European Refugee Integration Fund). There was a shift away from 'top down', deductive reasoning models of evaluation, whereby commissioners specify a set of questions to be investigated, to a new way of working and a somewhat revised evaluation paradigm, which acknowledged the importance of partnership working in the delivery of public services, and gave scope for a broader type of knowledge base to emerge. In the UK and in much of the developed Western world the policy landscape is once again changing as we enter an era of austerity. At this stage it is not clear what direction that policy evaluation will take nor what will be the future role of communities.

New ways of delivering services through partnership approaches have undoubtedly influenced ways of thinking which now recognise that a range of actors have valuable information, knowledge and ways of working that can feed into policy development and implementation. The emphasis on partnerships also links to ideas of participative and deliberative democracy, which aims to 'design institutions and processes for collective decision-making that compensate for the power imbalances between different stakeholders' (Skelcher et al, 2005). In recent years, public sector reform, the move to a mixed economy of welfare provision (see Rowson et al, 2010; Jordon, 2010; Norman, 2010), has seen the resurrection of the localism agenda and a shift of responsibility for services from the state to the private and community and voluntary sectors and ultimately the individual (Taylor-Gooby and Stoker, 2011). Alongside the restructuring of the public sector, personalisation has become a central tenet of service delivery (CLG, 2008). This move brought issues concerning community engagement to the forefront of public policy. It is in the context of community engagement that community research methodologies are particularly useful. They have helped bridge a gap between community members, who often lack understanding of the policy process and ways to shape service delivery, and government agencies that often have little understanding of the implication of policy interventions at a grass roots level (Goodson and Phillimore, 2010).

Changes in the policy process raise questions about methodological protocols used in policy evaluation. As the inclusion of service users has become more commonplace, policy evaluation has become more of an interpretative rather than a positivist pursuit, whereby multiple perspectives and experiences need to be considered and understood in reaching conclusions and in producing policy recommendations. Fischer (2009) raises questions about policy expertise in a democratic society, and especially the legitimacy of different forms of knowledge, whether technical, professional, political, or lay. As participative forms of governance provide opportunities for new methodologies such as community research, at the same time the type of knowledge created has become more contested and generally open for challenge, as the technical knowledge of paid experts is reassessed and repositioned.

When and why community research is appropriate

Community research can be used as a community engagement method, and a policy evaluation tool as well as a research approach in its own right. It has the potential to enhance the policy impact of research and help build stronger relationships with research users outside of academia. At the same time the approach also offers enormous potential for academics wishing to examine a range of processes, relationships and phenomena operating at a community level. The methodology is often used as a means to tackle the challenges and complexities of both involving and consulting with a range of individuals, often from 'hard to reach' communities, in decision-making processes. Community research draws on community researchers' own skills and networks to access data so is particularly attractive to those wishing to avoid accessing communities via traditional gatekeepers who 'choose' participants. Working with community members can give enhanced access to communities which traditional or 'outside' researchers find hard to reach (Elliott et al, 2002). Such privileged access is one of the impetuses for the use of community research, as it offers a doorway for 'traditional researchers' into the lives of people who may be outside of mainstream society or service provision (Griffith, 1998; McCabe and Ford, 2001). As the chapters in this book demonstrate the use of community researchers facilitates the collection of different forms of data through the ability to engage a wider sample and the use of shared languages and enhanced cultural understanding which can provide more authentic and richer accounts (Goodson and Phillimore, 2010).

While the involvement of community researchers not only overcomes issues of access, their engagement in other phases of the project can lead to a range of wider benefits. Their involvement in research design can increase the validity of research findings by introducing issues and themes which may have been overlooked by professional researchers who do not have the lived experience of community researchers. In addition, insights and involvement in data analysis can also provide new perspectives and ways of presenting and interpreting findings, which some may argue can reduce marginalisation of some communities by policy makers, or help give a voice to different invisible/under-the-radar community groups within academia.

Methodological challenges

Paradigm shifts in both social science and policy evaluation methodologies have provided great opportunities for community research methodologies to flourish. Yet a review of the literature aimed at assessing the methodological progress made in the area demonstrated that there is a limited amount of work in the field. While there exists an established body of literature related to participatory action research (see Fals-Borda and Rahman, 1991; Kemmis and McTaggart, 2000; Reason and Bradbury, 2001; Jason et al, 2004; Lennie, 2005; Stoecker, 2005, 2009; Hilsen, 2006; Coghlan and Brannick, 2007; McIntyre, 2008; Stringer, 2007; Schensul et al, 2008), and research with 'hard to reach' communities (Kramer, 1969; Gilbert and Eaton, 1970; Piven and Cloward, 1977; McCabe and Ford, 2001; Elliott et al, 2002; Pitts and Smith, 2007; Ataöv et al, 2010), there is a dearth of information on community research per se and its methodological challenges. Like all other research methods, the community research approach presents challenges as well as opportunities. Sceptics of the approach concern themselves with issues concerning methodological rigour. On the whole, methodological issues have tended to be addressed in passing rather than dealt with in any substantive way. Research ethics, including the way in which community researchers have been used and remunerated has attracted some attention (Greenwood and Levin, 1998). In addition, concerns regarding the validity and reliability of community research, more specifically the impact of community researchers on the quality of data, have been discussed in the context of demand characteristics when matching researchers with their peers, for example, Elliott et al's (2002) reflection of a community research project with young substance and alcohol mis-users (see Kuebler and Hausser, 1997; Byrne, 2001; Hall et al, 2002; Convey et al, 2010). Sampling issues particularly concerning the constraints of using personal networks limited to certain geographical or social milieus and the problem of sampling bias have also called the validity of community research into question (Hall et al, 2002). Kuebler and Hausser (1997) have taken a more solution-based approach to consider ways in which research reliability can be safeguarded by implementing 'intra-questionnaire checks'.

The chapters that follow address different methodological issues. In each chapter authors reflect on the advantages and disadvantageous of community research and offer suggestions about how shortcoming can be addressed. Table 1.1 below provides a summary, based on our own experience of working on a range of community research projects (Phillimore et al, 2009; Goodson and Phillimore, 2010), of the advantages and disadvantages of community research alongside our response of how methodological challenges might be addressed. In summary, the key to undertaking high quality community research is little different to more general approaches to qualitative research and depends on involving and training the research team for each specific project, careful matching of researchers to respondents and close monitoring of fieldwork and research outputs. Some reflexive consideration is also necessary to ensure that the personal standpoints and biases of all researchers involved in each project, rather than simply those of the community researchers, are taken into account when analysing data and drawing conclusions.

Structure of the book

The chapters in this book provide accounts from different disciplinary backgrounds and projects based in a variety of countries, including the UK, Australia, Botswana, Canada, South Africa, India, Italy, Spain, Germany, Finland, Russia and the US. The community researchers involved in the projects discussed herein also come in a wide range of different guises from specific ethnic groups, including Polish, Roma and indigenous peoples, to more heterogeneous groups of young people, mental health or HIV service users, refugees and new migrants. The contributions demonstrate different levels and types of community involvement in research and how more heterogeneous involvement has an impact on the research or evaluation process. It is clear that the community research approach lends itself to a myriad of different research and evaluation objectives and settings but is not without challenges. This book aims to transfer some of the learning, by sharing the experiences of those who have led or worked as part of community research initiatives, to help strengthen the methodological foundations of the approach. With this in mind the book was designed with pedagogical themes, which consider the benefits and challenges of adopting a community research approach and summaries of the key learning from each project. The interdisciplinary collection covers a range of methodological issues, from ethical and data analysis concerns to the validity and reliability of community research findings, as well as broader epistemological and ontological issues concerning objectivity, subjectivity and the type of knowledge community research produces.

The book is structured into three parts. The first covers a wide range of theoretical and methodological issues including the theoretical justifications for involving communities in research in different roles. Given concerns about a lack of rigour in research projects where communities, rather than professionals, take a key role, chapters in this section explore issues around reliability, authenticity and validity. Consideration is also given to the importance of reflexivity and communication and the added value of insider–led research. In Chapter Two, Gómez and Sordé Marti take a critical communicative perspective to examine the process of community research. They look at two strategies that can help ensure the active involvement of community research across the entire research process. Next, Clark, Holland and Ward summarise key debates around authenticity and validity and reflect on the challenges associated with representing the perspectives of community researchers in research outputs. In Chapter Four, Brown, Scullion and Niner focus upon the mutual understanding between the professional researcher and the community researcher, and examine the implications of power relationships for reliability and validity. Chapter Five from Atfield, Brahmbhatt, Hakimi and O'Toole explores the differences between insider and outsider research undertaken in hard to research communities and discuss ethical and methodological issues while reflecting on the benefits and challenges of involving community researchers. The following chapter by Bell, Madew, Addy and Kainulainen looks at the ways in which universities can act as agents to empower their local communities and suggest a range of approaches for effective empowerment. In the final chapter in Part One, Blakey, Milne and Kilburn outline the ways in which data analysis can be undertaken with communities. Using examples, they show how a range of different tools, including visual tools and a policy workshop can be employed to ensure that community researchers can engage in data analysis at every stage of a project.

Table 1.1 Advantages and disadvantages of community research (CR)

Issue	Advantages	Disadvantages	Comments
Validity	Respondents more likely to be open with people with whom they can identify. Can produce richer insights.	Respondents may attempt to portray themselves in a particular light to their peers.	There is always some kind of demand effect, it simply differs depending on the interviewee/interviewer relationship.
Sampling	When using a database, representativeness is more likely to be achieved where all respondents have the potential to participate because they are able to understand requests to be interviewed. Sample bias is more likely if CRs are not used and those who do not speak researcher languages or lack the confidence to speak to researchers are not involved.	Use of personal networks can lead to a skewed sample.	Representativeness can be achieved using databases rather than personal networks providing all on the database have the potential and incentive to be involved.
Quality of data collected	CRs may be equally committed as professional researchers if a) they have a connection with the issue, b) they are seeking to professionalise or have formal educational backgrounds/ training.	Community researchers may be less committed and less professional.	Using CRs with a track record and close monitoring and mentoring can ensure quality is controlled
Confidentiality	Respondents may be more willing to divulge sensitive information if they feel that CRs understand their cultural context and will not judge them. CRs may find it easier to build trust and rapport with participants because of commonalities in their backgrounds.	Community researchers may know their respondents who may fear their confidences will be divulged and hold back key information. Fear of being judged by a community member may prevent sensitive issues from being discussed openly.	CRs should be trained in research ethics. Matching CRs with people unknown to them, even outside their own ethnic groups can overcome these concerns. The use of participant information and consent forms which gain CR and interviewees' formal agreement to confidentiality can reassure.
Research tool development	Involvement of CRs in research tool development can help ensure the most appropriate terminology is used and consistency between interviews is maintained. CRs' involvement in research design can strengthen the validity of research findings.	Participation in tool development makes the process more time consuming.	There is a tendency to simply use CRs as interviewers without getting their input on the whole research process.

Issue	Advantages	Disadvantages	Comments
Power relations	Interviewees participating in evaluations are often reluctant to criticise projects being evaluated if they think the research is part of the establishment associated with the project. They may be more frank with a community researcher.	Interviewees may feel that an interview with a CR is worthless if they question their authority, seeing non-professionals as being more powerful and influential. Communities are not homogenous – individuals may hold opposing affiliations.	Each situation must be assessed to explore the suitability of CRs. CRs should be matched carefully to interviewees.
Language	Using CRs enables those who speak poor English to fully participate in the research. The use of CRs overcomes the expense and extensive problems associated with using non-research trained interpreters. Even where respondents speak English it's useful to use an interviewer who can explain complexities in their own language.	Questions can be mis-interpreted by CRs so respondents asked for the wrong information. This can undermine research reliability and validity.	Training CRs about the specific questions being asked and the reasons why will help them translate correctly. Close monitoring of question responses will reveal any inconsistencies. Unsatisfactory interviews are repeated.
Subjectivity	CRs are more likely to spot and interrogate issues that are underplayed because of cultural nuances which would be overlooked by a researcher speaking a different language or from a different culture. This can greatly enhance the depth and richness of data collated.	CRs may have a particular interpretation of responses and report selectively.	Ensuring that CRs record all responses whether or not considered relevant can overcome selectivity/ subjectivity. Recording all interviews ensures that checking comprehensiveness is possible.

Part Two concentrates on ethics, power and emotion as key dimensions of community research. The chapters in this section use a wide range of examples to demonstrate how power relations can have an impact upon community research projects and how those relations can be managed, as well as the consequences of not attending to power in the research process. Attention is also paid to the role of emotions in the research process and the ways in which emotions can be employed or emotional involvement place community researchers at risk. The section begins with a powerful account from Maretha Visser about relationships, boundaries and emotions in a community research project with HIV-positive pregnant women. Visser looks specifically at the ways in which these issues have an impact on the quality of data and how community researchers can be supported in emotionally charged environments. In Chapter Nine Mannarini explores the issue of power in participatory community research and examines the benefits and risks associated with participation. Throughout the chapter she focuses on the dynamics of power relationships before making suggestions about the ways in which processes can be managed. The following chapter from Schwartz, van de Sande and O'Brien examines power, control and ownership of research projects bringing together students and community organisations with a focus on how relationships can be managed. Cartland, Ruch-Ross and Mason in Chapter Eleven explore issues concerning the use of community researchers in evaluation and the ways in which power dynamics have an impact upon research. Both Chapters Ten and Eleven question assumptions that the community participants in community research inevitably lack power relative to researchers. In the following chapter, Twelve, Brophy et al look at the challenges experienced by community researchers in conducting evaluation research, including ethical considerations, participant recruitment, role boundaries, power sharing and the effects of the environment. Chapter Thirteen, from Kawulich and Ogletree, then focuses upon experiences of trying to conduct ethical research with first nations people and outlines some guidelines to support research practice in this field. The final chapter in the section from Warr, Mann and Williams considers how community contexts are important for understanding the challenges and achievements of peer interviewer methods and looks at the ways in which becoming a community researcher has an impact upon the individuals involved.

In Part Three of the book we look at the management of the community research process focusing on a range of specific issues including how to engage community partners, how to recruit community researchers, how to address representation in cross-language research, and the way in which mentoring support can act as an empowerment tool. In Chapter Fifteen, Kavanagh, Davidson, Campbell, Daly and Harper use the example of a study of citizens' experiences of compulsory mental health laws to look reflexively on the different perspectives of academics, service users and carers. Comparing these different accounts they explore implications for the ways in which community research can influence policy and practice in these fields. The next two chapters provide detailed accounts of indigenous research projects. First, in Chapter Sixteen, Andharia and Hardikar describe the process of developing an indigenous research tool which inspired community members to undertake a research project which has an impact upon policy around food security in India. In Chapter Seventeen, Chilisa and Chilisa provide an account of a project using indigenous research techniques to understand and support the development of an intervention to reduce risky sexual behaviours among adolescents. In Chapter Eighteen, McCartan, Schubotz and Burns also discuss involving young people in community research, reflecting on some of the difficulties of working with young people and giving some practical examples of how to manage the process. The following chapter, from Temple and Koterba, examines the ways in which representation is addressed in cross-language research employing bi-lingual community researchers. They explore in some detail the epistemological assumptions that are made when researching language and identity and then suggest a method to help address issues of representation. The final chapter, from Jones and Joseph, analyses the relationship between mentors and community researchers and argues that mentoring can support the emancipation of community researchers and the communities to which they belong.

We hope that the range of accounts from across the world documented in this book will help stimulate new community research activity and help those with some prior experience to reflect on their learning and develop their approach.

References

Alcoff, L. and Potter, E. (1993) *Feminist Epistemologies*, London: Routledge.

Arnstein, S. (1969) A Ladder of Citizen Participation, *Journal of the American Institute of Planners*, 35: 216–224.

Ataöv, A., Brøgger, B. and Hildrum, J. (2010) An Action Research Approach to the Inclusion of Immigrants in Work Life and Local Community Life: Preparation of a Participatory Realm, *Action Research* September 8: 237–265.

Barnes, M., Davies, A. and Tew, J. (2000) Valuing Experience: Users' Experience of Compulsion Under the Mental Health Act 1983, *Mental Health Review*, 5(3).

Berger, P. and Luckman, T. (1966) *The Social Construction of Reality*, New York: Anchor Books.

Brodie, E., Cowling, E. and Nissen, N. (2009) *Understanding Participation: A Literature Review*, London: NCVO, IVR and INVOLVE.

Byrne, M. (2001) *The Learning Centre Peer Research Project*, Edinburgh Youth Social Inclusion Partnership and the Learning Centre, Craigmillar.

Coghlan, D. and Brannick, T. (2007) *Doing Action Research in your Own Organization*, Thousand Oaks, CA: Sage Publications.

Communities and Local Government (CLG) (2008) *Creating Strong, Safe and Prosperous Communities*, London: HMSO.

Convey, M., Dickson-Gomez, J., Weeks, M. and Li, J. (2010) Altruism and Peer-Led HIV Prevention Targeting Heroin and Cocaine Users, *Qualitative Health Research*, 20(11):1546–1557.

Cornwall, A. and Jewkes, R. (1995) What is Participatory Research? *Social Science and Medicine*, 41(12): 1667–1676.

Denzin, N. and Lincoln, Y. (2005) *Handbook of Qualitative Research* (3rd edn), Thousand Oaks, CA: Sage.

Elliott, E., Watson, A. and Harries, U. (2002) Harnessing Expertise: Involving Peer Interviewers in Qualitative Research with Hard-to-Reach Populations, *Health Expectations*, 5: 172–178.

Fals-Borda, O. and Rahman, M. (1991) *Action and Knowledge: Breaking the Monopoly with Participatory Action-Research*, New York: Apex Press.

Fine, M., Weis, L., Weseen, S. and Wong, L. (2005) For Whom? Qualitative Research, Representations, and Social Responsibilities, in N. Denzin and Y. Lincoln (eds), *Handbook of Qualitative Research*, 107–131, Thousand Oaks, CA: Sage.

Fischer, F. (2009) *Democracy and Expertise: Reorienting Policy Inquiry,* Oxford: Oxford University Press.

Freire, P. (1972) *Pedagogy of the Oppressed*, Harmondsworth: Penguin.

Gans, H. (1968) *People and Plans*, New York: Basic Books.

Geertz, C. (1973) Thick Description: Toward an Interpretive Theory of Culture, in *The Interpretation of Cultures: Selected Essays*, Clifford Geertz, 3–30, New York: Basic Books.

Geertz, C. (1983) *Local Knowledge: Further Essays in Interpretive Anthropology*, New York: Basic Books.

Gilbert, N. and Eaton, J. (1970) Who Speaks for the Poor?, *Journal of the American Institute of Planners*, 36.

Gonsalves, F. (2005) *Participatory Research and Development for Sustainable Agriculture and Natural Resource Management*, International Development Research Centre: Canada.

Goodson, L. and Phillimore, J. (2010) A Community Research Methodology: Working with New Migrants to Develop a Policy Related Evidence Base, *Social Policy and Society*, 9(4).

Gramsci, A. (1971) *Selections from the Prison Notebooks*, Hoare, Q. and Smith, G. (eds and trans.), New York: International Publishers.

Greenwood, D. and Levin, M. (1998) *Introduction to Action Research: Social Research for Social Change*, Thousand Oaks: Sage.

Griffith, P. (1998) *Qat Use in London: A Study of Qat Use Amongst a Sample of Somalis Living in London*, Home Office Drug Prevention Initiative: London.

Hall, D., Rae, C. and Jarvis, M. (2002) *Young Parent Peer Research Project*, report for Connexions Leicestershire in association with Sure Start Plus: Leicester.

Haraway, D. (1988) Situated Knowledges: The Science Question in Feminism and the Privilege of Partial Perspective, *Feminist Studies*, 14(3): 575–599.

Hilsen, A. (2006) And They Shall be Known by Their Deeds: Ethics and Politics in Action Research, *Action Research*, 4(1): 23–36.

Israel, B., Eng, E., Schulz, A. and Parker, E. (2005) *Methods in Conducting Community-Based Participatory Research for Health*, San Francisco, CA: Jossey-Bass.

Jacobsen, K. and Landau, L. (2003) *Researching Refugees: Some Methodological and Ethical Considerations in Social Science and Forced Migration*, Geneva: UNHCR.

Jason, L., Christopher, K., Suarez-Balcazar, Y., and Davis, M. (2004) *Participatory Community Research: Theories and Methods in Action*, Washington DC: American Psychological Association.

Jordan, B. (2010) *Why the Third Way Failed: Economics, Morality and the Origins of the 'Big Society'*, Bristol: Policy Press.

Kemmis, S. and McTaggart, R. (2000) Participatory Action Research, in N. Denzin and Y. Lincoln (eds) *Handbook of Qualitative Research*, 567–605. Thousand Oaks, CA: Sage.

Kemshall, H. and Littlechild, R. (eds) (2000) *User Involvement and Participation in Social Care: Research Informing Practice*, London: Jessica Kingsley.

Kramer, R. (1969) *Participation of the Poor*, Englewood Cliffs, NJ: Prentice Hall.

Kuebler, D and Hausser, D. (1997) The Swiss Hidden Population Study: Practical and Methodological Aspects of Data Collection by Privileged Access Interviewers, *Addiction*, 92(3): 325–334.

Lennie, J. (2005) An Evaluation Capacity-Building Process for Sustainable Community IT Initiatives: Empowering and Disempowering Impacts, *Evaluation*, 11(4): 390–414.

McCabe, A. and Ford, C. (2001) *Redresssing the Balance: Crime and Mental Health*, Manchester: Public Health Alliance.

McIntyre, A. (2008) *Participatory Action Research*, Thousand Oaks, CA: Sage.

Minkler, M. and Wallerstain, N. (eds) (2003) *Community Based Participatory Research for Health*, San Francisco, CA: Jossey-Bass.

Minkler, M. and Wallerstain, N. (eds) (2008) *Community Based Participatory Research for Health: From Process to Outcome*, San Francisco, CA: Jossey- Bass.

Norman, J. (2010) *The Big Society the Anatomy of the New Politics*, Buckingham: University of Buckingham Press.

Phillimore, J., Goodson, L., Hennessy, D. and Ergun, E. (2009) *Empowering Birmingham's Migrant and Refugee Community Organisations*, York: Joseph Rowntree Foundation.

Pitts, M. and Smith, A. (2007) *Researching the Margins: Strategies for Ethical and Rigorous Research with Marginalised Communities*, New York: Palgrave MacMillan.

Piven, F. and Cloward, R. (1977) *Poor People's Movements*, New York: Pantheon.

Reason, P. and Bradbury, H. (2001) *Handbook of Action Research: Participative Inquiry and Practice*, Thousand Oaks, CA: Sage.

Rowson, J., Broome, S. and Jones, A. (2010) *Connected Communities: How Social Networks Power and Sustain the Big Society*, London: RSA.

Schensul, J., Berg, M. and Williamson, K. (2008) Challenging Hegemonies: Advancing Collaboration in Community-Based Participatory Action Research, *Collaborative Anthropologies*, 1: 102–137.

Silverman, D. (2005) *Doing Qualitative Research* (2nd edn), Thousand Oaks, CA: Sage.

Skelcher, C., Mathur, N. and Smith, M. (2005) The Public Governance of Collaborative Spaces: Discourse, Design and Democracy, *Public Administration*, 83: 573–596.

Stoecker, R. (2005) *Research Methods for Community Change: A Project-Based Approach*, Thousand Oaks, CA: Sage.

Stoecker, R. (2009) Are We Talking the Walk of Community-Based Research? *Action Research*, 7: 385–404.

Strand, K., Marullo, S., Cutforth, N., Stoecker, R. and Donohue, P. (2003) *Community-Based Research and Higher Education: Principles and Practices*, San Francisco, CA: Jossey-Bass.

Stringer, E. (2007) *Action Research*, Thousand Oaks, CA: Sage.

Taylor- Gooby, P. and Stoker, G. (2011) The Coalition Programme: A New Vision for Britain or Politics as Usual?, *The Political Quarterly*, 82(1): 4–15.

Tolley, E. and Bentley, M. (1996) Training Issues for the Use of Participatory Research Methods in Health, in K. de Koning and M. Martin (eds), *Participatory Research in Health*, 50–61, London: Zed.

Vertovec, S. (2008) Super-Diversity and its Implications, *Ethnic and Racial Studies*, 30(6): 1024–1054.

Yanow, D. (2004) Translating Local Knowledge at Organizational Peripheries, *British Journal of Management*, 15(1): 9–25.

Two

A critical communicative perspective on community research: reflections on experiences of working with Roma in Spain

Aitor Gómez and Teresa Sordé Marti

Chapter aims

- To present the theoretical framework of the critical communicative methodology within the context of the dialogic turn, as identified in social science and societies
- To describe the move from hierarchical power relations to more egalitarian ones between researchers and community members, both theoretically and in practice
- To analyse key theoretical and practical aspects of the dialogic creation of knowledge between researchers and members of Romani associations
- To reflect on the scientific, social and political transformation that research carried out using the critical communicative methodology has achieved

Introduction

This chapter examines the process of creating knowledge using a critical communicative perspective, which advocates for the active involvement, throughout the entire research process of community researchers, that is those individuals or groups whose experience is being analysed. Two strategies, a multicultural research team and an advisory council are presented. In using these, it is argued that involvement and the conditions that allow moving beyond objectivism and subjectivism are sought as we look to developing intersubjectivity between researchers and community members. The chapter also examines in which ways the dialogic creation of knowledge tend to counter power relations within the community research process (academic and peer researchers, researchers and subject, institutions, organisations and individuals). Drawing on examples of working with the Roma, and Romani associations, it is argued that it is through intersubjective dialogue research findings that it is possible to inform political and social transformation.

Critical communicative methodology (CCM) is defined as intersubjective dialogue between researchers and those actors whose experience is being studied. Through undertaking such an approach, the subjects of the research, both researchers and those being researched, are enabled to become more active agents in the whole research process and obtain a more reflexive and rigorous analysis (Gómez, Racionero and Sordé, 2010). In this chapter, the presentation of the CCM is framed within the dialogic turn in societies and social sciences. After introducing what this transformation has represented in terms of social science research, particularly in the field of Romani Studies, we present its main theoretical aspects. This paper continues with some practical examples of how the CCM serves the purpose of including community researchers throughout the entire scientific process. The chapter ends with a description of various pedagogical tools which allows the readers to capture the main aspects of the CCM.

Dialogic turn in societies and social sciences

Our societies are becoming increasingly dialogic. In both the private and public domain, people try to resolve various social issues through mutual agreements and consensus. People have always had these communicative skills; however, the context of the Information Society provides more opportunities to extend dialogic practices. Indeed, a general trend is to find dialogue at the core of social relationships. This dialogic turn, for example, is becoming increasingly obvious in our private lives, in the way we reach agreements at home and with our families, or solve problems in our community. This does not mean that authority or hierarchies are eradicated from society, but rather that there is an attempt to substitute them with dialogue. More people now recognise the value of egalitarian dialogue, and when those who hold authoritarian positions refuse to engage in it, conflict arises (Aubert et al., 2008).

The importance of analysing these dialogic dynamics has become more commonplace in social science research in recent years. Social science research is helping to describe the way that previous power relationships have been challenged by dialogic dynamics (Habermas, 1984; Habermas, 1987; Beck, 1992; Touraine, 2000). A number of theories have been developed to overcome the traditional methodological gap between the researcher and those being researched (Habermas, 1984; Beck et al., 1994). Drawing from them, the CCM allows social research to overcome the traditional interpretative hierarchy that has existed between the researcher and the actors being studied (Freire, 1970; Habermas, 1984).

The Roma population has not been left out of the dialogic turn. As part of this, Roma organisations have openly rejected research that contributes to the perpetuation of their social exclusion. This has been denominated the 'Romani refusal to engage in exclusionary research' (Touraine et al., 2004). Exclusionary research, contrary to community research, is carried out about the Roma but without them, and tends to objectify the subjects and reproduce existing stereotypes and prejudices against the Roma. After years of seeing research carried out on them but without them, and not observing any positive outcomes for their community, an increasing number of Romani organisations have refused to become involved in any kind of research that reproduces this pattern (Flecha and Gómez, 2004). When researchers use CCM, however, Romani associations have noted that it is possible to participate in research that takes their voices into account and provides political and social recommendations that help to overcome their social exclusion (Gómez and Vargas, 2003).

In the following sections, we provide a theoretical discussion of the main underpinnings of the CCM, followed by various examples of this methodology in practice with Roma communities in Catalonia and Spain.

Theoretical discussion

CCM is a scientific response to the above-mentioned dialogic turn in societies. It builds upon the universal capacity for communication (Flecha and Gómez, 2004). The critical communicative perspective gathers contributions from several research traditions, such as Freire's dialogic action (1970, 1997) or Habermas' communicative action (1984, 1987).

Research methodologies have often been based on collecting information from subjects; and the researchers being the only ones interpreting data. Research participants were frequently uninformed about how the information provided would be used, and were given no opportunity to comment on the research outputs. At worst, in some cases, their statements were distorted. In that way, the respondents arrived at the conclusion that the real objective of these studies was to increase the curricula of the researchers and legitimise certain policies rather than to create new rigorous scientific knowledge. Past research on groups that face inequalities has been criticised for failing to take into account the voices of marginalised groups, and for providing conclusions that contributed to the reproduction of social exclusion and inequalities. Members of excluded groups argue that scholars analyse them for their own benefit, but without the basic objective of improving the group's overall situation (Touraine et al., 2004).

Contemporary sociological theories see society as being two-fold (Flecha et al., 2003). Structures and systems are important; however, it is also important to recognise that subjects and collectives can transform them, even partially, and make them more human. In the name of acting scientifically, researchers have traditionally appeared to exclude social groups as representatives of these structures and systems. From their perspective as experts, researchers have tended to act hierarchically from their positions of power, imposing their own interpretations without taking the subjects' ideas, feelings or opinions into account. Researchers use only the information that subjects provide as raw material rather than engaging in dialogue with them throughout the research process. Researchers have tended to analyse the information collected by themselves, without accounting for the participation of people from the community.

In contrast to this objectivist view, the subjectivist approach prioritises the perspective of those being studied over that of the expert. Sometimes, academics carrying out research from a subjectivist perspective have considered themselves to be participants (Gómez et al., 2010; Gómez et al., 2011). However, the professional position and activity of researchers is often so different from that of the research subjects that it is unusual for researchers to place themselves in equal terms with study participants.

CCM is based on dual perspectives, with importance being placed on both systems (the experts' view) and the subject's lifeworld. The scientific system provides the accumulated knowledge that is fundamental for the construction of new theories, while the voices of all the actors involved are taken into account. Since social transformation is the basic objective of CCM, just as it is also the objective of action-research, or participatory action research (PAR), the approach does not involve positioning oneself either in favour of, or against, the use of qualitative or quantitative data collection techniques. What is important is to achieve results which are socially useful, and which also contribute to the transformation of situations of exclusion. Along these lines, CCM recognises the significance which objectivism brings to accumulated scientific knowledge (systems) and the importance which subjectivism awards to the interpretations which the subjects makes of reality (lifeworld). CCM is different to other methodologies in that it is based on a dual conception of society, and also in that it uses qualitative and quantitative techniques as appropriate. However, CCM also relies on ongoing communication to ensure the participation of the subjects 'being researched' from the beginning to the end of the research process (Gómez et al., 2006).

CCM facilitates empowerment of community researchers beyond the active participation and transformation of social reality inherent in PAR. The researchers' responsibility is one of the differences between CCM and PAR. The communicative paradigm where the CCM is located conceives reality in a dialogical way. For this reason, the relation between researchers and researched people is based on egalitarian and intersubjective dialogue. In this dialogue, it is essential that each participant is actively contributing. The interpretation of reality is constructed through contributions from science (researchers) and visions from the researched people. The interpretation of reality is produced simultaneously, considering both system and lifeworld. Empowerment, reflection and critical action are integral to this exchange. Community researchers are empowered by critically engaging with what has been said about their own reality, and contributing to advancing existing knowledge. Empowerment comes from direct meaningful participation and providing the opportunity to challenge what was considered as true until then.

In CCM accountability is not something that is considered after or as a phase of the research process, but as thoroughly embedded in it. While participatory methodologies (for example, PAR, action research, evaluative action research) based on a socio-critical paradigm encourage the participation of the researched people with the purpose of obtaining, through a dialectical perspective, an interpretation of reality. CCM, rooted in a larger theoretical spectrum including objectivist, subjectivist and socio-critical paradigms, is aimed at integrating the participation of the community researchers in all phases of the process.

Beyond objectivism and subjectivism, CCM is based on the intersubjective dialogues between researchers and their scientific knowledge and subjects with their experiences and perspectives. The people who are the 'objects' of the research participate directly in these spaces as subjects able to articulate their own views, interpretations and impressions. It is important that both the researchers and the subjects contribute to the debate. The aim is to create an atmosphere where relationships are promoted based on the force of the arguments provided, instead of the power positions of participants. The hierarchy between the researcher, the 'subject', and the person being researched, the 'object', is broken down and replaced by an interpretation of reality based on intersubjective dialogue (Habermas, 1984). In the next section, we reflect upon the ways in which these spaces and the conditions for the dialogic creation of knowledge might be created.

Critical communicative methodology in practice

Two aspects of CCM in practice are presented here. The first one refers to the way in which the research team and other participants in the study are organised, showing that anyone can contribute to research because of the universal capacity of language and action. This organisation of the communicative research will be illustrated through the example of the WORKALO project from the European Fifth Framework Programme (CREA, 2001–2004). WORKALO was a project with a European perspective, where associated countries developed research on the Roma population using CCM. In that way, findings had transferability beyond national boundaries, illustrating how it is possible to work with community members from a dialogical perspective, breaking the epistemological gap between researcher and researched people.

The second aspect focuses on the dialogic creation of knowledge that is based on the establishment of particular conditions that make intersubjective dialogue possible between the experts (system) and the studied groups (lifeworld), moving beyond what is already known.

Communicative organisation of research

Traditionally research has been organised around the centrality of experts, leaving the studied subjects in the background, as mere information sources. The communicative organisation of research consists of setting up a structure that guarantees the participation of members of the studied group at every stage of the research process. A concrete example is provided here from the WORKALO project (CREA, 2001–2004).

Representatives and individual members of Romani organisations worked together with the research team throughout the entire process, from the project design to the data analysis. The collaborative process had been going on for several years previously. The WORKALO researchers were very much involved in Romani associations and had a thorough knowledge of the challenges and problems that Roma people were facing in relation to their labour inclusion. They were involved in Romani organisations in many ways, as volunteers or as advisors. Members of the Roma population trusted the researchers since they had a long-term relationship with them and were different to other researchers who came into their homes, obtained the information they needed, and then disappeared. Neither were they like others who took advantage of Roma hospitality and then produced research that perpetuated stereotypes about them. The researchers also trusted the Roma representatives who acted for their communities in a voluntary role, and were clearly committed to the improvement of the Roma situation. This is not to say that typical power relations simply disappeared, but they were diminished because of this mutual trust between the researchers and the Roma community members.

As a result of this collaboration, the research design emerged from various conversations, collaborations and shared experiences that led to the belief that there were crucial questions to be addressed for the Roma population in the 21st century. Both the researchers and the community members were used to participating in these types of settings. The first hypothesis consisted of the idea that the Roma population can contribute to the European goal of social cohesion through their strength, teamwork and cooperative organisation, flexibility and adaptation to change, intercultural competencies and dynamism, qualities developed over the years through working in traditionally Romani jobs. The recognition of these strengths breaks down prejudiced views and deficit-based interpretations and can serve for a better Roma labour inclusion. The second hypothesis consisted of recognising that there are discriminatory practices that prevent this labour inclusion from taking place. The researchers' initial idea was to develop a study placing greater emphasis on the latter hypothesis; however, through informal conversations between researchers and Roma community members on the demands of the Information Society labour market, the former hypothesis became most important. The participation of the Roma population was crucial in defining these hypotheses, since they contributed their own knowledge of traditional occupations among the Roma population and how the skills developed through them were potentially connected to the labour market demands of the time.

This informal collaboration between Roma people and researchers was formalised via the communicative organisation of research that involved the development of two main strategies: a multicultural research team, and an advisory council.

The creation of a multicultural team is one of the strategies that close collaboration with community members can be formalised. The WORKALO research team consisted of an international consortium involving five different universities. Clearly not all of them had experienced a long-established collaboration with the Roma community. However, an agreement was made to orientate the work in the project towards building relationships of trust with the Roma population. The strategy of incorporating members of the Roma community into the research team itself was welcomed by all of the universities, and three of them hired community members to work along with their national teams. In the case of Spain, the project coordination team consisted of Romani and non-Romani researchers. This became possible after years of taking a proactive attitude which included promoting access to university for Roma people, and also providing job opportunities for them. These efforts not only responded to the issue of social justice for Roma people but also constituted a strategy to improve the quality of the research carried out in this particular field. The diversity of the team in terms of the different experiences, backgrounds, trajectories and prospects enriched the research process, breaking away from the homogeneity very often found in scientific teams. The promotion of multicultural teams does not fully guarantee that research will not reproduce existing stereotypes and prejudices, but it does contribute to the creation of conditions that make it more unlikely for this to happen. Thus, the inclusion of community members into the research group was essential in order to achieve new insight into and knowledge of the exclusion of the Roma population from the European labour market.

The creation of an Advisory Council (AC) helped to redress some of the limitations found in terms of creating multicultural research teams. For example, it was very important to capture the reality of those Roma people who were unemployed or had been discriminated against in the labour market, or who had worked in traditional jobs. Therefore there was a need to create a formal space in which these voices would be heard within the research. In the case of the WORKALO project, the AC contained Roma people who are leading a similar life to that of the majority of Roma people in Europe and who were representative of the majority of the collective. Thus, representatives of Roma nongovernmental organisations (NGOs) and of other organisations working with Roma people facing the barriers being looked at in the project were also involved at this stage. The main idea of the AC was to incorporate the voices of groups which have been traditionally excluded from research in a more formal way. One of the criteria for inclusion was to integrate people without academic qualifications. The AC therefore gives voice to community members who would find participation in a multicultural research team difficult. Creating a space in which researchers can present and discuss their findings with people who represent the studied group also benefited the project. In both the multicultural teams and the AC, it was necessary to take account of gender, age, language, and geographical origin as well as ethnicity.

The AC took on the role of a consultative body for the research team. Several meetings were organised to enable the AC to monitor and revise the project findings process. Members of the research team were in charge of presenting their work, and engaging in a dialogue with the AC members on the data analysis, the main conclusions, or the policy recommendations. The AC members brought their knowledge to the discussion, revised documents, provided advice and guidance on the project, evaluated the research process and the conclusions, and ensured that the results would help to transform the reality of the collectives and people whom the project targeted. The AC served the purpose of guaranteeing that the findings and recommendations were relevant to the lives of the majority of the members of the studied group. The initial reluctance and resistance found among certain researchers in terms of being challenged by non-academic people was overcome through the realisation that the final outcomes will be much more rigorous.

In the case of WORKALO, the role played by the AC members was important, not only at a scientific level but also in terms of dissemination. The use of CCM encouraged dissemination activities to be undertaken by AC members. For example, Romani people presented the findings in seminars and conferences, and discussed these with non-Romani people. On 29 September 2004, at a round table in the final conference held in the European Parliament, a member of the AC, an illiterate Romani woman, presented the overall results of the project. Members of the European

Parliament, EC scientific officers and other stakeholders were present, and a Spanish MP made a commitment to that woman and to her people that he would bring a proposal to the Spanish Congress for the Roma population to be recognised in Spain. That historic recognition in the Spanish Congress became a reality in September 2005 (Congreso de los Diputados, 2005). Prior to that moment Members of the European Parliament, who were in the audience, also promoted a European Parliament resolution that contained some of the WORKALO recommendations (European Parliament, 2005). The fact that a Roma woman was present to share her experience of participating in the creation of new knowledge and political recommendations had a significant impact on the audience who were deeply and unexpectedly moved.

The same political impact was obtained in Catalonia. As a follow-up to the recognition of the Roma population as an ethnic minority, the Catalan Parliament asked some of the researchers involved in the WORKALO project to carry out a study on the situation of Roma people in Catalonia. This research team also contained Roma and non-Roma people, with both academic and non-academic backgrounds. An example of how to cope with the potential power claims between the research team and the Advisory Council is provided by the way in which this study was carried out (Sánchez et al, 2005). The first stage of the study consisted of distributing a survey to gain an overview of the major problems the population was facing. Because Spain does not officially collect data on ethnicity, there was no systematic data on the distribution of the Romani population to be used as the basis for developing a representative sample. Therefore, the research team gathered together all of the existing studies providing estimates of the Roma population, from city councils, social service organisations, local police forces, and other sources. This allowed the research team to identify the areas of Catalonia where Roma live. A stratified sample proposal was created based on the data from these sources.

At this point, Joan, a very well-known and respected Romani man, an AC member who became very close to the research team, came along to a meeting with a hand-written sheet of paper. Although Joan is barely literate and did not know what a sample means, he had drawn a map of the Romani population in Catalonia. He created it based on his knowledge of all the Romani families and their distribution throughout Catalonia. He presented his figures at the meeting, and the researchers contrasted these with their own. Everyone was surprised to note that both were very similar. Where small differences were found, Joan and the researcher discussed how to contrast the data gathered through official sources with the information he had provided. Contrasting the two sources enabled them to create a closer and more accurate approximation of the Roma population than would have otherwise been possible. From an objectivist perspective, the stratified sample created by the researchers would be the accepted one. From a subjectivist perspective, the one provided by Joan would be preferred. In the case of the critical communicative perspective, the sample created, based on dialogic intersubjective engagement between the two: the researcher and the community member. Thus, the involvement of Roma people in this study went well beyond the role of being key informants. The dialogue between the research team and the AC allowed a more accurate analysis of reality to be generated.

In this case, the fieldwork was coordinated by the local Romani associations; they took charge of distributing the surveys and conducting the interviews with the nearby Roma population, and explaining the main premises of the study to them. This study was used as the basis of the Integral Plan for Roma people in Catalonia (Generalitat de Catalunya, 2005). The research structure moved into the political domain, not only due to the recommendations it could make, but also due to the communicative way in which the study was organised. The political plan also contained a multicultural coordination team, an advisory council and working groups in which non-academic Roma people participate voluntarily in order to determine how the various actions would be implemented. The communicative organisation of research thus reached the level of policy (Munté et al., 2011).

The dialogic creation of knowledge: contrasting structure and human agency

The recognition that everyone can take part in the creation of knowledge is clearly supported by the evidence that the participation of lay people can help to achieve more scientific and rigorous research findings. The formalisation of dialogic spaces such as the multicultural research team and the Advisory Council can facilitate this process. They are not the only spaces in which expert knowledge can be improved, however, so it is important to create conditions that will enable the dialogic creation of knowledge to take place throughout the research process. Our experience suggests there are a number of ways these conditions can be promoted.

For example the research project on labour market inclusion strategies for Romani women (CREA, 2002–2004) required communicative observations to take place in order to identify the type of skills and competences that Romani women had developed in their traditional workplaces. It was clear that dialogic spaces needed to be created in order to include Romani women. These spaces allowed mainstream theories to be contrasted with the views of the women and for us to access their interpretations and experiences.

In order to carry out communicative observation, we agreed with a Romani woman, Carmen, that the researcher/s would spend some periods of time with her in the street market during the data collection period. During this time researchers told her about the entire project and its structure. Carmen knew some of the Roma researchers involved in the project and also some of us through our involvement in the Roma rights movement. After spending this time with her, we engaged in a dialogue about her own interpretations, attitudes, abilities, and incorporated elements of non-verbal language. As researchers, we described and brought into the dialogue certain thoughts from mainstream feminist theory and from Romani Studies expressing the belief that Roma culture is sexist and chauvinist. From the standpoint of these theories, it could have been argued that Carmen was facing alienation because, while she was working as a sales person, her husband was watching her attentively. Through dialogue with Carmen, the research team learned that this was not the case. On the contrary, it was part of a sophisticated shared marketing strategy that Carmen and her husband had developed. The communicative observation allowed us to learn through interaction that she had taken on that specific role because most of the customers in markets are also women and Carmen was better able than her husband to gain the attention of female customers. Through dialogue with Carmen, and other saleswomen and salesmen from street markets, the researchers learned that Romani woman and men work as a team, rather than men exploiting the women.

Another example of the contrast between what researchers expected and the real position of social actors can be found in the communicative daily life stories carried out within a study on school persistence and dropout among Romani girls (Sordé, 2007). In the communicative life story, the researcher and the subject of the research interacted and dialogued about the life and experience of the subject on equal terms, enabling each to bring different, but equal, knowledge into dialogue (Gómez et al, 2006). This study constituted a shared interpretation, identifying the situations, actions, or opinions, that could lead to social transformation and understanding how these girls had, or could, overcome situations of social exclusion through school persistence.

Many objectivist-based researchers have reinforced the idea that Romani culture is opposed to schooling. Explaining why Romani girls drop out of school, some point to the tradition of marrying at an early age, or say that parents do not allow their daughters to attend high school. However, when research is organised communicatively and includes the participation of Roma people at every stage, it can demonstrate that these explanations are not always valid. When these explanations were contrasted with the girls' life stories, it was clear that other crucial factors played an important role in shaping these girls' decisions to drop out. Critical dialogue allowed them to reflect and identify the real reasons. The fact that schools did not respond to their need for better opportunities lead them to believe that school is not an option. Thus, believing school dropout as a situation from which no Roma girl can escape leads them to believe that marrying and having their own family is a better option, not only because doing so is important in their culture, but because it is an area in which they can envision being successful. In a school improved situation, they said they would stay and succeed, and might also get engaged. Far from what had previously been believed, critical communicative research demonstrated that it is the families of Romani girls who support them the most in their endeavour to continue their schooling.

Key learning

Everyone, independently of their educational credentials, can contribute to the dialogic creation of knowledge. Thus, community research should be based on the recognition of people's universal capacity to explain and share their own reality (Chomsky, 1965). Rigorous research that aims to create new scientific knowledge cannot only take the views of experts into consideration (Beck et al, 1994). It is necessary to contrast what the scientific community says (system) with the lifeworld of the participants (Habermas, 1984).

Subjects such as Joan, Carmen or the Romani girls and their families are not merely self-interested, strategic agents. They are social subjects who are capable of language and action. Their contributions should be valued, based on the strength of their arguments, rather than the strength of the position of power held by the person formulating the argument. In order to gather together these contributions, it is important to create conditions of egalitarian dialogue, prioritising the arguments of non-traditional participants through advisory councils and multicultural research teams throughout the research process. Critical communicative methodology in responding to the dialogic turn in society, combines both objectivist and subjectivist perspectives and moves towards intersubjectivity. It responds to people's demands for science to provide them with the tools to support and carry out transformations in order to create a better world.

Summary

Advantages

CCM makes research findings more socially useful. When representatives of vulnerable groups are included, the research is more likely to reflect the reality being experienced by these people and it is easier to transform situations of social exclusion. When taking the participation of subjects into account throughout the whole research process and establishing spaces for egalitarian dialogue with the researchers, it is easier to achieve a political impact.

CCM promotes the inclusion of experiences and voices that have been traditionally excluded from research and combines it with the findings obtained from the academic community, in order to produce new rigorous knowledge.

Limitations

It can be difficult to gain access to those people who can represent a vulnerable group.

Researchers must constantly contribute to dialogue with social subjects, drawing in the most relevant theories and findings. The researchers should be open to being challenged and questioned by non-experts and non-academic people.

Conclusions

CCM provides a useful framework for researchers who want to research groups that have been traditionally excluded from the creation of knowledge. Contemporary theories in social sciences suggest everyone is capable of describing the reasons behind their behaviour. It is now time to move from researching 'on' to researching 'with', based on the recognition that anyone can be treated as a subject who can contribute to the analysis of society (Flecha and Gómez, 2004). People can engage not only as key informants, but also as active participants in the creation of knowledge through an intersubjective dialogue with the researchers.

The involvement of these actors makes the CCM innovative and more effective in overcoming inequalities, by always combining the arguments of excluded people with the knowledge generated through academic processes. Moving beyond the hierarchy between researchers and those being researched has led to significant progress in terms of scientific knowledge, in both the social and the political domain. The developments of particular policies targeting the Roma illustrate the potential impact of research conducted using CCM, and the critical importance of involving community researchers and the community at large throughout the process.

As mentioned earlier, the need to develop innovative methodological approaches to include the Roma's own reflections, perspectives and views of their reality has often been raised as crucial. Their reality needs to be included in both official settings and informal community settings. If we are to make claims about the high quality of our ethical approach and standard of our research we need to adopt methods that genuinely include those whose reality is studied.

Discussion questions

1. Why is it important in today's society to connect scientific knowledge and the voice of the voiceless?
2. What are the benefits and limitations of critical communicative methodology in comparison to other forms of research?
3. In what ways can you introduce dialogic elements into your own research?

References

Aubert, A., Flecha, A., García, C., Flecha, R. and Racionero, S. (2008) *Aprendizaje Dialógico en la Sociedad de la Información*, Barcelona: Hipatia.

Beck, U. (1992) *Risk Society*, New York: Sage Publications.

Beck, U., Giddens, A. and Lash, S. (1994) *Reflexive Modernization: Politics, Tradition and Aesthetics in the Modern Social Order*, Stanford: Stanford University Press.

Chomsky, N. (1965) *Aspects of the Theory of Syntax*, Cambridge: M.I.T. Press.

Congreso de los Diputados (2005) '*162/000320 Proposición no de Ley Presentada por el Grupo Parlamentario de Esquerra Republicana (ERC), Relativa al Reconocimiento de los Derechos del Pueblo Gitano*', Boletín Oficial de las Cortes Generales, 186: 42-43.

CREA (2001-04) WORKALÓ. *The Creation of New Occupational Patterns for Cultural Minorities: The Gypsy Case*, (I+D+I) RTD, 5thFP, European Commission, Barcelona.

CREA (2002-04) CALLI BUTIPEN: *Mujer Gitana y Mercado Laboral, Plan Nacional de I+D+I*, Comisión Interministerial de Ciencia y Tecnología. MTAS/ Instituto de la Mujer, Barcelona.

CREA (2006-11) INCLUD-ED. *Strategies for Inclusion and Social Cohesion from Education in Europe*, 028603-2. Sixth Framework Programme. Priority 7: Citizens and Governance in a Knowledge-Based Society, European Commission.

European Parliament (2005) European Parliament resolution on the situation of the Roma in the European Union. P6_TA-PROV(2005)0151.

Flecha, R. and Gómez, J. (2004) 'Participatory Paradigms: Researching 'with' Rather Than 'on'', in B. Crossan, J. Gallacher and M. Osborne (eds) *Researching Widening Access: Issues and Approaches in an International Context*, London: Routledge, 129-140.

Flecha, R., Gómez, J. and Puigvert, L. (2003) *Contemporary Sociological Theory*, New York: Peter Lang Publishers.

Freire, P. (1970) *Pedagogía del Oprimido*, Madrid: Siglo XXI Editores.

Freire, P. (1997) *A la Sombra de Este árbol*, Barcelona: El Roure.

Generalitat de Catalunya (2005) *Pla Integral del Poble Gitano a Catalunya, Barcelona: Departament de Benestar i Família*, Direcció General d'actuacions comunitàries i cíviques.

Gómez, A., Racionero, S. and Sordé, T. (2010) 'Ten Years of Critical Communicative Methodology', *International Review of Qualitative Research*, 1(3): 17-43.

Gómez, A., Puigvert, L. and Flecha, R. (2011) 'Critical Communicative Methodology: Informing Real Social Transformation through Research', *Qualitative Inquiry*, 17(3): 235-245.

Gómez, J. and Vargas, J. (2003) 'Why Romà do not Like Mainstream School: A Voice of a People Without a Territory'. *Harvard Educational Review*, 73(4): 559-590.

Gómez, J., Latorre, A., Sánchez, M. and Flecha, R. (2006) *Metodología Comunicativa Crítica*, Barcelona: El Roure Editorial.

Habermas, J. (1984) *The Theory of Communicative Action, 1: Reasons and the Rationalization of Society*, Boston, MA: Beacon Press.

Habermas, J. (1987) *The Theory of Communicative Action, 2: Lifeworld and System: A Critique of Functionalist Reason*, Boston, MA: Beacon Press.

Munté, A., Serradell, O. and Sordé, T. (2011) 'From Research to Policy: Roma Participation through Communicative Research', *Qualitative Inquiry*, 17(3): 256-266.

Sánchez, M., Giménez, M., Blasco, R., Fernández, M., Sánchez, C., Serentill, S., Vílchez, R., Llopis, R., Closa, A., Prozo, C., Carbonell, A. and Bergé, M. (2005) *Estudi de la Població Gitana a Catalunya, Fundació Pere Tarrés*, Barcelona: Departament de Benestar Social i Família, Generalitat de Catalunya.

Sordé, T. (2007) *'Quitarse de la Escuela': Processes of Persistence and Dropping out among Romaní Girls*, Doctorate edn, Harvard University.

Touraine, A. (2000) *Can We Live Together? Equality and Difference*, Cambridge, UK: Polity Press.

Touraine, A., Wieviorka, M. and Flecha, R. (2004) *Conocimiento e Identidad. Voces de Grupos Culturales en la Investigación Social*, Barcelona: El Roure Editorial.

Three

Authenticity and validity in community research: looking at age discrimination and urban social interactions in the UK

Andrew Clark, Caroline Holland and Richard Ward

Chapter aims

- To summarise key debates about authenticity and validity in social research and outline the challenges and opportunities that participatory ways of researching present to authenticity and validity
- To contextualise these issues in the authors' experiences conducting research with community researchers in two research projects: one about age discrimination, the other social interactions in urban public spaces
- To discuss the impact of participatory approaches on the outcomes of the research, particularly in efforts to produce knowledge that can be claimed to be 'valid' and 'authentic'
- To reflect on the challenges involved in adequately representing the voices of the community researchers in research outputs
- To consider implications for future collaborative research involving academic and community researchers

Introduction

This chapter addresses some of the challenges of producing valid and authentic data, analysis and findings in participatory research projects involving teams of community researchers. The discussion is based upon our experiences working on two projects. One, Research on Age Discrimination (referred to as RoAD)[1] was a two-year, UK-wide study that aimed to uncover evidence of age discrimination. Older people participated in a variety of ways including as diarists, panel respondents, members of discussion groups and as advisory group members. Twelve older people were also recruited and trained as paid fieldworkers and from their work several smaller, sub-projects emerged, some of which were developed and led by community researchers (Ward and Bytheway, 2008). The other, Social Interactions in

Public Places (referred to as SIPP)[2] was a year-long study in which 40 local people aged between 16 and 73 were recruited and trained to complete structured and ethnographic observations of social interactions in a range of public places in one British town. These community researchers also contributed to research design and analysis, and gave reflective accounts of their involvement in the research (Holland et al, 2007). We discuss the impact of working with community researchers in both projects on our claims to having produced valid and authentic knowledge, and reflect on the challenges of adequately representing myriad voices in research. Rather than prescribe how researchers should approach these issues, we present insights into how we negotiated them through the research process.

Validity and authenticity in research

There has been considerable debate about the nature of validity and authenticity in social research, framed broadly in inter-related concerns about the nature of truth, the justification of research findings and data quality. Creswell and Miller (2000) suggest that issues of validity are rooted in the paradigms within which researchers work and, while cautious of over-simplification, it is broadly possible to differentiate between positivist and interpretivist and naturalistic approaches. In positivist research, validity is achieved through the rigour of the research instrument, such as the quality of the survey or the degree of objectivity of the researcher. Here, achieving reliability becomes a matter of obtaining repeatable or consistent results across a sample through the use of the same tool or method, such that different researchers can arrive at the same conclusions using the same approach or techniques. Validity concerns the strength of conclusions or inferences, and is often framed in relation to the accuracy of the analysis, the extent to which findings are generalisable to other contexts, or the accuracy of any causal relationships that are identified (Denscombe, 2007). As Kerlinger (1979: 138) puts it, 'validity is often defined by asking the question, 'Are you measuring what you think you are measuring?' (that is, internal validity), and, 'Are these findings generalisable to other populations?' (that is, external validity).

In naturalistic and interpretive inquiry making and assessing claims about validity are less straightforward, not least because producing either 'measurable', or objective facts, is rarely the intended outcome. Ascertaining the quality of interpretivist research is based upon a different set of assumptions. In part this is because the use of (predominantly though not exclusively) qualitative methodologies produces subjective and/or co-constructed data that is difficult to replicate, but because a demand for reliability is replaced by a desire for more 'authentic' understandings of experience (Seale and Silverman, 1997). Consequently, a variety of different criteria have been developed to ascertain the quality of qualitatively-driven research. For example, Maxwell (1996) argues that validity ought to refer not to data or methods, but rather to representations of accounts of findings. Others suggest researchers should be concerned with credibility rather than validity (Silverman, 2006), with confirmability and dependability (Lincoln and Guba, 1985), or with addressing the 'fidelity' of the data and its interpretations (Gobo, 2008). As such, internal validity becomes, broadly, a matter of credibility, trustworthiness and authenticity rather than a concern about objective truth, while generalisability and concerns about external validity are questions about the transferability of data and findings to other social milieux (Lincoln and Guba, 1985; Heron, 1996).

Ensuring the quality of such research can be achieved in several ways, including treating validity as an ongoing process from the selection of theoretical presuppositions through to the role that readers play in their own interpretation of research findings (Kvale and Brinkman, 2009). The use of thick description has been claimed to offer authentic insight into the experiences of research participants (Geertz, 1973), while member checking and peer-debriefing (Lincoln and Guba, 1985) and triangulation (Denzin, 1989; Seale, 1999) have been applied in order to enhance the credibility of accounts. However, these techniques are not necessarily concerned with whether the data collected and the knowledge presented represent 'truth'. For instance, Denzin and Lincoln (2008) suggest that techniques such as triangulation represent 'attempts to secure an in-depth understanding of the phenomenon in question' (page 7) rather than any attempt to capture an objective reality. Others have questioned whether notions of validity should be applied to qualitative research, arguing that the notion is bound to ideas of positivism and a discourse of replicability, measurement and universal truths (Lather, 1994; Schwandt, 1996; Wolcott, 1996). Denzin and Lincoln (2008: 26) term this a 'legitimation crisis' about how researchers can present qualitative research findings in ways that best represent the varied experiences of participants. Here, knowledge becomes situated, subjective and entangled in relationships of power, with the question of, 'Is this research valid?' perhaps more appropriately phrased as, 'For whom is this research valid?'

Questions about whose truths or realties are represented in research, is in part a matter of authenticity (Guba and Lincoln, 1989). In calling for attention to be paid to the authenticity of research, it has been suggested that qualitative researchers aim to demonstrate that:

> Informants have equal access to the inquiry process, being involved from the outset about the choice of salient questions and how to answer them… they have enlarged their personal views about their culture… have improved understanding of the views of others in the culture… [and] have been stimulated and empowered to act

> to reshape their culture on the basis of their expanded awareness. (Heron, 1996: 161)

Research with community researchers raises specific challenges for validity and authenticity beyond 'conventional' research practices. This includes ensuring different viewpoints are incorporated into research without succumbing to relativism, and enabling community researchers to have input across the research process through 'authentic participation' (Nolan et al, 2007). Bradbury and Reason's (2001) contribution to 'broadening the bandwidth of validity' in action research raises two issues that are particularly salient to our own learning here. These are a 'relational-praxis' that reflects the degree to which participants are free to be fully involved in the research process; and a 'plurality of knowing' that builds on different experiential and theoretical knowledge. As we reflect below, entangled in these are issues of power and empowerment, competing ontological bases for understanding the world, and appropriate ways of managing, doing and presenting research with community researchers. Being satisfied that we can claim research that is valid and authentic (however defined) requires iterative negotiation and dialogue between academic and community researchers in order to accommodate competing epistemologies and experiences.

Community research in practice

In the two research projects discussed here we worked alongside community researchers in the design, implementation and analysis of research. In SIPP the community researchers had no, or very little, experience of academic research. In RoAD they had a little more experience of conducting interviews, though not necessarily in a research context. In both projects these researchers were recruited from the communities we were seeking to understand. We refer to the community researchers as co-researchers. This is partly to avoid contention over who or what represents 'the community', but also to mark the equal value we placed on lay and academic knowledge. Our discussion is structured in relation to research design, data collection and analysis and dissemination, and addresses issues of participation, alongside questions of how the data and findings were produced.

Validity and authenticity in research design

The projects began as responses to calls for proposals from the Joseph Rowntree Foundation (for SIPP) and Help the Aged (now Age UK), funded by the National Lottery Community Fund (for RoAD), both of which emphasised community involvement. Although there were different degrees of non-academic input in their initiation, in neither project did co-researchers have direct input into the initial research design. This created an initial imbalance in the participatory nature of the research and raised issues about who had ownership, and control, over the research (Clark et al, 2009; see also Bagnoli and Clark, 2010). Nonetheless, once funding was obtained, we aimed to include the views of co-researchers in developing research design and modifying methods, as well as in data collection and analysis and, to a lesser extent, dissemination. Establishing open dialogue with co-researchers was key to this process and we sought their views on important substantive and theoretical ideas, issues to focus upon during data collection, and training in social research principals.

In SIPP, potential co-researchers were given a brief synopsis of the research and invited to a training day for more detailed discussions. This included an outline of research questions about the nature and use of public spaces by different social groups; an introduction to the nature of observation methods and data; and discussion of how we hoped the co-researchers would apply a specific method of non-participatory semi-structured observations. Instruction and advice was also given on ethical issues that might arise while working in the field. We stressed to the co-researchers that we were interested in learning from them whether the approach could collect the sort of data required to answer the research questions. In doing so, we hoped to achieve a more authentic degree of participation to research design despite the lack of participatory input in the initial design stages. As a result, co-researchers suggested different public spaces to include in the study, which were implemented. However, co-researchers arguably had most impact on research design while they were collecting the data, when they developed their own distinct ways of recording ethnographic observations, with many choosing to focus observations on particular interactions and groups (such as teenagers or older people) or features of the built environment (such as activities around public seating or monuments) that they found most interesting.

The RoAD project began by engaging in a dialogue with a network of older people's forums throughout the UK with efforts made to establish links to varied kinds of location (such as rural/urban, affluent/deprived). Twelve co-researchers were recruited and attended a two-day introductory training session where the broad aims of the project were presented, though from the outset the research team tried to avoid being prescriptive with regard to more specific objectives for the research. As the study unfolded new research questions and topics also emerged, often at a local level, which the co-researchers pursued themselves. For instance, the significance of taking into account multiple discrimination became clear as the co-researchers began to analyse and report back on the interviews they were conducting. We gathered profile information on participants: age, gender, disability/ health, sexuality, ethnicity and religion, work history and housing tenure.

This revealed that many of the social and political networks in which older people are involved were clustered around common characteristics (such as culture, ethnicity and sexuality) and exposed potential 'gaps' in the research. These efforts to build a profile of study participants underlined the tensions between authentic participation and questions of inclusivity. Co-researchers were supported in developing and leading sub-projects addressing specific issues which included considerations of sexual orientation and ethnicity and ageing, though we remained conscious that many standpoints remained under-represented or absent from the research, and we were careful to communicate these deficits when disseminating findings.

A significant challenge to achieving what we hoped would be authentic participation was the variety of ways of knowing that the co-researchers brought to the projects. Although not couched in the language of epistemology, many of our discussions focused upon competing views of how we might come to know the world, about what might be considered 'research' (rather than say, what was dismissed as anecdote or opinion), and about how we might assess the quality of the data being produced. In SIPP some co-researchers worked within a kind of positivist hegemony: that is, a search for objective truth and a commitment to conducting social scientific inquiry that mirror methodologies applied in the natural sciences. Discussion frequently focused on different hypotheses we could pursue, how we would generalise from the results, and concerns about what 'answer' we were going to come up with. Some co-researchers questioned whether their own data were 'correct', and whether we were going to transform the qualitative data being produced into numerical values for statistical analysis. This questioning of how to do research, and of what constituted appropriate data, was sometimes at odds with our initial aims (proposed in the funding application) about producing data that reflects the interpretations and significance of local, and everyday, knowledge and experience. We addressed these differences through group discussions about the nature of qualitative inquiry and in one-to-one conversations with co-researchers. Consequently, and as others have observed (Heron, 1996; Bradbury and Reason, 2001), these discussions were not simply about how to interpret what co-researchers observed, but also involved debate about different standpoints from which we could best describe, examine and understand the social world.

The nature of evidence was also central in the development of RoAD. We issued a request to older people's forums across the UK to submit accounts of specific instances of age discrimination as a form of reliable 'hard evidence'. A pro-forma was designed that recorded details of time, place and who was involved and suggested to contributors that they think of the type of evidence that might 'stand up in court'. In this way, RoAD maintained a focus on social practices rather than on attitudes or generalised reflections on the nature of age discrimination. This emphasis upon courtroom-like evidence enabled us to negotiate the positivist public hegemony that shaped the understanding and beliefs of many co-researchers, though at the same time created tensions as it underplayed the subjective and interpretative nature of the accounts we elicited. In some cases this meant that co-researchers reported being unable to 'find' or 'see' instances of age discrimination, suggesting that it was perceived as something fixed and unambiguous rather than a matter of interpretation.

Validity and authenticity in data collection and analysis

The RoAD co-researchers gathered data through interviewing diarists and composing reports based upon those interviews. These reports were based upon analysis by the co-researchers of the diaries and interviews and formed part of the broader analytic process for the study. Given limited time and funding available, a decision was taken to select fieldworkers with some prior interviewing experience. These fieldworkers' evolving understanding of age discrimination was central to the study. Each time they conducted an interview and reflected upon it while writing up the report, their insights were added to their own experiences as older people subject to discrimination. This meant that the co-researchers were required to play dual roles of researcher and researched. For relatively inexperienced researchers this required negotiating their anxieties about doing a good job, with a requirement to be reflexive about their own understanding. This was achieved through exchanges with the academic team where guidance and feedback were offered. However, care was taken to ensure that co-researchers adopted their own approach to the research rather than simply following instructions. A more formal debriefing process followed the completion of the fieldwork when the co-researchers collectively discussed their experiences and reflections with the input of the academic team and the project's steering group.

Establishing open dialogue was vital not only to sustaining interest and momentum in both projects, but also to maintain the quality of the data and analysis. RoAD unfolded in a sequence of iterative cycles: a design intended to ensure that older people were involved throughout the research process so that interpretations of the data were grounded in their perspectives and experiences. Through this, illustrative instances of age discrimination were extracted from the data and woven into short vignettes. Through regular newsletters participants were asked whether the vignettes 'rang any bells' with them, so eliciting comparable experiences in response. These efforts to achieve resonance reflected our attempt to shape findings into a format meaningful to non-academic audiences. By responding to the vignettes participants assisted in checking the credibility of our representations of age discrimination and, by drawing on their own experiences, contributed to the authenticity of our interpretations. Nonetheless, such activities also highlighted the tension between maintaining rigour and incorporating subjectivity. In response to certain vignettes we received a spectrum of opinion revealing the contested, and at times uncertain, meanings attached to age discrimination. For instance, when we offered an account of a son making age-related jokes in the presence of his mother, contrasting opinions were expressed on whether this type of exchange constituted age discrimination. In many instances respondents set out their reasons for why they believed the incident to be discriminatory, or not, and in so doing offered insights into the process and the criteria they applied in judging such encounters. This dissonance between individual responses and overall lack of consensus provided insight into the labelling of discriminatory encounters but subsequently challenged our efforts to provide a coherent narrative, along the lines of describing what age discrimination is or how it manifests itself.

Managing the data collection process in both projects was more complex than we initially envisioned. In part this was due to the logistics of coordinating a network of community researchers, but it was also due to the varied nature and quality of data being produced. In SIPP the majority of co-researchers produced thoughtful, detailed accounts of what they observed, but some occasionally struggled. A minority decided that the project was not for them because they found the methods too difficult, which raised questions about the inclusivity of our participatory endeavours. Rather than providing a single, generalised picture using a large number of co-researchers, the research revealed multiple ways of seeing, questioning and interpreting. For example, the most common activity in public spaces noted by researchers was of people just 'being there': sitting, waiting, passing the time, chatting with others. Violence, abuse and intimidation, regardless of location or researcher, were rarely reported (Holland et al, 2007), and remarked upon with surprise by co-researchers. Yet on occasions when something 'unusual' occurred, researchers would reflect on whether they attributed appropriate descriptions and explanations for what they observed. For instance, one co-researcher recalled noting but otherwise ignoring 'a homeless person asleep in an alleyway' whom she later observed being treated by paramedics: an episode that encouraged the co-researcher to reflect on both her ethical decision-making and the 'accuracy' of her interpretations.

Aside from the 'accuracy' of the observations and interpretations in SIPP, we also remained ignorant of activities that were not reported by the co-researchers. Here, our worries about 'missing data' were at odds with our interpretivist stance. On occasions, less experienced researchers would comment simply that 'nothing happened' in particular spaces at particular times. There was little indication as to whether this meant no individuals were present, or whether individuals were present but doing nothing 'of note'. Likewise, at other times researchers commented on how so much activity was happening that they could not record it all. At such times co-researchers recorded aspects of the scene they found of interest and this prompted considerable discussion about what this might mean. We came to recognise the contradiction with on the one hand, our aspirations for a 'complete' data-set of activities, people and happenings with our equally strong desire to focus on the community researchers' interpretations of situations, events and what they found 'of interest'. Consequently, we had to balance our expectations about data quantity with the ability to produce contextually nuanced interpretive accounts, though while it was initially frustrating for us to discover that some co-researchers had not probed a scene as much as more experienced researchers might, by the end of the project several co-researchers were producing data that went beyond initial expectations.

Assessing the internal validity of the data in SIPP became a process of repeated dialogue with the co-researchers about the robustness of the research methods. The academic team occasionally carried out observations alongside co-researchers, not to check that they were 'seeing the right things' but rather in anticipation of conversations about what was observed, and in the hope that co-researchers would be reassured of their own capabilities with the method. We also held informal meetings with co-researchers to collect and discuss the data. Aside from providing opportunities to probe for deeper insight into observed situations, these provided an important analytical practice that enabled co-researchers to present prominent or unusual themes and issues to pursue. During analysis we presented some of the themes we thought were emerging from the data to groups of co-researchers for scrutiny and comment. Of course, this may have influenced the nature of subsequent observations, encouraging co-researchers to intentionally seek out activities that appear to concur with findings from preliminary analysis. However, rather than becoming concerned with the potential 'bias' in the ensuing data, this worked to corroborate or refute our analysis. Moreover, this process proved important for guiding further analysis and provided opportunity for co-researchers to analyse their own, and others', assumptions, interpretations and perspectives on what was observed. Finally, the volume and scope of data produced in the SIPP project meant that we became less reliant on individual observations and competencies of individual co-researchers and more on the collective weight of the trends and patterns.

Ensuring the external validity of the findings for both projects proved more challenging. In part we had addressed this within the design of the projects by including other methods to produce comparative data. In SIPP we conducted public-space user surveys and stakeholder interviews. This enabled us to clarify and amplify the co-produced data on observed patterns and norms. The charity that commissioned the RoAD research also funded an opinion poll on the issues it raised. Statistical data from this was used in the final report to complement qualitative findings. Accounts from research into other forms of discrimination also enabled us to verify our findings. For instance a 20-year-old study of 'everyday racism' (Essed, 1991) that focused upon the experiences of black women, presented many comparisons to our own findings and supported our analysis and interpretation of the data, while a concurrent participative study based in Brighton that looked at the experiences lesbian, gay, bisexual and transgender individuals, similarly reported on the significance and impact of 'everyday' forms of discrimination (see www.countmeintoo.co.uk). Identifying resonance with other research thus helped to place our own findings in context and lend greater validity to our interpretations.

Validity and authenticity in dissemination

It was in aiming for authentic participation in dissemination that we faced our main challenge: how could we give voice to as many different co-researcher perspectives as possible while still presenting coherent narratives of our findings? As alluded to, the nature of our contracts with the research funders meant that we exercised editorial authority over outputs from both projects. While this raised vexed questions over who has control over research and about our advocacy of a participatory approach to research, for the SIPP project in practice we found that few co-researchers expected a say in determining the key findings or disseminating the results. Yet co-researchers anticipated that, as academics, we would be the ones completing the bulk of the analysis; first, because our access to the full data set provided us with an 'over-view', and second because they assumed that we would have the appropriate skills to analyse it (Clark et al, 2009). In RoAD, some co-researchers voiced expectations that we brought specific 'expertise' to the implied contract of co-working while others questioned who were the 'experts' on age discrimination. At one level, this raises issues about the value of different skills and practices in research (such as the value placed on academic expertise), but it also demonstrates the extent to which community researchers have expectations about the roles of academic researchers in research.

On reflection, while we involved co-researchers in dissemination to a limited extent (such as in university seminars and a conference presentation) we would have liked to have done more. Reflecting on both studies, it is clear from both that to fully realise a truly participatory approach will often require greater levels of funding and certainly more flexibility with time than might apply to other approaches. Here, time and financial constraints were confounding factors, but is also important to recognise that not all co-researchers were inclined to become involved in promoting the findings. One of the challenges of dissemination is that its duration is undetermined. Non-academic researchers do not necessarily have the time, once direct involvement with the project itself has ended, to revisit, reformulate and re-present findings. Although we were disappointed with the degree to which we could include co-researchers in dissemination activities, we found that their involvement on the project did have an impact upon how the research was received. Rightly or wrongly, the findings may have had more credibility with funders because of their pre-disposition to value user-involvement rather than any intrinsic quality in the substantive findings themselves. Given that this approach to research is relatively novel, we also found a 'twin-track' interest in both the research findings and the research process, with the latter having the potential to divert attention from the former. However, while we may have been interested in the methodological lessons of the research, co-researchers were far more interested in the substantive outcomes, and in particular, in how organisations and institutions would use them to bring about change.

While 'catalytic authenticity' (Guba and Lincoln, 1989) and the ability to act on research to change individual circumstances has begun to enter the debate, we would argue that how and when impact is assessed is a difficult process. As Frankham (2009) argues, a full understanding of impact could be both costly and complex and would require detailed ethnographic work 'in order to identify and trace the intricate webs of issues raised over time' (page 22). Nonetheless, in both projects, debriefings with co-researchers revealed the personal 'impact' of the research and of being involved in the research process, in part through raising awareness of issues and having assumptions and core beliefs challenged.

In RoAD some co-researchers reported that the experience had turned them into anti-age discrimination 'champions'; putting age discrimination on the agenda with their local older people's forums and other networks as well as feeling more confident to challenge instances of it in their own social encounters. In this respect, while we might claim that the study influenced the social capital of the communities to which the participants belonged, providing tangible evidence for this becomes difficult without an evaluative methodology. In SIPP, researchers commented on how their attitudes towards their town, their expectations about public places and their practices in them, had changed as a result of becoming more intimately aware of the places, people and activities they observed. However, and avoiding debate about the semantic differences between participatory and action research, it is worth distinguishing between action research, in which an emancipatory methodology is intimately and directly tied to both findings and impacts of research, and our attempts to incorporate 'non-academic' ways of knowing into research that has a public policy orientation. In this respect we draw upon and contribute to what Jasanoff (2003) describes as 'civic epistemologies'. While some co-researchers in RoAD may have altered their awareness of age discrimination in their lives, and in SIPP changed their attitudes towards public spaces and certain groups within it, we cannot really claim that these changes were due to any deliberate emancipatory methodology. Rather, we found that working with co-researchers was a reflexive endeavour insofar as the research process became the study. Given that reflexivity and internal scrutiny are central to assessing the quality of interpretivist research, we argue that placing such emphasis on the research process with community researchers contributes to our endeavour to produce valid and authentic knowledge.

Although authenticity (with its concern for the ways in which data, analysis and findings can represent that which it seeks to understand) is not the same as validity (and the concern for robust, defensible data and analysis), the two overlap in the projects discussed here insofar as what is considered authentic to the community researchers will, presumably, also be considered valid. Community research raises a number of issues around power then, particularly given its emphasis on accommodating a plurality of voices and experiences, and its intentions to give more power and/or voice to research participants, in order that knowledge might help develop insights into authentic, if subjective, realities.

Consequently, issues of authenticity and validity come into play throughout the research process, and concern not only technical matters of data and analysis quality, but also about the extent to which we can claim to have enabled authentic participation. Of course, enabling participation reveals a tension in the power-relations between academic and community researchers, for it implies that one group is in a position to encourage the participation of another. In both projects discussed, as academic researchers we initiated the participation, in part because the institutional and funding structures that prefaced the research initiated these roles. In this sense, community researchers were entering into a research relationship from a less powerful position. Similarly, we offered payment to the co-researchers for their time on both projects based on a standard consultancy rate offered by our host institution. While this raises inevitable questions about potential power imbalances, with the co-researchers effectively becoming the paid employees of academics, we were committed to involving a range of people with different backgrounds in the research, including those with very low incomes, and we believed it important to acknowledge the commitment required of, and ultimately demonstrated by, the community researchers (Clark et al, 2009).

The authenticity of participation, much like participation itself, is not about binary positions or an 'all or nothing' process, but rather about how roles, activities and experiences are negotiated throughout the research process. We have discussed here how achieving authentic participation is not always possible given structural constraints, but also because, as we found, community researchers did not always want to have the lead on some parts of the research. Involvement at different stages of a research project allows participants to develop confidence skills and interests to take on either more activity at a later stage, or to begin their own projects. In this sense, we are confident that our research offered an opportunity for capacity building that can lead to greater emancipatory research. Communities may be fortunate to already include individuals with the confidence and skills to conduct credible and rigorous research (however defined), but it is important that models of participatory and community-based research are also able to accommodate, and nurture, those who might choose to get involved in different aspects of the work, or who hope to develop skills or make a change to their lives and those around them. At the same time, by engaging in a processual model of involvement, academic researchers are also perhaps better able to learn the skills required for working with community researchers at a pace they find more comfortable. Of course, in both projects, and in an ideal funding and research world, we could have brought together a group of community researchers and framed the bid with them, or designed with them the methods and reach of the research rather than encouraged them to modify the methods between themselves and with us.

Community researchers are not a form of low-cost research labour. In our experience, the community researchers offered invaluable support and insight into the process, offering their own views on issues such as the formulation of the research problem and their experience of the research process and they challenged perceived misrepresentations arising out of analytical interpretations that they felt did not appropriately reflect their own experiences, contributing to a deeper, (perhaps more authentic) awareness of the phenomena we were collectively trying to understand. That said, this was not an easy process, and while we aimed to achieve what Guba and Lincoln (1989) term fairness to all stakeholders by involving them in constructions and interpretations of data (see also Milne, 2005), we were nonetheless conscious that those community researchers who could perhaps 'speak most loudly' or articulately about their experiences and interpretations during the group analysis sessions were the ones who were listened to most. While we tried to mitigate this through triangulation with other observations and data collected through other methods, such practices remind us of the power imbalances in striving to enable authentic, cooperative analysis.

Key learning

Our experiences of working with community researchers produced several recommendations about managing authenticity and validity in the community research process:

- Build flexibility into research design that allows for different (and unknown) inputs by community researchers while maintaining clear, consensual research goals. These can be developed solely by co-researchers or in dialogue with academics, and can be broadly or narrowly defined.
- Find ways of building the co-researchers' confidence. In both projects community researchers drew upon skills and experience to meet some of the challenges associated with research. The confidence building process fed into the iterative design which allowed for increased scope for independent working as the research developed.
- Work towards transparency in the concern for rigorous data and analysis, ensuring that methodological principles are expressed in lay terms.
- Be open to, and encouraging of talk about, power relations and make imbalances explicit within the academic/lay relationship and in the broader context of the study.
- Accommodate competing views through dialogue. Engage with co-researchers' ideas about appropriateness in methodology, establishing a genuine dialogue about knowledge that questions conventional ways of doing research. Be prepared for different types of data: community researchers bring their own (perhaps unexpressed) ways of knowing, positionalities and politics to the research. Here, being open to scrutiny and criticism is vital, as is being candid with community researchers about the potential failings of particular theories, approaches, or chosen research methods and approaches. At the same time, all involved in a project need to be able to understand why a particular approach, theory, or technique is considered the most appropriate.
- Ensure sufficient resources, time and funding to support co-researchers including planning and setting boundaries and establishing protocols and systems. In RoAD co-researchers were linked to local forums for immediate sources of contact and support. SIPP required a flexible and efficient process for recruiting and paying researchers that was somewhat at odds with existing, perhaps rather cumbersome, institutional payroll and human resource systems designed to work in different contexts.
- Ensure sufficient resources, time and funding to support collating the volume and variety of data that may be generated. This includes building into the research design capacity for the analysis, writing up and dissemination of data.

- Anticipate complexity in navigating research ethics, health and safety, recruitment and training. Ensure the accommodation of participants' commitments outside of the project. Develop 'training' materials and protocols for fieldwork and set up clear systems to deal with the interface between institutions and community researchers.
- Manage expectations by maintaining good working relationships among and between funding bodies, and academic and community researchers. The collective aim should be to achieve more authentic participation, greater motivation among researchers and, consequently, increased credibility of research findings. The collective anticipation should be that the unexpected will occur and require flexibility and creative thinking in response.

Summary: Advantages and limitations of working with community researchers

Advantages	Limitations
Allows multiple views	Recruitment and training of community
Challenges assumptions	researchers likely to be time consuming
Potentially more inclusive in terms of diversity and experience of researchers	Community researchers are not 'value-neutral' but bring their politics and positionalities to
Creates opportunities/spaces to hear voices that would not otherwise participate in debate	the research
	Administrative complexity: may divert attention from the research
Contribution of local or community-of-interest knowledge	Potentially more expensive
Potentially higher local profile for the research	Unanticipated challenges of producing results within time and budget
Capacity building at community level	Tensions over accountability within the team
Additional person-power in the field/when collecting data	Organisation and management of data production (and possibly analysis) more complex
Greater amount/coverage of research possible in the time available	
Provides a standpoint from which to critically view more authorised and authoritative constructions	Need to manage expectations of those taking part; funders; academic audiences; and the wider community

Conclusion

It is tempting to claim that involving community researchers produces research that is somehow more credible of, valid for, or authentic to the voices of those it purports to represent. However, we do not claim that working with community researchers produces research that is intrinsically more valid than other approaches to research, not least because this raises debate about whether different sorts of knowledge are better than others. Rather, the data produced in this way are different. Throughout the projects we described here, we encountered different views on what constitutes valid knowledge that we negotiated when striving to produce credible accounts of the worlds we were investigating. Key to this was engaging with different perspectives through open dialogue rather than dismissing or promoting particular views. Consequently, we suggest that the challenge of working with community researchers should be presented not so much in terms of whether some interpretations and experiences are more or less valid than others, but in how can we work within a research process that enables these different experiences to be shared and incorporated or translated into coherent findings. Overall, the validity and authenticity of our research lies not only in the extent to which the different outcomes encapsulate and express the range of explanations for the phenomenon we sought to understand, but also in providing insights into the processes through which such explanations are reached.

Discussion questions

1. Does working with community researchers require that we re-think definitions of validity and authenticity in research?
2. What counts as valid knowledge in participatory research and is all participant knowledge equally valid?
3. Given imbalances in power between funding bodies, academic researchers and community researchers, how is it possible to achieve an authentic sense of participation?
4. How can academic and community researchers negotiate differences in opinion to present credible research findings that concur with the experiences of community researchers?

Acknowledgements
The research was funded by the Joseph Rowntree Foundation and the National Lottery Community Fund. Thanks to all the co-researchers for their dedication and enthusiasm; and to Professor Sheila Peace, Dr Bill Bytheway and Dr Jeanne Katz.

Notes
[1] The academic team conducting this research was Bill Bytheway (Principal Investigator), Richard Ward, Caroline Holland, and Sheila Peace, all then based at The Open University, UK. The work was funded by the National Lottery Community Fund.

[2] The academic team conducting this research was Sheila Peace (Principal Investigator), Andrew Clark, Caroline Holland, and Jeanne Katz, all then based at The Open University, UK. The work was funded by the Joseph Rowntree Foundation.

References

Bagnoli, A. and Clark, A. (2010) Focus Groups with Young People: A Participatory Approach to Research Design, *Journal of Youth Studies*, 13(1): 101-119.

Bradbury, H. and Reason, P. (2001) Conclusion: Broadening the Bandwidth of Validity: Issues and Choice-Points for Improving the Quality of Action Research. In H. Bradbury and P. Reason (eds) *Handbook of Action Research: Participative Inquiry and Practice*, London: Sage, 447-455.

Cho, J. and Trent, A. (2006) Validity in Qualitative Research Revisited, *Qualitative Research*, 6(3), 319-340.

Clark, A., Holland, C., Katz, J. and Peace, S. (2009) Learning to See: Lessons from a Participatory Observation Research Project in Public Spaces, *International Journal of Social Research Methodology, Theory and Practice*, 12 (4): 345-360.

Creswell, J. W. and Miller, D. L. (2000) Determining Validity in Qualitative Inquiry, *Theory into Practice*, 39(3): 124-131.

Denscombe, M. (2007) The Good Research Guide for Small-Scale Social Research Projects (3rd edn), Maidenhead: Open University Press.

Denzin, N. (1989) The Research Act, New York: Prentice Hall.

Denzin, N. and Lincoln, Y. (2008) Introduction: The Discipline and Practice of Qualitative Research. In N. Denzin and Y. Lincoln (eds) *Collecting and Interpreting Qualitative Materials*, Thousand Oaks: Sage, 1-43.

Essed, P. (1991) Understanding Everyday Racism: An Interdisciplinary Theory, London: Sage.

Frankham, J. (2009) *Partnership Research: A Review of Approaches and Challenges in Conducting Research in Partnership with Service Users*, ESRC National Centre for Research Methods Review Paper, http://eprints.ncrm. ac.uk/778/1/Frankham_May_09.pdf

Geertz, C. (1973) Thick Description: Toward an Interpretive Theory of Culture. In *The Interpretation of Cultures: Selected Essays*, New-York: Basic Books: 3-30.

Gobo, G. (2008) *Doing Ethnography*, London: Sage.

Guba, E. and Lincoln, Y. (1989) *Fourth Generation Evaluation*, London: Sage.

Gustavson, B. (2001) Theory and Practice: The Mediating Discourse. In H. Bradbury and P. Reason, P (eds) *Handbook of Action Research: Participative Inquiry and Practice*, London: Sage, 17-26.

Heron, J. (1996) Co-operative Enquiry: Research into the Human Condition, London: Sage.

Holland, C., Clark, A., Peace, S. and Katz, J. (2007) *Social Interactions in Urban Public Spaces*, Bristol: Policy Press / Joseph Rowntree Foundation.

Jasanoff, S. (2003) Breaking the Waves in Science Studies, *Social Studies of Science*, 33(3): 389-400.

Kerlinger, F. (1979) *Behavioral Research: A Conceptual Approach*, New York: Holt, Rinehart and Winston.

Kvale, S. and Bruntman, S. (2009) *Interviews: Learning the Craft of Qualitative Research Interviews* (2nd edn), Thousand Oaks: Sage.

Lather, P. (1994) Fertile Obsession: Validity After Poststructuralism. In A. Gitlin (ed) *Power and Method: Political Activism and Educational Research*, London: Routledge, 36-60.

Lincoln, Y. and Guba E. (1985) *Naturalistic Inquiry*, Beverley Hills, CA: Sage.

Lincoln Y. (1995) Emerging Criteria for Quality in Qualitative and Interpretive Research, *Qualitative Inquiry*, 1(3): 275-289.

Maxwell, J. (1996) Qualitative Research Design: An Interpretive Approach, Thousand Oaks, CA: Sage.

Milne, C. (2005) On Being Authentic: A Response to 'No thank you, not today': Supporting Ethical and Professional Relationships in Large Qualitative Studies [8 paragraphs], Forum Qualitative Sozialforschung / Forum: Qualitative Social Research, 6(3), Art 38, http://nbnresolving.de/urn:nbn:de:0114-fqs0503382.

Nolan, M., Hanson, E., Grant, G., Keady, J. and Magnusson, L. (2007) Introduction: What Counts as Knowledge, Whose Knowledge Counts? Towards Authentic Participatory Enquiry. In M. Nolan, E. Hanson, G. Grant and J. Keady (eds) *User Participation in Health and Social Care Research: Voices, Values and Evaluation*, Maidenhead: Open University Press, 1-13.

Schwandt, T. (1996) Farewell to Criteriology, *Qualitative Inquiry*, 2(1): 58-72.

Seale, C. (1999) Quality in Qualitative Research, *Qualitative Inquiry*, 5(4): 465-478.

Seale, C. and Silverman, D. (1997) Ensuring Rigour in Qualitative Research, *European Journal of Public Health*, 7: 379-384.

Silverman, D. (2006) *Interpreting Qualitative Data* (3rd edn), London: Sage.

Van der Riet, M. (2008) Participatory Research and the Philosophy of Social Science: Beyond the Moral Imperative, *Qualitative Inquiry*, 14: 546-565.

Ward, R. and Bytheway, B. (2008) *Researching Age and Multiple Discrimination*, London: Centre for Policy on Ageing.

Wolcott, H. (1996) On Seeking and Rejecting Validity in Qualitative Research. In E. Eisner and A. Peshkin (eds) *Qualitative Inquiry in Education: The Continuing Debate*, New York: Teachers College Press, 121-152.

Four

Community research with Gypsies and Travellers in the UK: highlighting and negotiating compromises to reliability and validity

Philip Brown, Lisa Scullion and Pat Niner

Chapter aims

- To consider particular issues of, and threats to, reliability and validity in community research
- To explore community research in a politicised context
- To highlight the importance of mutual understanding between the researcher and the community interviewer throughout the research process and the implications for reliability and validity
- To look at strategies for working with members of excluded groups within community research

Introduction

This chapter explores issues around achieving reliability and validity in the context of policy-oriented community research with Gypsies and Travellers in England (Brown and Scullion, 2010).

Gypsies and Travellers are acknowledged as one of the most socially excluded groups in England (CRE, 2006). After a number of years of policy inertia on Gypsy and Traveller issues which illuminated a significant shortage of culturally-specific accommodation, the Housing Act 2004 heralded a new, more pro-active approach to meeting accommodation needs. Local authorities were given the duty to assess the accommodation needs, preferences and aspirations of Gypsies and Travellers (as they do for the wider population), and to devise housing strategies and local development plans to facilitate meeting those needs. Consequently, research studies, known as Gypsy and Traveller Accommodation Needs Assessments (GTAAs), have been carried out across the whole of England.

Many GTAAs that were carried out over this period directly involved Gypsy and Traveller community members in the research process as project advisors and/or interviewers (Greenfields and Home, 2006; Brown and Scullion, 2010). While some researchers are strong supporters of such community involvement (Greenfields and Home, 2006), Niner (2008) has reported that others are equally strongly opposed.

Bancroft (2005) identifies two broad populations within Gypsy and Traveller communities. The first are Roma, many of which are based in Central and Eastern Europe (CEE), although increasing numbers have settled in the UK, particularly since accession of CEE countries in 2004 and 2007. The second broad groupings are often accommodated in caravan-based accommodation, as opposed to bricks and mortar, and self-identify as Gypsies and/or Travellers. While we recognise that UK Gypsies and Travellers often share cultural characteristics with Roma, the research that we refer to here does not include Roma primarily as the GTAAs focused on UK Gypsies and Travellers. Indeed, in England, Roma have often been subsumed within research focusing on Central and Eastern European migration more broadly (see for example, Scullion and Morris, 2009a, 2009b; Scullion and Pemberton, 2010). Furthermore, research has highlighted concerns among Roma at being included with UK Gypsy and Traveller populations largely due to their understanding of the racist stereotypes that exist towards UK Gypsies and Travellers, particularly around living in caravans, criminality, and so on (Horton and Grayson, 2008). Indeed, a study in Leeds highlighted no formal contact between Roma communities and the UK and Irish Travellers living in the city (Travellers Health Partnership, 2006).

The authors undertook a number of GTAAs as contractors engaged by local authorities, and it is on this experience that the chapter draws to illustrate some of the benefits and concerns of community-based research in this context. In their GTAAs, the authors worked with members of Gypsy and Traveller communities who acted as paid interviewers in questionnaire-based surveys designed to identify caravan-based accommodation needs among Gypsies and Travellers. The approach proved to have a number of benefits, but also raised issues around reliability and validity in research. We will look in depth at a selection of the most common issues which arose, namely: ethics and confidentiality; implications for representativeness; and the impact of a community-based approach when dealing with 'sensitive' issues. This chapter will highlight how important it is to achieve mutual understanding at all points between the researcher and the community interviewer, and some of the challenges to this in a context of sometimes hidden cultural differences. Overall, we aim to identify and examine strategies for working with members of excluded groups within community research within a highly politicised context. Mirroring their social exclusion, Gypsies and Travellers (and Roma) are arguably one of the enduring political hot potatoes of all time. It would be hard to find another issue of similar scale which raises as much conflict and emotion (Turner, 2000); recent events at Dale Farm in Essex, which received hours of media air and print time, serve as reminders of this. This is the canvas upon which this work with community interviewers took place and where issues of reliability and validity were negotiated.

Identifying the accommodation needs of Gypsies and Travellers

Guidance on producing GTAAs (CLG, 2007) is not specific about exact methods to be used. It makes clear, however, that GTAAs must have an element of quantification, to estimate future caravan pitch requirements, and must include surveys of Gypsy and Traveller households. Such an approach follows the methodology for Housing Needs Assessments, which are well established tools for determining mainstream housing shortfalls. However, in the context of Gypsies and Travellers, such an approach places certain constraints and responsibilities upon researchers.

Gypsies and Travellers have long been described as 'hard to reach' (MORI, undated; Van Cleemput and Parry, 2001). While the term 'hard to reach' should always be critically examined, it is fair to say that engaging Gypsies and Travellers in research can be challenging (Brown and Scullion, 2010). There are practical issues involved in 'accessing' Gypsies and Travellers. For example, no-one knows how many Gypsies and Travellers there are, or where they live. Consequently, there is no available sample frame and a significant task in any GTAA is to inform the selection of a representative sample to act as a base for estimates of future requirements. In any study area, numbers of Gypsies and Travellers are likely to be small and scattered between many localities and types of accommodation, including bricks and mortar housing.

Additionally, the generic term 'Gypsies and Travellers' encompasses many different communities, for example, Romany Gypsies, Irish Travellers, New Travellers and Travelling Showpeople, all of whom have different cultures, characteristics, requirements and aspirations. Thus, diversity adds complexity to small numbers and scattered locations with implications for sample selection, design of survey instruments and fieldwork.

Crucially, there are also issues arising from general relations between Gypsies and Travellers and the 'settled' (that is, non-Gypsy/Traveller) community. At different times and places throughout history, being a Gypsy was punishable by death, slavery, imprisonment or deportation. Not surprisingly, history has left its mark with a culture of secrecy and elusiveness, and considerable mistrust for 'authority'. Researchers have recognised the legacy, which discrimination and tension has left for those attempting to engage Gypsies and Travellers in policy issues (Greenfields and Home, 2006; Levinson, 2007). Implementing a community-based approach has been seen as a key way to ameliorate some of these tensions and challenges while providing a vehicle to engage a broader population.

The importance of a community-based approach when assessing accommodation needs

Participatory research approaches emerged from a number of studies that involved working with oppressed or powerless people and groups in developing countries (see Fals-Borda and Anishur Rahman, 1991; Hall, 1993). Building on these foundations, researchers who are interested in enhancing the voice of marginalised people and ensuring their research resembles what is being played out 'on the ground' – or in other words has validity – have increasingly opted to involve community members in the research process (Temple and Edwards, 2006; Jacobs, 2007; Lomax, 2008). Indeed, it has been argued that research without the involvement of the community being researched cannot be entirely valid (Temple and Steele, 2004).

It is often anticipated that participatory approaches not only benefit the research in the short term, but also lay a foundation from which greater engagement and dialogue can occur in the future (Temple and Steele, 2004).

> Research has shown that when engagement with communities is based on the long term, is adequately resourced and leads to observable change, communities become less hard to reach and less antagonistic towards future research. Such positive moves have been based on community development and capacity building rather than on parachuting in outsiders with pre-defined, often inappropriate, measurement tools and objectives. (Temple and Steele, 2004: 553)

Our experiences of working with Gypsies and Travellers as interviewers and involving them in the production of GTAAs, suggest that this has enabled access to a wider and more diverse population, higher numbers of interviews and improved insights into the data and findings. Involving members of Gypsy and Traveller communities helps to ensure that the questions being asked are appropriate and that the methods of consultation are as unobtrusive as possible. It provides the research team with an understanding of some of the subtle cultural 'dos and don'ts' to engaging with Gypsies and Travellers and helps make contact with people who are 'hidden' and/or difficult to engage. Community involvement has also helped to increase 'buy-in' to the studies by 'community leaders' who often argue that Gypsies and Travellers are reluctant to communicate with 'outsiders' (Brown and Scullion, 2010). Finally, the very knowledge that members of the community have been involved has appeared to make the findings more credible to Gypsy and Traveller communities.

The challenges for community-based approaches when assessing accommodation needs

As with other social research studies, GTAAs must seek to produce reliable and valid findings. However, GTAAs are more than social research studies, they are also a policy creation. Because of their role as evidence base for planning policy formulation, GTAAs must yield 'robust' and 'credible' findings which can withstand challenge during public inquiries and examinations which are built into the land-use planning system (ODPM, 2004). In particular, GTAAs should provide a numerical estimate of future requirements for Gypsy and Traveller pitches. Unsurprisingly, the topic of providing additional accommodation for Gypsies and Travellers is highly contentious. Therefore, the 'robustness' and the 'credibility' of estimates is likely to be challenged, and any methodological shortcomings seized upon by those seeking to discredit unwelcome findings (that is, that the estimates of requirements are too high or too low). Thus, reliability and validity are doubly important in GTAA studies: as social science research and as part of a planning evidence base.

The key challenges facing GTAA researchers include identifying the target population, drawing a representative sample, designing a comprehensive yet accessible questionnaire, and carrying out fieldwork interviews in a way that builds rapport and elicits full and honest answers.

Community involvement in the architecture of research methodology

Although there are undoubted benefits to a community-based approach with Gypsies and Travellers, this approach rarely goes unchallenged. For example, where there is no basic information on population numbers or the extent, or nature of, community sub-divisions, it is impossible to say with assurance whether improved access and higher numbers of interviews has achieved increased representativeness or introduced bias. The involvement of community members in the research process may therefore increase credibility with Gypsies and Travellers, but reduce credibility with members of the settled community, local politicians and decision makers. Indeed, awareness of such tensions was one reason given by Horton (2007) for choosing not to work with researchers/interviewers from the Gypsy and Traveller communities.

A more immediate aspect of 'validity' concerns the design of the research. Tensions have sometimes arisen between effective community involvement in the research process, and the practicalities of carrying out GTAAs. As we will argue, these have the effect of reducing the role of Gypsies and Travellers in the research process.

There is a basic tension concerning choice of research methods. Some argue that the most successful approaches to working with Gypsies and Travellers should be broadly qualitative and less structured (Lomax, 2008). This, however, is problematic for GTAAs. As already noted, GTAAs must collect quantifiable data, which cannot be readily achieved with purely qualitative methods. In addition, local authority officers, politicians and the Planning Inspectorate may share common preconceptions that qualitative research, which takes a data 'generation' approach (Mason, 1996), is by nature 'subjective'. They are more likely to see quantitative surveys, based on structured questionnaires, as 'objective', and therefore more able to generate 'robust' findings.

In order to arrive at estimates of accommodation shortfalls which are perceived as 'robust', the current GTAA 'model' therefore involves a structured quantifiable questionnaire. Both 'robustness' and validity demand that the questionnaire asks about the 'right' things, phrased in ways which make sense to different members of the community both in terms of concepts (for example 'travelling') and words used (for example 'site', 'stopping place').

A further tension can arise over working arrangements. Community-based research is premised on the proposition that community members play significant roles in the process of information generation and knowledge creation (Westfall et al, 2006). Such approaches attempt to remove the barrier between the 'researcher' and the 'researched' (Gaventa, 1993). Where community-based research has seemingly been successful at breaking down boundaries between the researcher and the researched, opportunities are presented for mutual methodological design, including the design of questionnaires. This has been the approach in some community-based research with Gypsies and Travellers. Greenfields and Home (2006), for example, worked on a GTAA which aimed to include and engage with Gypsy/Traveller researchers throughout. This involvement influenced the development of survey instruments, as well as the style of fieldwork.

Subsequent GTAAs, however, have generally had smaller budgets and shorter timescales than this early study, which has reduced the level of engagement that researchers could realistically achieve, and the scope for community involvement throughout the research process, including questionnaire design. In addition, in the context of non-prescriptive government guidance, and a growing body of shared understanding of what works well and less well, both GTAA researchers and local authority clients have developed a clearer idea of what a GTAA questionnaire looks like. For some GTAAs, community involvement in survey design has therefore reduced to a form of piloting, in which a sample of Gypsies and Travellers are asked their view on the questions within the questionnaire, with no real opportunities to introduce significant changes. The resulting questionnaires represent a pragmatic approach to gain evidence for housing and planning policy. So, while they also seek to discover more about Gypsy and Traveller communities, understanding is limited by the confines of expected approaches to a survey intended and resourced for policy purposes.

Throughout this chain of developments, there are tensions between different aspects of reliability and validity, robustness and credibility, as well as budget or timetable constraints inherent in this sort of policy-generated study. As a consequence, the Gypsy/Traveller working with researchers becomes less a community 'researcher' and instead a community 'interviewer', at the extreme brought in to help access parts of the community otherwise inaccessible to time-poor GTAA researchers. Gypsies and Travellers therefore do not have the opportunity to shape the research goals, data collection process or the recommendations arising from the research. Participation on these terms can be seen as tokenistic at worst, and superficial at best.

Community research in practice

We have noted some of the limitations on the potential for genuine community-based research in the context of GTAAs. This section reflects on some key areas where working with community interviewers can potentially threaten the reliability and validity of GTAA research findings. The first issue considered relates to research ethics, in particular the issue of confidentiality within the context of a research team. The second issue relates to inter- and intra-community tensions and the implications these can have for sample selection in terms of inclusion and representativeness. The final issue relates to the approach the interviewer takes to carrying out the interview, focusing in particular on any (un)willingness to discuss 'sensitive' issues.

Ethics: understanding 'confidentiality'

The issue of confidentiality is a key concern for all social researchers. In the context of working with Gypsies and Travellers as community interviewers the issue has emerged in two very different ways. On the one hand there are concerns about interviewers divulging participant information, while on the other there are issues of interviewers being so 'secretive' about information that it has obstructed the research process. These conflicting aspects of confidentiality pose particular challenges in relation to quality control and have implications for the research sample.

All members of the research team must appreciate that knowledge gained from the study about individuals must not be used outside the research project. In relation to Gypsy and Traveller communities in particular, given the close-knit nature of communities, community interviewers often interview people they know directly or indirectly, even if recruited from another geographical area. Ensuring that any information provided during an interview is not discussed outside the interview setting is therefore essential. Although the training provided to community interviewers involves a clear discussion of this issue, the degree to which any one member of the research team adheres to these principles is very difficult, if not impossible, to monitor.

While it is recognised that community interviewers need to be able to keep information confidential, there is a need for understanding that some information must be shared within the context of a research team. In one particular study, community interviewers were reluctant to update team members about where, in terms of geography or type of site, the interviews had taken place, quoting 'confidentiality' as the reason for not divulging this information. Given that GTAAs are expected to yield quantifiable results, efforts must be made to interview a representative sample of people, which often involves setting quotas in relation to particular types of accommodation (for example, private, local authority and unauthorised sites and bricks and mortar accommodation). The reluctance of community interviewers to disclose which aspects of the quota had been fulfilled, even when the importance of the issue was explained, made it difficult to establish whether all known sites had been represented in the study, or even whether all the interviews carried out were actually in the study area.

Regardless of assurances, there was suspicion and mistrust in relation to members of the research team who were regarded in a similar way to others in official positions (for example, local authorities, government, or the Police). This situation made the usual quality assurance measures almost impossible to implement (for example, 'back checking', whereby a sample of respondents are contacted to ensure that the interview actually occurred, and that what is recorded reflects their views). It is also worth noting that, even where community interviewers do note the location, community reluctance to give names and precise address (if there is one) also makes back checking virtually impossible.

There are, of course, ways in which such issues can be managed, largely through tailored training on broader research practice and ethics. There is a wider and more general issue here relating to the need to ensure that community interviewers are embedded as part of a wider research team, where the team members all have a particular set of responsibilities; namely the collection of reliable data. Given the entrenched level of general mistrust between Gypsies and Travellers and the wider community, it is arguable whether it is possible for an equal partnership to emerge in a climate of inequality of accommodation and service provision. This, of course, is played out in the context of limited resources and time, which limits the opportunity for in-depth partnership building.

Ensuring representativeness

As highlighted earlier, the Gypsy and Traveller population is essentially a grouping of diverse communities brought together for a degree of policy convenience. Within and across communities there exists an array of different cultures and characteristics, but also a number of tensions. For example, within Gypsy and Traveller communities there are families identified as 'undesirable' with whom others do not want to associate. Across communities there are tensions that can even manifest themselves as actual discrimination. The tensions/discrimination that the authors experienced in their work ranged from the reluctance of English Romany Gypsies to interview Irish Travellers, to a complete refusal to recognise New Travellers as 'legitimate' Gypsies and Travellers. This poses particular challenges for GTAAs, which are meant to ensure the inclusion of all Gypsy and Traveller communities. If community interviewers are recruited from one section of the community (for example, Romany Gypsies) or are biased against particular families within a community, these tensions and the subsequent 'cherry picking' of interviewees can have the effect of over-sampling certain communities, while other voices within the communities remain ignored or hidden.

Issues of inter- and intra-community tension, and of gender representation, also proved difficult to manage. We attempted to ensure that the research teams included interviewers from a variety of backgrounds, facilitating the potential need to 'match' interviewers to interviewees (in terms of gender and/or community). However, this kind of 'matching' is sometimes contested (Edwards, 1998; Dunbar et al, 2000) and is not always achievable in practice due to difficulties in identifying community interviewers in some study areas and the wide number of groups present. Overall, we were aware of, and acknowledged the issues and tried to understand how the political and cultural milieu within which we were operating might have an impact on interviewer–interviewee relations. The 'outside' researcher could be seen to be at a disadvantage, but being aware and understanding possible tensions and the ramifications of cultural politics, means that the researcher can ask the right questions of the community interviewer in order to identify any issues that could potentially arise and, where needed, take appropriate mitigating or adaptive action.

Conducting the interview: tackling sensitive issues

The third challenge to validity and reliability that the authors experienced related to the willingness of community interviewers to engage with certain aspects of the questionnaire, particularly issues that were deemed 'sensitive' (for example, financial issues and employment). This manifested itself in two ways. Sometimes an overt reluctance to ask particular questions was verbalised to the GTAA researchers prior to the research commencing. However, in some cases, it only became apparent at the analysis stage that some questions rarely had informative answers recorded (in contrast to interviews conducted by non-community interviewers). In many cases, community interviewers, based on their own awkwardness or embarrassment, made assumptions that people did not want to discuss certain issues, or would be offended by them, and opted to 'skip over' such questions. Consequently, there was missing data relating to certain issues, making it hard to draw conclusions about particular aspects, such as affordability of accommodation.

Cultural barriers are clearly operating here. In many cases where a research team consisted of community interviewers and non-community members, the latter found that, on the whole, people were happy to discuss a wide range of issues, including those deemed sensitive by community interviewers. In some respects the community interviewers were acting to reinforce an entrenched idea about the unwillingness of Gypsy and Traveller communities to disclose certain types of information.

Clearly, it is possible that the some of the answers provided to non-community interviewers were inaccurate and thus no more 'use' than the uninformative ones provided by community interviewers. It could be argued that such difficulties arise out of a combination of the community interviewer–interviewee dynamic, the topic under question and methodological appropriateness. However, from our analysis over a number of studies, there does appear to be some discrepancy in the data generated by community interviewers and by other members of the research team.

Key learning

In order to avoid and manage threats to reliability and validity, researchers working with community interviewers, within a contentious, sensitive and politicised context, need to:

- Realise the importance of training – training needs to be on-going throughout the research, with regular briefing and debriefing appointments rather than a one-off session at the beginning of the process. There is also a need to support each interviewer throughout the process in a sensitive manner, in order to highlight errors/inconsistencies while at the same time maintaining their confidence. However, training is not a one-way street and researchers need to be open to adapting their approach, ideals and world view in line with the advice of communities, within the constraints of the study, in order to present more authentic community accounts.
- Ensure that interviewers have a full appreciation of the wider research agenda (that is, what the research aims to do and its limitations).

Our experience has taught us the value of ensuring that community interviewers are fully aware of the sensitivities surrounding the research process in a contentious area. Rather than insulating interviewers from 'pressure', which sees interviewers as vulnerable researchers, they should be encouraged to introduce a more empowering approach of full disclosure. Understanding the pressures upon the research and the researchers, as well as how the information will be analysed and used, will help overcome some of the barriers and help guide the actions and behaviour of interviewers in the field.

- Consider the most appropriate recruitment strategy to avoid problems associated with the tokenistic recruitment of community members. In particular, there is a need to move away from a 'usual suspects' approach whereby the people who become involved in research are the people who feature most prominently in the communities. Our experiences have demonstrated the importance of focusing on the existing skills of individuals rather than simply the 'contacts' they have and the gates they keep. Often the most skilled community interviewers have been people who have not previously represented any community or been 'linked in' to extensive networks. The recruitment strategy also needs to take account of age and gender, and to be as representative as possible of intra-community divisions.

These strategies can have significant implications for research funding, with a number of the potential resolutions requiring additional resources. Researchers therefore need to discuss the significance of these issues with funders in order for such strategies to be seen as fundamental to reliable and robust data, rather than simply 'academic perfectionism'. The box following provides an overview of implications of a community research approach for reliability and validity.

Summary: overview of the implications of a community research approach with regards to reliability and validity issues

Advantages

- Allows access to hidden or inaccessible sections of the communities
- Provides vital 'insider' information on cultural dos and don'ts
- Helps build trust with the idea of research and the research team
- Fosters longer term buy-in for research or other 'official' activities

Limitations

- Identifying capable interviewers that do not have a particular agenda is challenging and labour intensive
- The training of interviewers has to be robust, thorough and on-going, which is significantly resource intensive and unlikely to be funded in its entirety
- Working with community interviewers can raise the suspicion of particular stakeholders with regards to the credibility of the findings. Researchers need to work hard to provide absolute reassurances as to the reliability and validity of the research

Conclusion

Given that this is a new area of research there is a general acknowledgement, from researchers at least, that recent GTAA surveys and the evidence they provide are as good, and perhaps as 'valid', as can be expected at the present time (Niner, 2008). The findings, although not always 'welcome', are generally accepted as accurate as can be reasonably expected, given the difficulty of the subject matter. Compromises to the reliability and validity of the work exist, but these can be reduced if the research team is willing to respond to them, and be open about their presence.

However, the various challenges presented in this chapter have led us to confront difficult questions about our approach to community-based research with Gypsies and Travellers. We have consciously used the term 'community interviewer' rather than 'community researcher'. This reflects the role we believe people have played in the studies in which we have been involved. As a consequence, most roles for Gypsies and Travellers have, unfortunately, been superficial. While they have been paid for their data collection role, they have not been in a position of leadership. Overall, we see this as regrettable but unavoidable given the relevant skills currently available within the communities (which are constantly improving) and the presence of historical mutual misunderstandings and mistrust. A more important limiting factor, however, were the timescales and budgets available to undertake GTAAs. Our dilemma when producing GTAAs was either that we employ community members – albeit in a less than fully empowering manner – or we do not employ community members and become one of the many helicopter research teams involved in research on communities; we chose the first option.

Our conversations with interviewers have led us to be reasonably confident that their involvement in GTAAs has led to some positive reflections on the role they have played. We are reminded by some recent correspondence with an interviewer who worked extensively to assess needs in one local area who spoke of her pride in witnessing a number of pitches being developed and the local accommodation need being addressed because of her involvement. This was significantly empowering for that individual.

The next objective would be to progress to a position of 'community researcher', where people are working on studies not as a result of being in a particular community, or by being in the right place at the right time, but from their ability to appreciate the research endeavour and to be a credible component of the research team in the eyes of the policy maker. Ultimately, Gypsies and Travellers would take their place as 'researchers', without specific reference to 'community'.

This is a difficult area of social research but we are confident that awareness of the broader polity around accommodation needs has been created with the Gypsy and Traveller communities. There is much more Gypsy and Traveller activism than there used to be and many more organised associations have taken root. In turn, there are signs that the community interviewer role for Gypsies and Travellers has left, in some areas, a valuable legacy in the form of potentially more sustainable relations between members of the communities and local officialdom. In areas where there was previously no contact with Gypsies and Travellers there are now recognised community leaders or contact points. While in areas where such leaders or contacts were present, there is more diversity.

To date, our GTAA experience cannot be seen as a robust community research process but as something more embryonic. However, it can be seen as a vital stepping stone towards greater engagement with marginalised communities and something for which, at least at the outset, it may be worth sacrificing strict reliability and validity. We would argue that community research may not always produce the best (most robust) research results when judged against the indicators of reliability and validity. However, what it does produce is research that has more meaning to those whom it concerns and greater inclusion of minority groups within mainstream policy and practice.

Discussion questions

1. When planning a research study with members of the Gypsy and Traveller community, what are some of the key factors that need to be tackled when: identifying suitable interviewers, during training, during fieldwork, after fieldwork?
2. What are some of the benefits and disbenefits of working with community members already linked to 'officialdom'?
3. How would you tackle a community interviewer over concerns about the quality of their interviewing or survey completion?
4. Is a lack of reliability and validity in research ever justified?

References

Bancroft, A. (2005) *Roma and Gypsy–Travellers in Europe: Modernity, Race, Space and Exclusion*, Aldershot: Ashgate.

Brown, P. and Scullion, L. (2010) '"Doing research" with Gypsy-Travellers in England: Reflections on Experience and Practice', *Community Development Journal*, 45(2): 169–185.

Commission for Racial Equality (CRE) (2006) *Common Ground: Equality, Good Race Relations and Sites for Gypsies and Irish Travellers*, Commission for Racial Equality.

Communities and Local Government (CLG) (2007) *Gypsy and Traveller Accommodation Needs Assessments: Guidance*, London: Communities and Local Government.

Dunbar Jr, C., Rodriguez, D. and Parker, L. (2000) 'Race, Subjectivity and the Interview Process.' In N. Denzin and Y. Lincoln (eds) *Handbook of Qualitative Research*, Thousand Oaks, CA: Sage, 279–298.

Edwards, R. (1998) A Critical Examination of the Use of Interpreters in the Qualitative Research Process, *Journal of Ethnic and Migration Studies*, 24(1): 197–208.

Fals-Borda, O. and Anishur Rahman, M. (1991) *Action and Knowledge Breaking the Monopoly with Participatory Action Research*, New York: The Apex Press.

Gaventa, J. (1993) 'The Powerful, the Powerless, and the Experts: Knowledge Struggles in an Information Age'. In P. Park, M. Brydon-Miller, B. Hall and T. Jackson, (eds) *Voices of Change: Participatory Research in the United States and Canada*, Westport, CT: Bergin, Garvey, 21–40.

Greenfields, M. and Home, R. (2006) 'Assessing Gypsies' and Travellers' Needs: Partnership Working and 'The Cambridgeshire Project', *Romani Studies*, 16(2): 105–131.

Hall, B. (1993) 'Introduction', in P. Park, M. Brydon-Miller and B. Hall et al. (eds), *Voices of Change: Participatory Research in the United States and Canada*, Toronto: OISE Press, 13–22.

Horton, M. (2007) 'Health and Home Place: Close Contact Participatory Research with Gypsies and Travellers'. In A. Williamson and R. DeSouza (eds), *Researching with Communities: Grounded Perspectives on Engaging Communities in Research*, Auckland: Muddy Creek Press, 25–38.

Horton, M. and Grayson, J. (2008) 'Roma Research – the Context', in M. Horton and J. Grayson (eds) (2008) *Roma New Migrants: Local Research in the UK and European Contexts*, www.redtoothcreativesolutions.com/aded/docs/Roma_Conference_Report.pdf

Jacobs, G. (2007) 'Participation in Health Research: The Need for a Second Mirror'. In A. Williamson and R. DeSouza (eds) *Researching with Communities: Grounded Perspectives on Engaging Communities in Research*, Auckland: Muddy Creek Press, 151-165.

Levinson, M. (2007) 'Literacy in English Gypsy Communities: Cultural Capital Manifested as Negative Assets', *American Educational Research Journal*, 44(1): 5-39.

Lomax, D. (2008) 'Accommodating Gypsy/Travellers: Inclusive Approaches for Collaborative and Peer-led Research with Gypsy Travellers'. In P. J. Maginn, S. Tonts and S. Thompson, (eds) *Qualitative Housing Analysis: An International Perspective*, Emerald: London, 161–184.

Mason, J. (1996) *Qualitative Researching*, London: Sage.

MORI (undated) *Researching Hard-to-Reach and Vulnerable Groups*, London: MORI.

Niner, P. (2008) *Gypsy and Traveller Accommodation Assessments: Perceptions of Progress*, Birmingham, University of Birmingham. www.curs.bham.ac.uk/research_consultancy/pdfs/Niner_Report_Final.pdf (accessed 18 January 2011)

Office of the Deputy Prime Minister (ODPM) (2004) *Planning Policy Statement 12 : Local Development Frameworks*, London: ODPM.

Scullion, L. and Morris, G. (2009a) *Migrant Workers in Liverpool: A Study of A8 and A2 Nationals*, Salford: The University of Salford.

Scullion, L. and Morris, G. (2009b) *A Study of Migrant Workers in Peterborough*, Salford: The University of Salford.

Scullion, L. and Pemberton, S. (2010) *Exploring Migrant Workers Motivations for Migration and their Perceived Contributions to the UK: A Case Study of Liverpool*, Salford: The University of Salford.

Temple, B. and Edwards, R. (2006) 'Limited Exchanges: Approaches to Involving People who do not Speak English in Research and Service Development', in B. Temple and R. Moran (eds) *Doing Research with Refugees*, Policy Press: Bristol, 37-54.

Temple, B. and Steele, A. (2004) 'Injustices of Engagement: Issues in Housing Needs Assessments with Minority Ethnic Communities', *Housing Studies*, 19(4): 541–556.

Travellers Health Partnership (2006) *Roma Families in Leeds: A Social Audit of their Situation, Needs and Services*, www.grtleeds.co.uk/home/downloads/Final-Report-Roma-in-Leeds.doc.

Turner, R. (2000) 'Gypsies and Politics in Britain', *Political Quarterly*, 71 (1): 68–77.

Van Cleemput, P. and Parry, G. (2001) 'Health Status of Gypsy Travellers', *Journal of Public Health Medicine*, 23(2): 129-134.

Westfall, J.M., Van Vorst, R.F., Main, D.S. and Herbert, C. (2006) 'Community-Based Participatory Research in Practice-Based Research Networks', *Annals of Family Medicine*, 4(1): 8-14.

Five

Involving community researchers in refugee research in the UK

Gaby Atfield, Kavita Brahmbhatt,
Hameed Hakimi and Therese O'Toole

Chapter aims

- To explore the distinction between insider and outsider research in relation to community research
- To consider the ethical implications of research on and with community researchers in light of this distinction
- To discuss ethical, methodological and practical issues relating to community research that arose in a project exploring refugee integration
- To reflect on the benefits and challenges of involving community researchers in light of the experiences from this project

Introduction

This chapter considers theoretical, methodological and practical aspects of research involving refugees as community researchers, based on our experiences of working on a partnership project between the Refugee Council and the University of Birmingham on Refugees' Experiences of Integration (Atfield et al, 2007). This two-year qualitative project explored social aspects of refugees' integration.[1] The study was based on 116 qualitative semi-structured interviews with refugees in Haringey and Dudley, carried out by a research team which included academic, practitioner and refugee community researchers. The research was conceived as a 'joint endeavour' between a refugee welfare organisation, a university and refugee groups, who were involved in the development of the research proposal and its aims and, as we discuss below, refugees contributed, as researchers, to the design, fieldwork, analysis and dissemination of the project. In this sense, the research set out to involve researched communities in the processes of knowledge production (see Goodson and Phillimore, Chapter One), with the aim of ensuring that the knowledge generated practical benefits for refugees – as well as informing the welfare and campaigning work of the Refugee Council, and contributing to the academic field of refugee studies.

In this chapter, which is co-authored by academic, practitioner and community researchers involved in the research, we discuss some general theoretical considerations concerning 'insider' and 'outsider' research in light of our experiences of conducting research in a team comprised of 'insider' refugee and 'outsider' non-refugee researchers. We reflect on the rationale for adopting this approach and the particular issues that arose for refugees acting as community insider researchers. We consider the relationships between researchers and respondents and how insider and outsider identities shifted across the interviews. We discuss the contribution of the refugee community researchers at different points in the research process and the impact their involvement had on its process and outcomes. Finally, the chapter offers some critical reflections on the (unstable) distinctions between insider and outsider researchers and some of the ethical and practical issues these raise for those considering, or involved in, community research.

Theoretical reflections on insider/outsider research

There is a critical social research literature exploring the dynamics of 'insider' and 'outsider' research (Back, 1996; Gans, 1997; Gunuratnam, 2003; Young, 2004). Broadly speaking, insider researchers are regarded as sharing particular characteristics or experiences that make them a 'community member' and give them a particular understanding of the people they are researching, which outsider researchers do not necessarily share. Insider research has emerged as an area of interest within research particularly as a consequence of critical methodologies (such as feminist methodologies) which question both the feasibility and ethics of seeking to conduct 'objective' research, where distance between the researcher and researched is viewed as essential for achieving an impartial and thus more valid perspective.

Arguments for insider research have tended to refer to its instrumental benefits, such as enhanced disclosure and gathering of more reliable data as a consequence of increased trust between researchers and respondents, or the benefits of using insider researchers to overcome language or access problems. Ethically oriented arguments focus on the need to include researched groups within the research process to 'give voice' to marginalised groups, address power-differentials between researchers and researched, or provide opportunities to groups who otherwise lack institutional power to shape the kind of research that is carried out on them.

As many (Gans, 1997; Gunuratnam, 2003; Islam, 2000) point out, the distinction between 'insider' and 'outsider' researcher can be an unstable one. In engaging with questions of researching across race, for instance, Gunuratnam (2003) challenges positivist assumptions that black interviewers are uniquely positioned to elicit the 'truth' from black interviewees, arguing that the relationship between researchers and interviewees and interview data should be seen as situational. This is because of the multiple identities and positionings that researchers occupy in relation to their gender, age, origins, cultural and political dispositions, or social and cultural capital. This echoes Young's account of the research literature on the insider–outsider distinction that has tended to assert:

> that there is no singular insider or outsider position that researchers occupy during the course of fieldwork, but rather myriad positions and statuses that can be viewed by respondents either as insider or outsider depending on the social circumstances or conditions affecting the research endeavour. (2004: 191–2)

A key aim of community/insider research is to bring to bear the experiences of powerless and 'othered' groups, that is groups who do not exercise control over representations of themselves and who are routinely portrayed as having identities, values or practices that are different, inferior or threatening, to that of 'mainstream society'. The failure to give space to these othered groups' self-understandings and perspectives within research processes can exacerbate problems of lack of self-representation (see, for example, Braithwaite et al, 2007). The position of othered groups can be highly situational and complex, however (Fawcett and Hearn, 2004); this is certainly the case among refugees, who are an extremely diverse group (even 'super diverse' in Vertovec's (2007) sense). Thus, the ways in which refugees come to be othered, and the extent to which this occurs, can potentially arise generally from their status as refugees, but may vary also according to their specific legal status (for example, whether as asylum seekers or refugees), class positions, professional resources, social and cultural capitals (or lack of them), or religious, cultural and racialised identities, all of which are context-dependent.

Although literature on involving refugees as community researchers is somewhat limited, this way of working has become a subject of interest in refugee research and policy-making circles (Jacobsen and Landau, 2003; Temple and Moran, 2006), particularly as means of addressing the highly marginalised status of refugees in British society. Nevertheless, methodology, models of good practice and ethics are still under-developed (Brahmbhatt, 2008).

We suggest that there are some challenges common to all researchers conducting community research, as well as some that are specific to those interviewing refugees. For instance, some refugees may be in precarious legal positions that give rise to anxieties about their involvement with institutions or research processes or disclosing their experiences of settlement, placing a particular onus on the researcher to attend to risks and sensitivities that may be associated with their participation. While insider researchers may be able to present a less institutional face to interviewees, when refugees become researchers their identities, and how they are seen by their communities, may be shaped by their role as researcher and this may have important implications for their status as 'insider'. In becoming associated with academic, policy or governmental institutions that are commissioning or enabling the research, insider researchers themselves may come to be regarded as powerful or 'expert'. In the case of our research, the fact that community researchers were commissioned by a refugee support agency and a university meant that their role and purpose in undertaking research sometimes formalised their relationships with their respondents, which at times distanced them from respondents, as we discuss below.

Additionally, all researchers need to consider the impact of research on refugee interviewees who may be traumatised by experiences in their country of origin or by their experiences of settlement in the UK, although this may have particular resonance for refugee community researchers who may have undergone similar experiences (Ghorashi, 2007). This presents some distinctive questions concerning reflexivity, (appropriate) roles, support and well-being for researchers involved in such research. These, and the ethical issues that arise with respect to the community researchers' relationships with their communities, networks, gatekeepers and interviewees, are explored in the following section.

In considering the impact of working with insider researchers on a project, Gunuratnam (2003) points out that the ethical objectives and impact of working with insider researchers should not be reduced to interview interactions, but require the participation of interviewers in the ongoing processes of research design, analysis and implementation. Thus we should not assume that community researchers endow research with 'methodological capital' and an insider's perspective by virtue of their presence within the interview – if their participation does not inform the wider orientations, aims and practices of the research.

In this chapter we suggest that there are very significant ethical and practical benefits to working with community researchers, but that:

1. we need to be clear that the boundaries between 'insider' and 'outsider' can be unstable and about what assuming the role of researcher involves;
2. consequently we need to be careful about making assumptions about what is involved when researchers and respondents share aspects of their identities and recognise that there are practical and ethical issues present when researchers share identities with their respondents, as well as when they do not;
3. there are some distinctive ethical issues which can arise for community researchers;

4. the ethical issues raised by involving community researchers need to be seen within the wider context of the research and not just within the confines of the interview;

5. the issue of power differentials between researchers and respondents do not disappear when the researchers are community researchers, while power differentials within a research project also need to be addressed.

These issues give rise to a layered ethical account of working with refugee community researchers that needs to address the ethical demands of including the researched, the ethical obligations to the researchers who participate, as well as the ethical relationships between respondents and community, academic and practitioner researchers.

Community research in practice

In this section, we consider these issues in light of our research, in which we discuss: our rationale for working with community researchers; the issues that arose in relation to recruitment, training, design, fieldwork, analysis, writing and dissemination activities; and the impact of community researchers on the research process.

Rationale for conducting research with community researchers

An important aspect of the project's work was the inclusion of refugees within the research as active participants in the project's aims, design and implementation – rather than as research respondents only (Gunuratnam, 2003; Temple and Moran, 2006). Our rationale for working with refugee community researchers grew out of the need to develop research as a shared concern between academics, agencies and refugees.

Our approach differed then from participatory research action approaches, which seek to close the gap between institutions and grass-roots communities and remedy the power inequalities inherent in processes of knowledge production, by using professional researchers to put research into the service of marginalised groups, and institute the research process as one of consciousness-raising, with the aim of achieving change by and for the powerless (Gaventa and Cornwall, 2001). In this project, we set out to generate a dialogue between academics, practitioners and refugees about the purposes and practices of refugee research, and this underpinned our decision to approach the research as a 'joint endeavour'.

The project set out to achieve this dialogue by working with refugees as consultants, researchers, commentators, critical audiences, research users and beneficiaries at each stage of the research project. Four community researchers were recruited and trained to work on the project as members of the research team and they were involved in the research design, fieldwork, analysis and dissemination phases of the project.

This rationale was also governed by the logic of our funders – in this case, the Big Lottery Fund's Community Fund research programme. Under the terms of this programme, research projects had to be carried out through partnership between a charitable/voluntary sector and a research organisation, with the charitable/voluntary sector organisation acting as the lead partner, with the aim of conducting research that: promoted social inclusion; brought practical benefits to researched communities; and increased the research capacity of the community/voluntary sector.

We also wanted to recognise the (sometimes uncredentialised) skills that refugee community researchers possess and to find ways of recognising these for the benefit of both the research and the researchers (through career development, CV building, training and the opportunity for acquisition of qualifications). We regarded this as particularly significant given the barriers that many refugees face in accessing employment that is commensurate with their skills and experiences (Bloch, 1999, 2002). The community researchers who were recruited had high skills levels and some had prior experience of carrying out research (and see Mestheneos, 2006), from which this research benefited, as well as attempted to build on.

Finally, we identified clear benefits to composing a team with different skills (including language), experiences and insights into refugees' lives. Refugee research is complex because refugees are themselves highly diverse – in terms of their ethnicity, language, religion, cultural identity, countries of origin, migration routes, settlement experiences, education, skills, and so on. In our case, the inclusion of community researchers enhanced the project's capacity to interview in a wide range of refugee languages (which included Arabic, Azeri, Dari, Farsi, French, Kiswahili, Kurdish, Pashto, Serbo-Croat, Somali, Turkish and Urdu), brought an experiential understanding of many respondents' countries of origin and cultural, religious and ethnic identities, as well as direct experience of seeking refuge and settling in the UK, which strengthened the research team's understanding of these issues.

Recruitment and training

The project recruited four part-time researchers with the aim of creating these positions as career developmental posts. Typically, then, these researchers were engaged in other forms of education, training, volunteering or employment, and the team did face challenges in combining these commitments over the life of the project.

The training programme designed for the community researchers was a part of the project's aim to promote career development. It was also a key element to ensuring the quality of the research data, and essential for preparing community researchers for the challenges, risks and ethical demands that they would encounter in being involved in the research.

The training was provided by the University of Birmingham and was delivered with the option of achieving accreditation of 20 credits of a Higher Education level one undergraduate degree programme on successful completion. The course covered topics on: the use of qualitative methods – particularly semi-structured interviewing; research ethics; reflexivity and the role of the researcher working from and with communities; sampling, negotiating access and working with gate-keepers; and dissemination practices with communities. The key principles of the approach adopted within the programme were:

1. an emphasis on research with rather than on communities/groups;
2. understanding how researchers' identities have an impact upon the research process and developing approaches that utilise aspects of shared identity to maximise benefits of research for all concerned (paying attention to issues of reflexivity and insider/outsider status);
3. developing confidence to become researchers and understanding how individuals' experiences can be used as assets in research processes, by developing, identifying and valuing the skills that people have;
4. developing practice-oriented outcomes to research projects and contributing to disseminating research findings;
5. an emphasis on carrying out ethically driven research that is concerned with practically benefiting researched groups.

Feedback from the researchers on the training course indicated that in general they felt it had been beneficial because it gave them skills that they did not previously possess, or formalised skills that they had but for which they did not have accreditation. In a practical sense, the training prepared them and helped them to feel more confident about conducting interviews and enabled them to engage critically with issues of objectivity and empathy within research. In the training, researchers reflected on their role as researchers, the significance of different as well as shared identities between them and their respondents, and the extent to which they could provide support to respondents beyond the research context. However, some researchers felt that the credits that were awarded for the course would have been more useful if they had been awarded at postgraduate rather than undergraduate level.

Working as insiders/outsiders

Academic, practitioner and community researchers were all engaged in the fieldwork, and this gave us an opportunity to reflect on some of the common as well as distinctive issues that arose for community and non-community researchers on the team. As noted above, all researchers have important differences, as well as sometimes similarities, with their respondents, in terms of their gender, age, origin, language, religion, or social and cultural capitals – in addition to refugee status. Thus all fieldworkers needed to be reflexive about their own identities vis-à-vis their respondents.

Our team included refugee community researchers with high levels of social and cultural capital, including excellent language skills, high educational achievements, and experience and understanding of British society and institutional systems and practices of various kinds. There were issues then of what expectations respondents had when approached by researchers who were seen as 'successful' or 'well-integrated'. For instance, community researchers sometimes came under pressure from interviewees to help them in expediting their asylum claims, when the researchers were not in a position to provide advice or help in this way. All team members were briefed to refer these queries to the Refugee Council's specialist services, but nonetheless the request for advice indicates the presence of power differentials between researchers generally and their respondents, with respondents perceiving researchers to have privileged access to institutional capitals.

With regard to the insider–outsider researcher distinction, the blurred lines between these positions were apparent in the research. As noted above, community researchers' association with institutions can affect how they are seen by respondents. In some interviews these relationships raised issues of trust when respondents perceived researchers as working for the government or the state. In practice, it was often necessary to clarify the role of the researchers as independent from government, as well as to reassure respondents that participation in the research would have no implications for their current or future access to services or benefits.

Community researchers did note that expectations regarding their status among the communities that they were researching could be somewhat dichotomous. Thus entering communities as researchers could build community researchers' status (see Ganga and Scott, 2006), but it could also potentially damage it. Key to such concerns was how the research was perceived by researched communities and this can be strongly affected by perceptions of who is funding the research. For example, one community researcher reported diffusion of concerns throughout particular networks of Muslim refugees to whom he had access about other research projects that were funded by the government's Preventing Violent Extremism agenda, which had implications for how these networks responded to invitations to participate in research more generally.

Given the highly networked nature of refugee communities, views about research and researchers can spread (sometimes quite quickly) beyond immediate local community contacts. While it is a common experience for researchers to face questioning about the nature, agenda, funding and motivations of research, the implications of this for insider researchers can be far-reaching and enduring for their ongoing relationships with their communities – in ways that are slightly different for 'outsider' researchers. While outsider researchers take care to avoid damaging their relationships with researched communities, they do not necessarily have to face the implications of their involvement beyond their role as researcher.

In a similar way, the title and terms of research can also have an impact on insider researchers' relationships with their communities and networks. In our case, the project title 'Refugees' Experiences of Integration' posed some difficulties in that many refugees perceived integration to be specifically a government concern, with 'integration' sometimes seen as the government's terminology. We recognised that the term 'integration' is a difficult one with different and contested meanings and this had been much discussed within the team and with our External Advisory Group. Our project aimed to uncover what integration meant to refugees themselves and to give them an opportunity to define the term within their own framework. This helped to allay fears about the project being focused on the government's notion of integration. It should be noted though that there was a fine line between stressing that we were not working for the government or implementing its agenda on integration, while also suggesting that the research would have practical outcomes and impact.

Personal experiences of being a refugee were helpful in sensitising the research design and interview schedules to refugee respondents. It was also beneficial for team members to enter the field as community researchers in terms of their access and ability to negotiate with gate-keepers and meet respondents – for example, in understanding expectations about how to approach and address people, conduct oneself in particular spaces, when to contact people and so on. Shared identities were at times important for building relationships with respondents and generating trust between researchers and interviewees, although these could raise other issues – for example, the need to assuage anxieties about confidentiality when respondents occupied the same social or community networks as researchers.

It is important to recognise that being a refugee was just one part of a researcher's identity, and that in an interview sometimes other commonalities or differences came to the fore. For instance, on some occasions, young people's views were expressed better in conversation with younger researchers, women interviewees felt more comfortable being interviewed by another woman, it was easier for male researchers to enter some community spaces, and we had to address male respondents' concerns to find suitable places to participate in interviews with women researchers – and these issues arose across the research team. In other interviews, shared experiences of being Londoners or getting married were more key to the building of relationships than refugee status alone. For these reasons, the team did not seek to 'match' interviewers and respondents, given the difficulties in judging which shared characteristics would be most salient in any interview. Furthermore, we found interviewees' perceptions of interviewers could change – and thus shift between being perceived as an insider or outsider – over the course of their interaction in a single interview, as well as differ across interviews (and see Islam, 2000). Thus, we took the view that 'matching' was not the optimal strategy for building relationships of trust with respondents, but we focused instead on developing reflexivity among all team members throughout the research.

While community researchers' links to networks were clearly beneficial for access negotiations, it is important to have reasonable expectations of community researchers in terms of their access to communities, for example, an Afghan researcher should not be expected to have better access to refugee communities from other countries of origin or to Afghan communities in different parts of the UK. Additionally, teams should reflect on whether over-dependency on those connections may be problematic. The issue of reliance on our researchers' networks was significant for our project, because the research aimed to explore refugees' social networks, and how the diversity of refugee experiences affected access to social networks and in turn their experiences of integration. Thus it was important that the project was not over-reliant on the access to networks that community researchers enabled, excluding people who were not in the same network or not as well-networked as our researchers, and for the team to seek access to less well-networked refugees.

Participation of community researchers beyond and outside the interview

As noted above, it was an objective of the project to involve refugees and community researchers at all stages of the project, including before, during and after the fieldwork process. In order to achieve this, we held regular team meetings before the fieldwork to discuss research design and during the fieldwork to share and reflect on experiences in the field across the team.

While we aimed to include community researchers in the analysis and writing processes, and their time for this had been budgeted, it was not always practical for researchers to be involved at these stages, in part due to their other commitments but also because of the time involved and specialist nature of some of the analysis processes. Some specialised and fairly labour-intensive tasks, such as using NVivo to code and analyse the very large data-set that we had gathered, were performed only by two academic and practitioner researchers. This meant that community researchers were not involved in the analysis in the same way as the academic and practitioner researchers, instead they were consulted on analytical themes to apply to the coding process and then gave feedback, examples and impressions after the coding and analysis had been done. One consequence of this was that they were less familiar with all of the data, although very familiar with the data they had themselves directly collected. It would be beneficial to consider other ways in which community researchers might be able to become familiar with a full data-set, while having a manageable strategy for the technical tasks of effectively organising and coding large data sets.

Although time constraints meant that some community researchers were less involved in the writing stage, their input into this stage was important, particularly in drawing closer links between the research findings and recommendations with the lives of refugees. As one community researcher put it, the involvement of refugees at this stage helped to focus the implications of the research on the lives and perspectives of refugees rather than only on benefiting or informing policy-makers. In addition to the researchers' input into the report's content, involvement at this stage is important in terms of building community researchers' transferable skills. What is important is that for them to benefit in this way, they should be involved at the drafting stage – to shape the report – rather than only in commenting on finished drafts.

The project also developed a dissemination strategy aimed at sharing the experiences, reflections and perspectives of our respondents with refugees more widely, in which the community researchers were involved. This involved workshops, the development of interactive web pages, the production of posters, a DVD, advice cards, and a document 'how research can help you' that was disseminated to refugee community organisations (RCOs) discussing how our findings could be used in their lobbying and advocacy work. In relation to dissemination, and reflecting the discussion above of the implications of becoming an insider researcher for researchers' ongoing relationships with their communities and networks, research teams should also pay attention to how the research findings are reported and whether these may have any particular implications for community researchers and the communities they research.

Impact of community researchers

The impact made by community researchers on the project at various stages was significant, although it varied at different points of the research. The fact that we recruited community researchers after the funding bid had been successful meant that they were not directly involved in setting the broad terms and purposes of the research – although many of our academic and practitioner researchers were not involved in this stage either. Instead, the bid grew out of close collaboration between the partner organisations, working with refugees at the application drafting stage by utilising the Refugee Council's established links with refugees and refugee community organisations in order to determine the broad purposes of the research.

The community researchers were involved at the research design stage of the study and their experiences and perspectives informed the aims, objectives, methods and analysis. Additionally, community researchers advised on issues that were likely to be sensitive to participants and on more appropriate, sensitive or coherent wording of interview questions. One refugee team member suggested that during the principle stages of the research and the training course in particular, his experience of having been a refugee and been through the process of integration in the UK made him able to put himself in the shoes of respondents and in this way comment on the appropriateness and the validity of the questions.

The experiential knowledge of these issues was significant for community researchers' ability to negotiate access to respondents and in building trust with them. Snowballing techniques (that is, asking interviewees for referrals to other potential interviewees) were used very effectively in accessing respondents from within community researchers' own networks (for example, in working through mosques or being able to reach failed asylum seekers).

There were also practical benefits in greatly expanding the range of refugee languages and cultural knowledge that the team could employ, which increased the diversity of our sample and meant that the project benefited from not being reliant on interpreters in the interview. There were many advantages to this, including enhanced rapport between researchers and respondents, which is more difficult to achieve if both are reliant on an interpreter, or concerned about the interpreter's role and position. Interviewing in the respondent's mother-tongue, rather than in English, also enhanced interview interactions, and these interviews were much richer and more detailed than those that were conducted in English. Furthermore, researchers were able to transcribe the interviews themselves, so that these were first-hand rather than only translated accounts.

All team-members, and community researchers perhaps particularly, had to manage respondents' expectations that they could provide sometimes very specialist support that lay outside their knowledge or expertise. It is common for people working with refugees to find themselves asked about a range of issues outside of their area of expertise, given the difficulties refugees often face in accessing institutions and forms of social and cultural capital. All team members were able to provide some forms of advice, although community researchers reported also being able to share many experiences that respondents had been through, which meant that they could provide informal advice on whom to see or talk to, or what to do, in relation to a range of aspects of refugee experience.

Generally, the experiences for all researchers of working in a mixed team were positive and developmental. For academic and practitioner researchers with experience of working in several research teams, in many ways working with community researchers was similar to working with other researchers, but it tended to highlight the 'real-world' implications of the research.

Refugee research team members reported having developed career relevant skills and experiences as a consequence of participation in the training and the research. They tended not to be as involved in analysis and writing as they were in design and fieldwork. This was partly as a consequence of time, skills and resources constraints, and the fact that many had other commitments. We also found that some researchers perceived this stage to be less important than involvement at the interviewing stage, although it was remunerated at the same rate.

Despite this, some refugee team members have gone on to do more research and make use of their training and experience, with some suggesting that they also employ interview techniques in non-research settings since the project. However, while the experience gave researchers good credentials for their CVs, the appointments themselves did not constitute a career trajectory due to the short-term nature of the research funding, and some management of career expectations, goals and progression should be incorporated into projects based on teams with community researchers.

Key learning

An understanding of why and how to involve community researchers in a range of projects should be developed on the basis of explicit discussion with the communities concerned, rather than being developed through conversation only among academic or practitioner researchers. While this is of particular importance for researchers working with refugees as researchers, due to the under-developed nature of the literature in this area, many of the issues raised have implications for all those undertaking community research. The key learning points that emerge from our experience are that:

- involving community researchers brings ethical and practical benefits to research;
- the distinction between an 'insider' and an 'outsider' researcher is a fluid one and we need to be careful not to make assumptions about shared identities;

- a researcher's identity and how he or she is seen by respondents may be shaped by his or her role as a researcher;
- community researchers should not be pigeon-holed as only interested in or available to conduct research on their own community;
- training is important, as is ongoing support in the field, and the associated work-loads and roles that this involves should be taken into account within the team;
- insider researchers often have unique access to communities, but the implications of being involved in research for their ongoing relationships with those communities should be taken into account;
- it is important to have reasonable expectations of community researchers in terms of their access to communities;
- research cannot be reduced to interview interactions, but the participation of interviewers in the ongoing processes of research aims, design, fieldwork, analysis and dissemination also needs to be addressed, as do the time, resources and training implications this involves;
- ways of involving communities in shaping research at its inception, and prior to achieving funding, should be considered;
- research should pay attention to how research findings are reported and their implications for community researchers' relationship with communities;
- how participation facilitates community researchers' career progression needs wider discussion on the part of funders and commissioning organisations.

Summary

Advantages

- Community researchers contribute to research design, bringing a different perspective and understanding on what is important/relevant/useful/insensitive/poorly worded, etc.
- Community researchers bring practical benefits, such as language skills, experiential knowledge of communities, access and the ability to build relationships of trust with interviewees.
- Community researchers can be more aware of how research can help them and their communities.
- Community researchers can help communities learn how to conduct their own research for their own needs.
- Working in a diverse team can be developmental for all team members, and can help non-community researchers develop a better understanding of the social pressures that result from working within communities as an insider researcher.

Limitations

- It can be difficult to ensure that all people feel that they are part of the team when they are not working on the project on a day-to-day basis, or on all tasks associated with the project, and have other commitments.
- It is important to avoid making too many assumptions about the role that shared identity can play, what constitutes a 'community', or privileging particular status or ethnicity over all other forms of identity someone has, simply because it suits the project to do so.
- We should have realistic expectations about what shared identities and common experiences between researchers and the communities they are researching can bring (for example, we were all working in geographical areas with which we were not necessarily familiar, thus it was not inevitable that community researchers would have better access to those communities because they shared certain aspects of their identity with them).
- The time, resources and strategies needed for inclusion in all aspects of the research, including analysis, writing and dissemination need planning at the outset
- The short-term nature of funded research, and frequent lack of follow-on funding, has implications for community researchers' career progression.

Discussion questions

1. How can communities' inclusion in the early stages of research (that is, before funding, recruitment and project starts) be increased?
2. How best can community researchers be more effectively included in analysis and writing stages and are there more creative ways to include people in these?

Note

[1] For the purposes of this chapter, the term 'refugee' is used in an inclusive way to refer to those who are seeking refuge (including asylum seekers) as well as those who have been formally granted refugee status.

References

Atfield, G., Brahmbhatt, K. and O'Toole, T. (2007) *Refugees' Experiences of Integration*, London: Refugee Council.

Back, L. (1996) *New Ethnicities and Urban Culture: Racisms and Multiculture in Young Lives*, London: Routledge.

Bloch, A. (1999) 'Refugees in the Job Market: A Case of Unused Skills in the British Economy'. In A. Bloch and C. Levy (eds) *Refugees, Citizenship and Social Policy in Europe*, Basingstoke: Palgrave.

Bloch, A. (2002) *Refugees' Opportunities and Barriers in Employment and Training*, Department for Work and Pensions Research Report 179. Leeds: Corporate Document Services.

Brahmbhatt, K. (2008) *Evaluating Community Research*, London: Refugee Council.

Braithwaite, R., Cockwill, S., O'Neill, M. and Rebane, D. (2007) 'Insider Participatory Action Research in Disadvantaged Post-Industrial Areas: The Experiences of Community Members as they become Community Based Action Researchers', *Action Research*, 5(1): 61-74.

Fawcett, B. and Hearn, J. (2004) 'Researching Others: Epistemology, Experience, Standpoints and Participation', *Journal of Social Research Methodology*, 7(3): 201-218.

Ganga, D and Scott, S (2006) 'Cultural "Insiders" and the Issue of Positionality in Qualitative Migration Research: Moving "Across" and Moving "Along" Researcher–Participant Divides', *Forum: Qualitative Social Research*, 7: p 3.

Gans, H.R. (1997) 'Toward a Reconciliation of "Assimilation" and "Pluralism": The Interplay of Acculturation and Ethnic Retention', *International Migration Review*, 31(4): 875-892.

Gaventa, J. and Cornwall, A. (2001) 'Power and Knowledge', P. Reason and H. Bradbury (eds) *Handbook of Action Research: Participative Inquiry and Practice*, London: Sage.

Ghorashi, H. (2007) 'Giving Silence a Chance: The Importance of Life Stories for Research on Refugees', *Journal of Refugee Studies*, 21(1): 117-132.

Gunaratnam, Y. (2003) *Researching 'Race' and Ethnicity: Methods, Knowledge and Power*, London: Sage.

Islam, N. (2000) 'Research as an Act of Betrayal: Researching Community in an Asian Community in Los Angeles'. In F. Winddance Twine and J.W. Warren (eds) *Researching Race: Methodological Dilemmas in Critical Race Studies*, New York: New York University Press.

Jacobsen, K. and Landau, L. (2003) 'The Dual Imperative in Refugee Research: Some Methodological and Ethical Considerations in Social Science Research on Forced Migration', *Disasters*, 27(3): 185-206.

Mestheneos, E. (2006) 'Refugees as Researchers: Experiences from the Project "Bridges and Fences: Paths to Refugee Integration in the EU"'. In B. Temple and M. Moran (eds) *Doing Research with Refugees: Issues and Guidelines*, Bristol: Policy Press.

Temple, B. and Moran, M. (eds) (2006) *Doing Research with Refugees: Issues and Guidelines* Bristol: Policy Press.

Vertovec, S. (2007) 'Super-diversity and its implications', *Ethnic and Racial Studies*, 30(6): 1024-1054

Young Jr, A.A. (2004) 'Experiences in Ethnographic Interviewing About Race: The Inside and Outside Of It'. In M. Bulmer and J. Solomos (eds) *Researching Race and Racism*, London: Routledge.

Six

Universities as agents in the empowerment of local communities in Germany, Finland and Russia

Patricia Bell, Tony Addy, Melinda Madew and Sakari Kainulainen

Chapter aims

- To outline a model for community empowerment through university research
- To examine the theoretical base which informs such work including working definitions of community and empowerment
- To consider the challenges of community research as empowerment such as ethical considerations and structural obstacles
- To suggest elements of a model for community research including alliance building, provision of training and redefinition of goals

Introduction

In 2006 a group of academics, researching and teaching in the field of social work, from universities of applied sciences in Germany and Finland began to construct a model of community-based research designed to empower communities and increase their influence on local social planning. Our aim was to incorporate the principles of social inclusion into university research and move from a tradition of research on the problem of social exclusion, to a model of research with excluded communities, in a way which promoted sustainable inclusion. This chapter examines the progress made and some of the pitfalls encountered along the way.

Theoretical background

Traditionally, the privileged status of academic knowledge rested on the presumption that through the rigorous application of scientific method, untainted by opinions or values, objective facts could be uncovered (Stanley and Wise, 1993: 151–4; Haraway, 1991: 183–4). Throughout the past half century successful challenges to academic claims of objectivity have come from many quarters. Feminists, for example, have questioned the ontological impossibility of what Haraway has named the 'God trick of seeing everything from nowhere' (Haraway, 1991: 189) and also asserted the indexical and contextual nature of truth claims about the social world (Stanley and Wise, 1993). In other words, this is the impossibility of knowing anything independent of the 'interests, competences, experiences and understandings of knowledge producers' (Stanley and Wise, 1993: 191) or as Haraway expresses it, without consideration of the embodied nature of perception (Haraway, 1988: 578). Qualitative methods of social inquiry have increasingly included the voices of the researched. Nevertheless the contexts within which the perspectives of the researched are produced and presented continue to be framed by researchers. Thus, research about a community can often alienate the very people it claims to represent. Furthermore, research findings disseminated through scientific journals and conferences are not readily accessible to communities outside academia (Gray, 2003: 53).

In considering how community engagement in the research process can be improved it is useful to look at the works of Guitiérrez (1971) 'A theology of liberation' and the related works of Freire (1996) 'Pedagogy of the oppressed'. Both these authors, writing nearly 40 years ago, stress the importance of harnessing the critical and creative ability of the socially excluded to make decisions about their inclusion. They argued that socially excluded people should be engaged in a process of education to provide them with the tools to liberate themselves. If education involves engaging the community in a learning dialogue aimed at the development of critical consciousness and social change, then a community research approach, too, must involve the 'conscientisation' of the researched community. Freire's (1996) 'conscientisation' process begins with the acknowledgment that empowerment cannot be disassociated from the act of knowing and re-learning. It proclaims a trust in people as subjects capable of critical analysis and reflective action. The conscientising approach rests upon a dialogical methodology with marginalised sectors of society and aims to break the culture of silence that has consigned many to being treated as incapable of involvement in procedures designed to have an impact on their existence (Freire, 1996: 35–46).

No one liberates herself/himself alone; but neither is anybody liberated by others (Freire, 1996: 153). To promote liberation through empowerment people need to be accompanied in encountering new paradigms which broaden their context of awareness and experience. The liberative approach to research is a collaborative exercise in searching together for new paradigms and discourses, comparing realities, and creating a synthesis of diverse experiences to produce an account of the phenomena under investigation, which can be accepted as adequate and sufficient explanation.

Social work academics interested in community research can learn much from this approach. The objective of research becomes not the delivery of an ahistoric product (Stanley, 1990: 11) but engagement in a dialogical process of creating situated knowledge (Haraway, 1991). Situated knowledge, which reflects and makes transparent the conditions of its production, is not about transcendence, it is not divorced from the conditions of its production, but actively reflects on these, creating a responsible knowledge, through which 'we might become answerable for what we learn how to see' (Haraway, 1991: 190). Researchers operating within this paradigm do not seek objective detachment, rather respectful engagement and re-engagement in the experiences that communities bring. The process of reflexivity comes to bear on the researcher and community's ability to co-discover aspects of knowledge that otherwise might have escaped consideration when a rigid subject–object dichotomy is imposed on the methodology (Oakley, 1993: 224). Freire's dialogical approach provides people with a voice to name their world and thereby transform it. By naming their experience they take ownership of it and become the experts on how it can be transformed (Freire, 1996: 69). 'Within the word we find two dimensions, reflection and action, in such radical interaction that if one is sacrificed – even in part – the other immediately suffers. There is no true word that is not at the same time praxis. Thus, to speak a true word is to transform the world' (Freire, 1996: 68). Research can be a tool for inclusion when it brings to the surface feelings, perceptions and insights, which are all sources of knowledge that can be overlooked when exploring the experience of people located at the margins of society (Stanley and Wise, 1993). Through a dialogical process the once unknowing become the authorities in knowing (Freire, 1996: 93).

This is not to say that Freire's (1996) reification of the 'knowledge of the poor' fits easily to the complexity and fluidity of European life today. Freire (1996) himself acknowledged that disempowered communities can also be mired in attitudes that give rise to racism and other exclusionary practices. As Haraway (1991) states, there are no 'innocent positions', all knowledge as situated is communal, contextual and socially constructed. It can, and should be, subjected to critical examination and deconstruction (Haraway, 1991: 191). What is most important to note is that situated knowledge is an achieved perspective. It is not a superficial, immediately obvious unmediated perception. Thus the creation of situated knowledge is a process. Knowledge about the social world is embodied and provides, therefore, a partial perspective which opens up the possibility for connections enabling the 'joining of partial views and halting voices' into a 'collective subject position' (Haraway, 1991: 196). 'Situated knowledges are about communities, not about isolated individuals' (Haraway, 1988: 590).

Defining community

For the purpose of this chapter 'community' is understood both as, a) a definable contiguous location (Hooper and Dunham, 1959: 19), and b) a community of interests (Hoggett, 1997: 7) which transcends spatial borders connecting people who relate to common needs. As Cohen (1985) has pointed out, both kinds of community have boundaries (Cohen, 1985: 12). Researchers must be aware that key informants may represent established power structures and seek access to less powerful or visible community members (Bennett and Roberts, 2004: 26; Cornwall and Jewkes, 1995: 1673). While communities may be represented, and may represent themselves, as homogeneous, in reality they may be internally heterogeneous, divided and/or polarised (Ramji, 2008: 113; Cornwall and Jewkes, 1995: 1673). A researcher may need to identify 'connectivities' (Ramji, 2008) or as Addy (in Geht et al, 2011) prefers to call them, 'convivialities' which enable communities to identify and focus on specific elements of common ground.

Defining 'empowerment'

The validity of perspective, of knowledge, is related to power (Maguire, 1987; Bennett and Roberts, 2004). Empowerment may be understood as elevating people's knowledge, in particular their situated and communal knowledge (Haraway, 1991). Valuing knowledge in this way is an epistemological shift and requires a research methodology which seeks the involvement and cooperation of silenced and voiceless communities in the process of giving, gathering and analysing information. Community organisations need to be built and supported so that people can express their own point of view and their own interests (Cornwall and Jewkes, 1995: 1669; Bennett and Roberts, 2004: 58–9). Working for change involves encouraging communication between excluded or marginalised groups and the institutions which shape their lives and environment. Rather than motivating local communities to conform to institutional values, norms and expectations, empowerment opens up the possibility to create change, not only in the community but also in the institutions. This long-term commitment goes beyond project-based finite funding and requires a shift from the perception of theorising and practice as separate and distinct activities. This radical shift opens up the possibility for practice researchers, schooled in social work and research methods, to bridge the gap between universities and the communities they serve.

Commenting on the outcomes of government initiated community consultations on public policy, Bennett and Roberts (2004) support the argument that such exercises 'often start by thinking that the result will be to increase public confidence in the experts – but that what the experience often does in practice is to increase the experts' confidence in the public' (Bennett and Roberts, 2004: 55–6). Similarly Addy's experience of 'Put Yourself into Integration', a training course for agencies working with migrants and refugees, demonstrated the necessity of employees being open to change themselves as a prerequisite to promoting change in 'the other'.[1] Thus empowerment, linked to transformation occurs through a process of mutual reinterpretation.

Empowering methodologies have gained considerable popularity in policy oriented science research. In their review of participatory research in the fields of health and international development, Cornwall and Jewkes (1995) assert that this method is increasingly being promoted by funding bodies to enhance effectiveness and efficiency (Cornwall and Jewkes, 1995: 1667). Researchers looking at the fields of poverty (Bennett and Roberts, 2004) and social exclusion (West, 1995; France, 2000) are additionally motivated to adopt such an approach by what Gray (2003) terms 'a democratic impulse' (Gray, 2003: 30). Cornwall and Jewkes assess the depth and breadth of 'ownership' and 'participation', which they identify as two essential features of empowering methodologies. In 'shallow' research, the researchers retain control, 'deep' refers to projects where the researched develop ownership of the process. Similarly, 'narrow' research describes projects with few participants, and 'wide', many participants. From their review they conclude that 'much of what passes as "participatory" research goes no further than contracting people into projects which are entirely scientist-led, designed and managed' (Cornwall and Jewkes, 1995: 1669).

Social inclusion, the overriding priority of social work, is an ongoing interactive process. Therefore, Faculties of Social Work are ideal locations for the development of a research strategy which aims to empower communities by strengthening the structures which support a process of sustainable social inclusion. Practitioner researchers, recruited from experienced practitioners could be encouraged to re-enter education either full or part time and work collaboratively on research projects. Additionally, these could be jointly supervised and assessed by academics and practitioners. Thus a fluidity between social work practice and academic social work teaching and research could be achieved which could change the face of social work.

Factors for a working model

Empowerment research requires that universities have a clear commitment to developing partnerships with communities both in terms of values and ideology, and in terms of staff time.

Long-term alliances

From the university perspective the benefit of developing longer term alliances or partnerships is that they have the potential to provide opportunities for students and staff to work in real life situations and build up experience of research in context over many years. From the community point of view it demonstrates that the university is a committed partner, and is not just in the business of data extraction.

One successful example is the ongoing work between Diaconia University of Applied Science in Finland and communities in Karelia, Russia. This cooperation was initiated in 2000 and focused at first on developing health services. Between 2001 and 2004 a multi-agency, user-oriented approach to outpatient facilities for alcohol and drug abuse was developed. As a consequence of this the community became involved with healthcare professionals and municipal planners in developing healthier communities. Phase 2, from 2005 to 2007, focused on involving civil society in creating a communal intoxicant damage prevention plan. One aspect was an inter-generational local history project to identify what social, economic and political resources the communities had previously enjoyed. The findings were presented in an exhibition and people were encouraged to respond to this using 'post-it note' voting. From this the research team developed a three dimensional physical model of the community and people were asked to use flags to indicate how they felt about spaces, buildings, and so on. Once specific needs, in terms of activities, events and social networks had been identified, wall chart calendars of community activities throughout the year were displayed locally and new grassroots developments were encouraged.

The researcher's role was as mentor and consultant on practical research methods and the community developed a sense of ownership of the project which stimulated wider involvement. In contrast to 'drive-by research projects' (McIntyre, 2008: 12) whereby researchers engage with the community for data collection and then depart, the Karelian model supports sustainable change. The local community were involved at every stage and by 2008 felt optimistic and able to generate their own momentum to continue achieving their goals.[2]

This kind of longer-term collaboration is an antidote to the problem of co-option identified by Cornwall and Jewkes (1995: 1669). In the field of social work much research funding is focused on delivering solutions to problems identified in Berlin, Helsinki or Brussels. Once funding has been granted the researchers will enter the field to explore the community response to specific research questions which have been generated by academics. External contacts to communities and service providers can, therefore, be episodic and centred on exploring deficits.

An unintended, but often exploitative, consequence of episodic problem-oriented research on social exclusion is the tendency to 'feed off' the community. Areas of high long-term unemployment have been the focus of intense research interest. Residents in one area in North West England responded by renaming academics 'epidemics' (experienced by Addy in Geht et al, 2011). Similarly, at a meeting in North East England in 2000, a research team including Bell were asked by residents why yet another research project was being proposed for their estate. From the researchers' perspective they were residents of a 'sink' estate, topping the tables on every indicator of chronic and multiple deprivation and prime candidates for research funding on social exclusion. From the community's perspective they were a community living under difficult circumstances and sceptical about whether any benefit would accrue from cooperating with yet another research project. As Grey points out, research in the first instance benefits the career prospects of researchers (Gray, 2003: 53). The tension is not just an ethical issue, but has an impact on the quality of research and on the impact of the research findings on the community.

Ownership

Cornwall and Jewkes (1995) have identified that the engagement of members of a community may be limited by their scepticism, lack of time and a lack of knowledge and confidence (Cornwall and Jewkes, 1995: 1673). The problem of scepticism can be counteracted by a long-term commitment by universities to community development. Nevertheless, the community development skills necessary to an empowerment approach to research may exceed the ability of even the most committed researcher. In the longer term, the expansion of practitioner researchers who embody both practical experience of social work and research competence is a solution. In the meantime, joint (or tandem) working with community organisers and front line service providers is advantageous. An example of how this can be facilitated is provided by Darmstadt. In 2006 the Darmstadt University of Applied Sciences in Germany established a 'Social Science Quality Transfer Network' (SWQT) with representatives of the major service providers in the area and local social policy makers. This Network meets twice a year to discuss social problems facing the city and also to explore opportunities for collaborative projects with joint or external funding. This cooperation provides the university with a constant link to practitioners working with local communities and is further strengthened through the lengthy student placements required for social workers. A recent development aimed at encouraging practice based research from students, is the establishment of a monetary prize for undergraduate theses on topics of relevance to the Network.

In Finland the Diaconia University of Applied Sciences has a similar solution. 'Community Based Learning Environment' contracts are created with communities both locally and internationally. Within this structure students gain practical and research experience and through such a dialogical approach, researchers get in touch with everyday life of community members, their norms, expectations and needs. This model is sustained not only through student placements and undergraduate theses, but also through externally funded research projects. A similar collaboration between the Freiburg Protestant University of Applied Sciences, Germany, and a multicultural neighbourhood development, was initiated by making the community development project the focus of a seminar for social work students. This, plus student placements, undergraduate theses and externally funded research projects maintained a mutually beneficial collaboration for over 20 years (Maier and Mauch, 2005).

A further hindrance to involving members of the community in research is a lack of training and confidence (Cornwall and Jewkes, 1995: 1675; McIntyre, 2008: 57). Thus researchers should provide some training in data gathering and analysis skills and also adopt low threshold methods of data gathering such as photo text exhibits, storytelling, collages and paintings.

The need to combine community development and research skills highlights the need to develop career paths for practitioner researchers in social work similar to practitioner researchers in healthcare. Expanding the role of Universities of Applied Sciences in promoting doctorates for social workers would further this goal and, at the same time, counteract the trend to reduce social work to case management and social policy enforcement.

The authors' collective experience of research with or on communities within existing academic structures has highlighted the need for structural change in universities to ensure their relevance to current social policy. Within the existing structures of research funding in higher education, efforts can still be made to expand the opportunities for genuine community involvement in research and for this, honesty and realism are essential. If researchers are not prepared to relinquish control of analysis and dissemination it is better to be open about this at the outset as people can feel exploited if they are excluded from these crucial aspects. As was noted earlier, community research can vary in depth and width and being clear about the scope of participation throughout the process is essential for maintaining community involvement.

Encouraging members of the community to be actively involved in every phase of a research project does not, however, make the researcher redundant. Considerable skills are required, to produce a research proposal, which is on the one hand, academic enough to ensure the support of the institution and funders and, on the other hand, does justice to the interests of the community.

Training community members to actively participate in designing and delivering the research, and not just be present at meetings where academics take decisions, requires resources and is time consuming. For example, community members need training in rigorous and reliable methods, a robust structure for group reflection and ongoing appraisal to avoid a too individualistic approach and enable them to gather high quality data in a sensitive manner. This was done in the Karelian Project described above and other researchers, in the field of youth studies, have incorporated training in peer research in their projects (see West, 1995 on young people in care and France, 2000 on youth transitions). The extent to which the community have a sense of ownership of the research process has an impact on the extent to which they are able and motivated to make use of the knowledge gained from the research.

Redefining goals and aims

A second hurdle to community research is the way in which research funding is organised. Increasingly, research funders demand not only evidence of community engagement but also defined milestones, benchmarks and deliverables within funding applications. The focus is not on the research process but on clearly defined products, which contradicts a Freireian methodology by which the subjective experience of the community and their learning processes are central. There is a need to persuade funding bodies to support process oriented community research, and to challenge the commodification of research in the field of social welfare. Sustained networking with local policy makers, for example as described in the SWQT example above, can go some way to ameliorating this problem.

The goal of community research is not just holding up a mirror to the community but creating the possibility for change and democratising knowledge. One way to do this may be to redefine the aims of research and allow communities to decide what constitutes a research outcome and to what ends they should be used. McIntyre (2008) referring to participatory action research (which can be considered a synonym for community empowerment research) goes so far as to suggest that success should not be judged on whether objective truths have been established but on whether or not the participants have benefited from the experience (McIntyre, 2008: 62). This poses a considerable difficulty within the existing constraints of research funding, nevertheless, such openness can enhance a research project by broadening its perspective and impact. Encouraging the community to be involved in determining the ways in which a research project serves their needs opens up a wider range of possibilities than may have been apparent to researchers.

The community and the researchers are often drawing on different knowledge bases which can result in differing understandings of issues and possible conflicts about necessary strategies. The specific ways in which community participants frame issues and the strategies they use in everyday life do not have to be accepted by the researcher, but they have to be acknowledged as contextually important base lines to be taken seriously as data. If professional researchers embark on a process of research and change without understanding the community's analyses and strategies they will be starting from a false premise. Long-term collaborations promote mutual understanding and minimise this problem.

On a very practical level the timetable for funding applications discourages community engagement. A community which is active in the project planning and funding application phase, may have lost interest or moved on in the many months elapsing between application and start date.[3] Researchers committed to getting funding for empowerment based research work with an identified community may need to constantly redesign projects to fit funding priorities. A consequence can be a drawer full of funding applications and a community that has lost interest. In the field of social work, alliances with community organisations or service providers can be a way of maintaining contact with the community during the long months of waiting.

An inclusive approach to research methodology

The choice of what to research determines the research methods chosen. Community research does not preclude any method or approach. A community could decide on a research question and then commission a university to do the data gathering for them. For example, a 'narrow' project in Cornwall and Jewkes (1995) termed the Dutch Science Shops, which aimed to democratise science and contribute to social change through providing expertise to local communities, originally operated on this basis. This model emerged in the Netherlands in the early 1970s and grew out of the student movement of the 1960s. Initially they provided groups interested in improving their environment with research data free of charge. Despite the decline of this model in the Netherlands (Hellemans, 2001; Wacholder, 2003) the idea has been adapted and adopted by many countries throughout Europe and beyond (Worthington et al, 2008; EC European Commission 2003). At the other end of the scale, a wide project would involve the community doing the data gathering themselves. Neither the broader nor the narrower approach can be said to provide better data, they just generate different kinds of data. Some people may find peer interviews and taking part in a group discussion on a particular issue less intimidating than being interviewed by a stranger from a university. We have found that some people find the word 'interview' intimidating, rather like a job interview. Some seek reassurance after the interview that they 'passed' the test by providing the 'correct' answers. On the other hand, others may feel more able to reflect critically on their community in a one-to-one interview with an outsider (Ramji, 2008: 109). Ramji, in particular, notes the pitfalls when interviewees presume a common knowledge base with the researcher and fail to make explicit taken-for-granted assumptions, or worse, make assumptions about what the researcher wants or expects to hear. Similarly, being asked to give your opinion on an issue within a group can run the risk of being challenged or subject to hurtful criticism. If the group is known to you, disclosure within the group can have negative longer term consequences (Kitzinger and Barbour, 1999: 17).

Creating situated knowledge involves drawing out and drawing together knowledge which the participants did not know they had (Lundgren, 1995: 363). The role of the researcher is crucial in asking the 'innocent' outsider questions to provoke, be critical, and highlight taken-for-granted assumptions among the community. Such collaborative working may involve a mix of data gathering and analysis rather than a series of clearly delineated phases in a project (Maguire, 1987: 158).

Explaining the range of research methods available and organising appropriate training can be time consuming for researchers and members of the community. Many years of academic training cannot be condensed into a handful of workshops on research techniques and inevitably the academic will take the lead role in writing the research report (McIntyre, 2008: 57). Similarly, locating the research in the context of current academic debate is often of little immediate interest to researched populations. It is an important task for academics, not only to add to a body of knowledge, but also in terms of their own career prospects. Involving the community in these stages of a project requires a time commitment from academics and others that may be difficult to make. Wacholder (2003) identifies increasing pressure on academics to publish as one factor contributing to the demise of science shops in the Netherlands (Wacholder, 2003: 256).

Some handbooks on community research emphasise that if the community own the research the analysis should be based on categories and concepts used by informants (Cornwall and Jewkes, 1995). The first difficulty with this approach is that it may produce a very good description of lived experience which, although useful for explaining a community to outsiders, may not provide new insights or provide the community themselves with additional resources. The second is that if communities are experiencing exploitation, for example, domestic violence, the analysis may not be able to take a perspective outside the oppressive hierarchy (Müller, 1991: 78). Researchers on poverty have similarly noted that an analysis solely in terms of the categories and concepts of the poor may suffer from the low expectations of the chronically disadvantaged (Bennett and Roberts, 2004: 49). Some researchers advocate using the analysis of the community as raw data for an academic analysis. In our opinion, however, this secondary analysis reasserts a superiority of academic knowledge. There is no easy solution to this dilemma and the extent of community involvement is something that has to be continuously communicated and negotiated throughout the process. As with all teamwork, achieving consensus can be time consuming and is fraught with difficulties and it may not be possible to arrive at one definitive analysis of the data.

Empowerment, as communities claim their ability to chart their own directions for change, can result in groups opting out of the research process altogether. Living with social exclusion may significantly restrict people's ability to maintain consistent involvement throughout the project. Researchers may be required to step in at different times in order to keep the project on target, and targets may not be met (McIntyre, 2008: 64; France, 2000: 26). Being creative and offering a range of opportunities to become involved, such as contributing comments to an 'ideas wall' or mapping their past year, as was done in the Karelia project described above, gives a voice to people who would otherwise be excluded.

Key learning points

- Empowerment can never be a singular act, the freedom of individuals to make decisions and choices about their lives can only be achieved within a community which provides a range of opportunities to its members.
- The challenge for social work community research projects is to remain true to the complexities of diverse histories and culture whilst, at the same time, teasing out the commonalities around which people can form strategic alliances.
- The starting point for effective research on social inclusion is recognising the competencies of the people involved and the strategies they have developed in response to structural changes affecting them. Moving away from a deficit model requires taking as a starting point the strengths and resources a community has developed to cope with a particular challenge.
- To ensure the broadest participation various visual methods can be employed in data collection, such as painting, clay modelling, photography etc. Interviews can be complemented by storytelling, oral history and small scale contributions, for example, using video to communicate with a wider audience and get feedback.
- Community research is not product oriented. It is a process, the consequences of which cannot be anticipated in advance. Similarly, the impact may not be quantifiable in the short term.

• Keeping the community involved may require negotiating time limited involvement at different stages of the research process or adopting a kaleidoscope design of independent mini projects around one central research question.

Summary: Advantages and disadvantages of a community research approach

Advantages

1. The act of knowing is empowering. Knowledge relates to power when research methodology seeks the involvement and cooperation of silenced communities in gathering and analysing information.

2. Research is empowering when situated knowledge in communities is transformed into action for social change.

3. Community research empowers excluded communities by engaging them in a dialogical methodology of articulating, understanding and reflecting on their collective situations and developing a critical awareness. This dialogical method is a tool in transcending a culture of silence as the subjects of research become active producers of knowledge.

4. Participatory research enables the inclusion of contextual knowledge. Contextual knowledge is derived from the experiences, interests, competences and understandings of the community being researched.

5. Community research opens up the possibility for change in communities and academic institutions by bridging the gap between universities and the people served by social workers. Training social workers as researchers brings about radical change in social work theory, teaching and practice.

Limitations

1. Community research is process not product oriented. Producing results for research funders can be difficult in the short term.

2. Communities are not homogenous and key informants may represent established power structures in their communities. There are polarities and divisions within their internal structures as well as connectivities which allow them to build strategic alliances. These polarities and connectivities can pose a major challenge to community research and require considerable time investment.

3. The process of empowerment is possible when communities claim ownership of the research process and results. Transformative change occurs when communities and researchers go through a process of mutual reinterpretation. This reinterpretation can result in projects departing from, or even abandoning, original aims.

4. The challenge of building trusting relationships and developing long term alliances between social work researchers, universities and the communities they serve can reduce universities to the business of data extraction.

5. Well intended research focused on delivering solutions to social problems can result in contact to communities becoming deficit oriented and episodic. This not only affects the quality of research findings but also diminishes their impact and raises ethical questions.

Conclusion

This chapter has discussed some possibilities for increasing community participation in academic research and also outlined some obstacles that may be encountered. It also describes the emergence of strategies to encourage empowering methodologies in the field of social work research in Germany and Finland. Community research is neither easy nor straightforward. The transformative character of community research is often circuitous and protracted because communities devise their own discourse. Individuals may contradict each other, have competing interests and will not engage in a process of change from a unified and coherent standpoint. Throughout the process the researcher has to re-engage in a community dialogue which allows for an examination of the researcher's own status. In short, community research is not an easy option; it requires a high level of commitment in terms of resources. It does, however, deliver a more lasting impact by empowering people to take action on behalf of their community.

Discussion questions

1. Why is it important to ensure that communities own the process of research?
2. Define a marginalised community and identify the greatest challenges that a community empowerment approach to research would encounter.
3. How would you empower communities in such a place to get involved in the research process?

Notes

[1] See the project website www.ekscr.cz for details of the project.

[2] Kainulainen, S. (unpublished) 'The effect of projects on society: an evaluation of the preconditions of influence'.

[3] This can take up to 21 months, for example, Hessian LOEWE Programme www.hmwk.hessen.de.

References

Bennett, F. and Roberts, M. (2004) *From Input to Influence*, York: Joseph Rowntree Foundation.

Cohen, A. P. (1985) *The Symbolic Construction of Community*, London: Tavistock.

Cornwall, A. and Jewkes, R. (1995) 'What is Participatory Research?', *Social Sciences and Medicine*, 41(12): 1667–1676.

Diaconia University of Applied Sciences, Finland, (2008) *Guide Book for Theses*, www.diak.fi

European Commission (EC) (2003) *Science Shops: Knowledge for the Community*, EUR 20877, Office for Official Publications of the European Communities, Luxembourg.

France, A., (2000) *Youth Researching Youth*, Leicester: Youth Work Press and Joseph Rowntree Foundation.

Freire, P., (1996) *Pedagogy of the Oppressed*, London: Penguin.

Geht, E., Kainulainen, S., Pakkasvirta, T. (2011) *Joint Efforts for Healthy Life: Experience of the Finnish-Russian Project 'Addiction Problems and Health in Saint Petersburg and in the Karelian Republic'*, Diakonia-ammattikorkeakoulun julkaisuja. D Työpapereita 55. Helsinki. www.diak.fi/files/diak/Julkaisutoiminta/D_55_ISBN_9789524931458.pdf.pdf.

Gray, A., (2003) *Research Practice for Cultural Studies*, London: Sage.

Gutiérrez, G., (1971) *A Theology of Liberation*, New York: Orbis Books.

Haraway, D. (1988) 'Situated Knowledges: The Science Question in Feminism and the Privilege of Partial Perspective', *Feminist Studies*, 14(3): 575.

Haraway, D. (1991) *Simians, Cyborgs and Women. The Reinvention of Nature*, London: Free Association Books publishing.

Hellemans, A. (2001) Special Report Science Shops Provide Non-Profit Alternative, *In Nature*, 412: 4–5.

Hoggett, P. (1997) 'Contested Communities'. In P. Hoggett (ed) *Contested Communities. Experiences, Struggles, Policies*, Bristol: Policy Press.

Hooper, E.H. and Dunham, A., (1959) *Community Organization in Action: Basic Literature and Critical Comments*, New York: Association Press.

Kitzinger, J. and Barbour, R.S. (1999) 'Introduction: The Challenge and Promise of Focus Groups' in R.S. Barbour and J. Kitzinger (eds) *Developing Focus Group Research: Politics, Theory and Practice*, London: Sage.

Lundgren, E. (1995) *Feminist Theory and Violent Empiricism*, Aldershot: Ashgate.

McIntyre, A. (2008) *Participatory Action Research*, Thousand Oaks: Sage.

Maguire, P. (1987) Doing Participatory Research: A Feminist Approach, Amherst: University of Massachusetts.

Maier, K. and Mauch, D. (eds) (2005) Rieselfelder Welten, Porträts von Migrantinnen und Migranten im Stadtteil, Verlag, Freiburg: Forschung, Entwicklung, Lehre.

Müller, U., (1991) 'Gleichheit im Zeitalter der Differenz', *Psychologie und Gesellschaftskritik*, 3/4(59/60).

Oakley, A., (1993) *Essays on Women, Medicine and Health*, Edinburgh: Edinburgh University Press.

Ramji, H. (2008) 'Exploring Commonality and Difference in In-Depth Interviewing: A Case-Study of Researching British Asian Women'. *British Journal of Sociology*, 59(1): 99.

Stanley, L. (ed) (1990) *Feminist Praxis*, London: Routledge.

Stanley, L. and Wise, S. (1993) *Breaking Out Again. Feminist Ontology and Epistemology*, London: Routledge and Kegan Paul.

Wachholder, J. (2003) Democratizing Science: Various Routes and Visions of Dutch Science Shops, *Science, Technology and Human Values*, 28(2).

West, A. (1995) *You're On Your Own: Young People's Research on Leaving Care*, London: Save the Children.

Worthington, R., Balazas, B., Cupsa, D., Georgescu, L., Holas, J., Holasova, V., Telcean, I. (2008) Science Shops in Central and Eastern Europe: Challenges and Opportunities, *International Journal of Community Based Research*, 8.

Seven

Data analysis and community research: capturing reality on housing estates in Bradford, UK?[1]

Heather Blakey, E-J. Milne and Louise Kilburn

Chapter aims

- To explore the value and realities of doing 'data analysis' with communities, rather than as academics in the university 'ivory tower'
- To show that analysis within community research takes place throughout every stage of the project; it should be an inbuilt component of research planning, data collection and dissemination
- To consider the potential that working with community researchers and visual tools have for facilitating community involvement in research analysis
- To share learning from one community research project, in the hopes that it will raise helpful questions for other researchers

Introduction

This chapter is not a 'how-to guide' to community analysis. The most important thing about community research is that it must be flexible. Methods which work in one setting or at one time may not work in other circumstances. Involving community members in analysis develops from an attitude to research; the methods vary depending on the community with whom you are working. Our methods evolved throughout the project: our participatory video project turned into a community meeting about the choice not to participate (Milne, 2012); and the community meeting evolved into outdoor research events, because some communities did not feel comfortable in the community centre. Our methods developed as a result of the particular contexts in which we were working, as well as our experiences, knowledge and personalities.[2]

In this chapter, we draw on learning from one research project that took place over 18 months in Scholemoor and Braithwaite and Guardhouse, two traditionally 'white' (but changing) housing estates in the Bradford

Metropolitan District, one large (c. 2000 houses) and one small (c. 500 houses). Both have a negative local image, and often a negative self-image, with a deep-seated distrust of 'outside(r)' agencies. Both estates have a strong community spirit, but they are also divided – by age, ethnicity and territory.[3]

Our discussion of community analysis is based on our approach to community research, which we define as laid out in Box 7.1:

Box 7.1

Community research tries to offer opportunities for involvement to a *whole* community, at all stages of the research: planning, data collection, analysis and dissemination, with the aim of generating community, as well as academic, outcomes.

Our definition evolves as we continue to learn about and engage in community research, but it captures several ideas for us, in particular the importance of inclusiveness: involving as many people as possible, and at all times, not relying on community researchers as 'voices' for their community. This is an ideal; we recognise that funding and time constraints on academics complicate efforts to involve community members, particularly during the earliest and latest stages of the research, that is, in preparing the proposal and dissemination. However, it acknowledges that community research is about offering opportunities, rather than about numbers involved. People may have many reasons for not participating (see White, 2003; Milne, 2012); we should not presume it is because we did not ask in the right way. It recognises that community research is an attempt at inclusion. As with any 'living' process, it is not always possible to do it perfectly. Finally, it recognises the importance of community outcomes, which motivate community involvement, as an aim alongside academic outcomes.[4] The overall aims of our research evolved through the process. They included an attempt to build community confidence to participate in local decisions, and improved local understanding of the communities. We recognise that the process of bringing together the various community and academic aims is a process in itself. However, recognising the need to do this, and giving time to discussing aims and goals, is an important first step.

Like any research, community research has its limitations; it captures some realities. Community research is not about putting 'community' viewpoints on a pedestal, but about valuing and giving space to community members' experiential knowledge – all too often undervalued. We also worked to include other important viewpoints, such as agency workers and policy makers.

This chapter is based on a particular understanding of analysis, although it can be difficult to untangle data collection and analysis in community research as they are often intertwined. We recognise that our definition differs from mainstream academic definitions of analysis. However, it includes a focus on patterns and causation which we believe is the basis of academic analysis (see Box 7.2).

> **Box 7.2**
>
> Analysis is what happens when you put your personal knowledge and understanding into a bigger picture of the knowledge and understanding held by others; this encourages you to question your assumptions and to look for patterns, reasons why and possible answers.

In our experience, community analysis is a collective process: bringing people together (including different ages and different ethnic backgrounds) to share and discuss their experiences. This helps us to challenge collectively our own and each other's assumptions, and to understand what it is that we do know, and realise what we do not. In this chapter, we explore what helps community analysis happen and why we believe it is worth doing.

Our research used visual methods, including map-making, photovoice and participatory video, and involved four community researchers and three academic researchers. The community researchers were members of the community employed on the project, with no previous research experience.[5] This chapter has been written by one community researcher and two academics, although we have benefited from the insights of the whole team. The writing process has been undertaken collaboratively; some sections have been written communally and others individually. You may hear our different voices as one section moves into another.

Analysis in participatory research

Community research literature is somewhat muted on the subject of data analysis, largely because it is not always seen as a distinct activity within the community research process. Reason (1998: 271–2), who has written extensively on participative inquiry and action research, suggests that we cannot think in conventional terms when doing this kind of research. He says that 'methodologies that in orthodox research would be called research design, data gathering, data analysis and so on, take second place to emergent processes of collaboration and dialogue that empower, motivate, increase self-esteem and develop community solidarity'. Thus traditional academic analysis, which includes an emphasis on formal coding – working through the data word by word and grouping similar theoretical ideas, is typically replaced in participatory forms of research with a deliberative process of 'sense-making' (Greenwood and Levin, 1998). Similarly, traditions of participatory research which include conventional data analysis, for example within the field of health, involve collective processes of reflection as well as the more typical 'lone researcher immersed in the data' (see for example, Chung and Lounsbury, 2006; Cashman et al, 2008). The contrast between traditional and participatory approaches to analysis fits with Mauthner and Doucet's view that data analysis techniques are not neutral, but carry with them assumptions about knowledge (2003: 415).

Conventional analysis is based on the understanding that knowledge is an object to be 'uncovered' from data via analysis (knowledge exists distinct from the knower), whereas participatory research sees knowledge as socially constructed and embedded. Participatory research emphasises the process of 'knowing' rather than the knowledge product (see for example: Law, 2004; Gaventa and Cornwall, 2008); knowledge is therefore indivisible from the knower.

The challenge to traditional views of knowledge has been facilitated by Heron's discussion of four different types of knowing (Heron, 1996; Heron and Reason, 2008). The first is experiential knowledge, gained through lived experience, in our view the basis of community research. The second is presentational knowledge: shaping experience into a communicable form such as dance or poetry. The third is propositional: knowledge about things – the conceptual form of knowledge recognised by academia. The fourth is practical knowledge: knowing how to do something.

Our approach to analysis recognises the value of different forms of knowledge, and aims to encourage local as well as academic 'knowing', rather than to discover or create knowledge without reference to who knows it. Accordingly, while we embrace a wide range of methods for both data collection and analysis, we avoid the detailed conceptual coding of traditional analysis.

This is for two reasons. First, formal coding excludes research participants, resting as it does on particular academic skills which community members may not have. For us, the purpose of community research is increased understanding within – not simply about – the communities. In this vein, Freire (1972) links people's ability to analyse oppression in their own lives with their ability to challenge it, and to effect change. Therefore, it is essential that opportunities for analysis are accessible. University-based coding analysis does not encourage widespread ownership of the knowledge generated. However, we recognise that analytical processes of reflection within the community do include the informal sorting and categorisation of data, processes that are themselves based in conceptual knowledge.

Second, formal coding privileges academic perceptions of the data and in the process devalues experiential knowledge, in a way that conflicts with the community research ethos of equal respect for different forms of knowledge. For Reason (1994: 35), 'since the process of classifying and labelling separates us from our experience, conceptual language can be a powerful source of alienation'. While we could have trained community researchers in academic analysis skills, this project was not about asking community members, involved due to their experiential knowledge, to become academic researchers. To do so would have been to reinforce the widespread perception that conceptual knowledge is more worthwhile than experiential knowledge. It was critical to our project that we valued this knowledge as it stood, not to the extent that we were able to turn it into conventional academic 'knowledge'.

We recognise there is a balance to be found, that our inclusive approach to analysis has a cost in terms of academic perceptions of the 'validity' of our research. Both academic and community analysis are important. However, academic theories should not be contradicted by lived experience (Greenwood and Levin, 1998: 81). We believe that community-based analysis, while not replacing academic research, can stand alongside it.

Community analysis in practice

Our approach to community analysis is based on the recognition that every time you connect with a community member is an opportunity to involve them in analysis. Analysis, therefore, happened at every stage of our research, from thinking together as a team about how and where to do the research, to gathering feedback on our findings as we shared them with research participants. As Figure 7.1 shows, data collection and analysis were often simultaneous.

Community analysis happened at different levels at different times. Sometimes it involved all the research participants, while at other times we had longer analytical conversations within the research team, in which we shared our reflections on the data. There is a balance between numbers involved and depth of engagement. Ideally, the research process allows for easy movement between levels and forms of engagement. In this section we talk about our attempts to engage, though we recognise that there were gaps in the breadth of our engagement. We struggled to hear from adult, working-age men, and while we engaged well with indigenous 'white' and newly-arrived Slovakian communities, we found it harder to engage Asian residents in the research.

Figure 7.1 Community analysis timeline

Training	• Involved 2 academics and 4 community researchers • 'We did everything we expected the residents to do': maps, photovoice, visual focus groups, listening skills, how to analyse, note-keeping • Rich source of data as community researchers shared information; site of analysis as the team discussed insights together
Small Community Maps	• Involved residents (recruited through word-of-mouth and 'snowballing'), youth and community groups and agencies • Participants produced individual maps of their community and discussed them with researchers, generating research data • Maps were discussed analytically by the team
Team Meetings (throughout the project)	• Involved academics and community researchers • After each stage the team brought their data and reflections to team meetings • Key analytic space, but also generated new data as researchers contributed new information from their own experience
Large Community Maps	• Involved many residents of all ages and some agency workers • Informal and inclusive map-making: outside shops, on roundabouts, in community centres and with local groups • Generated data through the stories which accompanied contributions; analysis mainly by the research team
Photovoice	• Involved participants aged between 7 and 90, mainly women and young people, through flyers, presence on the streets and word-of-mouth • Individual residents took photos of their community, gave them a caption, and discussed with a member of the research team • Generated data for the project; analysis mainly undertaken by the research team
Visual Focus Groups	• Involved three groups of residents (all photovoice participants invited) • Residents presented and discussed their photos • Generated new data as participants spoke; key analytic space for shared community reflection
Participatory Video	• Involved two groups of primary school pupils • Majority of the people invited to participate (through door-to-door flyering, posters and word-of-mouth) made an active choice not to participate • Video process involved data collection and analysis as participants developed the story they wanted to tell
Community Booklets	• Involved community researchers and academics in production, and residents and agency workers in commenting on drafts • Developing the booklet text was an analytic process for academics and community researchers, who organised the data by theme • Feedback on drafts involved community members in analytical discussions
Community Discussion on Safety on Scholemoor	• Involved agency workers and residents in a three-hour discussion at a time of high tension on the estate • Participants invited through flyers and word-of-mouth; process instigated by residents and local businesses • Data collection and analysis (and action) combined in a reflective discussion
Policy Workshop	• Involved residents, funding agency, councillors, statutory services, community workers, by invite • Intended as a reflective discussion of findings, though only partially effective
Community Photo Exhibition (Scholemoor)	• Involved people from all ethnic communities on Scholemoor and all age ranges • Exhibition of photos taken by residents with their comments in local community centre • Primarily dissemination, but opportunity for shared reflection by participants

We illustrate the relationship between community data collection and community analysis through four examples from our research: visual focus groups, community map-making, research team meetings and analysis with agencies and decision-makers.

Community map-making

We found map-making to be an effective means to help people recognise and express what they know about their communities. Of the three forms of map-making used in this research (see time-line), it is the large-scale community maps that we focus on here. We took hand-drawn maps out to public places in the communities, from community centres to roundabouts. We asked residents to place green sticky dots to indicate places to which they go, red dots to show where they would not go, and blue for where they lived. The involvement of community researchers in particular brought a freshness and enthusiasm to the research design, taking the research onto the streets and to the people who lived in them.

The maps had three main benefits. First, they acted as a gateway to further involvement with the research. Seeing people participating publicly made it easier for other residents to join in, despite their fears over what others would think, or doubts about their own contribution. The presence of community researchers was effective here, as they helped create a sense of familiarity and trust. The short time spent by individual participants, the instant results and the fact that it was fun, meant they were then often more inclined to make a further commitment to involvement in the research in order to continue the conversations, for example through the visual focus groups.

Second, the maps generated rich data as people shared stories of the estate and talked to fellow residents around the map-table. They shared feelings, often reflecting how the estate and their participation within it had changed over time. The presence of academic researchers at this stage allowed participants to 'be the expert', often correcting the map, which revealed different perceptions and areas of knowledge, as well as telling the estate's history. This helped them value their own knowledge, and contributed to a sense of active involvement with the research process. Thus the different ways in which academic and community researchers were seen by community members brought different benefits to the research process, a trend which developed throughout the project.

Third, the maps were useful in analysis. As visual objects, they showed patterns of inclusion and exclusion which residents and research team members spontaneously reflected upon. The maps have also become a visual representation of our understanding of analysis, placing each individual's knowledge within the collective expression of knowledge about the estate. However, the short time spent by individual participants meant that this type of map-making was often not a deeply analytic space, although within closed areas such as community centres and cafes, more reflective conversations were able to develop. The main analytic benefit of this tool was in its use by the research team, discussed in more detail below. The highly visual nature of the maps, and the rich stories that hung from them, generated both more data from within the team and allowed for fertile discussion.

Finally, the map-making process built community researchers' sense of ownership of the research, publicly identifying them with the project, and helping them contribute confidently to research design, as the maps illuminated issues important to many residents.

Visual focus groups

During the project, residents were asked to take three photographs of how they saw their communities and the message they would like to pass on to their own communities or to the world outside their estate. When the images were collected, the photographers discussed the images with a team member and were invited to choose one to discuss at a visual focus group in one of the community centres. Three visual focus groups were each attended by between eight and 16 residents. One was cross-generational, one for 8–19 year olds, and the third for adults.

The visual focus groups were designed as a site of analysis within the communities. The research team acted as facilitators, though community researchers also contributed as residents. Each image was projected onto a screen and the photographer invited to discuss why they took the image, and what it meant to them. After this, other participants were able to share their interpretations. As the discussions evolved the research team fed in additional significant images taken by other residents, and our preliminary findings, which participants were invited to discuss.

The interactive discussion meant that we gained detailed data while hearing different analyses of the same images, which contextualised or countered the photographers' stories. The analysis became collaborative as we interpreted what others said, and asked questions of ourselves and each other. These discussions fed into community feedback booklets which the team wrote and distributed around both communities, and local agencies and policy makers. We continued these conversations through discussions about the booklets before producing a final booklet to create conversations between groups on each estate, local agencies and policy makers.

The visual focus groups, as well as becoming spaces for analysis, also became spaces of ownership and action. The images, discussion and shared analysis meant that the visual focus group was an active, not passive, experience. This generated tangible outcomes, including inter-generational and inter-ethnic encounters, participants volunteering to help in their communities, and agencies responding to previously unmet local needs, for example around inter-ethnic youth provision.

Team meetings

Team meetings were a key analytic space. We met frequently to share data and discuss research events. The presence of community researchers meant new information often emerged in addition to analysis. These discussions were recorded and became further data for the project. Team meetings built on prior individual reflection by each team member. Analysis took place as a discussion between team members. Different roles, each played at different times by academic and community team members, included:

- sharing additional research information;
- contextualising the words or images before us;
- speaking from an illuminating lack of knowledge: a fresh perspective which helped other team members see differently;
- keeping it real: not allowing us to pursue theory for its own sake;
- pointing out absences or assumptions in each other's narratives, which are often easier to see in someone else's conversation than in our own;
- asking questions which drew out our individual and shared understanding.

The trust between team members, built up through working and thinking together, was crucial in allowing this process to develop effectively.

Working together in this way, with community researchers integrally involved as members of the research team, rather than as data collectors or subsidiary team members, meant that all the team members felt able to contribute, and had some sense of control. As one of the community researchers said, 'It was like a working family atmosphere; we were able to tackle problems openly and as a team'. Seeing the community researchers so centrally involved affected ownership from the wider community, as illustrated by the response of one active resident to the question of what the university would do with the findings: 'They're not going to do anything with it, they're researchers, they're gonna move onto their next project. We're the ones who are gonna do something about it, it's our research.'

Sustained and in-depth community involvement in analysis has two major benefits for the research findings. First, research users such as local decision-makers have two reasons to trust the findings, making them harder to undermine. It has credibility in both academic and grassroots settings. Second, and perhaps more important, the analysis remains within the communities beyond the life of the research. The findings exist not only in the university and in a policy report on a council shelf, but are held by community members, who can, if they wish, use what they have learned in their own efforts for change on the estate. In this way the research leaves a footprint behind, of skills, materials and knowledge.

Policy workshop

At the end of the research we held a workshop where the director and co-ordinator of the research presented the research findings to invited residents, activists, agency staff and policy makers. This presentation was followed by responses from a panel of four residents from three Bradford estates. After this panel, participants were split into tables of eight, with each table hosted by a resident from one of the estates.

The intention in the design of the workshop was to allow spaces for residents, agency workers and policy makers to engage in discussions with each other, to challenge each other and question our research so that we could add another level to the previous forms of analysis. We also wanted to provide space where outside agencies and those not living on the estates could talk in direct ways with residents in order to enable changes in decision making processes to begin. Unfortunately such a level of analysis did not noticeably occur.

We observed three different forms of interaction which hampered open and honest analysis. In some cases, agency workers, particularly when relatively junior or inexperienced, were reluctant to question residents, taking their comments as 'truth' and privileging lived experience over the knowledge that they had as practitioners. As a result, they were unable to engage in a process of collective analysis, which involves both trust and mutual challenge. In other cases, agency workers, particularly when relatively senior, listened to residents' experiences, but turned to one another to discuss solutions, demonstrating their lack of respect for alternative forms of knowledge and analysis. Finally, the public nature of the event meant that some agency workers and policy makers, even those who had previously engaged in critiques and spoken out for change, felt obliged to speak as representatives of their organisations, and became entrenched in a public defence of their roles and organisations.

As a result, we felt that the event produced little in the way of analysis or suggestions for future directions and collaborations between residents and agencies/policy makers. This is not a criticism of the people present, but a criticism of the environment, which was formal and public, and did not lend itself to building the trust necessary for shared analysis. Our attempts to create a more constructive environment were constrained by a number of factors, not least that the agency-funded event was designed to meet the needs of policy makers over the needs of community members. This highlights the difficulties of undertaking genuine analysis in traditional or formal spaces.

Key learning

As mentioned earlier, this is not a 'how-to guide' to doing community analysis. However, in this section we would like to share with you some of the understandings we have learnt through experience, and which we bring to community research design.

First, while we believe community research is an attitude not a technique, it remains true that choice of methods increases or decreases community participation. Visual research techniques can be particularly effective in engaging participants who are sceptical towards or unused to research. It is helpful to offer a variety of levels of engagement, ranging from instant involvement to more reflective discussion.

Second, in order to involve community members in analysis, it is important to think holistically. Academics are used to thinking in terms of stages of research: design, followed by data collection, followed by data analysis, and so on. However, most community members are not going to share information, and then return to analyse it weeks or months later. To maximise community involvement in analysis, data collection and analysis must be seen as inseparable.

Third, and perhaps most important, community research is about collaboration. It is not led by academics or community members, but values both kinds of knowledge without prioritising either. We recognise there are different truths, different realities; our analysis needs to capture that diversity. Individually, we cannot know the 'truth', so it is the shared analysis of the team that makes the research work. For this reason, and because different members of the team have access to different places, through knowing the communities in different ways and being trusted in different ways, it is important to see data collection and analysis as shared activities, rather than creating a division of labour with community members doing data collection and academics doing data analysis.

Finally, we think an attitude of intellectual respect towards participants is vital. If we want people to contribute ideas, rather than simply extracting information from them, supporting them to 'know what they know' is essential. Community analysis is about facilitating thinking, not finding out what people know: it's different to ask yourself a question than to be asked. This affects the language we use, so that people don't feel under-educated or unintelligent, as well as the way we work. This attitude leads to ownership; it helps people feel that what comes out of the research is their knowledge.

Summary: Community analysis methods

	Advantages	Limitations
Community map-making	• Generates a collective product which illustrates community knowledge and stimulates analytic discussion • Engages participants easily • Allows people to value and express their knowledge	• Not always a collective process – this can lead to misunderstandings, as people can make assumptions about other people's reasons for placing dots • Doesn't allow complexity
Visual focus groups	• Generates immediate individual sense of involvement and ownership developing into collective ownership • Allows in-depth discussions producing both data and analysis	• Some residents can feel excluded because of a) fear of speaking in public with their photos or b) the spaces where they are held, for example, some people will not go to certain areas or buildings on the estate
Team meetings	• Sustained and in-depth engagement in analysis • Combines academic and community knowledge effectively • Builds ownership and legitimacy of research	• Accessible to very few community members
Policy workshop	• Brings residents and agency-workers/policy-makers together to start or continue conversations • Combines many levels of knowledge about the communities, all of which are needed in processes of change	• People attend in a particular role; this can lead to a performance of these roles rather than an ability to reflect, learn and be challenged • The size of such events can make the occasion impersonal, allowing participants to distance themselves from becoming involved • People present do not necessarily all value experiential knowledge; therefore expertise celebrated within the project can be undermined

Conclusions

The development of community involvement in analysis is based on wide opportunities for involvement, a shared valuing of different knowledges and a focus on local knowing and local action and outcomes. As such, community researchers cannot 'deliver' community analysis for a project. They are facilitators, bringing their knowledge of the community or communities to the research team. They work with academic team members on all stages of the project; they cannot ensure access or represent the community.

This understanding helps us to work as equals within a collaborative community research project, and reminds us to pay attention to issues of power within the research team and also the wider project. Getting this right is essential for building relationships and trust. It is this, not tools or techniques, which is the core of effective community analysis. Listening to and knowing the communities are therefore crucial to community analysis, alongside flexibility and responsiveness.

We tend to think of analysis as the step in the research process which creates knowledge, and community analysis is about a different kind of knowledge, or more accurately, a different kind of knowing. However, it is also about the purpose of the research, and the use of the findings. In community research, we cannot separate analysis from the overall ethos and values of the project. A danger here can be unrealistically raised expectations, as we of course cannot guarantee the community outcomes that we rightly value and for which we aim. This can have a most severe impact on community researchers who are embedded within the community and do not 'move on' at the end of the project. Therefore, it is important to pay equal attention to managing the ending of the project as it is to developing involvement and inclusion throughout.

Community analysis is not an easy option or a straightforward one. However, we believe that a joint research team involving academics and community members can be much stronger than a research team which only holds one form of knowledge, and can lead to valuable outcomes and greater local ownership, as well as robust and useful knowledge.

Discussion questions

1. What do you see as the potential advantages and limitations of undertaking community analysis, to communities and to academics?
2. What are our responsibilities as academics, given that joining the research team can have repercussions for community researchers?
3. Can we undertake community analysis in such a way that other important actors (e.g. agency staff and local decision-makers) are not excluded?

Notes

[1] The authors would like to thank the Joseph Rowntree Foundation who funded the research.

[2] For a more comprehensive overview of the research, including methodology, methods and findings, see Pearce and Milne, 2010.

[3] People living in one neighbourhood may not consider another area of the same estate as part of 'their' community.

[4] We do not claim that we were entirely successful in achieving community outcomes, but it is important that they were present as an aim with equal status to academic outcomes.

[5] Two of the community researchers left the project part of the way through, one for a permanent position in his former area of employment, the second as a result of personal circumstances. We were also joined half-way through the project by one long-term volunteer.

References

Cashman, S.B., Allen, A.J. III, Corburn, J., Israel, B.A., Montano, J., Rhodes, S.D., Swanston, S.F. and Eng, E. (2008) 'Analysing and Interpreting Data with Communities'. In M. Minkler and N. Wallerstein (eds) *Community-Based Participatory Research for Health: From Process to Outcomes* (2nd edn), San Francisco: Jossey-Bass: 285–301.

Chung, K. and Lounsbury, D.W. (2006) 'The Role of Power, Process and Relationships in Participatory Research for State-Wide HIV/AIDS Programming', *Social Science and Medicine*, 63: 2129–40.

Freire, P. (1972) *Pedagogy of the Oppressed*, Harmondsworth: Penguin.

Gaventa, J. and Cornwall, A. (2008) 'Power and Knowledge', in P. Reason and H. Bradbury (eds) *The Sage Handbook of Action Research*, London: Sage: 172–89.

Greenwood, D.J. and Levin, M. (1998) *Introduction to Action Research: Social Research for Social Change*, London: Sage.

Heron, J. (1996) *Co-operative Inquiry*, London: Sage.

Heron, J. and Reason, P. (2008) 'Extending Epistemology Within a Co-operative Inquiry', in P. Reason and H. Bradbury (eds) *The Sage Handbook of Action Research*, London: Sage: 366–80.

Law, J. (2004) *After Method: Mess in Social Science Research*, London: Routledge.

Mauthner, N.S. and Doucet, A. (2003) 'Reflexive Accounts and Accounts of Reflexivity in Qualitative Data Analysis', *Sociology*, 37(3), 413–31.

Milne, E.-J. (2012) 'Saying 'NO!' to Participatory Video: Unravelling the Complexities of (Non)Participation', in E.-J. Milne, C. Mitchell and N. deLange (eds) *The Handbook of Participatory Video*, Lanham MD: AltaMira Press. Forthcoming.

Pearce, J. and Milne, E.-J. (2010) *Participation and Community on Bradford's Traditionally White Estates*, York: Joseph Rowntree Foundation.

Reason, P. (ed) (1994) *Participation in Human Inquiry*, London: Sage.

Reason, P. (1998) 'Three Approaches to Participative Inquiry', in N.K. Denzin and Y.S. Lincoln (eds) *Strategies of Qualitative Inquiry*, Thousand Oaks: Sage: 261-91.

White, S.A. (2003) 'Involving People in Participatory Processes', in S.A. White (ed) *Participatory Video: Images that Transform and Empower*, Thousand Oaks: Sage, 33-62.

Part Two

Ethics, power and emotion

Eight

Participation in community research: experiences of community researchers undertaking HIV research in South Africa

Maretha Visser

Chapter aims

- To reflect on the challenges and advantages in using community researchers (CRs) to interact with respondents in a community research project
- To illustrate the importance of training and supervision for community researchers
- To indicate that a balance between maintaining the wellbeing of respondents and research team members and conducting quality research should be included in ethical guidelines for community research

Introduction

Participation in research has an impact on all participants, including the research team, community researchers and respondents. The experiences illustrated in this chapter show that this is especially true when research is conducted regarding sensitive issues such as HIV/AIDS. The advantages and challenges involved in community research is presented using the experiences of community researchers who took part in a longitudinal study that was conducted with women diagnosed as HIV positive during pregnancy in Tshwane, South Africa. The research, by a multi-disciplinary team, investigated the medical, psychological and social impact of HIV on the lives of women diagnosed during pregnancy. The study was undertaken with a view to developing interventions to assist and empower women to take responsibility for their own health and for that of their children. The research was done in two phases. Phase One was a baseline study which followed 317 HIV infected women for two years after the birth of their babies. Interviews were conducted between one and four weeks after diagnosis during pregnancy, six weeks post-partum and then three, six, nine and 18 months post-partum. These follow-up intervals were chosen to coincide with scheduled clinic visits for immunisation of the infants (Makin et al, 2008). The knowledge gained during Phase One of the research was used to develop interventions to assist HIV infected women during Phase Two. For the sake of brevity Phase Two is not included here, but interested readers may review it independently (see Mundell et al, 2011).

The research took place in two multicultural communities in South Africa consisting of mainly black, isiZulu-, Sepedi- and Setswana-speaking members. The communities were of very low to middle socio-economic status. When working in multicultural communities it is necessary to have members of those communities in the research team to understand the cultural context, to gain access to the respondents and to obtain legitimate data (Vertovec, 2008). Members of the community who could speak two or three of the local languages and had some training in psychology, sociology or nursing, were identified. Ten women with such backgrounds were recruited as community researchers (CRs) and included in the research team for a five-year period. Throughout the research they received intensive training and supervision in interviewing and related research skills outlined later in the chapter.

The research was not classic participatory action research (PAR) – a strategy to empower disadvantaged groups through collective action (Bhana, 2006; Fals-Borda, 2006). This research followed a custom research design where researchers involved themselves in a community to understand behaviour and to provide appropriate health services. It displayed characteristics of community research as defined in Chapter One by studying sensitive issues in a community and by involving members from the community as CRs. This chapter focuses on the experiences of the CRs and on the challenges they were confronted with during the research process.

Description of the research project

Study context

South Africa has the largest population of HIV infected adults in the world. It is estimated that about 5.6 million people (between 5.4 and 5.8 million) in South Africa are infected, this is about 12–15% of the population as a whole, or 17.8% of the population aged 15 to 49 years (UNAIDS, 2010). Women account for an estimated 59% of adults living with HIV in South Africa (UNAIDS, 2008). Almost one in three women aged 25–34 years and over a quarter of men aged 30 to 34 years are living with HIV (Shisana et al, 2009). People with HIV are found in every race group in South Africa, although it is more prominent in black communities (13% compared to less than 2% in other communities) (Shisana et al, 2005). HIV-infection is more common in low socio-economic areas where a lack of health and social services exists. There is a pressing need for social and psychological services that can help HIV-infected people to come to terms with their diagnosis and develop a healthy lifestyle.

This research started in 2003 at a time when the South African government did not provide anti-retroviral therapy (ART) for infected patients. AIDS was then seen as a death sentence because no medication was available. This perspective influenced the climate around HIV in communities as well as in the project. During the research period, in 2004, the roll-out of ART started for patients with low CD4 counts. Thereafter, the community attitude towards HIV changed somewhat, although the stigma related to HIV remained (Visser et al, 2009).

Recruitment of participants

Pregnant HIV-infected women were recruited from four antenatal clinics in Tshwane. HIV counsellors at the clinics were trained to recruit newly diagnosed HIV-positive pregnant women for the study. Over the period of two years the counsellors approached 438 qualifying respondents to determine whether they were amenable to participation in the research project. Those respondents who agreed met with a CR who explained the study aims and procedures extensively. A total of 317 newly diagnosed HIV-positive pregnant women agreed to participate. They signed consent forms and an appointment was made for their first interviews. To enable

Figure 8.1 Posed photo of women attending an antenatal clinic

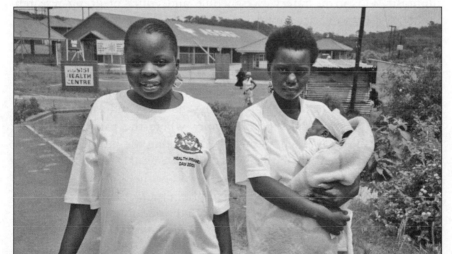

respondents to attend interviews at the clinics, concomitant transport costs were carried by the project.

Role of the community researchers

CRs recruited from the target communities, had a dual role in the research. As part of project planning they provided insight into cultural understanding, knowledge and social life in these communities. They contributed to the development of research instruments to ensure that questions were culturally sensitive and that important issues and themes were not overlooked. While the questionnaires were translated into the local languages by language experts, the CRs had to adapt the formal translations into the spoken language and employ the most appropriate terminology to make it easy for respondents to understand the questions. Furthermore, they had to build relationships with respondents and conduct the interviews with each HIV positive respondent in her preferred dialect. It was assumed that respondents would feel more comfortable speaking to someone from their own cultural background. This could smooth access to the participants and enhance the validity of the data.

Training of community researchers

CRs were trained and supervised to build trusting relationships with the respondents to enhance the quality and validity of data. A five-day training programme for CRs was presented by the senior researchers. The content of the training included information regarding the research process, collection of data, interviewing and relationship building techniques, general administration of the interview schedule and ethics of doing research about HIV. They received information about HIV and AIDS to enable them to answer women's basic questions during interviews. CRs practised interviewing skills through role play. In addition, each CR was required to conduct at least two interviews under the supervision of a senior researcher in order to ensure that the correct procedures were followed.

After conclusion of the training programme, the CRs conducted interviews independently as scheduled at the clinics where the participants were recruited. At the end of each research day a meeting was held to discuss the interviews and review the challenges of the day. Weekly project meetings attended by the whole research team were also held to deal with the challenges that were encountered and to plan ahead.

At first, interviews were tape recorded with the permission of respondents to assist CRs in keeping records. As time progressed the CRs became adept at capturing information directly onto printed interview schedules. Interviews took between one and two hours each.

Figure 8.2 A training session for community researchers

Even during training and progressively through the first few interviews the research team became aware that interviewing had a profound emotional effect on CRs. The daily meetings were consequently used to debrief, advise and support them in this regard. Additionally, the research team organised weekly interactive sessions with a psychologist to help support CRs with the emotional impacts of interviewing. The psychologist regularly took stock of the emotional experiences that took place during the preceding week and proceeded to prepare the CRs to deal with the emotional expressions of the participants during the interviews. They were also assisted in dealing with their own emotional experiences. This continued throughout the baseline study.

CRs' experiences and challenges

This section draws on the minutes of weekly project meetings and a focus group discussion held with CRs to reflect on their experiences and the challenges encountered during the data collection phase of the project. The following questions were asked during the focus group and a thematic analysis of findings was conducted upon completion (Smith and Osborn, 2007):

1. What kind of problems were the participants experiencing?
2. How did the participants benefit from participation in the research?

3. How did the interviews affect you personally?

Participation in the research presented the CRs with a number of challenges that had an impact on them on various levels.

Privacy and confidentiality

Due to the stigma surrounding HIV and AIDS (Visser et al, 2009), many HIV positive women do not disclose their HIV status to anyone, or they disclose selectively. It is therefore incumbent upon researchers to protect the confidentiality of the respondents' HIV status. As a result of this obligation, interviews had to be conducted in a private area in the clinic. If there was no private room available, temporary office space had to be arranged and funded to enable interviews to take place in privacy. Respondents risked exposure by simply being seen to partake in the research. The researchers therefore adopted an image not associated with HIV, but with the promotion of women's health in general, to ensure that the women's status would not became known through their participation. Telephone calls and home visits to remind respondents of appointments were done with discretion so as to not reveal the status of the women.

Informal contact between the CRs and the respondents could also expose the women. CRs agreed to be friendly when they met the respondents informally during community interaction, but not to talk to them or reveal any information that could expose the women's status. If respondents wanted to talk to them they could come to the research office or contact them by telephone.

Support requirements and expectations

To obtain valid information from respondents, CRs had to build trusting relationships with them. Good relationships developed over time as CRs met with respondents on several occasions (up to six times) during the course of the project. After being informed about the research objectives, the participants shared their stories and expected practical help to deal with their psychosocial problems. CRs were faced with a number of issues during interviews:

- Women were very emotional because it was often the first time that they shared their experiences of being HIV+.
- Women did not always understand what their diagnosis meant and needed information about HIV. One woman (in the words of the CR) "wondered whether her family might be bewitched or some ghosts were taking her child. Every bad thing has happened to her family."

- Women shared problems in their relationships with partners, such as abuse and financial dependency. One CR said "It was worse when it comes to relationships, the story of condoms and the difficulty they encountered with their partners."
- Women discussed their financial difficulties which was often the root of many other problems. In addition, during the research period eight mothers and 33 babies died. This included two still births. There were also 39 babies that tested positive for HIV. These incidents had severe emotional effects on both CRs and respondents.

The intense emotional pain and poverty experienced by the HIV+ women evoked a sense of responsibility in the CRs. They wished to help the women. This created a dilemma of defining boundaries between the research (to gain information) and the necessity to intervene. Because Phase One was not an intervention but a baseline study, the policy was not to intervene in order not to compromise research results. However, because of the intense needs and the lack of community resources which limited what could be offered, the research team decided to introduce a system of referrals and provide some direct help. Referrals were made for necessary medical services, such as ART (49 women were referred) and to social workers for survival resources such as food parcels, nappies and clothes for the babies (25 women were referred to social workers and 46 received food parcels). CRs also provided HIV information and advice on how to live with HIV and how to protect themselves. In this way the role of the CRs extended to being educators, supporters, medical advisors, counsellors and advocates for the participants.

The need for specialised interviewing skills

It was difficult to interview recently diagnosed HIV positive women because of the emotional content discussed. The CRs needed good interpersonal skills to understand what women wanted to say. As one CR put it, "It is difficult to get information, because you have to read the clients and almost play with that to get information," and "I would ask a question and they would give an irrelevant answer that doesn't make sense. But you have to go back and try until you finish the interview."

At times some of the women were too emotional to take part in interviews. In such cases CRs would comfort the women and then organise alternative arrangements. They said the following: "Some women have just received the news that they are HIV positive. They become so emotional that they cannot even talk. So we ended up stopping the interview and giving them other appointments."

On a few occasions the CRs had to break the news to the mother that the infant was HIV positive, as testing the infants was part of the research protocol. This was very difficult for CRs: "Now I must face this mother ... we were crying. You know, you don't even have a starting point, you don't know how to open your mouth and say this."

Research as an emotional burden

The emotional content of the interviews resulted in the CRs becoming emotionally involved with the experiences of the women: "You become emotionally involved with the person and you want to help the person and sometimes you get angry and then it goes up and down." The high level of involvement with the participants led to emotional stress for some. At times they felt trapped between their responsibility to get research data and the moral obligation they felt to help participants in need. It became necessary to organise individual debriefing and counselling sessions for CRs to deal with their own emotions and to learn how to deal with the experiences of the respondents. This was done to protect the CRs and to safeguard the quality of data obtained.

During the focus group discussion CRs spoke about their feelings of sadness, anger, frustration and exploitation. CRs explained how they experienced intense sadness when the women were crying, especially when the babies were HIV positive. One CR said "It actually breaks your heart. I was in tears and she was in tears about her baby. I know it was not very helpful but sometimes it tears your inside out." Another one said "You cry, you are emotionally disturbed. You want to say it shouldn't have happened. Why did it happen this way? You want to change things around." It was difficult for them not to cry with the participants: "You don't want to become emotional yourself. You wish the tears don't appear because you have to listen and support. You have to make them at ease, make them tea so that they feel better before you can complete the questionnaire."

CRs experienced some of the anger expressed by the women for being treated badly by family members or medical staff or for being infected by an unfaithful partner. They also became angry when they believed that the women had lied to them. As one CR explained "When she tells you one thing and lives another" or "You can see she is pregnant but she does not admit it." CRs also spoke of how they felt frustrated, but had to hide it, when the women did not understand the questions or did not answer consistently so that they had to rephrase questions. Sometimes interviews took up to four hours because the respondents told their whole life stories and elaborated on every answer. They also felt frustrated when they tried to help the women by informing them about the consequences of high risk behaviour and how to protect themselves, but some women did not take responsibility. One said "She does not even take it seriously that she is HIV positive, she needs to take care of herself." At times some said that they felt exploited when respondents expected favours from them or tried to manipulate them. For example, one woman requested the CR to write a letter to her employer to disguise her HIV status. "Because we are so nice, accommodating and accepting, these patients will ask you something that you could never do. You have to phone this, you have to phone there. And you know when she started crying… but I said NO. No, things were going too far." CRs felt a few women became overly dependent and demanded too much help from them: "They do not want to go out for themselves, they rely completely on us. They demand nappies and food parcels and they will toi-toi (protest) to get them."

Effect on their personal lives

The stories of the respondents affected the CRs personally in various ways. They spoke of how they experienced a 'heavy load', since they had many roles to play – that of interviewer, educator and counsellor. They felt responsible to help the women. They internalised some of the feelings and fears of the women which contributed to their feeling of vulnerability. Seeing the mistrust in the relationships of the women they interviewed, made them vulnerable to mistrust in their own relationships. The following are examples of what CRs said:

'You sort of hope your partner is not doing what you hear out there.'

'I am able to talk to him but I cannot trust. I think the stories have affected my trust in him.'

'The stories I have heard from women about HIV and how they got infected, it actually makes me to become more afraid of HIV and vulnerable at the same time. So I started educating those who are close to me more about it and even I tried it with my husband. I think I am vulnerable because I am living with another person who is my husband.'

Some CRs started to educate their family, friends and their children about HIV and the risks involved, in an effort to avoid the impact of HIV in their own families. They took their work seriously and it became a life mission:

'I have two boxes of condoms in my house. I took them to my two sons. I preached the gospel of HIV to them.'

'I preach HIV so much at home I am waiting for the day my husband will tell me that he is tired of hearing about it.'

Some of the CRs described how they experienced 'burnout', 'emotional exhaustion' and 'distancing' because of too much emotional exposure in the work situation. In relation to the excessive exposure to emotions one CR said the following:

'Some women always cried. When you start asking a question, not even a question that can elicit any emotional stuff, they start to cry. Then you give a tissue and you turn around and say to yourself, "I am not going to cry this time." Then you don't even probe. You just want to complete the interview.'

Some CRs spoke of how they felt overwhelmed by HIV, because they were confronted with it wherever they went: at work, at home and through the media. One CR indicated that she was emotionally exhausted and distanced herself emotionally when a family member passed away: "A relative was buried recently and in that household it was the fourth HIV-related death. I think it comes to a point where you are exhausted, I did not want to go through the sadness of the funeral." Another CR said "At work and at home, you have to bear with it, you can't run away from it, if you say you don't want to work here anymore... you go home, it hits you out there." Another CR expressed burnout in a form of disillusionment:

'I wanted to change the world at first. You have all this energy, because you want to educate these women and empower them, but nothing happens. She does not take it seriously that she is HIV+. My heart is as hard as a rock now. When they start crying, I know it is normal for them. It is like I don't care. I know I care, but there is nothing I can do for them.'

Another said "I realised that there is only so much that you can do. You cannot change the world. We have given them information; it is up to them to improve their lives."

The rewards CRs experienced

Despite various challenges, the research was an enriching experience for most of the CRs. They coped with the intense emotional experiences by supporting one another: "Working as a team really helped us to go on even when things were difficult; you always know that someone is there to talk to." The CRs discussed how they discovered strength in themselves: "You sort of gain momentum of strength. You feel you have dealt with this case today; tomorrow it will be another case. Maybe today will be better than yesterday. God will give me the strength to face this." Some CRs expressed awareness and gratefulness for their privileges because they saw people less fortunate than themselves: "It certainly makes you more grateful for what you have. There are people with a lot of problems out there." Another said "It makes me more appreciative that I am in a relationship that I can talk to my husband." They felt appreciated and proud of themselves when they received feedback that they had helped someone: "She came in one day and it was like a miracle. There was this woman who put on weight and she was absolutely glowing. It was a miracle."

Effect on research results

The sensitivity of the research topic and experiences of all participants, could have had an influence on the quality of the research results. Even though no specific intervention was offered, the research became an intervention in itself and respondents benefited in various ways. The interviews became a source of emotional support where women could share their emotional experiences and CRs listened and supported them:

> 'We talked to them, listened to them; we showed empathy and supported them. If they had nobody else to go to, we listened and tried to help even when it was difficult. We never said "We are tired of your problems," we referred them to the appropriate place and we let them know that the doors are open for them. Even afterwards they still came to us.'

The questions that were asked prompted the participants to become knowledgeable about HIV and they could track their progress through the CD4 counts that were done as part of the research. They were sensitised to healthy living simply by being part of the research: "I think we instilled in them the importance of taking care of their health and knowing what is going on in their bodies." CRs felt that women were empowered through participation in the project: "I think they have gained a lot because they feel so empowered, they know their rights, they feel they have a role to play in their families and to empower other women by sharing information with them."

Reflections

Although extensive training and supervision of the CRs was crucial in obtaining valid and reliable research data, the involvement of CRs from the target community had major advantages in this research. They made an invaluable contribution in building relationships with the respondents to gain understanding of their emotional experiences. They also contributed to the formulation of culturally appropriate questions and brought an understanding that enhanced the depth and richness of the data. The trusting relationships that developed over time enhanced the validity of the data.

The most important challenge in using CRs was that they had to deal with serious emotional trauma without having had formal counselling training to help them to process it. The CRs experienced difficulty in establishing boundaries between themselves and the clients as well as between the research and their need to help the participants. CRs over-identified with the problems of the respondents so that it affected their personal lives. They felt so overwhelmed by the emotional response and the impact of HIV that they had difficulty attending to their own family traumas. It is possible that this could have affected the quality of the data in a negative way. Because of confidentiality involved in the research, CRs could not discuss these feelings with anyone outside the research team. They therefore had to rely on each other and on the debriefing structures provided as part of the research to deal with their emotions.

Additionally, the most difficult dilemma for the CRs was defining the boundaries between research and intervention. This project was aimed at obtaining baseline data to develop interventions, but participating in the baseline research benefited the women. Respondents found someone who was interested in them, who was listening to them and was building good relationships with them. Some of them were referred to additional services to address their most pressing needs. They also learnt more about HIV and general health care which they could apply in their own lives. The high level of involvement of CRs in the lives of participants could cast some doubt about the accuracy of longitudinal data because the research became an intervention in itself.

Key learning

Community research is complex because it involves various multifaceted relationships and dimensions of cultural knowledge. The lessons learned through reflecting on this research project may also be applicable in other community research initiatives:

- The intimate relationships that developed between CRs and the respondents were an important advantage and at the same time created various challenges.
- The training and consistent supervision of CRs as well as debriefing and counselling sessions assisted the CRs to deliver quality work despite the challenges.
- Research in underserved communities may easily result in dichotomies in defining the boundaries between research and intervention. The interviews themselves may become a source of support for the

respondents. Additional support structures to address some of the most pressing needs of all participants (researchers and respondents alike) may be required.

• Researchers should take into account the effect of the research on the processes in communities. Involvement in communities has an effect on interaction in communities. This is a circular process.

Summary

Advantages:

• Being from the target community CRs can easily build trusting relationships with respondents
• CRs from the target community understand the culture and contributed to the cultural relevance of the research
• Their understanding of the cultural background of respondents enhanced the richness and validity of the data

Challenges:

• CRs had to deal with emotional trauma without any training in counselling skills
• CRs over-identified with the emotional trauma of the respondents so that it had an influence on their personal lives
• CRs working in research projects involving a highly emotional topic, need ongoing debriefing and supervision to enable them to deliver quality work.

Conclusion

To do community research ethically, researchers cannot only attend to privacy and the rights and interests of respondents as specified in guidelines for ethical research (World Medical Association Declaration of Helsinki, 1996; Shamoo and Resnick, 2003; Resnick, 2005). Instead, there should be a balance between the responsibilities towards the quality of the research, the wellbeing of the respondents, and the wellbeing of all members of the research team.

Experiences from this research emphasised that achieving such a balance can present a challenge. Trying to protect the rights of the respondents in a resource-poor environment may confront the researchers with the challenge of delivering unintended services. This again places a heavy burden on the researchers to assist respondents and may require additional project resources. Helping respondents may influence the scientific validity of baseline research results. In such a context the research can be an intervention in itself which can result in change in the behaviour that is monitored and may influence the behaviour of the researchers.

In planning research in resource-poor communities, researchers should be aware of the needs of participants and form linkages with existing helping organisations or assist in developing infrastructure in these communities. CRs dealing with sensitive topics also need regular debriefing and counselling to cope with the intense emotional demands of the research. Project managers should aim at striking a balance between the help provided, the protection of resources available to the project and the quality and integrity of research data.

Discussion questions

1. Who benefited most from participating in the research project discussed in this chapter?
2. Name the key factors to empower community members for roles as community researchers.
3. Can all community research be defined as community interventions? Is it possible to do community research without intervening or changing aspects of community life?

References

Bhana, A. (2006) 'Participatory Action Research: A Practical Guide for Realistic Radicals', in Terre Blance, M., Durrheim, K. and Painter, D. (eds), *Research in Practice, Applied Methods for Social Sciences*, Cape Town: University of Cape Town Press, 429–442.

Fals-Borda, O. (2006) 'Participatory (Action) Research in Social Theory:

Origins and Challenges', in Reason, P. and Bradbury, H. (eds) *Handbook of Action Research: Participative Inquiry and Practice*, London: Sage.

Makin, J., Forsyth, B., Visser M., Sikkema, K., Neufeld, S. and Jeffery, B (2008) 'Factors Affecting Disclosure in South African HIV-positive Pregnant Women', *AIDS Patient Care and STDs*, 2(11): 907-916.

Mundell J., Visser, M., Makin, J., Kershaw, T., Forsyth, B. and Sikkema, K. (2011) 'The Impact of Structured Support Groups for Pregnant Women Living with HIV', *Women and Health*, 51: 546-565.

Resnick, D. (2005) What is Ethics and Why is it Important? Retrieved from: www.niehs.nih.gov/research/resources/bioethics/whatis.cfm

Shamoo, D. and Resnick, D. (2003) *Responsible Conduct of Research*. New York: Oxford Press.

Shisana, O., Rehle, T., Simbayi, L. Parker, W., Zuma, K., Bhana, A., Connolly, C., Jooste, S., Pillay, V. et al. (2005) *South African National HIV Prevalence, HIV Incidence, Behaviour and Communication Survey*. Cape Town: Human Sciences Research Council.

Shisana, O., Rehle, T., Simbayi, L., Zuma, K., Jooste, S., Pillay-van-Wyk, V., Mbelle, N., Van Zyl, J., Parker, W., Zungu, N. Pezi, S. and the SABSSM III Implementation Team (2009) *South African National HIV Prevalence, Incidence, Behaviour and Communication Survey 2008: A Turning Tide Among Teenagers?* Cape Town: Human Sciences Research Council.

Smith, J. and Osborn, M. (2007) 'Interpretive Phenomenology Analysis', in Smith, J.A. (ed) *Qualitative Psychology: A Practical Guide to Research Methods*, London, Sage Publications Ltd, 53–80.

UNAIDS (2008) *Fast Facts About HIV*. Retrieved from www.unaids.org/en/media/unaids/contentassets/dataimport/pub/factsheet/2008/20080519_fastfacts_hiv_en.pdf

UNAIDS (2010) *Global Report – UNAIDS Report on the Global AIDS Epidemic*, Geneve: UNAIDS.

Vertovec, S. (2008) 'Super-Diversity and its Implications', *Ethnic and Racial Studies*, 30(6): 1024–1054.

Visser, M., Makin, J. Vandormael, A., Sikkema, K. and Forsyth, B. (2009) 'HIV/AIDS Stigma in a South African Community', *AIDS Care*, 21(2): 197–206.

World Medical Association Declaration of Helsinki (1996) *Ethical Principles for Medical Research Involving Human Subjects*, http://ohsr.od.nih.gov/guidelines/Helsinki.html

Nine

Power and participation in community research: community profiling in Italy

Terri Mannarini

Chapter aims

- To highlight the rewards as well as the risks entailed in participatory community research
- To identify and discuss dynamics and devices through which inequality, exclusion and power asymmetry are created and preserved in the research process
- To make suggestions about the ways in which community research participation processes can be managed
- To formulate recommendations concerning ways of increasing the reflexivity of community researchers

Introduction

The main aim of this chapter is to explore the issue of power in participatory community research (CR). After a brief introduction about the importance and benefits of participation, and of ensuring the participation of citizens in community research, the dynamics of power relationships will be addressed and the risks and problems associated with the adoption of a participatory approach highlighted. Specifically, issues concerning inclusion, manipulation, reproduction of social inequalities, quality of participation, and influence will be discussed, with examples from projects that have utilised community research.

Advantages of participation in CR

According to the community psychology and community development literature, citizen participation in community life and citizens' contributions to collective problem identification and problem solving are desirable both for people and institutions (Montero, 2004), as well as for society at large

(Clary and Snyder, 2002). Citizen participation plays a relevant role in many community settings, ranging from workplaces to health programmes, urban planning interventions, and public policies (Wandersman and Florin, 2000), as well as in community research (Balcazar et al, 2006). Participation, as a transformative concept, forms the basis of the processes aimed at improving the environmental, social and economic conditions of a community (Ledwith and Springett, 2010). As a fundamental part of active citizenship, participation in CR can enhance the quality of life of the community's members. In addition, participation can contribute to social cohesion and to both individual and collective well-being: as Cantor and Sanderson (1999) put it, not only participation increases social contacts and thereby fulfils the need for affiliation, but it also provides people with meaningful aims to achieve. Moreover, participation can increase social well-being (Keyes, 1998) by reinforcing the perceptions of individuals and groups of being socially integrated and accepted and strengthening their belief in the possibility of benefiting themselves and society. Kagan (2007) argues that bottom–up participation, or in any case those community research practices that include bottom–up processes, is the most influential form of action that can foster well–being and change the material circumstances of people's lives.

Disadvantages of participation in CR

Although community psychologists claim that community participatory research should be considered as a gold standard, they often fail to deal with a set of critical issues raised by the practice of citizen involvement. Among such issues, power stands out as one of the most striking. There are many ways in which power affects community research. At a very general level, we can rely on the notion of psychopolitical validity. Psychopolitical validity refers both to the validity achieved by a systematic account of the role of power in political and psychological dynamics affecting the phenomenon of interest (Prilleltensky, 2003), and to the potential of community research and action to promote well-being and reduce power inequalities (Prilleltensky, 2008). Indeed, communities are characterised by multiple and conflicting perspectives, with power operating within, between and upon communities (Sandler, 2007). As will be discussed in the following sections, these aspects of power can be either underestimated or neglected in CR. At a more specific level, there are other forms in which power dynamics enter the community research setting. For example, the degree to which the research setting is inclusive and accessible depends on crucial questions about 'who' represents the community and how researchers can grant access to groups and individuals that are likely to remain, and mostly do remain, on the fringe of the community (see also, Jewkes and Murcott, 1998; Botes and van Rensburg, 2000; Regonini, 2005). Moreover, the status and power differences observed in the larger community are likely to persist in the 'small community' directly involved in the research process. When the people involved are remarkably diverse as regards their education, income and gender (Baiocchi, 2003), as well as their expertise credibility (Ulbert and Risse, 2005), and cognitive and communicative skills (Burkhalter et al, 2002), the process through which meanings are co-constructed is not immune from the effects of the dynamics of power (Cornwall 2002) which can result in asymmetries or even exclusion (Campbell and Jovchelovitch, 2000).

In addition, the asymmetry between professional researchers and community researchers has to be taken into account as a potential source of oppression and manipulation. The status of professional researchers as alternatively insiders or outsiders (Bartunek, 2008) is also likely to affects group dynamics, with consequences for both process and outcomes (Arieli et al, 2009). One more issue related to power dynamics concerns the quality of participation. Variations over time in individual and group commitment, conflicts within the community, stress and burnout can intervene in the research process, thereby affecting the quality of knowledge generated in the research setting, as well as motivations for sustaining participation (Kagan et al, 2005). Finally, the actual influence that citizen participation, and specifically community researchers, can exert on institutions and the larger community raises a more general question about the amount of power attributed to community members and their capacity for having an impact on public choices and policies (Abelson and Gauvin, 2006).

Examples of each of these facets will be discussed in the light of a specific research experience consisting of a participatory community profiling carried out in a municipality of 17,000 inhabitants in southern Italy. The goal of the study was to provide the local administration with a list of priorities to be used for implementing local development actions.

Theoretical discussion

The community psychology, community development and deliberative democracy literatures mostly agree that participatory CR has to deal with a set of critical issues. Kothari (2001) suggests that participation has become a 'new grand narrative', a myth that researchers should demolish, and a theory and a practice that should be rescued from the pitfalls of rhetoric. One of the assumptions that needs to be acknowledged is that every participatory practice is based on an implicit theory, which in turn is grounded in a certain conception of society, power and social change (Ciaffi and Mela, 2006). Whatever the participatory practice, its aims and features vary according to the specific view that institutions and professional researchers share about how society evolves and who are the protagonists of change.

A further critical issue to be considered is the quality of participation. As shown by an overview of a large number of experiences of participatory development in undeveloped countries (Tommasoli, 2001), in CR the risks of manipulation, as well as the emergence of populistic tendencies, are real (see also, Esteva, 1992; Carmen, 1996; Botes and van Rensburg, 2000). Exploitation by power élites and lobbies is also a possibility (Stokes, 1998). The quality of participation also depends on the quality of knowledge produced: in some cases, what is presented as 'local knowledge' is more a construct of the planning context than an expression of community needs, interests and priorities (Mosse, 2001). Moreover, some of that knowledge may also be a source of obstacles to transformation necessary for the community (Montero, 2006). Finally, careful thought should also be given to factors favouring the sustainability of commitment. Since participation is stressful and time- and energy-consuming, its quality is likely to decrease over time (Cornwall and Jewkes, 1995), and disempowerment is likely to occur if insufficient or inappropriate resources are provided to community members (Kagan, 2006). In CR, community members and community researchers need to be supported by professional researchers, who can provide them with information, expertise, supervision, hard resources, and leadership so as to 'decrease the likelihood of burnout' (Kagan, 2007: 13). The power dynamics permeating communities are reflected in the degrees of inclusiveness and accessibility of the research setting. It has often been noted that community researchers are likely to belong to privileged or high-status social groups and cannot be regarded as representatives of the community (Jewkes and Murcott, 1998; Baiocchi, 2003; Regonini, 2005). The recruitment of community members as researchers and participants is often distorted by either effects of self-selection or failure in outreach activities. As a result, underprivileged groups may be excluded. This happens partly because they lack the resources (for example, time, social networks and competencies) for negotiating the costs of participation and also because they may have internalised disadvantage and accepted it as an unmodifiable condition of life (Jost et al, 2004). Professional researchers need to acknowledge that power operates at the psychological level, creating internal barriers to participation and change, even in those individuals or groups who would benefit most from being involved in community research and action.

Power also emerges within the research setting in group dynamics, in which individual and social differences on the one hand, and social influence processes on the other, play significant roles (Van Stokkom, 2005). Income, education and gender are likely to create disparities among participants and community researchers (Baiocchi, 2003), as are personal traits such as credibility (Ulbert and Risse, 2005) and cognitive and communication skills (Burkhalter et al, 2002). Those participants who tend to be socially dominant (Reykowski, 2006) are often more active and persuasive than others.

Moreover, social influence can drive group processes toward unexpected and in some cases unwanted outcomes, such as risky shift phenomenon (also known as group polarization) (Stoner, 1968) and false agreement (Harvey, 1988). Studies on group decision-making, moving from Stoner's (1968) discoveries, showed that group discussion can lead group members to take more risky decisions than they would take as individuals. At a more general level, interactions among group members can make most of them move towards a more extreme point, thereby becoming more and more aligned in the direction to which they were already tending. False agreement refers to unconscious collusion among group members concerning the nature of the situation being faced and the action that need to be undertaken. Miscommunication and unverified assumptions made by each member about what the other members of the group think and wish to do, leads the group to a misleading, though shared, view of reality. Both polarization (Sunstein, 2000, 2002) and false agreement (Cooke, 2001) have been mentioned as concrete risks entailed in participatory research processes. The impact of participatory CR on public policy and the influence that citizens can exert on institutions and the larger community are further facets of the power issue. At a general level, reviews of citizen participation from different countries (Canada, UK, Italy, US) (Burton, 2003; Irvin and Stansbury, 2004; Abelson and Gauvin, 2006; Bobbio, 2007) suggest that the impact of participation is modest, and that citizen involvement in CR often has a symbolic rather than a pragmatic value. Other acknowledged negative effects include the deterioration of relations between community members and professional researchers, or financing institutions, which is likely to occur when the goals of the research setting are not fully achieved or not clearly stated; and the emergence of new social conflicts within the community because of the voluntary or involuntary exclusion of groups or because of conflicting interests voiced by different groups (Botes and van Rensburg, 2000).

The last facet of power that we will address concerns the relationships between professional researchers, community researchers and community members. The importance of the quality of such relationships is well known among community psychologists (see Brodsky et al, 2004), and commentators often recommend that ensuring collaborative and non-exploitative relations is important when undertaking CR (Fawcett, 1991). However, some argue that no one can escape the 'paradox of participation' (Quaghebeur, et al, 2004; Arieli, et al, 2009). Participatory CR is caught in the dilemma of supporting bottom-up processes, emancipation and self-determination and at the same time of fulfilling the need for product, efficiency and effectiveness (Mannarini, 2009). Furthermore, power can define the identities of participants as 'citizens', 'users', 'beneficiaries' or 'clients' and may affect what people think they can or cannot do, know, or decide (Cornwall, 2002). Such power has the effect of 'tidying up' the setting so as to exclude people, types of knowledge and practices that are perceived as sources of disorder or do not fit into the logic of the research (Kothari, 2001).

Community research in practice

An experience of community profiling

In this section, examples of power dynamics and effects in community research will be presented, drawing on a specific research experience carried out in a local community in southern Italy. The examination of the project will highlight how power dynamics manifest and generate their effects when community researchers are involved in participative projects. The research was designed and implemented according to the principles of the community profiling method (see Francescato et al, 2007). Community profiling is a participatory research process aimed at analysing different facets of the community (geography, demography, economics, services, institutions and psychology). Techniques of data gathering vary from profile to profile, ranging from environmental walks, interviews of key informants and focus groups to surveys and analysis of secondary data (Francescato and Tomai, 2002). Data are collected and analysed by a core research group made up of community members and researchers, with the goal of identifying the assets and critical points of the community and setting a list of priorities for intervention.

The study was requested and funded by the local administration of Tricase (Lecce, Italy) and carried out in nine months by a research team composed of two external researchers and 15 community members involved as community researchers who either responded individually to a public call for volunteers, or were members of local associations. The research comprised of 26 key informant interviews, five focus groups involving 50 community residents, a questionnaire with a sample of 497 families, surveying their current perceptions of the community's strengths and weaknesses. Table 9.1 shows all the actors involved in the study and the tasks they performed. All data, along with social and economic indicators, were used to define both the assets and the problems of the community, and a set of priorities was defined. Results of the study (see Francescato et al, 2004) were presented in a public meeting and reported to local administrators.

Power dynamics emerged in different phases and facets of the research process. The main critical points in terms of power relationships are discussed here.

Table 9.1 Community research in practice: actors involved and tasks performed

Players	N	Task
Professional researchers	2	Leading the research team and providing technical and methodological support to community researchers
Community members involved as community researchers	15	Data gathering and data analysis
Community members involved as key informants	26	Providing data
Community members involved in focus group sessions	50	Providing data
Community members involved in completing a survey	497	Providing data

The relationship between the research team and the community (the power of the few)

CRs experienced mixed reactions upon turning to their fellow citizens to collect information on the community. While some respondents were helpful and willing to cooperate, others proved mistrustful and suspicious, challenging the legitimacy of the request. CRs reported that they were asked 'who they stood in for', 'what benefits they were provided with' and 'what kind of relationship they had with the local administration'. Such reactions induced community researchers to reflect on their role as 'representatives' of the community. They became aware that their decision to engage in the project as community researchers did not automatically grant them positive status in the eyes of their fellow citizens. Indeed, the local people's attitudes of mistrust and hostility were interpreted by CRs as the result of a lack of transparency in the recruitment campaign for community researchers carried out by the local administration. CRs learned from their fellow citizens that the recruitment campaign carried out partly through public calls and partly through the informal channel of personal networks, had been perceived by part of the community as instrumentally aimed at consolidating the electoral consensus. Such perception prevented sections of the community from participating in the research process and cast a shadow on the intentions and goals of the community researchers themselves. Community members who were willing to be involved in the project as researchers had voluntarily chosen to play an active role in the project. They had not been chosen because they belonged to any of the underprivileged groups existing in the community, but simply because they wanted to support the project.

Initially, CRs were not aware of the inclusion/exclusion dynamics, nor did they reflect on the different power structures and inequalities in the community. They were unaware that they themselves might inadvertently be partly responsible for enforcing these dimensions. However, they eventually realised that the frame of social hierarchies and power relationships in which the research was taking place had to be taken into account, and thus became critically conscious of their position within the community. This happened because professional and community researchers engaged in a group reflexive process in which all of the research team members enhanced their awareness of the researchers' contribution to the construction of meanings throughout the research process. They also increased their personal reflexivity, reflecting upon the ways in which their own values, experiences, interests, beliefs, political commitments and wider aims in life shaped the research.

The relationships within the research team (the power of leadership)

The exercise of power entailed in group dynamics became more and more visible as the research team proceeded through the stages that characterise team building: 'forming', 'storming', 'norming' and 'performing' (Tuckman, 1965). While at the beginning cohesion was high and CRs were willing to seek consensus and strengthen similarities among themselves, over time conflicting views and motivations emerged. Social as well as individual differences influenced both the group's productivity and satisfaction: older CRs, and those community leaders with more experience of participation, tended to have the most influence over group decisions. Younger and less experienced group members did not have the opportunity or the time to participate to the same degree, were on the whole less satisfied than the former, resulting in some of them leaving the programme. Although the professional researchers encouraged the group to reflect on its internal relational dynamics and attempted to repair relationships, tensions remained and resulted in progressive breakdown of the group. By the end of the research process, almost half of the people involved had left. There were several reasons for such an undesired outcome, which only partly depended on the group internal problems. Besides the length of the research process, which is an objective cost that not everyone was able to bear, two more factors contributed to the breakdown of the team: the lack of logistic and organisational support by the local administration who was supposed to provide it, and the consequent serious deterioration in relations between the administration and the community researchers. Due to the weak responsiveness of the administration to their requests for support, CRs felt that they were being abandoned by the administration, and even manipulated for undeclared purposes. Finally, managing group relationships proved to be exhausting and drew on resources that could have been spent on making the group more effective and efficient.

The relationship between professional and CRs (the power of roles)

The paradox of participatory community research mentioned in the theoretical section was apparent in the minds of the professional researchers for the whole duration of the process. Despite their efforts to promote a bottom-up process, emancipation and self-determination, and to enhance participation and empower people, they could not help pressing the group to reach its aims as efficiently as possible. This happened because the professional researchers were pressured by the local administration to accomplish their task within a set period of time. This prevented CRs from exploring new and different paths and plans of action in all of the phases and activities required by the research plan. Professional researchers provided CRs with ideas and instruments that were consistent with the research context, but time pressure made them less willing to innovate instruments and techniques. Above all, CRs accepted the authority of professional researchers in explaining 'how' to do research, as well as their subordinate role. CRs never questioned this hierarchy and did not propose different frames of thought. On the whole, the feeling of the professional researchers was that they had been much more directive than they had originally intended and that the 'local knowledge' produced was partly the result of rules, guidelines and implicit theories set out by the professional researchers. In light of this, it is not possible to be certain that community needs, interests and priorities were fully voiced.

The relationship between community members and political institutions (the power of citizens)

The participatory community profiling highlighted that community members had detailed perceptions of the problems affecting the community and knew how to single out and use the resources needed to cope with those problems. They suffered from a general sense of frustration, however, and had lost hope in the possibility of changing their community. They felt they could not exert an influence on collective choices and public policy, and that they had been given a negligible amount of power by the local government. The same feelings were expressed by CRs, who articulated their frustration and demotivation, as well as the fear of being exploited and manipulated by local political institutions. They were concerned that the local administration, which had funded the research, would not consider the citizens' proposals and that all of their efforts would have been wasted. These concerns were exacerbated by a lack of clarity in the intentions of the local administrators, who did not explicitly declare what use they intended to make of the research findings. Even professional researchers were not able to obtain from the administrators a definite and public statement about the use of the results, though they overtly invited administrators to take a clear stand. In addition, as CRs faced problems and difficulties in collecting the information they needed from local agencies and offices. For instance, when immigration services under the municipality proved unable to provide CRs with all the data requested, because of internal organisational and technical problems of the office itself, CRs interpreted such a situation as a sign that they had been abandoned by institutions and that no support, in terms of resources, information and competencies, was available for them. As a consequence, relations between CRs and political institutions deteriorated: CRs started complaining, some of them progressively lost motivation and withdrew the investment they had made as researchers. The most dissatisfied among them chose an exit strategy (Hirschman, 1970) and left the programme before its conclusion. These relationships could have been maintained had expectations and outcomes been explicit at the outset of the project.

Key learning

The research experience discussed in this chapter shows how the dynamics of power permeate community research settings and the relations between the actors involved, including professional researchers, CRs, community members, the community at large and political institutions. The issues raised by the participatory research model underlying the community profiling method suggest that the involvement of community members in the research process might involuntarily yield unexpected and undesired effects, such as knowledge disparities between professional and non-professional researchers, limited autonomy and mastery of the CRs over the research process itself, a globally weak impact at the policy level and new conflicts within the community. Although not all these effects can be regarded as a direct consequence of the theoretical model itself, but rather as the outcomes of the specific implementation strategies that were chosen, we believe that there is a lesson to be learned both from theory and from practice.

In the project discussed above, CRs were involved both as data collectors and data users, but not as leading researchers. Consequently, such a position entailed that from the very beginning, a disparity of power characterised the relationship between the CRs and the professional researchers. Nevertheless, unless we think of participatory research that can be conducted in the absence of professional researchers, this is a condition that is set at the theoretical level. Thus, the point is not that the CRs were not given the possibility to lead the research process autonomously, but that the professional researchers on the one hand were too directive and on the other hand complied with the CRs' expectations that they would have a guide. To be more precise, they were too directive because they felt that they were asked to interpret their role in this way, thereby colluding with the CRs. This psychological device yielded two main effects. On the one hand, it resulted

148

in lack of innovation: the knowledge produced was somehow constrained by the high-structured nature of the task, thereby leaving narrow margins for deviations and changes that might have added new knowledge. On the other hand, it ended up demotivating some components of the research team. Indeed, those CRs who felt comfortable with a high-structured setting were satisfied and persisted in the work, but those who needed a more fluid environment for their contributions to emerge left.

Having stated this dilemma, in our view, the key factor of disempowerment lay neither in roles or leadership nor in the absence of material compensation for time and effort, but in the symbolic relationships linking CRs to the political institutions that asked for the intervention. To cast the problem in terms of the 'power of citizens', the disempowering key factor was the CRs' perception that their work would not have made a difference on the policy level. Based on the belief that the political institutions that had involved them in the project did not really value their roles as important and useful for the community, they reduced their investment. At the same time, their political efficacy decreased as they realised that they were not acknowledged as influential interlocutors.

Finally, the last dimension of power we have analysed concerns the representativeness of CRs: who has the power to speak for the community, to stand for the community? In the project discussed above, little effort was devoted to involving the community at large. Consequently, there was a significant self-selection effect. As we said, this effect resulted in a tension between those who decided to volunteer and the remainder of the community, including both those who were not interested in participating and those who would have participated had they been asked to.

We can now briefly explore the key learning points that can be drawn from this experience to highlight what professional researchers and CRs should actively consider. We will assume as a general premise that in order to deal with the problems associated with disempowerment, it is crucial that both professionals and CRs improve their awareness of potential imbalances in peer relations and take steps to ensure as much parity as possible. This general premise entails that CRs should increase their awareness of the contradiction between the logic of empowerment and the logic of effectiveness, a dilemma entailed in every participatory top-down process. In particular, they should reflect upon a side-effect of the institutional framing of participation, that is, the risk that the logic of effectiveness might lead to the construction of a normative high-structured setting, which they themselves shape and direct. In these circumstances, 'participatory processes can produce not diverse and locally varied development programmes, but strong convergence into a fixed set' (Mosse, 2001: 25)

The role of the researcher encompasses an inevitable margin of asymmetry, which can be reduced but never completely eroded. Such asymmetry might be instrumental for the achievement of the fixed goals, but it might also involuntarily serve as a channel to restrain the autonomy and initiative of the participants. In addition, from the very beginning until the research process is over, group dynamics should be carefully monitored to prevent the occurrence of social influence mechanisms that can orientate the knowledge building process towards convergence and conformism instead of fostering divergent and innovative processes.

Furthermore, while accepting that even the most inclusive research setting is necessarily also exclusive, CRs should invest in thorough and accurate information and outreach activities that widen the range of potential participants, thereby addressing ex ante the issue of representativeness. CRs should also engage in thorough analyses, both of the conflicts and inequalities within the community – even when they are not immediately connected to the specific research goal – and of the relationships between citizens involved in the research process and the financing institutions, ensuring that the two parties clarify and meet their reciprocal expectations, needs and duties. This action will help define the conditions for the symbolic reciprocal acknowledgement of the parties involved, that is, institutions and community members, conditions that are, in turn, the premise for the exercise of influence at the policy level.

Summary

Advantages of carefully considering power issues in CR

- Increased reflexivity of professional and community researchers
- Sustained participation over time
- Prevention of risks of voluntary/involuntary manipulation of citizen participation by political institutions/professional researchers
- Increased quality of research processes
- Comprehensive view of the ongoing processes (within the research setting, within the community and between the research setting and the community)

Limitations

- Highly demanding task, entailing the analysis of power configurations at multiple levels and the use of relational skills, as well as the ability to deal with group dynamics
- Possible trade-off between empowerment and effectiveness

Conclusions

Power and participation are key factors in community research. In this chapter we have argued that the goals of participatory community research may not be met if power issues are not given full consideration. We have also tried to elaborate on the visible and subtle forms in which power can affect the research setting and highlighted the drawbacks that can hide behind an insufficient consideration of the values underpinning the notion of citizen participation. The issues and the examples discussed confirm the complex nature of community research, emphasise the centrality of relationships and demonstrate the need for improving the reflexivity of all researchers involved in the process.

Discussion questions

1. What are the main manifestations of power that researchers need to be aware of when planning and carrying out a community research project?
2. What are the undesired effects generated by insufficient consideration of power issues?
3. What are the actions that researchers need to undertake to prevent such undesired effects?

References

Abelson, J. and Gauvin, F. P. (2006) 'Assessing the Impact of Public Participation: Concepts, Evidence and Policy Implications', *CHEPA Working Paper Series*, 8, Paper 08-01, Ontario: McMaster University.

Arieli, D., Friedman, V.J. and Agbaria, K. (2009) 'The Paradox of Participation in Action Research', *Action Research*, 7(3): 263-290.

Baiocchi, G. (2003) 'Participation, Activism, and Politics: The Porto Alegre Experiment'. In A. Fung and E.O. Wright (eds) *Deepening Democracy: Institutional Innovations in Empowered Participatory Governance*, London: Verso, 47-84.

Balcazar, F. E., Taylor, R.T., Kielhofner, G.W., Tamley, K., Benziger, T., Carlin, N. and Johnsons, S. (2006) 'Participatory Action Research: General Principles and a Study with a Chronic Health Condition', in L.A. Jason, C.B. Keys, Y. Suarez-Balcazar, R.T. Taylor and M.I. Davis (eds) *Participatory Community Research: Theories and Methods in Action*, Washington DC: APA, 17-35.

Bartunek, J.M. (2008) 'Insider/Outsider Team Research', in A.B. Shani, S.A. Mohrman, W. Pasmore, B. Stymne and N. Adler (eds) *Handbook of Collaborative Management Research*, Thousand Oaks, CA: Sage, 73-92.

Bobbio, L. (2007) *Amministrare con i Cittadini: Viaggio tra le Pratiche di Partecipazione in Italia*, Torino: Dipartimento di Studi Politici–Università di Torino.

Botes, L. and van Rensburg, D. (2000) 'Community Participation in Development: Nine Plagues and Twelve Commandments', *Community Development Journal*, 35(1): 41–58.

Brodsky, A., Senuta, K., Weiss, C., Marx, C., Loomis, C., Arteaga, S., Moore, H., Benhorin, R. and Castagnera-Fletcher, A. (2004) 'When One Plus One Equals Three: The Role of Relationships in Community Research', *American Journal of Community Psychology*, 33(3–4): 229-241.

Burkhalter, S., Gastil, J. and Kelshaw, T. (2002) 'A Conceptual Definition and a Theoretical Model of Public Deliberation in Small Face-to-Face Groups', *Communication Theory*, 12(4): 398-422.

Burton, P. (2003) *Community Involvement in Neighbourhood Regeneration: Stairway to Heaven or Road to Nowhere?*, Paper no.13, Bristol: ESRC Centre for Neighbourhood Research.

Campbell, C. and Jovchelovitch, S. (2000) 'Health, Community and Development: Towards a Social Psychology of Participation. *Journal of Community and Applied Social Psychology*, 10(4): 255-270.

Cantor, N. and Sanderson, C.A. (1999) 'Life Task Participation and Well-being: The Importance of Taking Part in Daily Life', in D. Kahneman and E, Diener (eds) *Well-being: The Foundation of Hedonic Psychology*, London: Sage, 230-243.

Carmen, R. (1996) *Autonomous Development. Humanizing the Landscape: An Excursion into Radical Thinking and Practice*, London: Zed Books.

Ciaffi, D. and Mela, A. (2006) *La Partecipazione*, Roma: Carocci.

Clary, E.G. and Snyder, M. (2002) 'Community Involvement: Opportunities and Challenges in Socializing Adults to Participate in Society', *Journal of Social Issue*, 58 (3): 581-592.

Cooke, B. (2001) 'The Social Psychological Limits of Participation?', in B. Cooke and U. Kothari (eds), *Participation: The New Tyranny?*, London: Zed Books, 102-121.

Cornwall, A. (2002) *Making Spaces, Changing Places: Situating Participation in Development*, Working Paper n.170, Brighton: Institute of Development Studies-Brighton University.

Cornwall, A. and Jewkes, R. (1995) 'What is Participatory Research?', *Social Science and Medicine*, 41(12): 1667-1676.

Esteva, G. (1992) 'Development', in W. Sachs (ed) *The Development Dictionary: A Guide to Knowledge as Power*, London: Zed Books, 6-25.

Fawcett, S.B. (1991) 'Some Values Guiding Community Research and Action', *Journal of Applied Behavior Analysis*, 24(4): 621-636.

Francescato, D. and Tomai, M. (2002) 'I Profili di Comunità Nell'era Della Globalizzazione'. In M. Prezza and M. Santinello (eds) *Conoscere la Comunità*, Bologna: Il Mulino, 39-66.

Francescato, D., Gelli, B., Mannarini, T. and Taurino, A. (2004) 'Community Development: Action-Research Through Community Profiles'. In A. Sánchez-Vidal, A. Zambrano and M. Palacín (eds) *European Community Psychology: Community, Power, Ethics and Values*, Barcelona: Publicacions Universitat de Barcelona, 247-261.

Francescato, D., Arcidiacono, C., Albanesi, C. and Mannarini, T. (2007) 'Community Psychology in Italy', in S. Reich, M. Riemer, I. Prilleltensky and M. Montero (eds) *International Community Psychology: History and Theories*, New York: Springer, 263-281.

Harvey, J.B. (1988) *The Abilene Paradox*, Lexington: Lexington Books.

Hirschman, O. (1970) *Exit, Voice, and Loyalty: Responses to Decline in Firms, Organizations, and States*, Cambridge, MA: Harvard University Press.

Irvin, R.A. and Stansbury, J. (2004) 'Citizen Participation in Decision Making: Is it Worth the Effort?', *Public Administration Review*, 64(1): 55-65.

Jewkes, R. and Murcott, A. (1998) 'Community Representatives: Representing the "Community"?', *Social Science and Medicine*, 46(7): 843-858.

Jost, T.J., Banaji, R.M. and Nosek, B.A, (2004) 'A Decade of System Justification Theory: Accumulated Evidence of Conscious and Unconscious Bolstering of the Status Quo', *Political Psychology*, 25(6): 881-919.

Kagan, C. (2006) *Making a Difference: Participation and Wellbeing*, Liverpool: RENEW Intelligence Report.

Kagan, C. (2007) 'Pillars of Support for Wellbeing in the Community: The Role of the Public Sector', Paper presented at the Wellbeing and Sustainable Living Seminar, Manchester, May 17.

Kagan, C., Castile, S. and Stewart, A. (2005) 'Participation: Are Some More Equal than Others?', *Clinical Psychology Forum*, 153: 30-34.

Keyes, C.L.M. (1998) 'Social Well-being', *Social Psychological Quarterly*, 61(2): 121-140.

Kothari, U. (2001) 'Power, Knowledge and Social Control in Participatory Development', in B. Cooke and U. Kothari (eds) *Participation: The New Tyranny?*, London: Zed Books, 210-231.

Ledwith, M. and Springett, J. (2010) *Participatory Practice*, Bristol: Policy Press.

Mannarini, T. (2009) *Cittadinanza Attiva: Psicologia Sociale della Partecipazione Pubblica*, Bologna: Il Mulino.

Montero, M. (2004) *Introducción a la Psicología Comunitaria*, Buenos Aires: Paidos.

Montero, M. (2006) 'New Horizons for Knowledge: The Influence of Citizen Participation'. In L.A. Jason, C.B. Keys, Y. Suarez-Balcazar, R.R. Taylor and M.I. Davis (eds) *Participatory Community Research*, Washington DC: APA, 251-262.

Mosse, D. (2001) 'People's Knowledge, Participation and Patronage: Operations and Representations in Rural Development'. In B. Cooke and U. Kothari (eds) *Participation: The New Tyranny?*, London: Zed Books, 16-35.

Prilleltensky, I. (2003) 'Understanding and Overcoming Oppression: Towards Psychopolitical Validity', *American Journal of Community Psychology*, 31 (1–2): 195–202.

Prilleltensky, I. (2008) 'The Role of Power in Wellness, Oppression, and Liberation: The Promise of Psychopolitical Validity', *Journal of Community Psychology*, 36(2): 116–136.

Quaghebeur, K., Masschelein, J. and Nguyen, H.H. (2004) 'Paradox of Participation: Giving or Taking Part?', *Journal of Community and Applied Social Psychology*, 14(3): 154–165.

Regonini, G. (2005) 'Paradossi della Democrazia Deliberativa', *Stato e Mercato*, 1(1): 3–31.

Reykowski, J. (2006) 'Deliberative Democracy and 'Human Nature'? An Empirical Approach', *Political Psychology*, 27(3): 323–346.

Sandler, J. (2007) 'Community-based Practices: Integrating Dissemination Theory with Critical Theories of Power and Justice', *American Journal of Community Psychology*, 40(3): 272–289.

Stokes, S. (1998) 'Pathologies of Deliberation', in J. Elster (ed), *Deliberative Democracy*, Cambridge, MA: Cambridge University Press, 123–139.

Stoner, J. (1968) 'Risky and Cautious Shift in Group Decisions: The Influence of Widely Held Values', *Journal of Experimental Social Psychology*, 4(4): 442–59.

Sunstein, C. (2000) 'Deliberative Trouble? Why Groups go to Extremes', *The Yale Law Journal*, 110(1): 71–119.

Sunstein, C. (2002) 'The Law of Group Polarization', *The Journal of Political Philosophy*, 10(2): 175–195.

Tommasoli, M. (2001) *Lo Sviluppo Partecipativo*, Roma: Carocci.

Tuckman, B. (1965) 'Developmental Sequence in Small Groups', *Psychological Bulletin*, 63: 384–399.

Ulbert, C. and Risse, T. (2005) 'Deliberately Changing the Discourse: What Does Make Arguing Effective?', *Acta Politica*, 40(3): 351–367.

Van Stokkom, B. (2005) 'Deliberative Groups Dynamics: Power, Status and Affect in Interactive Policy Making', *Policy and Politics*, 33(3): 387–409.

Wandersman, A. and Florin, P. (2000) 'Citizen Participation and Community Organizations', in J. Rappaport and E. Seidman (eds) *Handbook of Community Psychology*, New York: Kluwer Academic/Plenum Press, 247–272.

Ten

The pedagogy of community research: moving out of the ivory tower and into community organisations in Canada

Karen Schwartz, Adje van de Sande and Ann-Marie O'Brien

Chapter aims

- To describe a model of teaching/preparing students to engage in community research
- To focus on the collaborative elements of the project
- To examine power issues associated with communities setting the research agenda
- To discuss the relationships that emerge between student researchers and community organisations as they collaborate on research

Introduction

Universities are increasingly engaged in community research (CR) as a means of attracting and retaining students (Gallini and Moely, 2003). The approach to preparing researchers discussed in this chapter has benefits for the university, students and community organisations. Students receive relevant training and experience when engaged in the community and engagement is seen as an indicator of academic success (Billig, 2009). In an era of downsizing and budget restrictions there is increased emphasis on fiscal accountability. Funders are demanding evidence of effectiveness as a prerequisite for continued resources. Community organisations can benefit from students' expertise in evaluating their programmes and defining effectiveness in order to meet their funders' demands. In this context universities and students can make a significant contribution to services provided to service users, but they must acquire the necessary skills to form collaborations that embrace the research agendas of the community.

This chapter considers a number of key questions: how do you prepare students to collaborate with community organisations in research projects? How do the various research partners (faculty, students, community organisations, service providers, service users) experience this collaboration? What are the power issues that students face when engaging in research when the community sets the research agenda? We will address these questions based on several years of experience teaching about community research to social work graduate students while they engage in research with social service community partners in the Ottawa region in Canada.[1] We will use examples of projects where the collaboration was equitable and successful as well as where it has been more problematic.

There are challenges inherent in universities and communities engaging in community research (Ahmed et al, 2004; Savan, 2004; Seifer and Calleson, 2004). CR seeks to democratise knowledge by validating multiple sources of knowledge, promoting the use of multiple methods of discovery and dissemination with the goal of social action (Strand et al, 2003).[2] It has been suggested that the more collaborative the research process is the more effective it can be, both as scholarship and as a service to society (Arches, 2007; Stanton, 2008). Flicker (2008) found that the benefits of CR include the improved quality of research and sense of accomplishment of the various research partners.[3]

CR does, however, pose some important challenges in terms of control, ownership of the data and the power relations between the university and community organisations. The literature on research between universities and communities identifies such issues as the systemic barriers in the academy (Ahmed et al, 2004), conforming to university time lines (Hyde and Meyer, 2004), monitoring whether the research is truly community initiated and driven (Flicker et al, 2007; Minkler, 2004, 2005), and negotiating ownership and dissemination of the research results (Seifer and Calleson, 2004). Students experience tension with respect to their perceived lack of power in their relationships with the university and community organisations (Schwartz, 2010). This chapter will examine these issues of control, ownership and the power relations related to CR.

Theoretical context

Our theory is related to participation and power. Tew examines power as a social relation between people, one that 'may potentially open up or close off opportunities for individuals' (Tew, 2005: 71). In analysing how power operates he asks two questions which intersect. First is the question 'Does power limit opportunities or produce new opportunities?' Second, 'Does power operate over an individual, for example, in the case of systemic oppression and exploitation, or together with an individual, for example, when groups organise in solidarity to resist oppressive powers?'This matrix was adapted from Tew's model (2005) to reflect the power relations that can occur in community research when utilising our approach; each cell in the power matrix defines a specific mode of power relations (see Figure 10.1). Oppressive power can be enacted in various ways in research, for example, research that fails to acknowledge cultural diversity in formulating research questions and methodology. Research citizens are reduced to research 'subjects' rather than 'participants'. In the Canadian context, research conducted in aboriginal communities often failed to engage the community in identifying the problems to be explored or methods of inquiry (Smith, 1999; Sinclair, 2004). This research could be experienced as exploitive and would provide little useful information that is relevant to the community being studied.

Figure 10.1 Power relations matrix in community research

	Power Over	Power Together
Productive Modes of Power	Protective Power Guiding the involvement of research partners to safeguard them in areas where they are vulnerable but still enable them to be part of some aspects of the research process.	Co-operative Power In research terms this means employing principals of community research, involving community members in all stages of the research.
Limiting Modes of Power	Oppressive Power Limiting access to research results and excluding some community groups from participating in the research process.	Collusive Power In terms of research, this means banding together to exclude certain groups from the research process or to suppress part of the research process.

Source: Adapted from Tew (2005)

Protective power involves safeguarding vulnerable people and their possibilities of advancement. Forming an advisory committee of service users and involving them in programme evaluation is an example of protective power when the advisory committee acts as consultants rather than becoming involved in all steps of the research. In this way, the service users are empowered by having their experiences valued.

Cooperative power involves building social movements that gain strength from dialogues around points of commonality and difference. An example from research involves blurring identities of 'service user/ traditional research respondent' and 'university student/researcher' in order to work together. Cooperative power involves sharing knowledge and information so that service users can actively participate in all aspects of the research process.

Service users may learn new skills such as interviewing, data entry and presentation skills.

Community research in practice

In this section we consider approaches to teaching students how to engage in community research. We believe that the most effective way to teach students community research is to have students and faculty leave the 'ivory tower' and connect directly with the community. For the past several years our research course at Carleton University School of Social Work in Ottawa, Canada has been structured so that students in small groups engage in research with community agencies.

Following is a brief description of how we organise this course. Each July, we send out a letter to community organisations inviting them to submit a request for research. The majority of these requests involves programme evaluation, assessing best practices, assessing community capacity and needs assessments. Community organisations are interested in other research questions, for example: 'What are the costs and impacts of social enterprises?', 'What are the structural barriers facing mentally ill offenders?'

Over the summer, we review these requests and select a shortlist of projects based on appropriateness in terms of learning opportunities, academic timelines and giving preference to organisations with few resources to meet their research needs. In September, students are organised into research teams. They are allowed to identify three choices of the projects on which they would like to work. The student teams begin by getting background information to take to the initial meeting. At that time the teams expand to include the community members who wrote the original proposal and others that are seen as necessary to carry out the research. Each research team chooses a spokesperson who will contact the organisation and set up an initial meeting. This meeting is attended by the instructor, students, organisational representatives and individual service users and/or an advisory committee of service users or community members (when possible). The purpose of this initial meeting is to discuss the research request in more detail and develop a contract, which spells out the level of collaboration, details of the project, including the research question, the research design, the data gathering process and the dissemination of the results. We encourage as much collaboration as the organisation and advisory committee is willing to engage in. They drive the decision making.

The team then develops a detailed research proposal[4] for the approval of the community organisation and the instructors. The proposals are presented in class for discussion and feedback. At times members of the organisation and/or advisory committee attend these presentations. The teams also develop an ethics review proposal for approval by the Research Ethics Board of the University.[5]

Once the proposal has been cleared by the Research Ethics Board and has been accepted by the organisation, the student teams start gathering and analysing data. In January a further meeting is held with the instructor, student team, organisational representative and advisory committee to check if any aspects of the initial contract need to be renegotiated and to discuss how the data collection is progressing. Depending on the initial contract with the community organisation the student portion of the teams may be collecting and analysing the data on their own, or in collaboration with other members of the broader team. Once the data has been collected and analysed, all of the above partners can be involved in writing the final report which is presented in class for discussion and feedback. The project concludes with the team presenting their final report to the broader organisation.

In addition to conducting the research, students are required to attend weekly classes. Lectures are presented in the first hour and a half of the research class, and supervision and consultation is provided in the second half. Data analysis is part of the curriculum and we encourage the participation by advisory committee members. A number of advisory committees have attended the classes on SPSS and data analysis so that they can participate in the analysis with the students. This training is provided in an attempt to equalise power by balancing knowledge related to data analysis.

An important part of the learning is the reflective exercises. On two occasions, once in the Fall/Autumn and again in the Winter semester, each student writes a reflective paper in which they explore their biases about research, their feelings about dealing with the power issues, and their struggle in trying to meet the needs of the organisations while respecting ethical guidelines. These reflective exercises are often the first occasion for most students to engage in some introspection and many report that they found them quite challenging.

Description of one research collaboration

This section reflects on a recent project carried out by some of our students. This research project explored the sexual and reproductive health information needs of Muslim youth in collaboration with Planned Parenthood of Ottawa (PPO), an established community organisation. Since this was a new area of interest for PPO an advisory committee was formed of youth and adult members of the Muslim community. The students, advisory committee and PPO collaborated on the design of the interview schedule and recruitment of youth participants. As negotiated with the research team, the students conducted the interviews, analysed the data and composed the report with input from the youth members of the advisory committee and PPO. The results of the research were posted on their website and distributed to members of the advisory committee who distributed it within their networks. In addition PPO incorporated the results of the research into a funding proposal and was able to obtain one time funding from the United Way to run a group for Muslim females that would address the needs identified in the interviews. The following year a new group of students worked with PPO to evaluate the programme they had designed in the hopes of gaining sustainable funding.

Reflections on the community research approach adopted

The learning from our experiences of offering the course is now discussed in the following section. We have learned that community organisations come with different degrees of willingness and capacity to conduct research. We receive a broad range of requests which call for varying degrees of participation on the part of service users. We constantly strive for the maximum possible service user involvement.

We have also learned that the identification of research partners and participants is particularly important when researchers are exploring sensitive topics (Renzetti and Lee, 1993) or when the research in question has the potential to have an impact on a particular population with a history of oppression (Sin, 2007). Rather than treating service users as an afterthought the interests of the service users should be paramount. Therefore, while it is important to identify all research partners and their respective agendas, we place the service users and their interests ahead of all others. In this way we can build allies in fighting oppressive forces. Some of the organisations that we work with are not always comfortable with involving service users in the research. We attempt to work with them to demonstrate the benefits in this approach. One of the limitations of the course is that we work within university deadlines and the students need to complete their work in time to get a grade and credit for the course. If the organisation is unwilling to put the service users in the foreground we reach a compromise so that the students can complete their coursework.

Our research projects have involved a high level of collaboration with a range of participants including labour unions, feminist and anti-racist organisations, anti-poverty groups and mental health organisations. One example of this collaboration is the evaluation we conducted of the Banking Accessibility Project (BAPP). BAPP was launched by the Canadian Mental Health Association (CMHA) in partnership with a local bank. The objectives of the project were to identify and remove barriers that people with serious mental illness encounter when accessing banking services. A primary goal of BAPP was to have participants feel financially independent and confident in the ability to manage money and access banking services.

Four clients of the CMHA were engaged in this participatory research evaluation, along with two MSW students and a project evaluator. All members of the research team were responsible for the evaluation design, data collection, data analysis and reporting of results. The evaluation found that the benefits of this project included banking staff feeling more knowledgeable and positive about providing services to previously excluded customers, for example, to people living with serious mental illness. For their part, the clients experienced a sense empowerment on being able to manage their own finances and access mainstream banking.[6]

Participation from the students' perspective

This section draws on findings that emerged during focus groups with students that we conduct at the end of each academic year. Findings suggest that students conducting community-based research may feel vulnerable about expressing their opinions or disagreeing with the community organisation representative because their focus is on achieving high grades and publishing the research results. They are concerned about their reputation in the community, and often hope to be employed by the community agency with which they are collaborating. This combination can result in an organisation treating decision making in a top-down manner ('power over' according to the adapted model by Tew, 2005) by the organisation and/or a perceived lack of power on the part of the students in any negotiations between students and the community agency. Seifer (2006) discusses the need to balance power among partners, as well as build community and campus capacity to engage each other as partners.

Balancing the student's perceived power and community perceived power, needs to be part of this equation. One project exemplifies the importance of acknowledging this power differential. The students were asked to conduct a survey of employees in a large city organisation after there had been a labour dispute that resulted in a strike. The management of the organisation did not want the results of the survey distributed to the union. They wanted to decide on a strategy to address the concerns that employees raised without input from the union, an obvious employment of 'power over'. The students did not feel comfortable with this use of power as they had promised their research participants that they would be able to share the results of the survey. The students also knew that for the employees to have any power to make the changes as a result of the survey the labour union needed to have access to the results. Notwithstanding the objections of management, the students shared the survey results with the union. The study was helpful in informing the discussion in the labour negotiations, however, we have subsequently never received another research request from that organisation.

At times the students want to have much more control over the research process. Organisations who want to take a very active participatory role in the analyses and discussion of research results have been perceived by the students as either lacking trust in their capabilities or as potentially jeopardising the results. The fear was that objectivity would be jeopardised by focusing on favourable results. At other times, the students had concerns about the agency's understanding of the university's ethical procedures that they were expected to follow.

Dealing with these power and ethical challenges can have positive outcomes. Strand (2000) believes that her students learned more about designing ethical research procedures by dealing with these challenges than they could ever learn in a textbook. However, one possible consequence is that the students feel the need to exert more control over the research process. One of our research groups was concerned about the ethics of the perceived gate-keeping role the agency played in recruiting participants for the research project and questioned whether the participation was truly voluntary. This is reflective of the tension between the organisation's need to protect the privacy of their service users and the students desire to ensure that the research participants did not experience coercive power because they felt that their future services would be jeopardised since the organisation knew they might be participating in the research.

Participation from the community perspective

Community organisations have traditionally seen the university as controlling the research process. Historically, university faculty would design, fund and execute their research agendas with little input from the community. The results would be analysed and often not reported to the community at all, or if a report was given to community members or research participants it was not written in language that was easily accessible (van de Sande and Schwartz, 2011).

For a number of years we conducted phone surveys to get feedback from our partner organisations about how they utilised the research data and how the collaboration could be improved. It was reported that the research produced was useful to the organisation and several stated that they would integrate the results into funding applications. Others responded that they planned to use the findings to create new programmes or develop training for staff and volunteers. Some organisations incorporated the data into conference presentations and programme improvements.

One community partner stated that, 'Without the participation of the School of Social Work, I think we never would have come this far in the programme development for this award winning project,' (Schwartz, 2010).

Some of our community partners found that time constraints limited their availability to engage with students, contribute to the research project and resolve collaboration dynamics. Another challenge is being unfamiliar with the culture of research and not appreciating the ethical dilemmas that the students perceive. The benefits of engaging in CR from the perspective of our community partners are (1) being able to evaluate and reflect on practice (2) to demonstrate effectiveness of interventions, (3) to move the research forward, (4) to build research knowledge and expertise (5) to support/coach others to enable them to feel more confident in their research skills and (6) to have fun.

Key learning

The course offers a number of key learning opportunities and challenges for students and community organisations alike. Students identified the benefits of this research programme as providing important practical skills which improve their chances for future employment and further their academic careers, for example, the ability to carry out a research project from start to finish. Some of the challenges from the students' perspective included the heavy workload, having to share power with community organisations and trying to meet university ethical guidelines which do not always match the priorities of community organisations.

Feedback from the community indicates that they view this programme as providing an important service that allows them to enhance the level of accountability required by their funders, and that it improved the service to their service users. Many organisations do not have the capacity to carry out the research themselves or the funds to hire research consultants. The main challenge from the perspective of community organisations is getting the results they need from the research to meet their programme planning objectives or which satisfies their funders.

One of the tensions in having the community drive the research agenda is that community partners are typically interested in research to address practical problems such as service improvement, while university-based researchers are typically interested in knowledge production (Wallerstein and Duran, 2006). On a few occasions, there was tension between the student researchers and the organisation when the organisation requested a programme evaluation but wanted confirmation of existing practices. Some organisations explicitly stated that they only wanted positive results. This request from the organisation was viewed as a coercive use of power. Students were empowered to state that they could not guarantee that their findings would be positive. In a few other cases, community organisations requested a high degree of control over the research design, ownership of the raw data and the dissemination of the results. These challenges were dealt with most effectively when there was open and honest communication throughout the research process with the instructors occasionally intervening to mediate the discussions.

The tensions between some community organisations and the students seemed to be more present in community organisations who requested programme evaluation rather than those who requested needs assessment. The former had more of a need to confirm the effectiveness of the agency's current policies and practices and less interest in change. There were the fewest tensions where the original understanding was that a true community research process would take place, for example, the project with PPO and the BAPP project that we discussed earlier. In order to sustain these community–university partnerships these issues need to be better addressed in the initial meeting between the team, organisation and instructor, as well in the course content.

Summary

Challenges in creating a successful project

- At times it is difficult to find community members willing to be part of an advisory committee or some organisational representatives may be anxious about including an advisory committee.
- Frequent communication is time consuming when people are very busy.
- It is not always possible to resolve power imbalances and at times the research cannot be completed because of this.

Elements of a successful project

- Inclusion of advisory committee of community members and/or service users.
- Frequent communication and collaboration at every stage of the process.
- Cohesiveness and trust among members of the research team.
- Frank discussion of ownership of research results, how they will be used, by whom and when. Ensure that all participants' names appear on conference presentations. Discuss publication of the report on the organisation's website and whether they will be allowed to use the results at a later date.
- Confront unintentional/ intentional instances of oppressive and collusive power. Deal with misunderstandings right away.
- Invite advisory committee members to the class to learn with students.

Conclusion

In this chapter, we have explored how to prepare students to collaborate with community organisations in research projects, how the various research partners experience this collaboration, and the power issues that students face in engaging in research when the community sets the agenda. In spite of the challenges of the heavy workload, of working within the constraints imposed by the university schedule, meeting ethical requirements and dealing with organisations coming with a broad range of needs, we found that the benefits of teaching and engaging in community research far outweighs the challenges. The students are learning valuable research skills which further their professional and academic careers. The reflective exercises help students to examine their biases about research and explore their feelings about the power issues that invariably arise. Asking students to present their work to the class provides everyone in the class with excellent opportunities to learn from each other. From the perspective of community organisations, the course provides an important service. The research has helped many organisations to demonstrate the effectiveness of their programmes, identify unmet needs and satisfy the expectations of funders all for little or no cost. The course also meets our university's strategic priority of promoting community engagement. We feel that we are making an important contribution to the community, social work clients and our students by teaching research in way that is more enjoyable than the standard lecture. Finally, from our perspective as instructors, the course has truly been an enjoyable and rewarding experience.

Discussion questions

1. What do you see as the potential advantages and limitations of teaching students about community research in this manner? What are the benefits and limitations of students being involved in community research as part of a research course?
2. What do you think might make you uncomfortable with sharing power with respect to important research decisions?
3. In reflecting on the Power Relations Matrix have your experiences with community research been characterised by productive mode of power or limiting ones; power over or power together ?

Notes
[1] Two of the authors are academics and one is a service provider and adjunct professor with whom we have collaborated and extensively discussed the process of collaboration.

[2] These authors use the term 'community engaged research' not 'community research' but we believe that the goals of CR are the same.

[3] This author used the term 'community based participatory research'.

[4] This is done in collaboration with the organisation and advisory committee based on the level of collaboration specified at the first meeting.

[5] REB in Canada, Institutional Review Board- IRB in the United States

[6] From the research report of Hadas Elkayam, Lindsay Snow, Bessa Whitmore and CMHA, 2008.

References

Ahmed, S., Beck, B., Murana, C. and Newton, G. (2004) 'Overcoming Barriers to Effective Community Based Participatory Research in U. S. Medical Schools', *Education for Health*, 17(2): 141-151.

Arches, J. (2007) 'Youth Take Charge: Social Action in a Community-University Partnership' in Hofman, N. and Rosing, H. (ed), *Pedagogies of Praxis: Course-based Research in the Social Sciences.* Boston, Anker Publishing Company, Inc., 59-77.

Billig, S. (2009) 'Does Quality Really Matter?', in Moely, B., Bilig, S. and Holland, B. (eds), *Creating our Identities in Service-Learning and Community Engagement.* Charlotte, North Carolina, IAP-Information Age Publishing, 131-158.

Elkayam, H., Snow, L., Whitmore, B. (2008) *Creating Change by Saving Change: A Participatory Evaluation of the Banking Accessibility Pilot Project*, report to Canadian Mental Health Association.

Flicker, S. (2008) 'Who Benefits from Community-Based Participatory Research? A Case Study of the Positive Youth Project', *Health Education and Behavior*, 35(1): 70-86.

Flicker, S., Savan, B., Mc Grath, M., Kolenda, B., Mildenberger, M. (2007) 'If You Could Change One Thing… What Community-Based Researchers Wish They Could Have Done Differently', *Community Development Journal*, 43(2): 239-253.

Gallini, S., and Moely, B. (2003) 'Service-Learning and Engagement, Academic Challenge, and Retention', *Michigan Journal of Community Service Learning*, 10(1): 5–14.

Hyde, C.A., and Meyer, M. (2004) A Collaborative Approach to Service, Learning, and Scholarship :A Community-Based Research Course, *Journal of Community Practice*, 12(1/2), 71-88.

Lundy, C. (2004) *Social Work and Social Justice*, Peterborough, ON, Broadview Press.

Minkler, M. (2004) 'Ethical Challenges for the Outside Researcher in Community-Based Participatory Research', *Health Education and Behavior*, 31(6): 684–697.

Minkler, M. (2005) 'Community-Based Research Partnerships: Challenges and Opportunities', *Journal of Urban Health*, 82(2): ii3–ii12.

Moreau, M. (1979) 'A Structural Approach to Social Work Practice', *Canadian Journal of Social Work Education*, 5(1).

Mullaly, B. (2007) *The New Structural Social Work*, 3rd edn, Toronto, Oxford University Press.

Mulroy, E. (2004) 'University Civic Engagement with Community-Based Organizations: Dispersed or Coordinated Model', in Soska, T. and Butterfield, A. (eds) *University-Community Partnerships: Universities in Civic Engagement*, The Haworth Social Work Practice Press, Haworth Press, Inc., 35–72.

Renzetti, C. and Lee, R. (eds) (1993) *Researching Sensitive Topics*. London: Sage Publications.

Savan, B. (2004) 'Community–University Partnerships: Linking Research and Action for Sustainable Community Development', *Community Development Journal*, 39(4): 372–384.

Schwartz, K. (2010) 'Community Engaged Research: Student and Community Perspectives', *Partnerships: A Journal of Service Learning and Civic Engagement*, 1: 1–16.

Seifer, S. (2006) 'Building and Sustaining Community-Institutional Partnerships for Prevention Research: Findings from a National Collaborative', *Journal of Urban Health-Bulletin of the New York Academy of Medicine*, 83(6): 989–1003.

Seifer, S. and Calleson, D. (2004) Health Professional Faculty Perspectives on Community-Based Research: Implications for Policy and Practice', *Journal of Interprofessional Care*, 18(4): 416–427.

Sin, R. (2007) 'Community Action Research: Lessons from the Chinese Communities in Montreal', in Baines, D. (ed), *Doing Anti-Oppressive Practice: Building Transformative Politicized Social Work*, Halifax, Nova Scotia: Fernwood Publishing.

Sinclair, R. (2004) 'Aboriginal Social Work Education: Decolonizing Pedagogy for the Seventh Generation'. *First Nations Child and Family Review*, 1(1).

Smith, L. (1999) *Decolonizing Methodologies: Research and Indigenous Peoples*. London: Zed Books, Ltd.

Stanton, T. (2008) 'New Times Demand New Scholarship: Opportunities and Challenges for Civic Engagement', *Education, Citizenship and Social Justice*, 3: 19–42.

Strand, K. (2000) Community-Based Research as Pedagogy, *Michigan Journal of Community Service Learning*, 1: 85–96.

Strand, K., Marullo, S., Cutforth, N., Stoecker, R. and Donohue, P. (2003) 'Principles of Best Practice for Community-Based Research', *Michigan Journal of Community Service Learn*, 9(3): 5-15.

Tew, J. (2005) *Social Perspectives in Mental Health: Developing Social Models to Understand and Work with Mental Distress*, London: Jessica Kingsley Publishers.

van de Sande, A. and Schwartz, K. (2011) *Research for Social Justice: A Community-Based Approach*, Halifax, Nova Scotia: Fernwood Publishing.

Wallerstein, N. and Duran, B. (2006) 'Using Community-Based Participatory Research to Address Health Disparities', *Health Promotion Practice*, 7: 312-323, http://hpp.sagepub.com/cgi/content/abstract/7/3/312.

Eleven

Engaging community researchers in evaluation: looking at the experiences of community partners in school-based projects in the US

Jenifer Cartland, Holly S. Ruch-Ross and Maryann Mason

Chapter aims

- To explore key means of engaging community partners in evaluation
- To understand barriers to participation in evaluation and community research
- To identify ways to promote participation that is seen as optimal from the perspective of community partners

Introduction

The field of community-based participatory research (CBPR) is relatively new but fast developing (Israel et al, 2005). Evaluation research, broadly defined as an investigation intended to assess the impact of an intervention, is an older field of endeavour which continues to evolve, particularly in areas related to community engagement and participation (Weiss, 1998). Although CPBR and participatory evaluation have clear differences, CBPR borrows many elements from participatory evaluation in its approach to community partnerships. This chapter examines 20 participatory evaluation projects undertaken over a three-year period to explore themes that can inform CBPR.

We report qualitative data from a three-year project examining evaluators' engagement of their lead community partner in the process of evaluating a complex set of community-based interventions. The evaluators, who were responsible for bringing research methods and protocols to the question of the impact of the interventions on their target population, were not typically members of the community that was the subject of the evaluation (a number were academic researchers, others were independent evaluation contractors).

The lead community partners were typically highly experienced leaders in their communities (such as a former school superintendent or senior mental health services planner). Twenty evaluators and their lead community partners were interviewed at three points in time. The interviews focused on the goals, successes and failures of the evaluation.

In an earlier piece of work, we explored what optimal evaluation is from the perspective of the 20 evaluators studied and found that each of the evaluators fell into one of three groups (Cartland et al, 2008). 'Academically-oriented' evaluators held the view that optimal evaluations assured that decisions made by community partners were evidence-based. 'Programme-oriented' evaluators contended that optimal evaluations would provide constant feedback to the programme implementation or community change process so that new programmes would function as well as possible. 'Client-oriented' evaluators believed good evaluation builds capacity in community organisations to serve clients well. It is clear from our small sample that there is little consensus on what an 'optimal' evaluation achieves from the perspective of evaluators.

The current chapter examines the lead community partners' side of these expectations. As the 'clients' of the evaluator, and as representatives of the community, the lead community partners determine whether the evaluation meets the needs of the community. They may identify problems with the evaluation product that the evaluator may not see. It is likely that the lead community partners and the evaluators themselves will have different views about what an 'optimal' evaluation is.

Theoretical discussion

What constitutes 'good' evaluation research in a community-based setting? We are told that good evaluators engage community partners, or stakeholders, in defining the research questions and in deciding the overall goals for the evaluation project (for example, American Evaluation Association, *Guiding Principles for Evaluation*). But does such an approach lead to an improved evaluation of the intervention under study, with 'products' that better serve community needs?

To understand what community partners expect from evaluation research, and how well evaluations meet these expectations, we begin by exploring the literature that focuses on what happens during the participatory evaluation process. Our study seeks to understand what pieces of the process play a role in the perception among community partners that the evaluation portion of their project was worth their effort.

While it is rarely explored empirically, evaluation theory presupposes that evaluation takes place in a social context that is dominated by complex social dynamics, perhaps made more complex by the very presence of the evaluation researcher (Weiss, 1998; Chouinard and Cousins, 2009). Communities are never simple, but one could argue that the most complex side of the community is revealed when change is contemplated, implemented or reflected upon (for example, King, 2008) – which are all evaluative moments, whether or not they involve a specific research presence. Evaluators choose how to engage the social context they confront in the community with whom they are working, either as an observer who measures or manages the impact of the social context on the study or as a facilitator of an improved social context (Abma and Widdershoven, 2008).

By employing participatory and collaborative methods, evaluation can do for the community what Stern calls for it to do for academic and policy circles: it can open a space in the community within which many practitioners, policy-makers, clients and other stakeholders can generate new knowledge for the community, and perhaps for other communities as well (Stern, 2008). When the evaluator engages in a participatory process, he or she brings to the community a set of skills and resources. Community stakeholders bring knowledge of the community, their own personal and professional skills, and other forms of local knowledge. The evaluator works with the stakeholders to 'co-construct' new knowledge through an evaluative or research process (Symonette, 2004), and to do so he or she must create a learning space in which it is safe for collaborators to speak frankly and radically about their community programmes and institutions.

There is growing acceptance that effective evaluators adopt three principals in order to engage stakeholders fully in the evaluation process (House, 2005). The first principle is inclusion, which requires the evaluation researcher to work to expand the voice of less powerful stakeholders (for example, children or the poor). The second principle is dialogue, by which is meant that the researcher facilitates dialogue among stakeholders in reference to the evaluation. The third principle is deliberation, which asks the evaluator to facilitate the building of consensus around the evaluation process and product.

One of the challenges of putting the principles of inclusion, dialogue and deliberation into practice is that not every community and not every group in each community is prepared to participate in evaluation research. It is not enough to create a space for deliberation and invite stakeholders to the table, evaluators most go further and prepare both the stakeholders and the 'space' for collaboration. For instance, evaluators are encouraged to train participants for participation in evaluation, especially if they represent less powerful stakeholders. They should accommodate the unique preparation needs of less powerful stakeholders (Plottu and Plottu, 2009). In preparing the space, evaluators must assure that the dialogue among groups can be and is inclusive, respectful and productive. One of the challenges facing evaluators is whether they have the capacity to engage community partners in this manner and whether they believe that it is an appropriate role to take on (Cartland et al, 2008).

Beyond case studies, little empirical work has explored specific strengths and weaknesses in participatory processes for evaluation research (Diagneault and Jacob, 2009) – the extent that participatory practices are employed, what they look like in community settings and how well they work. This chapter examines 20 evaluations taking place in 20 communities based on interviews with the lead community partner at three points in the projects to explore a range of issues inherent in the participatory evaluation process. It considers the extent to which the studies serve the communities for whom they are working.

Community research in practice

About our study

Over a three-syear period, 20 pairs of evaluation researchers and their lead community partners from local Safe Schools/Health Students (SSHS) sites were followed.

SSHS grants have a unique structure and function that shapes how the evaluator interacts with the community. SSHS grants are funded by the United States Department of Education and awarded competitively to school districts who demonstrate specific capabilities and characteristics. These include the willingness and capacity to improve school-based services for youth, to collaborate with community partners to improve the integration of and access to mental health services, to conduct primary and secondary prevention of peer violence and substance use, and to promote healthy, positive youth development (Furlong et al, 2003).

The funding level of SSHS grants is substantial, with school districts receiving between $1,000,000 and $3,000,000 per year for three years. Between 20 and 40 school districts are chosen for new funding each year. Each school district is required to hire a researcher to evaluate its activities, spending not less than 7 per cent of the overall budget on evaluation.

While all SSHS sites have the freedom to organise their internal relationships in a way that best meets their needs, most sites employ the organisational structure described in Figure 11.1. The lead community partner is the SSHS project director; he or she oversees the entire SSHS project for the school district and any other community agencies involved and is the main contact between all of the other community partners and the evaluator. The lead community partner is the prime contact person representing the community to the evaluator. The evaluator often develops relationships with other community leaders, but these relationships are usually mediated by the lead community partner. Because the evaluator is directly accountable to the lead community partner, this individual is generally in the most equal power relationship with him or her and therefore may be best able to balance the power of the evaluator's research expertise and position.

Figure 11.1 Typical organisational structure for SSHS projects

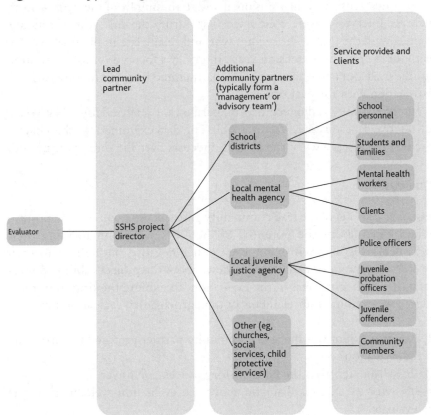

An evaluation plan must be submitted as part of any SSHS funding proposal as this is a part of the application criteria. The degree to which community partners have a say in the evaluation plan varies by site. All sites involve the lead community partner in choosing research questions and in identifying how the evaluation research will be carried out. Because of the time constraints of the application process, a full participatory process is not practical until after funding has been achieved. Many sites include a fuller range of community partners in revising the research questions and in finalising the evaluation plan after funding is achieved. The evaluator is responsible for reviewing and balancing the requests and recommendations made by community partners and then drafting the final evaluation plan. He or she is also responsible for assuring the scientific rigour of the evaluation, as well as its implementation. Our study began with a survey of the 20 evaluators and lead community partners to explore their notions of the role of evaluation in the SSHS projects during the first six months of funding. Our goal was to understand the complexity of the role-sharing process. We focused on the role of the lead community partner rather than other community partners because we hypothesised that this is where we would see the greatest tension and confusion, if any, stemming from the participatory process. Interviews were conducted first during the first year of funding, then toward the end of the second year, and finally late in the final year (or early in the no-cost extension year). Interviews focused on role definition for the evaluator and lead community partner, and lead community partner's satisfaction with the evaluation.

Interviews were audio recorded, transcribed and analysed using NVivo 7.0 qualitative data software (Victoria, AU). The data examined for this chapter include the interviews of the project directors over the three-year period.

Findings

Just over half (11) of the lead community partners were consistently positive when asked about the potential of their evaluations in meeting their intended goals. The remainder were either negative throughout in their overall assessments or had differing views about the project's ability to meet its goal at different stages of the evaluation. To explore the origins of these views, we examine four elements of the participatory evaluation process:

1. To what extent was the lead community partner prepared to participate in evaluation?
2. To what extent was the participatory process inclusive?
3. To what extent was dialogue about the evaluation welcomed by the evaluator?
4. To what extent did the evaluator foster deliberation about the evaluation?

Preparation

Because the evaluators were hired and evaluation plans were put into place before our data collection began, we are unable to speak in detail about the efforts evaluators made to prepare the lead community partner for making decisions about the evaluation. However, it is clear that, for most lead community partners, confidence in the evaluation was won or lost early in the project. Lead community partners who had been through large evaluations before or who had a previous working relationship with their evaluator generally felt more comfortable with the evaluator and the evaluation from the start. Little was new in the evaluation or the participatory process for them, and so they were prepared to participate in shaping the evaluation.

However, for lead community partners who did not have these experiences, the capacity of the evaluator to earn their confidence early was determined to some degree by the evaluator's willingness to be methodologically creative and flexible with the lead community partners, and other community partners, in the early stages of the project. Because the timeline was very tight to put a research plan together, the time for full participatory preparation was not available. Even so, from our data, it was clear that some evaluators entered the participatory arrangement with more ability to be flexible and creative than others, which optimised the little time the project had to put the plan together. The following quote is from a lead community partner whose evaluator could be quite creative and flexible about developing an evaluation plan that responded to the community needs:

"It's good to bounce off ideas with [the evaluation team] because usually I bounce off an idea and I'm not quite sure how to get there. They help me get there. They're like, 'Okay we could do X, Y, Z.' I'm like, 'Oh, that would be great.'" Some evaluators begin projects with specific strengths and interests, and with a narrow range of methodological experience or knowledge (for example, being qualitative researchers with little expertise in surveys or statistical analysis). These researchers struggled more than others with responding well to their community partners in the short timeframe they had to put the evaluation plan together. As this next example shows, the lead community partners in these cases discussed the need to find a compromise with the evaluator, rather than expressing that the evaluator was fully responding to their needs.

"[The evaluator] was looking more at analysing environmental data, like has the number of suspensions decreased? . . . And I was looking more at impact, have we impacted kids' lives? . . . And ultimately, as time passed, we sort of implemented some of both."

Our data indicate that evaluators regarded as effective benefited from having lead community partners who were prepared for the planning process by having participated in other evaluation projects. If the preparation time was not available, effective evaluators were methodologically flexible and creative, and were willing to change the shape of the evaluation plan to closely meet the expressed needs of their community partners.

Inclusion

A major supposition of participatory evaluation is allowing stakeholders, in this case the lead community partner, to be involved with the design of the evaluation. One of the major themes of the interviews with lead community partners is that those who were permitted to engage more fully had a higher level of confidence in the evaluation and the evaluator.

"I feel like I am a collaborative partner. [The evaluator] and I speak by email or telephone at least once or twice a week. He keeps me up to speed and I give my two cents. . . I trust him implicitly."

In contrast to this lead community partner's sense of inclusion in the evaluation process, other lead community partners felt less included and more distanced from the process of research plan development. Besides not benefiting from the insights of the community partners, evaluations that did not include the lead community partner in the planning process suffered another, more significant problem: when lead community partners reported not having much say in the course of the evaluation, they also reported that the evaluation product was less useful. Sometimes, the lead community partner had to go out of his or her way to intercede to make sure that the evaluation would fit what the project needed. For example, in the following quotes, we see two ways in which lead community partners described evaluators who did not include the lead community partner in the planning process.

> 'We had trouble with our evaluator . . . she kind of made up her mind which way she thinks is best, which design is best. But the project coordinator and myself really – because there's so much pain involved from the programme point of view, from the service point of view – we didn't want to just have her tell us what is the best design [sic].'

> 'I'm not sure if [the evaluation has] done what it's supposed to do because I'm not sure what it was supposed to do [in the first place].'

In the first example, the evaluator had a design in mind for the evaluation plan and refused to consider alternative ideas. In the second example, the evaluator appears not to have communicated the evaluation plan to the lead community partner at all.

Inclusion is a two-way street. Where evaluators were effective at including their lead community partners in the evaluation process, lead community partners included the evaluator in their own community planning process. Many evaluators ended up advising lead community partners on programme changes, helping the lead community partner think through stakeholder issues, and became 'sounding boards' for the lead community partner, as this quote indicates:

'Our local evaluator is somebody who's intimately involved in the programme and she is here all the time. We speak frequently. I think that she is very, very good about giving us ongoing feedback.'

When evaluators were not involved in the programme at this level, the lead community partner felt that they were missing an important resource that other SSHS sites had, as is exemplified by the following lead community partner statements:

'I heard what other [SSHS] evaluators are doing. They seem to be more hands–on, really knowing what is going on . . . They seem to be right there, close by, accessible, very visible. I don't have that.'

Our study is able to document that evaluators who include lead community partners in the process of designing the evaluation are more likely to be seen as effective. The long–term payoff for this is two–fold: the evaluation is more responsive to community needs and the evaluator becomes a trusted partner to the community representatives. The latter ensures that the evaluator is kept up to date on changes in the programme and ensures that the community is able to continually take advantage of the evaluator's expertise.

Dialogue

Early exchange of ideas about the evaluation plan ensures that the plan developed is clearly linked to the goals and objectives of the project. Some evaluators opened a dialogue about the evaluation plan and engaged the lead community partners, and perhaps other community partners, in the process of developing the plan, a process reflected, for example, in this statement by one lead community partner:

'We met with the lead evaluator . . . along with some other folks like someone from our Mental Health Department and the Safe and Drug Free school coordinator and the director of student services and just kind of went over the goal, what we wanted. I don't know – [it was] kind of a group effort. Then from there, you know, . . it's been a work in progress, I think. But we had a good base plan figured out by meeting face-to-face a few times.'

Sometimes, the open dialogue was not fully welcomed by the lead community partner, or perhaps the evaluator did not know how to move to a more deliberative stage. The following quote shows that for one lead community partner, the open-ended nature of the dialogue with the evaluator was not welcome.

> 'I would like them to be a little more directive. But that's not their style. If I'm in a room with other executive decision makers, I want them to come and tell me what they know and where they think we should go. And then we'll decide together if we're going to take a piece of that or all of it or none of it. What's harder, though, is if you have six people in a room and two of them are like, "Whatever you want to do is fine." I don't like that as much.'

Clearly, this lead community partner expected that an effective evaluator would come with a concrete plan to which they and other community partners could respond. Instead, the evaluator expected the lead community partner to take the lead in setting priorities for the evaluation plan.

There was a second way in which dialogue was not welcomed by lead community partners: when it came to articulating how the evaluation would actually be carried out. Lead community partners who had positive assessments of the evaluation tended to report that they understood the evaluation plan, what they needed to do to support it, and what deliverables would be provided. For example:

> 'I feel very comfortable with our evaluation. I feel like I know what's going on. . . the best thing for us was that we knew it upfront, so . . . the teachers [who would need to participate in the evaluation] knew from day one they were going to have to pre-test and post-test or do whatever was going to be the assessment of that programme.'

Finally, some evaluators were not able to open a dialogue at all. This limitation, in our study, typically related to disciplinary divides between the evaluator and community partners. For example, a quite exasperated lead community partner commented:

> 'There's definitely some language and cultural barriers just between evaluators and human beings.'

In this case, attempts at dialogue about the evaluation plan failed because the evaluator and lead community partner could not find a common language with which to speak. In one instance, the lead community partner brought in another team of researchers to 'translate' the evaluator's ideas to the community partners. This opened a dialogue with the evaluator that was not able to be opened in previous efforts.

Deliberation

When lead community partners expressed confidence in the evaluation, they inevitably spoke at length about the role of the evaluator as advisor and trusted colleague. Lead community partners gave many examples of evaluators facilitating conversations among community partners about how to develop the evaluation or how to use the results of the evaluation for making better decisions. This was especially evident in two moments in the project's life: when evaluation findings were presented to community partners and when the community partners began the process of planning for sustainability.

Lead community partners who expressed confidence in the evaluation and the evaluator reported that their evaluators provided interpretations of data that were intended to make the data more useful for programme development. More than just providing the data, effective evaluators facilitated deliberations about the meaning of the data from a programme point of view, for example,

> 'We want the evaluators to walk us through [the evaluation findings]. And that's what they've been doing at the advisory meetings. They've been kind of breaking it down and just actually showing us where we have made progress and what programs appear to be creating a difference in the performance of our children.'

Evaluators who could not provide the data in a way that closely fitted with decisions the lead community partner was making, or who could not do so on a timely basis, delivered an evaluation in which the lead community partner had less confidence. For example: "[The data have] been helpful, but it feels like we're kind of late in the game in getting some of this data to schools and making it meaningful for them."

For some projects, the evaluator took a central role in sustainability planning. Evaluators who took such a role had typically already conducted a fair amount of facilitation around decisions for the community partners. The transition to sustainability planning was natural in such cases, since the evaluator had proven himself or herself as an effective and unbiased facilitator in prior discussions. Thus, when painful and politically complicated discussions were held about which programmes would be sustained with local funding, the evaluator was seen an unbiased partner in the deliberative process.

Key learning

This study suggests that community partners feel that they receive more value when in engaging in research with researchers who:

1. Are transparent and communicative about the products that the research will produce and the role of community partners in collecting the data These researchers are more inclusive when it comes to involving community partners in the research planning process. Often, the effort that the researcher makes to include community partners in the development of the research plan results in the community partners including the researcher in their community decision-making process. This keeps the researcher informed about changes in the community and provides community partners fuller access to the expertise the researcher brings to many different parts of their decision-making processes.

2. Present findings to community partners in a way that they can put the findings into actionResearchers are considered more effective by their community partners if they have the ability to facilitate deliberation about the findings from the research and the implications of the findings for local community decisions. This facilitative capacity ensures that the findings will be used during the community planning process, and that the researcher is seen as an unbiased consultant during what can be a politically difficult process of deciding which programmes will be sustained.

3. Use a wide range of methods and research resources to meet community partner needs, even if that means evaluators need to learn new methods themselvesResearchers and evaluators who enter a community partnership with a strong commitment to one set of research methods or one approach to understanding the community's challenges are perceived as being of limited use to their community partners. Researchers who are methodologically creative and flexible, on the other hand, are able to find approaches to answering most questions that the community partners want to have answered. This increases their value and perceived effectiveness significantly.

4. View their role broadly, and understand that one of their contributions to the partnership is the promotion of data-driven thinking beyond the narrow focus of the research project at handFor many of the projects we studied, the lead community partner welcomed having an expert engaged in the community planning process who did not have a stake in the outcome of the research. This meant that the researcher was often welcomed as a partner who could facilitate complex discussions among partners by keeping the focus on what the research findings meant for the community, rather than on the narrow, competing interests of many

community partners. The ability to facilitate deliberation around the meaning of the research findings allowed community partners to make decisions that were more data-driven and ultimately more beneficial for the community.

Summary

Advantages

The community-based approaches discussed here (preparing community partners for planning the research, being inclusive, opening a dialogue and facilitating deliberation) gave the lead community partners more confidence in the evaluation and made sure that the evaluation more closely met the needs of the community.

Limitations

Although community-based participatory research (CBPR) has learned much from evaluation research, the two continue to have differences. For example, evaluation research is often concerned with making judgments about the progress of a community initiative, which naturally makes community leaders feel more vulnerable and exposed than perhaps other forms of research (Weiss, 1998). Such differences may limit the applicability of this study to CBPR.

Conclusion

In examining these findings, it is worth pausing to note a few limitations or conditions to our data. First, in studying participation in a community setting, we examined the participation of only one stakeholder, the lead community partner. This stakeholder is unique in that he or she (a) oversees the contract with the evaluator and thus in some sense has a unique capacity to hold the evaluator accountable, and (b) is the gatekeeper between the evaluator and all other community partners. It is not clear how typical this is for communities engaged in participatory research.

This study offers a view of the participatory research process between evaluators and their lead community partners. While there is more work to be done to understand the complexities of the participatory process, several important themes emerge that indicate what successful participation may look like. Evaluators and researchers who are creative and flexible about their approach and methods, and who take the time to increase stakeholder inclusion from the earliest stages of planning are more likely to build confidence in the evaluation or research process. In addition, evaluators whose lead community partners report them as having an excellent ability to create dialogue and deliberation about the evaluation plan and findings were far more likely to build confidence in the evaluation. Where evaluators did not have the capacity to open a dialogue and facilitate deliberation, lead community partners reported having much less confidence in the evaluation.

Returning to the claim made by Plottu and Plottu (2009) in regards to evaluators needing to prepare stakeholders to participate in evaluation, it is clear that not all evaluators have the capacity to do this. Not all evaluators studied had the capacity to communicate in lay terms about evaluation; they could not open a dialogue about the evaluation plan. Thus, it appears that before evaluators approach a community to discuss evaluation, some practical training in working with non-researchers on research issues seems warranted. Once these communication skills are in place, the process of preparation is fairly straightforward. While lead community partners with more research experience generally had more confidence in the evaluation, none of the lead community partners, regardless of their past experience, reported needing to learn much about the technical aspects of evaluation in order to collaborate fully. The findings suggest that the preparation evaluators need to do for community partners in order to bring them into the participatory process need not be highly technical and should focus more on speaking in lay terms about the research process and how it interconnects with community decision-making.

Finally, evaluators and researchers who work in communities must remain mindful that the product that is most useful to community partners tends to be applied and concrete research findings perhaps not at the level that would interest the evaluator or their research peers. For example, counting the number of individuals getting services in one community mental health agency may be of most interest to community partners, but would typically hold little interest to an academic journal. Nonetheless, having research findings that can inform community decisions not only builds confidence in the evaluation, but is also one of the most important rewards community partners receive for participating in research.

Lead community partners (and other community partners) gain confidence in evaluations and research when evaluators and researchers express a commitment to the community and a willingness to engage their effort fully for the benefit of the community. This may mean that the evaluators and researchers learn new skills, change their data collection plan, or advise the community on a broader field of issues than just the research itself. Once this partnership is in place, the evaluator or researcher has the potential to bring into the community decision-making process a respect for data-driven thinking, and help support a commitment among stakeholders to move beyond local competition for resources by making decisions based on concrete community outcomes.

Reflections

This study was aimed at understanding how participatory research happens in practice. Because the variety of the SSHS was great, we chose to study one relationship in depth: how the evaluation tasks were shared by the evaluator with the lead community partner. We believe this tells a small, but necessary, part of the story of how participatory research works in practice. Additional study is required to explore more fully the optimal methods for engaging community partners in research, and the extent to which community partners consider that participating in the research was both worthwhile for them and led to a research product that was of high value to the community.

Discussion questions

1. To what extent does the participatory approach to evaluation pose advantages and disadvantages for rigorous evaluation?
2. What does the term 'data-driven thinking' imply in a community setting?
3. What limits are there or should there be, if any, to participation in an evaluation of a programme that you direct?
4. Are there certain aspects of participation you believe would be crucial to the evaluation being well conducted?
5. What additional tensions or challenges might exist for community-based participatory researchers that perhaps evaluators do not contend with?

References
Abma, T. A. and Widdershoven, G. A. (2009) 'Evaluation and/as Social Relation', *Evaluation*, 14(2): 209-225.

Cartland, J., Ruch-Ross, H. and Mason, M. (2008) 'Role-Sharing Between Evaluators and Stakeholders in Practice', *American Journal of Evaluation*, 29(4): 460-477.

Chouinard, J. A. and Cousins, B. J. (2009) 'A Review and Synthesis of Current Research on Cross-Cultural Evaluation', *American Journal of Evaluation*, 30(4): 474-494.

Daigneault, P.-M. and Jacob, S. (2009) 'Toward Accurate Measurement of Participation: Rethinking the Conceptualization and Operationalizations of Participatory Evaluation', *American Journal of Evaluation*, 30(3): 330-348.

Furlong, M., Paige, L. Z. and Osher, D. (2003) 'The Safe Schools/Healthy Students (SS/HS) Initiative: Lessons Learned from Implementing Comprehensive Youth Development Programs', *Psychology in the Schools*, 40(5): 447-456.

House, E. (2005) 'Promising Practices: The Many Forms of Democratic Evaluation', *The Evaluation Exchange,* 11(3): 7.

Israel, B. A., Eng, E., Schulz, A.J. and Parker, E.A. (eds) (2005) *Methods in Community-Based Participatory Research for Health*, San Francisco: Jossey-Bass.

King, J. (2008) 'Bringing Evaluative Learning to Light', *American Journal of Evaluation*, 29: 151.

Plottu, B. and Plottu, E. (2009) 'Approaches to Participation in Evaluation: Some Conditions for Implementation', *Evaluation*, 15(3): 343–359.

Stern, E. (2008) 'Evaluation: Critical for Whom and Connected to What?' *Evaluation*, 14(2): 249–257.

Symonette, H. (2004) 'Walking Pathways Toward Becoming a Culturally Competent Evaluator: Boundaries, Borderlands, and Border crossings', *New Directions for Evaluation*, 102: 95–109.

Weiss, C. (1998) *Evaluation*, Upper Saddle River, NJ: Prentice Hall.

Twelve

Are we recovery oriented?
An Australian encounter of learning
from people with lived experiences

*Liam Buckley, Nadine Cocks, Matthew Scott,
Michael Stylianou, Lisa Brophy, Jayne Lewis,
Kieran Halloran and Melissa Petrakis*

Chapter aims

- To describe an evaluation of the recovery orientation of an innovation model of service delivery for people with multiple and complex needs.
- To illustrate the value of collaborative partnerships in conducting community research (CR).
- To highlight the value of CR to a project seeking to engage vulnerable and marginalised participants.
- To explore the challenges experienced by community researchers in conducting research, including ethical considerations, participant recruitment, role boundaries, power sharing and the effects of the environment.

Introduction

This chapter describes the experience of community researchers as active participants in the evaluation of an innovative new model of service delivery, the Adult Mental Health Initiatives: a collaboration between St Vincent's Mental Health (SVMH) and Mind Australia in Melbourne, Australia. Both organisations support people with severe and enduring symptoms of mental illness and complex needs. The initiatives are funded by the Victorian State Government and are aimed at people who move between service providers in an uncoordinated manner, often at risk of poor outcomes including repeated hospital admissions, homelessness and/or incarceration. Both services aim to embed a recovery model to achieve service user-focused, integrated, holistic and targeted service delivery.

To develop and improve the service being provided, the evaluation team utilised two service user-rated recovery-orientation-of-the-service measures: the Recovery Enhancing Environment measure (REE) and the Recovery Self-Assessment (RSA) (service user version). The experience of the service users in completing the measures was also investigated by inviting them to rate the relevance of the tools and their preference to determine the more appropriate recovery measure for future programme evaluation.

In Australia 'consumer consultants' are employed in mental health services to ensure that a service user perspective is included in all aspects of mental health service planning, delivery and evaluation. Their role is to improve mental health services' responsiveness to service user needs. The evaluation team in the current project included consumer consultants working as community researchers recruited from both organisations. This evaluation design affirmed the value of consumer consultants extending their role into research activities. It also affirmed the merit of a service user perspective throughout, service user-to-service user research processes, and provided important learning about facilitating people considered 'vulnerable' and 'complex' to be involved in research and evaluation activities. This chapter will discuss the value of service user research, participation and leadership in this project.

Embedding a recovery approach to mental health service for people with serious and enduring symptoms of mental ill health and complex needs

Recovery has become an important emerging concept in mental health services in Australia and has significantly influenced policy and practice developments. It is increasingly influencing research and encouraging greater involvement by service users in research activities (Ramon et al, 2007). Recovery has been described as:

> A deeply personal, unique process of changing one's attitudes, values, feelings, goals, skills and roles. It is a way of living a satisfying, hopeful and contributing life even with limitations caused by the illness. Recovery involves the development of new meaning and purpose in one's life as one grows beyond the catastrophic effects of mental illness. (Anthony, 1993: 12)

Recovery is a paradigm shift whereby mental health services move away from traditional service delivery models characterised by professional experts providing treatments to patients in an effort to cure them or relieve them of their symptoms, to an approach that emphasises collaboration, partnership, citizenship and finding meaning and purpose with or without ongoing episodes of illness. This way of conceptualising recovery has been particularly driven by the service user movement who have advocated increased recognition for service users as experts through recognition of the wisdom and insights they have gained through their lived experience.

The Victorian Government in Australia recently produced a framework for recovery-oriented practice (State Government of Victoria, 2011). The framework encourages all specialist mental health services in Victoria to adopt recovery principles in practice. The principles are identified as self-determination and personalised care, and recovery-oriented practice is implemented through emphasising hope, social inclusion, community participation, personal goal setting and self-management.

St Vincent's Mental Health: achieving a paradigm shift to a recovery orientation in clinical services

St Vincent's Mental Health (SVMH) is a comprehensive area-based service, providing public specialist mental health services to the inner-urban east area of Melbourne. Since 2004, SVMH has adopted a recovery-oriented approach for service users, based on the 'Strengths' model of case management, as outlined by Rapp and Goscha (1998) and implemented in a smaller clinical service in Timaru in New Zealand. After having initially been introduced in community-based mental health teams the Strengths model is now being implemented in the acute setting.

The Strengths model focuses on a person's strengths and personal goals rather than on the deficits associated with mental health problems and the model assumes that the service user is in charge of directing their care, that growth and change are always possible and that the community is an oasis of resources.

Mind: supporting mental health recovery

Mind Australia is the largest community managed specialist mental health service in Victoria and South Australia and delivers a broad suite of recovery-focused services to young people, adults and families. The organisation has grown considerably in recent years and anticipates further growth over the next decade.

The Mind Strategic Plan 2010–15 articulates a commitment to: 'Establish a robust and effective research and programme evaluation capability shared with academic and service delivery partners'.

The Strategic Plan documents a far-reaching approach to developing and repositioning Mind. The plan involves refining the approach to recovery and social inclusion, restructuring to enable services to be better tailored to individual needs and changes to the workforce to utilise and recognise the skills of staff more effectively.

Service-level recovery-orientation evaluation instruments

State and national mental health policies in Australia emphasise the importance of services providing opportunities for service users to recover from mental illness and associated disability. There has also been considerable effort to develop ways of investigating the degree to which mental health services are recovery oriented (O'Connell et al, 2005).

In February 2010 the Australian Mental Health Outcomes and Classification Network (AMHOCN) completed a review of recovery measures in the treatment of mental illness. Burgess et al (2010) investigated the suitability of a recovery outcome measure for use across all specialist mental health services. This scope led to significant limitations regarding the criteria for assessing a measure that would be suitable for such broad application and the findings of the review are indicative of the issues. Their finding was a diversity of measures that were inconsistent in approach and not necessarily compatible with the Australian context.

A distinction between the measurement of individual recovery and the recovery orientation of the service, and an emphasis on the importance of distinguishing between these two different types of recovery measures, was also found. Of the four service-level evaluation instruments that appeared the most promising, only one had versions that seek feedback from service users, family members/carers, service providers and managers, the Recovery Self Assessment (RSA). SVMH planned to trial the RSA with both a group of service users and a group of carers to ascertain the usefulness and meaningfulness of its use in an Australian public mental health service, and in conjunction with the Strengths model of care. Further, the plan was to trial a second measure, the Ridgeway Recovery-Enhancing Environment measure (REE) (Ridgway and Press, 2004) with the same group of service users to ascertain which was preferred by or more useful to service users.

In an earlier audit of recovery measures, among the 13 measures provided by Campbell-Orde et al (2005), the REE stands out as being one of the few that examines both individual recovery and the service environment that supports recovery. The REE was developed using service users' accounts of recovery and what environmental factors supported them and it is recommended that the measure be completed using service user researchers.

Mind had previously conducted a pilot study in order to ascertain the suitability of the REE as a measure of both recovery outcomes for service users and the recovery orientation of the service. One of the most innovative aspects to the pilot study was that it was service users themselves who were employed and trained by Mind to administer the survey. Four community researchers were recruited along with two consumer consultants from Mind. The REE was administered to 72 clients who consented to participate in the study. The pilot data provided a voice for service users to provide feedback directly and specifically about what was being done well, and where more support was needed. The REE was identified as a potentially valuable tool for Mind as a feedback and planning mechanism.

Background to the research project

The project had five main objectives:

1. To obtain feedback from service users using two different recovery orientation of the service measures: the REE and the RSA – person in recovery version
2. To obtain service user preferences about the two different measures
3. To use the findings to make recommendations for service development
4. To use the findings to identify the most appropriate tool that measures the recovery orientation of the service for service users under the Adult Mental Health Reform Initiatives
5. To repeat the process with the preferred tool and monitor change in the recovery orientation of the service over time

A key feature of the project was the involvement of service users. While seeking the views of service users and employing service users were both becoming more common in the mental health field, employment of service users within the research field itself remained highly limited. Participatory action research is one approach to enabling the active involvement of service users in research that is focused on their needs (Ramon et al, 2007; Rethink, 2010). According to Davidson et al (2010): 'These methods require a collaborative approach to involving people with experience of the phenomena of focus to participate as partners throughout all stages of a study' (pages 101–2).

Diana Rose pioneered service users undertaking the role of researcher (Rose, 2001) – particularly in evaluation exercises to enable service users to feel sufficiently safe to honestly discuss their experience of services. Rose reported in her study that:

> The consumer researchers reported back that service users visibly relaxed and opened up once they knew the consumer researcher had also 'been through the system' and understood their own situation. (2001: 4)

The research team reflected the structure of both services, involving managers, researchers, workers and consumer consultants. Both organisations employ two consumer consultants and it was decided to invite all four to participate as community researchers recruited to the research. They were staff employed within each service because of the combination of their interpersonal skills, administrative skills and lived experience as service users. These four individuals carried out various roles including: orientation of new service users to the service and systems of care, co-facilitating psychoeducation and support meetings, conducting satisfaction surveys with service users regarding projects and programmes, membership on programme implementation and service evaluation committees, and at times reviewing applicants for suitability for employment within the service.

For their role within the current research project, the two consumer consultants from Mind had the responsibility of choosing research tools since both are members of the Selection and Operations group which is a part of the clinical governance structure of the Initiative. They additionally had both previously been trained in and used the REE for the earlier pilot at Mind that has been mentioned previously. The SVMH community researchers needed to be trained in this evaluation tool. All four community researchers were unfamiliar with, and needed to be trained in the use of, the RSA.

A meeting with all four community researchers was convened to discuss the project and provide information on the tools and how to administer them. Feedback was sought; and some changes suggested that would improve the readability of the REE. The project officer contacted case managers to seek service user consent to participate in the research. The community researchers played a central role whereby they engaged service users who wished to participate, explained the process, and facilitated completion of the measures. One of the four community researchers then arranged a meeting time and location that was agreeable to both them and the service user. A member of the project team transported the community researchers to each interview to answer questions and provide support, and if needed, debrief before and after each interview. Both the project officer at SVMH and the manager at Mind acted as mentors to facilitate preparation for the interviews and debriefing shortly afterwards.

Involving four community researchers, with different levels of experience required planning, training, anticipation and support. Each was very familiar with the organisations involved in the project, which greatly assisted in terms of their confidence and capacity to undertake the research. The four community researchers also provided peer support as they shared experiences and developed confidence in conducting research.

'This project, I think, has been interesting and challenging at the same time. I really believe we have been very well supported throughout and I look forward to further developments as they occur. I found the interview process rewarding for myself as well as the consumer being interviewed.' (community researcher)

This comment is indicative of the importance of discussion and debriefing, which was an essential part of the process.

'I see it as vital that Mind and St Vincent's are informed by research of this nature (particularly client-centred). I also enjoyed the affirmation of having completed a task which was in "a new area of work", successfully.' (community researcher)

The two research fellows provided a consultation role to manage risk and reporting issues. This was activated when one service user expressed veiled suicidal thoughts to the community researcher during one of the interviews.

A shared commitment to the project, avoidance of a hierarchical structure and an emphasis on shared decision-making were supportive of collaborative, flexible and numerous discussions, rather than a limited number of formal meetings. The range of possible situations that might have arisen was unclear so an agreement to share responsibility was important between research fellows, managers and community researchers.

'The feelings of minor anxiety were short lived. I did feel better after each interview mainly because having gotten over the initial anxiety, I felt enthusiastic about the process of administering both these very fine surveys and asking clients to choose which one they prefer.' (community researcher)

Ethical considerations: meaningful informed consent

Since service users in the Adult Mental Health Initiatives were people with complex needs, both services recognised the need to undertake a formal ethics review process prior to commencing the research process. A plain language statement (PLS) was developed by the research fellow at SVMH, with feedback sought from the Strengths evaluation committee. This committee includes one of the community researchers in this study as a regular contributor to and member of the committee. On the PLS the potential benefits of the research were explained. Participants were made aware that the questionnaires would require reflection on the care they received and it was acknowledged that discussing personal issues and difficult life experiences may be upsetting.

Participants were informed of the supports available to them if they wished to discuss any concerns after completing the measures and they were informed of the systems in place to protect their privacy and confidentiality. The voluntary nature of participation was safeguarded and prospective participants were assured that they were free to withdraw at any stage and that this would not have an impact on their current or future treatment. Participants were also provided with a $20 gift voucher in appreciation of their time and feedback.

In reflecting on this research process all eight members of the project team, including the community researchers, identified some common themes including ethical issues. The following questions are based on 'real life' events the team had to work through. For example, how do members of the project team respond in a recovery-oriented way to people becoming distressed – even expressing suicidal ideation – when recalling their experience with a service? What do we do when someone wants to repeat their interview because they would like to be paid again? Is it more difficult for community researchers to establish 'boundaries' between themselves and the participants and is that a problem?

A potential outcome for community researchers involved in research with service users is that boundaries are sometimes difficult to establish. Community researchers informing service user participants that they have also been a service user may create a sense of camaraderie and shared experience. This promotes candid and honest responses. However, one particular story highlighted some of the challenges:

> 'A participant immediately wanted to know more about me. How much should I tell? Do I in fact have to tell anything? I decided to tell the participant a little and this seemed to put the participant at ease. I reminded myself that the participant was divulging a lot of information about themselves by participating in the research so this was the least I could do. When interview was over (it was in the secure unit of a psychiatric ward) I left with the participant to walk down the street (he wanted to spend his voucher) and this resulted in further conversation both about the participant and myself and ended with a hug to say goodbye. I should note that I pointed to my place of work and said I have to go back to work now. It was about a week later that I was told the participant turned up to my work wanting to complete the survey again to obtain another voucher. Should I have told the participant where I work? Had I been too honest and frank?' (community researcher)

These are some of the dilemmas that community researchers could face, especially around establishing boundaries with participants. There are definite advantages in community researchers disclosing some information about themselves, but the need to carefully establish appropriate boundaries remain.

It was important to feel safe enough to reflect with others on the team about ethical and boundary issues. As it happened there were times when boundaries seemed 'stretched' but no occasion when they were 'breached'. It might be that the preparedness to 'stretch' the boundaries accounted for the ease of engagement of which the community researchers were so aware. Perhaps it is consistent with Denhov and Topor's (2011: 1) findings that there were 'two core themes that described vital components of helping relationships: a non-stigmatizing attitude on the part of the professionals and their willingness to do something beyond established routines'. Doing something beyond established routines are described by the participants in Denhov and Topor's (2011) study as being extensions of boundaries that were simple acts of humanity, sometimes personal disclosure and often located in small everyday interactions that had a lot of meaning to the person.

Power sharing

In reflecting on the general experience of undertaking this research, it was found that community researchers confiding in participants that they shared a lived experience of mental health challenges lead to a change in the 'vibe' or feel of the research interview.

This was summarised by one of the community researchers below:

> 'Having consumer consultants administer the survey with each consumer seemed to overcome the power differential between consumer and worker quite well. The consumer consultants were aware of the positive feeling or vibe experienced by consumers of realizing the person administering the survey was also a consumer.
>
> 'On the other hand, it appeared helpful that the consumer consultants had the skills, experience and training in gathering the feedback. It would be a challenge for an untrained or unskilled consumer to administer the surveys.' (community researcher)

Case manager and support worker 'gatekeepers'

Since the ethics approval process required that service users be given the opportunity to decide whether to participate without coercion, a step was put in place to introduce the service evaluation via case managers and support workers.

A manager explained the process as:

> 'A member of the project team assisted by contacting all case managers to tell them about the project and encourage them to

ask their clients if they would be willing to receive a telephone call from one of the consumer consultants about potential participation in completing two surveys to rate the service they are receiving.'

The manager acknowledges, however, that,

> 'This particular step was one of the most challenging of the project. While team managers were very supportive of this project there was a real "road block" in terms of response from case managers and support workers. Despite a range of communication strategies there was very minimal initial response.'

Asking case managers and support workers to act as 'gatekeepers' by asking the service users if they would be willing to receive information about participating in the study seemed to produce barriers in the recruitment process. As one community researcher explained:

> 'The experience of depending on case managers or support workers to inform consumers about the request for their participation in giving feedback has generally proved less than effective in recruiting interested consumers. Having a means of approaching consumers directly would seem to be advantageous.'

The experience of another community researcher is similar, and additionally highlights how messages can become distorted if there are too many people between those conducting the research and the participants:

> 'A case manager who introduced me to a participant explained that the reason for the project was to identify how the person was coping so that staff could talk to them about it. I then had to explain that the project was actually to gauge how the person thought the service was performing for them and that the results would be de identified. Where the case manager got their idea from I don't know.'

One possible explanation for why this situation developed has been considered in recent, related research. Emmel et al (2007) suggest that patterns of trust and mistrust can develop between researchers, gatekeepers and participants. Case managers, even more so than support workers, could be perceived as, and act as, 'formal' gatekeepers, especially as elements of their role include statutory functions (for example supervising a Community Treatment Order). In some cases it seemed that a paternalistic stance was being taken, perhaps motivated by wanting to protect service users from any perceived or actual burden or risk associated with participating in the research. This is consistent with the issues raised by Smith (2008) who discusses paternalism as one barrier that limits access to vulnerable and disadvantaged groups in research. Our experience supports the need for what Smith (2008) calls 'responsible advocacy' to ensure that vulnerable and marginalised people such as our potential participants are not excluded from research and therefore the opportunity to contribute to service development.

Environment

In considering the best place to conduct this kind of interview a number of factors needed to be considered. Some of the potential interviewees were currently in hospital, secure units, or community residential units and this created dilemmas in attempts to provide an opportunity to participate while limited to environments that were considered potentially unfavourable or unsuitable. Questions we considered were:

- Where does the participant reside currently?
- Is this a suitable place?
- Are there going to be any interruptions?
- Is the space neutral, in particular, not the researcher's or the participant's home or place of work?
- Is the place familiar to the participant or a space the participant enjoys being in?

During this research project one of the interviews was conducted in the secure unit of a psychiatric hospital. This resulted in the following comment from the CR involved when compared with another interview that took place in the participant's own home:

> 'The effects of the environment in both situations couldn't have been more stark. The interview conducted in the secure unit of the psychiatric hospital did not present a quiet uninterrupted space and as a result the participant appeared uncomfortable and the interview was interrupted at several stages. It was also difficult to access the ward for the researchers.' (community researcher)

Creating a neutral, safe and relatively quiet place in which to conduct the interviews such as a café or even a public library would seem obvious choices but they bring their own difficulties such as privacy and confidentiality. It was anticipated that some participants may not feel entirely comfortable divulging personal information in a public place.

While conducting the interview in the participant's home seemed to be ideal in terms of comfort for the service user, there were safety considerations.

This was important given that the target group were people with serious mental health challenges who may have had concurrent behavioural or cognitive disturbance and substance abuse issues. As one of the research fellows noted:

> 'In my experience in the project the consumer consultants were much more confident and at ease about seeing people in their own homes. I could see in my own reactions how problem saturated and risk averse I had become in thinking about what might go wrong. In this research it was particularly challenging to take risks because there were ethics obligations and management expectations that had to be kept in mind. But I was aware that this way of thinking was further discriminating against and marginalising the consumers – it's a constant dilemma.'

Key learning points

1. Community researchers have the capacity and interest to conduct interviews with service users with multiple and complex needs.
2. Community researchers will experience challenges, including issues relating to ethics, recruitment, boundaries, power sharing and the effects of the environment to conduct research.
3. There is value in consumer consultants participating in research activities as community researchers, using their valuable skills in engaging service users and in extending their usual roles into a new area.

Summary: Advantages and disadvantages of using community researchers

Advantages

- The participation of the community researchers greatly enhanced this research activity. Along with managers and research fellows they were a vital element in a unique team within and across two organisations.
- The involvement of community researchers was pivotal to a meaningful engagement with service users. Their involvement affirmed the value of lived experience and its positive impact on reducing any power differential between participant and interviewer.
- A flexible and sensitive approach to role boundary considerations by community researchers was an important factor that contributed to strong engagement with service users, and decisions around the management of any delicate boundary issues were shared by the entire research team.

- The community researchers were able to extend and expand their usual roles into a new area; that of conducting research. While this was somewhat challenging, it was ultimately seen by them to be a fulfilling, satisfying and worthwhile experience.
- The community researchers provided mutual peer support through open sharing of ideas, expertise and encouragement in relation to their role; in this way a sense of isolation and performance anxiety, common for new researchers generally and in no way particular to consumers, was avoided or minimised.

Disadvantages

- There are challenges for community researchers in maintaining role boundaries and in navigating how much to share of their own lived experience with people who are simultaneously both peers in recovery and research participants.
- There are challenges for the organisations in providing enough resources and forethought to adequately train and support meaningful involvement of community researchers, who may not have undertaken graduate, let alone postgraduate, research education that more typically prepares staff to undertake such activities.

Conclusions

The participation of the community researchers greatly enhanced this research activity. The collaboration of the key stakeholders to engage recovery orientation of the service measurement was valuable. Each tool generated useful service user feedback to guide service improvement. The methods and process facilitated collaboration at multiple levels, between:

- Community researchers, managers and academics who formed a unique team within and across the two services
- Community researchers across the two organisations who could share expertise, ideas and increased the potential for mutual support and encouragement in what can sometimes be isolating and marginalised roles
- Research and academic linkages within each service, thus encouraging a research partnership that facilitated a responsive, embedded approach to research and evaluation
- Two different types of specialist mental health services: a large clinical service and a community managed service.

The contribution of the community researchers to this process enabled a rich appreciation of the value of a shared lived experience to engaging participants. The team also valued the consumer researchers' lived experience through demonstrating an emphasis on shared decision making and ensuring that the community researchers received the appropriate training and support to undertake this role. Community researchers also felt that they made gains. In the words of one researcher:

'I found this project both empowering and rewarding. The interviews I did were challenging but were a good experience and I think the consumers involved gained a sense of achievement and purpose from being part of this. They felt like they were participating in something worthwhile.' (community researcher)

Discussion questions

1. Is it more difficult for community researchers to establish 'boundaries' between themselves and the participants? Is that a problem?
2. In what ways might involving 'gatekeepers' potentially restrict the involvement of marginalised and vulnerable people in research?
3. Should research activity be encouraged to take place in community spaces and homes? If so, how can concerns about 'risk' be managed?

References
Anthony, W. (1993) 'Recovery from Mental Illness: The Guiding Vision of the Mental Health Service System in the 1990s', *Psychosocial Rehabilitation Journal*, 16: 11–23.
Burgess, P., Pirkis, J., Coombs, T. and Rosen, A. (2010) *Review of Recovery Measures. Final Report for Australian Mental Health Outcomes and Classification Network*, Parkville, Australia: The University of Melbourne.
Campbell-Orde, T., Chamberlin, J., Carpenter, J. and Leff, H. (2005) *Measuring the Promise: A Compendium of Recovery Measures, Volume II*, Cambridge: Human Services Research Institute.
Davidson, L., Shaw, J., Welborn, S., Mahon, B., Siorota, M., Gilbo, P., McDermin, M, Fazio, J., Gilbert, C., Breettz, S. and Pelletier, J.F. (2010) '"I Don't Know How to Find My Way in the World": Contributions of User-Led Research to Transforming Mental Health Practice', *Psychiatry*, 73(2): 101–113.
Denhov, A. and Topor, A. (2011) 'The Components of Helping Relationships with Professionals in Psychiatry: Users' Perspective', *International Journal of Social Psychiatry*, Published online 20 May, DOI: 10.1177/0020764011406811.

Emmel, N., Hughes, K., Greenhalgh J. and Sales, A. (2007) 'Accessing Socially Excluded People: Trust and the Gatekeeper in the Researcher–Participant Relationship', *Sociological Research Online*, 12(2), www.socresonline.org.uk /12/2/emmel.html.

O'Connell, M., Tondora, J., Croog, G., Evans, A., and Davidson, L. (2005) 'From Rhetoric to Routine: Assessing Perceptions of Recovery-Oriented Practices in a State Mental Health and Addiction System', *Psychiatric Rehabilitation Journal*, 28(4): 378–386.

Ramon, S., Healy, B. and Renouf, N. (2007) 'Recovery from Mental Illness as an Emergent Concept and Practice in Australia and the UK', *International Journal of Social Psychiatry*, 53: 108–122.

Rapp, C. and Goscha, R. (2006) *The Strengths Model: Case Management with People with Psychiatric Disabilities* (2nd edn), Oxford: Oxford University Press.

Rethink (2010) *Recovery Insights: Learning from Lived Experience*, Rethink Recovery Series 3, www.rethink.org/recoveryinsights.

Ridgway, P., and Press, A. (2004) *Assessing the Recovery-Orientation of Your Mental Health Program: A User's Guide for the Recovery-Enhancing Environment Scale (REE) Version 1*, Lawrence, KS: University of Kansas, School of Social Welfare, Office of Mental Health Training and Research.

Rose, D. (2001) *Users' Voices: The Perspectives of Mental Health Service Users on Community and Hospital Care*, London: The Sainsbury Centre for Mental Health.

Smith L.J. (2008) 'How Ethical is Ethical Research? Recruiting Marginalized, Vulnerable Groups into Health Services Research', *Journal of Advanced Nursing*, 62(2): 248–257.

State Government of Victoria (2011) *Framework for Recovery Orientated Practice*, Melbourne: Mental Health, Drugs and Regions Division, Victorian Government, Department of Health.

Thirteen

Ethics in community research: reflections from ethnographic research with First Nations people in the US

Barbara Kawulich and Tamra Ogletree

Chapter aims

- To share the historic implications of unethical research
- To discuss ethical considerations of importance to community research
- To share guidelines for researchers to follow in conducting research
- To discuss the dimensions and development of an Institutional Review Board (IRB) document

Introduction

Conducting ethical research may be considered one of the most important aspects of the research process. For community research, specific issues may arise that researchers must address. These are the focus of this chapter. The key methodological issues we consider in this chapter include the importance of collaboration with community members, informed consent and cultural considerations when conducting ethical research. Our experience with community research, in part, stems from our work conducting ethnographic research with the Muscogee (Creek) Nation of Oklahoma (US) and the Eastern Band of the Cherokee Nation (EBCN) of North Carolina (US) over the past 15 years. Examples from our work are included. In this chapter, the terms 'aboriginal', 'indigenous' and 'native' reflect the original people of a country.

Historical overview of ethical research concerns

During the last century, various studies have illustrated the need for the creation of Institutional Review Boards (IRBs) (Berg, 2001). The torture, dismemberment and experimentation on prisoners in Nazi concentration camps (Franzblau, 1995; Howell, 1999), the Tuskegee syphilis study (Christians, 2000) and the Milgram experiment (Christians, 2000; Berg, 2001), among others, serve as instances of exploitation of participants and communities. Concerns about such studies provided the impetus for the development of guidelines to oversee research, to prohibit, or at least limit, such exploitation. In response, the US National Research Act of 1974 required all institutions conducting research to establish IRBs to guard participant safety.

In response, various organisations developed 'Codes of Ethics', focusing researchers' attention on disclosure of research goals, methods and sponsorship, and assurance of non-coercive, voluntary participation of informants (Bernard, 1994). Confidentiality and respect for the community's dignity, integrity and worth, and the need for accurate reporting were also stressed. The resulting guidelines emphasised the interests of participants over those of the researcher, particularly issues of confidentiality and receipt of copies of the final product (Kutsche, 1998). Additionally, researchers' misrepresentation of themselves and/or their research projects to participants is discouraged; honesty and openness are encouraged from both researcher and participants (Bernard, 1994; Kutsche, 1998). Care must be taken to make participants aware of risk factors associated with participation and accommodations for treatment when injury or harm results. In certain instances, additional considerations include low literacy rates, language barriers, exclusion of certain groups and existing community health problems (Caballero, 2002).

Harm to the community by research studies

Various populations have been the object of research that today we would believe violates ethical standards. One example involved a study of radiation effects on Japanese atomic bomb survivors, in which no medical care was provided (Fischer, 2001). Another example occurred in the 1960s and 1970s, when the US Indian Health Service (IHS) allegedly sterilised 25 per cent of Native American women between the ages of 15 and 44 (Lawrence, 2000). This experimentation in birth control could be construed as eugenics (Smith, 2005), as the allegations included failure to properly inform women about sterilisation, use of coercion to obtain signed consent forms, use of improper consent forms and failure to implement a waiting period between consent and surgery. An investigation of IHS found that, while there was no proof of forced sterilisations, Health, Education and Welfare Department (HEW) regulations were not followed and informed consent did not adhere to HEW standards. It is not uncommon for Aboriginal communities, for example, to attribute negative events that occur in the community, such as illness or death, to members' participation in research studies in which they shared sacred information. Careless presentation of information can serve as a source of damage to both the individual and the community (Wax, 1971). These and similar studies, such as the Tuskegee syphilis study, a 40-year study in which black males were misinformed about the purpose of the study and, in some cases, treatment was withheld, underline the importance of informed consent in the research process.

Past studies have harmed communities by causing members and whole families to be stigmatised or ostracised or by causing adverse credit ratings for communities through insensitivity, intrusiveness and exploitation, and by leaving community members feeling hurt, angry (Quigley, 2006) and powerless to circumvent negative repercussions caused by research findings. In other instances, research results were not shared with the communities, research models were contrary to traditional mores, or researchers identified problems but failed to help the communities to solve them (Quigley, 2006). Such studies may not have benefited from the involvement of community members who could emphasise issues of importance to the community or voice concerns related to the research, resulting in oppression of the community.

Ethical research from a culturally respectful stance

Various scholars (such as Smith, 1999; Kievit, 2003; Mihesuah, 2005) stipulate that research should be carried out by community members themselves, rather than by outside investigators and that research should benefit the community, a stance in concert with Participatory Action Research. Researchers who simply jump into their study without regard for proper behavioural protocols related to cultural traditions and history may compromise the entire research process (Fixico, 1996, 1998). Community collaboration can facilitate research that is respectful of cultural traditions, the community and individual members. To achieve a collaborative research effort, Kievit (2003) suggests that community researchers visit, meet and live with the community for extended periods to become acquainted with members and their customs. For many reasons, particularly budget constraints, this is not always feasible. Yet it is clear that community members should be considered co-researchers with whom, not on whom, research is conducted (Kawulich, 2005).

While grant deadlines and publishing requirements are important, researchers are encouraged to remember that the interactions with the community members are the basis for the research process and hold equal, if not more, importance (Fixico, 1996, 1998). It is important that research be co-constructed through a participatory process, which heavily involves the community in the research process from development of the research question and protocols, analysis and interpretation of data, to dissemination of results (Castellano, 2004; Smylie, 2005). In doing so, a sense of community ownership of the research is enhanced, which may, in turn, serve as a catalyst for community action. It has become common practice for community researchers to include community members to assist with research, showing the community how the research benefits them, ensuring no harm is done, ensuring confidentiality and anonymity and encouraging community approval of results prior to publication. A collaborative approach to conducting research empowers the community (Burhansstipanov et al, 2005), giving them a voice, facilitating research that is beneficial to them and aiding in culturally appropriate research design, implementation and interpretation. Codes of ethics may be especially important when group property is involved, when leaders serve as key informants to suggest potential participants, when the research addresses group characteristics, or when individuals are used to speak on behalf of others (Castellano, 2004).

Issues of power and control should be considered by the researcher (Marshall and Batten, 2004), including questions of disposition of cultural materials and ownership of archaeological artefacts. A continuing relationship between researchers and communities stems from shared power and recognition of social justice issues that are important to community prosperity. According to the International Human Rights Instruments Article 29, Aboriginal peoples should be entitled to the ownership, control and protection of their cultural and intellectual property, and the Native language should be used to document traditional knowledge (Hansen and Van Fleet, 2003). Decisions about dissemination of findings should be collaboratively determined by the researcher and the community under study. Community involvement in the research ensures that issues of ownership and use are of central importance.

Ethical researchers seek to avoid ethnocentric and racist thought, try to view data through the eyes of the participants and be respectful of community customs. When seeking to achieve these goals it may be necessary to avoid some topics in one's writings (Fixico, 1996; Kawulich, 1998, 2010). Respect for traditional customs includes knowing to whom one should speak, when, and about what. Respect means understanding different ways of knowing, a different worldview, and understanding silence and other nonverbal communication (Marshall and Batten, 2004). Each community has its own customs and traditions, making broad generalisations difficult; yet many cultures share a history of colonisation, varying levels of poverty resulting from that colonisation and various social stressors that should be considered when conducting research with these communities (Smylie, 2005). Such factors may affect how research and researchers are perceived by community members.

Previous researchers' lack of respect has coloured the way some Aboriginal communities view non-Native researchers or researchers whom they do not know. For example, in a recent interview, a traditional Muscogee elder indicated that working with researchers, such as archaeologists, is frustrating when they fail to consider the oral history transmitted by elders and traditional tribal members, relying instead on historical reports for their interpretations (personal communication, 2005). He contends that oral history should take precedence over the written history, an idea echoed by Kievit (2003) and Ambler (1995). Yet, some scholars will not use oral testimonies, never visit the tribal communities about whom they write, and do not understand what hardships confront Native peoples (Mihesuah, 2003). Furthermore, some authors will not cite Native scholars' work that challenges written historical reports (Kievit, 2003). Respecting oral traditions is an integral part of ethical research, particularly in Aboriginal communities. For example, I (Kawulich) was asked to conduct a workshop for Creek Nation on conducting oral histories. We collaboratively developed interview materials, including interview guides, consent forms and archival forms for the project. I have conducted numerous interviews with Muscogee women over the years, but by teaching them oral history techniques, they were able to conduct their own interviews for their library's oral history collection. In a study of women's leadership (Kawulich, 2008), Muscogee women participated in interviews and focus groups, in which they emphasised the role of women leaders in mentoring youth. These discussions resulted in increased awareness of the important role these women play in cultural transmission and preservation, a goal of the collective group.

Guidelines for researchers to follow in conducting research

Ethical research protocols should be developed collaboratively through partnership and capacity building conversations and dialogue with community leaders and members (Quigley, 2006). In preparation, the researcher should discuss research goals and potential implementation procedures (Quigley, 2006) with an advisory committee, establish collaborative agreements (delineating researchers' accountability to the community), address equity issues, such as how to empower the community with resources and solutions and use cultural sensitivity. They should also ensure informed consent (both individual and community consent with full disclosure, comprehension, voluntary participation and understanding of potential harm or benefits). Data management and ownership issues must be resolved and reports shared. Quigley asserts that raw data belongs to the community; therefore, the community should determine how the findings are used and with whom they are shared. Typically, all data and findings should be presented with anonymity of individuals or community. There are, however, instances that should be negotiated: when, for example, the community members involved in the study choose to have participants' true names used.

In this situation, the researcher should provide advice about any potential harm that may arise from such actions. This is not an unusual situation to encounter when conducting research in Aboriginal communities; in several instances, we have been asked to use participants' real names. As a result, the initial discussions in the collaboration should include addressing the potential harms and benefits to using real names over pseudonyms. That is not to say that using real names is an unacceptable practice, as, for example, in oral history, it is expected; we simply suggest that the topic be a conscious subject for discussion in the initial stages of the collaborative research process. Researchers should co-author with participants to share authorship and a conflict resolution process should be established to rectify issues that may arise (Quigley, 2006). The community should also be left with the means to address problems associated with possible funding, direct economic benefits, improvements in health services, or improved research capabilities (Quigley, 2006). These issues might be addressed throughout the research process in collaboration with the community to ensure that they are considered as they arise. By giving 'voice' to the community, issues of inequitable power are diminished and a sense of partnership and common goal is established.

Individual informed consent may not be enough. Sometimes community interests may override the interests of individual participants (Murphy and Dingwall, 2002). The National Bioethics Advisory Commission (NBAC) advocates that human rights protection be extended to communities, rather than simply to individuals. This can be achieved by working with community representatives to seek to prevent harm to the group (Sharp and Foster, 2002). The needs of the community should dictate what research is undertaken (Kievit, 2003).

Various organisations in the US and Australia have put forward ethical guidelines and advocate sanctions for non-adherence. Common elements of these guidelines (American Indian Law Centre 1999; Aboriginal Healing Foundation, 2000; Australian Institute of Aboriginal and Torres Strait Islander Series, 2011) include that community researchers should:

- acknowledge family and community elders and tap into their knowledge and support;
- identify and establish links between community members and available services;
- share the potential benefits to the community of their participation in the study;
- use culturally relevant terminology and language;
- respect cultural and spiritual traditions, belief systems and intellectual and cultural property rights;
- ensure that participants understand their right to voluntary consent and withdrawal at any time;

- ensure on-going consultation and negotiation with community leaders, gatekeepers and participants to ensure mutual understanding and agreement of the proposed research study design and implementation; share results with both the participants and the community at large; and
- ask permission to use technology (recorders, cameras).

While these recommendations were suggested by organisations for indigenous/Aboriginal communities, they should be applicable to all communities in which researchers conduct research.

Dimensions and development of an Institutional Review Board (IRB) document

Universities typically have established protocols for faculty to follow to ensure that research is implemented ethically. In addition, some communities also have their own prescribed protocols to be addressed. Others, however, may not have established rules for researchers to follow. In these cases, researchers may need to establish a protocol in collaboration with community leaders or other designated community members. The emphasis in this process is on enabling the researcher to gain entry into the community, to protect their interests and to prevent potential harm to both community and individual participants.

There are several typical components of an ethics review or IRB that are advantageous to ensuring informed consent. For example, one should include the purpose of the research project. This is a description of the proposed study and its context, supporting literature, demographics, significance and rationale. An explanation of who will be included as participants and how they will be recruited and selected should be included. The potential risk/benefit ratio for both the community and individual participants should be discussed. Also included should be the actions that will be taken to protect the privacy of the participants (and the community, if applicable) and the confidentiality of the data collected. An unsigned copy of the written consent form should be included, with a separate consent form for adults and for minors (minors may not participate without written parental or custodial consent). These consent forms should include the purpose of the study, what participants can expect to be asked to do, the potential benefits, what potential harm may be incurred as a result of participating, how the data will be handled, stored and accessed, the ways the findings will be used and disseminated, and a statement indicating that participation is completely voluntary and that participants may withdraw at any time. Waived consent should be justified; for instance, a participant requests not to sign the consent form, but she agrees to have her consent to participate and her interview tape-recorded.

Case studies

Below we set out two case studies that illustrate the ways which we have used a community research approach to ensure ethical research in ethnographic studies with Aboriginal peoples.

Case 1

Kawulich

In 1996, my dissertation research with the Muscogee (Creek) women on their perceptions of work began with establishing friendships with key informants as gatekeepers. The first key informant introduced me to the Principal Chief who gave me permission to conduct research and shared names of potential participants to interview. Throughout the study, several community members served as peer reviewers. Results were shared with several community members without identifying the source of the information. They helped me to understand the data from a Muscogee perspective, taking into account the history of their people. This peer review process has continued with our subsequent studies together. Since then, our research has become increasingly collaborative, as I have established a large network of colleagues from various sectors of that culture. Because of the extensive interaction and 'hanging out' I have done with them, trust has been established. I cite below several examples of community partnership in research.

In one instance, two council women discussed with me some legislation they wanted the council to consider; I commented that they were showing me how Muscogee women lead. We discussed the roles of Muscogee women in past and present culture. They encouraged me to study the issue. After I obtained university IRB approval, I went to the Principal Chief to seek his permission and contacted the women as starting points for sampling. Through purposeful and snowball sampling, I was referred to women who held leadership positions throughout the culture. At one tribal council meeting I met with other female council members who invited me to hold a focus group with them. After I coded and analysed the interviews, community members served as peer reviewers to verify my interpretations. Findings were shared with various community members for corroboration and clarification. Several times, community elders who were not directly involved in the studies asked me to explain to them what we were doing and what we found; their concerns with knowing what was being written about them were addressed. When they have shown interest in the research, I typically have invited them to participate as interviewers, asked for their input on sample selection or otherwise invited them to participate. Such invitations are sometimes met with a simple nod of approval or with comments for improving the study. Their trust in me as a colleague, friend and researcher was further illustrated, when they asked me to teach them how to conduct oral histories. Together, we developed a protocol for data collection and maintenance, which their tribal members have implemented.

More recently, I visited Muscogee Nation's Veterans' Office, where a community member and I noticed that the contributions of women veterans had been omitted. Muscogee citizens, including representatives of the Veterans' Office, collaborated with me to develop the protocol, interview and record the stories of several women veterans whose stories would otherwise have been lost. Raw data from the interviews were shared with the Veterans' Office. Our intent is to put together clips from these interviews into a video in conjunction with other community members to help the Veterans' Office celebrate these women's sacrifices to our country through their military service.

Case 2

Ogletree

A Cherokee family from the Snowbird reservation invited me to study the effects of current educational trends on traditional culture of the Eastern Band of the Cherokee Nation for my dissertation research. I sought the proper tribal protocols for formal permission, but no Institutional Review Panel or contact person was in place at that time. After some fact finding, I found that seeking formal permission was not typical for researchers, because the process was not clearly established. Striving to be an ethical researcher, I felt uncomfortable with this common practice and wished instead to establish a collaborative partnership for my study. Over the next two years, I gained entry into the community, visiting on a regular basis without conducting formal research. As a result, I was contacted by the director of the newly-formed EBCN Institutional Review Board, who indicated that they wanted to create a standardised IRB document. The director, community members and I collaborated to develop an ethics protocol to facilitate future research approvals. My research was the first to be processed through the new committee. Two months later, the Tribal Council gave their approval for me to conduct my research and thanked me for the ethical stance I took on this issue. Our collaboration provided a catalyst for change within the system. After gaining the tribal council's permission, a formal gatekeeper was assigned to me as a community liaison officer to assist me in conducting the research within their cultural mores. Because of his involvement, I was able to establish solid relationships with community members and was given access to areas normally forbidden to researchers.

After transcribing the interviews, I sent transcripts to participants for review. Community participants served as peer reviewers, providing feedback on drafts and instructing me about what information should be shared with the public. While I conducted the actual interviews, community members serving in tribal administration collaborated on the research design and served as gatekeepers and key informants to open doors and ensure correct interpretations from a Cherokee perspective. This shared power facilitated stakeholders' active involvement in this research study on current trends in education and its impact on cultural preservation and tradition. As a direct result, they developed plans for a new school to emphasise language and cultural preservation. Through this collaborative approach, change occurred. Although it was difficult waiting for two years to begin formal research, the outcome of community involvement and collaboration was one in which we all benefited.

Key learning

The two cases illustrate the importance of gaining community permissions, both collectively and individually and the importance of shared power in the research process. Conducting ethical research in communities involves going beyond doing no harm and focuses on the establishment of an ongoing relationship with the community that engages them as an integral part of the research process. Research should be perceived by the community as beneficial and respectful of persons, cultural mores and oral traditions. It should be designed, implemented and interpreted collaboratively with the community members. Of equal importance is the fact that research should be approved by both community and university (if appropriate) ethics boards and by individual community members and include full disclosure of potential benefits and risks. Proper consent of all involved participants should be obtained. Ultimately, community research is a collaborative effort. In some instances, without their help, the researcher would not be able to access the participants. Community members assist in designing and implementing the research in a culturally appropriate way, and their participation assists researchers to conduct research that is of benefit to the community. Having community members collect the data encourages participants to share their feelings and emotions more than they would with an outsider. Having a thorough knowledge of the culture, community members may be able to ask specific questions about occurrences that are unfamiliar to others. Besides giving a voice to the participants, community research enables them to give back to their community in their own voice and language and empowers them as co-researchers to continue their research efforts beyond one study. Co-researching with community members facilitates a reciprocal learning process through which researchers are educated about community issues and cultural traditions, while community members are empowered to continue to conduct research in their own communities beyond the life of the research project.

Summary

Advantages of ethical community research

- Collaboration facilitates obtaining appropriate permissions.
- Community members feel included and may want to participate again.
- Collaboration makes (emic and etic) interpretation easier.
- Participant observation and collaboration facilitate a growing network of co-researchers.
- The community researcher has many cultural teachers willing to share their knowledge.
- A sense of shared power is established.
- Research is more apt to be of benefit to the community.

Limitations of ethical community research

- Sometimes gaining permission is time-consuming and difficult.
- Confidentiality and anonymity are difficult to ensure.
- Different people may construe data differently, based on cultural referents.
- Spending time in the community in order to establish rapport and learn the culture takes time.
- The community researcher must be careful about becoming embroiled in factionalism or taking sides on community issues.
- The community researcher does not plan for a quick entrance and exit: this is a long-term commitment.

Conclusion

Ethics Review Boards provide a beginning point for ensuring that research is ethical. Consideration for additional ethical principles discussed herein, such as respect, collaboration and reciprocity, is an important step in the implementation of research that produces quality results based on depth, rather than breadth. These results yield in-depth information that more fully explains various phenomena, particularly when researchers have community members as co-researchers. Gaining participation and involving community members in every aspect of the research process takes time, but provides more accurate data and interpretation than can be produced by a single researcher. Community members understand their own community better than outsiders, and they know which participants can inform the study, or which historical information is helpful to our understanding of the topic but can be misrepresentative. Oral histories, for example, particularly when conducted in conjunction with community members, facilitate sharing of information between and among researchers and community members. Collaborative research cements relationships and facilitates research that is beneficial and empowering. Consideration for ethical dimensions is integral to conducting quality research and requires collaboration between researchers and community members at every stage of the research process. When community members are involved in the research process, they are encouraged to think about how to solve community problems systematically, and their involvement in the process enhances implementation of ethical research. As a result of the shared findings, the impetus for change is initiated.

Discussion questions

1. To what extent do you think there are special ethical considerations when working with ethnic communities?
2. What ethical considerations do you think are most important for community research?
3. If you were planning a community research project, what are the key factors you would need to consider in order to conduct it ethically?

References

Aboriginal Healing Foundation (AHF) (2000) *Ethics Guidelines for Aboriginal Communities Doing Healing Work*, Ottowa: AHF, www.ahf.ca/downloads/ethics-guide.pdf

Ambler, M. (1995) 'History in the First Person: Always Valued in the Native World, Oral History Gains Respect among Western Scholars', *Tribal College*, 6(4): 8-14.

American Indian Law Center, Inc. (1999) *Model Tribal Research Code*, New Mexico: American Indian Law Centre.

Australian Institute of Aboriginal and Torres Strait Islander Series (2011) Guidelines for Ethical Research in Indigenous Studies, Australia: Australian Institute, www.aiatsis.gov.au/research/docs/ethics.pdf

Berg, B. L. (2001) *Qualitative Research Methods for the Social Sciences* (4th edn), Boston: Allyn and Bacon.

Bernard, H. R. (1994) *Research Methods in Anthropology: Qualitative and Quantitative Approaches* (2nd edn), Walnut Creek, CA: AltaMira Press.

Burkansstipanov, L., Christopher, S. and Schumacher, Sr. A. (November, 2005) 'Lessons Learned from Community-based Participatory Research in Indian Country', *Cancer, Culture and Literacy* Supplement to *Cancer Control*, 70-76, http://hlmcc.org/CCJRoot/v12s5/pdf/70.pdf

Caballero, B. (2002) 'Ethical Issues for Collaborative Research in Developing Countries', *American Journal of Clinical Nutrition*, 76(4): 771-720.

Castellano, M. B. (2004) 'Ethics of Aboriginal Research', *Journal of Aboriginal Health*, 1(1): 98-114.

Christians, C. G. (2000) 'Ethics and Politics in Qualitative Research', in N. K. Denzin and Y. S. Lincoln (eds) *Handbook of Qualitative Research* (2nd edn), Thousand Oaks, CA: Sage Publications, 133-155.

Fischer, M. M. J. (2001) 'In the Science Zone: The Yanomami and the Fight for Representation (part 3)', *Anthropology Today*, 17(5): 16-19.

Fixico, D. L. (1996) 'Ethics and Responsibilities in Writing American Indian History', *American Indian Quarterly*, Special Issue: Writing about American Indians, 20(1): 29-39.

Fixico, D. L. (1998) 'Ethics and Responsibilities in Writing American Indian History', in D. A. Mihesuah (ed) *Natives and Academics: Researching and Writing about American Indians*, Lincoln, Nebraska: University of Nebraska Press, 84-99.

Franzblau, M. J. (1995) 'Ethical Values in Health Care in 1995: Lessons from the Nazi Period', *Journal of the Medical Association of Georgia*, 84(4): 161-164.

Hansen, S. A. and Van Fleet, J. (2003) *Traditional Knowledge and Intellectual Property: A Handbook on Issues and Options for Traditional Knowledge Holders*, Washington: American Association for the Advancement of Science, http://shr.aaas.org/tek/handbook/.

Howell, L. (1999) '*Nazi Medical Experiments: Murder or Research?*' http://holocaust.hklaw.com/essays/1999/993.htm.

Kawulich, B. B. (1998) *Muscogee (Creek) Women's Perceptions of Work*, Unpublished dissertation, Atlanta, GA: Georgia State University, AAT 9903268.

Kawulich, B. B. (2005) 'Participant Observation as a Data Collection Method', *Forum Qualitative Sozialforschung / Forum: Qualitative Social Research*, 6(2), Art. 43, http://nbnresolving.de/urn:nbn:de:0114-fqs0502430.

Kawulich, B. B. (2008) 'Giving Back to the Community Through Leadership', *Advancing Women in Leadership*, 28(1), http://advancingwomen.com/awl/awl_wordpress/

Kawulich, B. B. (2010) 'Gatekeeping: An Ongoing Adventure in Research', *Field Methods*, 22(4): 1-20.

Kievit, J. A. (2003) 'A Discussion of Scholarly Responsibilities to Indigenous Communities', *American Indian Quarterly*, 27(1&2): 3-45.

Kutsche, P. (1998) *Field Ethnography: A Manual for Doing Cultural Anthropology*, Upper Saddle River, NJ: Prentice Hall.

Lawrence, J. (2000) 'The Indian Health Service and the Sterilization of American Indian Women', *American Indian Quarterly*, 24(3): 400-419.

Marshall, A. and Batten, S. (2004) 'Researching Across Cultures: Issues of Ethics and Power', *Forum Qualitative Sozialforschung [Forum: Qualitative Social Research]*, 5(3): Art. 39, www.qualitative-research.net/fqs-texte/3-04/04-3-39-e.htm

Mihesuah, D.A. (2003) *Indigenous American Women: Decolonization, Empowerment, Activism (Contemporary Indigenous Issues)*, Lincoln, Nebraska: University of Nebraska Press.

Mihesuah, D.A. (2005) *So You Want to Write about American Indians? A Guide for Writers, Students, and Scholars*, Lincoln, Nebraska: University of Nebraska Press.

Murphy, E. and Dingwall, R. (2002) 'The Ethics of Ethnography', in P. Atkinson, A. Coffey, S. Delamont, J. Lofland and L. Lofland (eds) *The Handbook of Ethnography*, Thousand Oaks, CA: Sage Publications, 339-351.

Quigley, D. (2006) 'A Review of Improved Ethical Practices in Environmental and Public Health Research: Case Examples from Native Communities', *Health, Education, and Behaviour*, 33(2): 130-147.

Sharp, R.R. and Foster, M.W. (2002) 'Community Involvement in the Ethical Review of Genetic Research: Lessons from American Indian and Alaska Native Populations', *Environmental Health Perspectives*, 110(2): 145-148.

Smith, A. (2005) *Conquest: Sexual Violence and American Indian Genocide*, Cambridge, MA: South End Press.

Smith, L.T. (1999) *Decolonizing Methodologies: Research and Indigenous Peoples*, London: Zed Books.

Smylie, J. (2005) 'The Ethics of Research involving Canada's Aboriginal Populations', *Canadian Medical Association Journal*, 172(8): 977.

Wax, R. (1971) *Doing Fieldwork: Warnings and Advice*, Chicago: University of Chicago Press.

Fourteen

Avoiding 'best' being the enemy of 'good': using peer interviewer methods for community research in place-based settings in Australia

Deborah Warr, Rosemary Mann and Richard Williams

Chapter aims

- To consider the methodological issues in using peer interviewer methods in the complex settings of place-based research.
- To consider how community contexts are important for understanding the challenges and achievements of peer interviewer methods.
- To present peer interviewers' perspectives on the benefits and challenges of the method.
- To reflect on associated ethical concerns.
- To demonstrate the benefits of promoting participatory processes even while community control across all stages of research may not be possible or desirable.

Introduction: peer interviewing as community research

In this chapter we consider the implications of community research in neighbourhood contexts of socio-economic disadvantage and examine the challenges these contexts present in achieving the ideals of community research approaches. Specifically, we discuss an initiative that used peer interviewer methods to conduct local community surveys with neighbourhood residents. We will argue that, while it can be difficult to achieve community research 'best' practice in these contexts, methods that promote collaboration and participation can still have 'good', if incomplete, outcomes for communities.

The neighbourhoods under consideration are part of the state government's 'Neighbourhood Renewal' [NR] initiative that targets the most disadvantaged areas in Victoria, Australia. A total of 22 NR projects have been implemented in urban and regional localities, each with a funding commitment of eight years (Klein, 2004; DHS, 2010b). While the local context of each of the NR sites is unique, there are commonalities across programme objectives and evaluation methods. A key plank in the NR evaluation is a standardised questionnaire or community survey (containing both close- and open-ended questions) held biannually in each project area. A team of approximately 25 local residents are recruited and trained as peer interviewers at each NR site to conduct 300 face-to-face interviews with local residents. University-based researchers from a range of Victorian universities work cooperatively with local NR committees (comprising resident representatives, NR personnel and local service providers) to provide training for peer interviewers, guide the data-collection process and analyse the survey data. The findings are returned to the community via local governance committees in the form of comprehensive community reports where they are used to identify residents' priorities for action and to evaluate the progress and impact of the projects (see DHS, 2006, 2010a for more detail of evaluation methodology).

The peer interviewer method involves an adaptation of a technique known as Privileged Access Interviewers (PAI) that enhances the reliability and validity of data collected (Griffiths et al, 1993; Kuebler and Hausser, 1997). PAI methods stress the importance of recruiting peer interviewers who share certain pre-determined sample characteristics but who also represent diverging characteristics that provide access into milieus within populations and communities. In the NR setting, local peer interviewers are recruited from a range of backgrounds to reflect the social, cultural and linguistic diversity in the community. Interviewers, in turn, recruit local residents through their own networks to complete the survey as well as using more standard recruitment strategies (for example, survey promotion via public notices, fliers, newsletters and letterbox-drops). University-based researchers provide peer interviewers with 12 hours of research training in workshops that cover general theoretical aspects of survey design as well as ethical and practical considerations. Peer interviewers are paid for their attendance at the training workshops and for each community survey completed. Resident-interviewees are also financially reimbursed for their participation.

Clearly, aspects of the peer interviewer method employed in NR settings fall well short of the ideals for community-controlled research – the survey is a standardised and highly structured instrument that allows only minimal modification to the set questions; it is implemented locally but is devised, regulated and scheduled centrally; and research 'participatory' roles are confined to data-collection. As other authors have argued in this volume and elsewhere, the hallmark of community research is an insistence on a cooperative approach that engages community members and researchers in a joint process in which both contribute equally (Wallerstein and Duran, 2003; Cameron and Gibson, 2005; Cameron and Grant-Smith, 2005).

Community research can also be embedded in social action paradigms where research is conceived as a catalyst for broader social change, transformation or redistribution of resources (Freire, 1993; Pyett, 2002). Such attributes may well be key indicators of community research 'best' practice. Applied to NR projects, such a conceptualisation would see residents with opportunities for a wider engagement across all the stages of research, including formulation of its aims, the development of research and evaluation questions and involvement in data analysis and research translation activities. However, while not best practice, we argue that the limited or partial involvement of peer interviewers in the NR initiative remains good practice and a valuable community research method that fosters benefits for peer interviewers and the community more widely. In contexts of place-based socio-economic disadvantage, such as NR settings, partial as well as 'best' community research approaches can be used to identify local issues and opportunities, build community capacities, facilitate active roles for community members in the co-creation of knowledge and, more pragmatically, enable access to 'hard-to-reach' and marginalised populations. In this chapter, we discuss the benefits and challenges that were generated through the NR peer interviewer method. However, because community research obliges researchers to interrogate the concept of community, particularly how it is best defined and conceptualised, we need to tease out the complexities and precarious qualities of 'community' specifically in relation to poor neighbourhoods. We begin our discussion by considering how the contexts of place-based socio-economic disadvantage are critical to understanding both the positive outcomes generated and the limitations such contexts impose for realising greater levels of community engagement in, and control over, research processes.

Theoretical discussion: the (im)possibility of community?

In place-based research, notions of 'community' are complex and often contradictory. Neighbourhoods can be both physical and social environments, dynamic and changing with many different qualities, comprising multiple and overlapping experiences forged through a shared sense of place, ethnicity or other circumstances. Anderson (1960: 26), for example, suggests that community 'has the quality of duration, representing an accumulation of group experiences which comes out of the past and extends through time, even though the individuals making up that community are forever coming and going'. However, more recently the idea of community has become less discernible. Walters and Rosenblatt (2008) and others have explored shifts in ideals for community in suburban living in which people prefer to live among others who are perceived to be similar to themselves while seeking a good life with one's family, not with one's neighbours (Lupi and Musterd,

2006). They suggest a 'hands off' experience of community, a 'co-presence' rather than a social environment arising out of participatory and cooperative interaction (Walters and Rosenblatt, 2008). Here, as Savage et al (2005) point to in their notion of 'elective belonging', community is a subjective experience that can be actively pursued or avoided. In neighbourhoods where geographic proximity may not entail a shared sense of community the various ways in which 'community' is conceptualised and deployed can be especially vexed. Housing tenure, ethnicity, economic and personal situations can serve to emphasise the differences between residents over their common interests (Atkinson and Kintrea 2004; Warr 2005).

While neighbourhoods are often referred to as 'communities', whether or not residents actually experience a shared sense of connectedness, in socio-economically disadvantaged neighbourhoods intense experiences of community can coexist alongside high levels of social isolation. As Warr (2005, 2006) and others suggest, generalised experiences of social exclusion from wider forms of social participation can promote high dependence on local networks of family and friends (Cattell, 2001; Lupton, 2003; MacDonald et al, 2005). At the same time, such dependence can strain local social relations and leave people vulnerable to social isolation if relationships break down (Warr, 2008). In response residents can practice forms of 'boundary maintenance' for self-protection, deliberately avoiding local involvement such as expectations to provide material and social support or managing inconsiderate or difficult neighbours because of the risks perceived to be entailed (Campbell and Gillies, 2001; Warr, 2005).

Research has also highlighted the increasing socio-economic-spatial divisions between neighbourhoods and, consequently, the diminishing social connections between people living in settings of place-based disadvantage and those living in higher socio-economic localities (Massey, 1996; McDonald, 1999; Wacquant, 1999, 2008; Atkinson and Kintrea, 2001; Graham and Marvin, 2001; Onyx and Bullen, 2001; Lash, 2002; Lupton, 2003; MacDonald et al, 2005;). Such scissions are linked to the socially and spatially fragmenting effects of globalisation and, in particular, to technological and infrastructure developments that enhance the capacities of the middle class to exercise strategies of disaffiliation from the poor (Burrows and Ellison, 2004; Atkinson, 2006). Madanipour (1998), for example, refers to the 'spatiality of social exclusion' that results in fewer opportunities for everyday cross-class interactions that promote insight into other lives and foster awareness of commonalities. As a consequence poor neighbourhoods are highly vulnerable to stigmatisation through what Wacquant (1999: 1644) refers to as 'discourses of demonisation' where misleading images of fact and hyperbole serve to emphasise the negative aspects of neighbourhoods (see also Warr, 2007).

Yet there is a further complexity to be considered here. Poor neighbourhoods are more heterogeneous than is often assumed because the category 'socio-economic disadvantage' increasingly references a wide range of social and economic circumstances such as involvement in low or unskilled occupations, unemployment, sole parenting, migration, disability and so forth (Massey, 1996; Wacquant, 1999). These issues – the diversity of circumstances among households living in neighbourhoods classified as disadvantaged and the heightened vulnerability to stigmatization – combine to form what Wacquant (2008) conceptualises as 'de-solidarising' effects in poor neighbourhoods. These effects weaken communal bonds and corrode possibilities for local solidarity and collective action. They arise through the strains on local social relations and through processes where residents absorb stigmatising images and interpret their own and others' situations as arising through personal deficits and fecklessness. In turn, this elicits strategies that tend to collude with the stigmatising images rather than challenging them. Such strategies can include displacing problems onto problematic – more vulnerable – others (for example, recent migrants or public housing tenants); local distancing strategies applied to immediate neighbours or within neighbourhoods; or coming to believe that moving out, rather than local action, is the only viable option for improving the situation. For Wacquant (2008: 184), the socially fragmenting effects that are linked to contemporary conditions of place-based poverty, and the destructive implications of place-based stigma for neighbourhoods and their residents, generates 'impossible communit[ies]' with diminished potential to recognise shared concerns or to collectivise for social action. Although, as Wacquant (1999) also notes, an important point is that such demonisation is frequently contradicted by the residents of disadvantaged neighbourhoods, many of whom express high levels of satisfaction with their neighbourhoods (Lupton, 2003; Warr, 2005; Palmer et al, 2004).

In summary, the notion of 'community' cannot be taken for granted. How the concept is theorised and understood is critical to community research approaches particularly in relation to place-based communities of socio-economic disadvantage. The strains within poor neighbourhoods and the increasing disconnections between neighbourhoods are critical to understanding the tensions, complexities and contradictions of neighbourhood communities. In place-based community research the social, cultural, economic, ethnic (and other) cleavages between residents can hinder participatory and collaborative research processes. Invariably there will be challenges in terms of reconciling the local contexts of place-based research and the aspirations of community research 'best' practice. At the same time, the potential of participatory research to build cooperative networks between residents, to highlight structural issues and to have empowering effects provides a strong incentive to find ways though the tensions that are presented (Warr, 2005; Warr et al, 2011). In the following section we look specifically at peer interviewing and its potential as a community research method. We draw on findings from a qualitative research study that explored NR peer interviewers' perceptions of the personal and local impacts of the method.

Community research in practice: peer interviewing in the neighbourhood

The data we discuss in this section were collected in semi-structured interviews with peer interviewers from six different NR sites. They represented a range of place-based settings (metropolitan and regional) and university-based research partners. All peer interviewers in the study sites were provided with information about the study and were invited to contact the researchers if they were interested in participating in an interview (see Warr et al, 2011, for further information on the method and sample for the study). Thirty peer interviewers were then interviewed by one of the authors (RM): 22 women and eight men, Australian and overseas born, across all ages and a variety of household circumstances.

The benefits and advantages of peer interviewing

While one of the benefits of the method (using PAI techniques) is that it encourages peer interviewers to tap into their own local social networks, many of the NR interviewers reported that they also engaged with people whom they did not previously know. The engagement promoted new local networks with many bridging ethnic and other differences. Peer interviewers' accounts of their involvement suggested that the method contributed to building bridging links between residents across culture, tenure and other circumstances – differences that might otherwise have been sites of fragmentation within neighbourhoods. A important point to note is that NR community workers were often critical in encouraging the participation of some peer interviewers, particularly those who had left school early or who were concerned they lacked adequate English-language skills (interviewers needed to be able to speak and write in English). A number of interviewers from migrant backgrounds reported feelings of isolation, of loneliness in the neighbourhood. Shanta, for example, from the Indian subcontinent who had being living in Australia for three years, described her initial trepidations:

'So the first day [of research training] I am scared. I can't concentrate, you know I'm sitting in the room but I'm think, okay, I can't do this ... When I went home I read the [survey] paper three or four times and I practised some questions about that. I practised with my children. My daughter told me, "Mum, you must change your voice, you must read like this, you must ask like this," so my daughter guided me. The second day [of the training] I'm nervous but I have confidence. Okay, I can do this one because, in my group, a few people are speaking English the same like me, so I can easily understand they are saying [...] I did 19 interviews, most of the interview were with Chinese people, especially Mandarin people.'

For Hansa, as for Shanta, her social network expanded through her interviewer role: "It does make me more friends ... they greet me going to their places and they know me and they just say 'Hi, are you going shopping?' and things like that. Before, they won't even talk to anyone or me."

Such a friendly greeting, as Shanta suggested, "is not a very big conversation" but it points to the ways in which the peer interviewer method had positive personal impacts. It initiated conversations between residents that, in turn, contributed to the building of local community connections, including cross-cultural connections. Peer interviewing encouraged the establishment of new local networks and enhanced a sense of neighbourliness and, perhaps, community:

'It makes the whole neighbourhood a hell of a lot better place to live in, because people get to know each other, and then from knowing that person you get to know some of their friends. I didn't know a couple that lived two doors down on the other side, and I've got to know them now, and they're good friends.' (Jack)

Lynne reflected on the opportunity of meeting residents across contrasting socio-economic circumstances, realising their shared enthusiasm for the neighbourhood:

'You have the other side where people are earning a good dollar, you know, are paying off a mortgage or own their home, but they'd only been here for a few years, and just love the area, just passionate about wanting it to grow and that was incredible [...] Yeah most of them were just, I was in shock that, from all different backgrounds, how passionate they were about the area. I mean it really made me feel good.' (Lynne)

The peer interviewer method represented important opportunities for new bridging links to emerge that could feasibly enhance a sense of place and community in the neighbourhoods. Other interviewers explained how their research conversations prompted new insights into other residents' situations and the neighbourhood more generally. Anna's reflections were interesting because she had only recently moved into her neighbourhood. She described how the insights she gathered as a peer interviewer served to challenge the negative stereotypes she held towards the neighbourhood:

'I guess I slightly had the stereotype that everyone has [...] I thought it's not that good an area, pretty much in my mind, and I didn't get the connection, I didn't get the community connection. Yet, like I'd met a lot of people, residents, and they were very nice people, but as a whole community? Then, when I started talking to all these different people I realized that they're quite happy, they're quite happy here, they're quite content people. They've lived here all their life, a lot of the families, and generations have grown up here all their lives and they have a lot of pride [...] I got to hear from their mouths what they like. I got to see a bit of their personality, which helps you know. I got to see what they really think and what they feel, what they're proud about and what they're not proud about and they're just like everybody else. They don't like walking along the street and seeing a lawn unmowed. They're just like a lot of other people, they're just the same as everybody else, you know. They whinge about speeding cars and wanting speed humps and all this sort of stuff. So yeah, they're just the same as everybody else. That's what I got, you know.' (Anna)

Peer interviewers identified benefits for the community that were linked to the ways in which the method encouraged recruitment and local engagement, demonstrated the value of local knowledge and promoted local action:

'I think they [residents] responded to me more because they know that I live in this area and I see it, I hear it, I feel it every day [...] so it was like we were on the same level. You weren't from the outside so you knew what they were talking about.' (Ruth)

'I made sure that they knew that I was obviously local. I think that was a good tool to start the interview because, you know, if you're from somewhere else people perhaps might not trust you.' (Riccardo)

'People had no idea what the area's got. So we would talk for an hour on just me letting them know that, "Yeah, you have got this and you have got that." They just didn't know because they don't know many people [...] Well, a couple of people said that there should be more education, like adult education, and [in the building] where were surveying, you could see the [adult education] sign and I said, "You just go down there." So it was heaps of things, it was about buses, you know, it was telling people, "Yeah, you can get the bus to that place." A lot of people obviously just keep to themselves, you know, or haven't had the chance to meet anyone, which is really sad.' (Lynne)

Our focus in this section has been the wider community benefits facilitated through the peer interviewer method. However, peer interviewers also consistently reported a range of positive personal outcomes and direct practical benefits for the NR survey process itself. In addition to the opportunities to engage with neighbours and others living in the neighbourhood, peer interviewers noted increased confidence and self-esteem as well as training and employment related skill development:

'Over the last six months I've taken medication and [my mental health] improved a lot. I think being involved with this helped me a lot too. Because, you know, there were things I kind of had to go to. There were days when I was on a down, you know, because it will last a week usually, but it sort of made me. Prior to that I didn't want to see a psychiatrist and stuff but doing this has kind of made me re-explore my life a little bit and it's been a very positive thing for me and family, too.' (Riccardo)

'I did get a fair bit out of it [being a peer interviewer]. I don't know if you've been in this position, but, you know how your confidence goes down? Well that brought it up, that brought it up.' (Shirley)

'At the end of it we were being trained in a little of something … When you haven't got any qualifications at all and you've got an opportunity to be trained in something, even if it's small, it looks good on a résumé. It's stepping stones.' (Peggy)

The peer interviewer method also enhanced recruitment, the reach of the survey into the community and the quality of the data that were collected. Peer interviewers as residents encouraged 'honest' responses. Being interviewed by a local person, as Phillip noted, "tends to make the interviewee more a part of it, being interviewed with, not being interviewed at, do you know what I mean?" Peer interviewers' knowledge and understandings of the local community also assisted in the administration of the survey, as Sarah identified:

'I know the questions were very governmentish because that's one of my things, where I keep saying to Neighbourhood Renewal, put it in English ... You're talking like government people ... bring it down to the level ... This time we could roughly change it, if people got stuck. Basically they'd be the same, similar questions, but just worded differently.' (Sarah)

In these place-based settings, the peer interviewer method extended key benefits to individual interviewers, the neighbourhood community and the data collection process itself. Invariably, peer interviewers reported that they 'enjoyed' the role and strongly supported the peer interviewing strategy. However, peer interviewers also highlighted a number of difficulties associated with the method. The following section examines these challenges in more detail.

The challenges and uncertainties of peer interviewing

For many peer interviewers unfamiliarity with the expectations and procedures of research presented initial challenges. With few exceptions, peer interviewers had little previous research or interviewing experience and, not surprisingly, many expressed nervousness and anxiety concerning the role. However, interview practice and increasing familiarity with the survey form quickly overcame these initial hesitations. Many also noted that technical aspects of the survey instrument itself, as well as features of the local organisation and administration, had proved challenging. For example, frustrations with the length and complexity of the survey with its 'governmentish' language, difficulties capturing and recording open-ended responses, and concerns with time-management in keeping the interview 'on track' were all highlighted. Peer interviewers also pointed to the importance of appropriate peer interviewer selection, provision of adequate training and equitable management in survey allocation.

However, more significant challenges identified by peer interviewers largely related to the key benefits noted previously, namely, managing issues raised by the proximity between interviewers and resident-interviewees. We focus on these concerns in this section, in part because of a number of important ethical issues they raise for both interviewers and university researchers. For many peer interviewers being a 'local' was clearly a double-edged sword. Preserving confidentiality in ongoing neighbourhood relationships, maintaining objectivity in the face of disagreeable opinions or offensive language as well as an increased awareness of social isolation and other distressing local circumstances were all identified as problematic.

Peer interviewers pointed to their difficulties responding to negative comments and often intolerant opinions expressed by some residents:

'I mean they could be your neighbour and their opinion could be totally the opposite of yours … I mean you can get on with your neighbour and be fine with them and then once you've surveyed them and know their ideas and what they think, that changes your opinion of that person to what you would know them as normally. That can be a downfall in interviewing someone in your local area.' (Amy)

'I interviewed some people that shocked me in some of their views. I had to really bite my tongue.' (Riccardo)

Peer interviewers also reported a heightened sense of risk associated with their local area after listening to the safety concerns and experiences of other residents.

'I did hear a lot of people say it's not safe, and since I've been doing this I suppose it has opened my eyes to the fact that I shouldn't duck around to my daughter's at midnight, on my own, walking. It tends to get inside you. You tend to think about it now when you walk out the door and I think that's terrible. That's one of the downsides to it. I heard a lot more bad stuff than what I ever imagined.' (Marg)

For others, witnessing the social distress experienced by some residents proved difficult. One interviewer recorded these notes on her survey form:

'This was a difficult interview. First I felt unsure and unsafe; second, the interviewee told me of personal problems and about her alcoholism. In the end, she was getting quite cross that the interview was taking so long. Eventually, I suspended the interview and gave her the $20. She told me she had no food, her son had died and I felt I needed to get her some help but really there was nothing much I could do.'

A significant ethical dimension underpins many of the concerns raised here by peer interviewers – their distress, uncertainty, disquiet over residents' responses, the tensions between interviewers that arose at times when individual reputations were questioned or the integrity of a peer interviewers' practice was challenged (although these often reflected pre-existing local relationships). These are all examples of what Guillemin and Gillam (2004: 262) have called 'ethically important moments … the difficult, often subtle, and usually unpredictable situations that arise in the practice of doing research'. Certainly many of the issues identified by peer interviewers are also common to more orthodox research methodologies, particularly research involving disadvantaged and marginalised populations. However, such ethically important moments have particular significance for community research (Liamputtong and Ezzy, 2005; Guillemin and Heggen, 2009). In conventional research the interviewer, at the completion of the research, leaves the field. However participatory community research engages community members in research practices within their own communities. Peer interviewers, as local community residents, remain in the neighbourhood after the interview process has been completed. As they return to their 'everyday selves' as fellow residents, the movement in and out of their research role required thoughtful and careful navigation. It demands 'ethical mindfulness' (Guillemin and Gillam, 2006). Ethical research practices and principles were important components of the initial training workshops provided for peer interviewers. However, ongoing support and debriefing sessions held throughout the data collection period, involving university researchers, local NR teams and fellow peer interviewers, were critical in assisting peer interviewers to navigate and respond to such ethically important, and everyday, moments.

Key learning

We have identified four key and interrelated factors that underpinned the success of the peer interviewing strategy.

First, the survey form itself was a highly structured instrument of, predominantly, closed questions. While such structure has its limitations, for residents who have little or no experience in conducting interviews it provides a secure platform to build interviewer confidence and skills while, at the same time, maximising confidence in the validity of the data collected.

Second, peer interviewing allowed flexible and partial participation in community research. It allowed interviewers to manage their involvement in ways that accommodated the complexities of everyday lives.

Third, research that encourages participation by often inexperienced community residents demands thorough preparatory training, ongoing support and debriefing sessions that address both the 'technical' aspects of survey and interview methods as well as ethically important moments that may be encountered.

Finally, the peer interviewer method was embedded in an on-going community-based programme. In contrast to other settings where peer interviewing has been used as a methodological research strategy to gain access to 'hard to reach' populations, where participation has been limited to the period of data collection (see for example Elliot et al, 2002; Chui, 2008; Garcia et al, 2008), the NR setting described encourages ongoing participation in the local NR initiative. Here peer interviewing offers the potential for continued community connection and participation (whether partial or wider).

Summary

Advantages of peer interviewer method

For the individual, peer interviewing can build skills, self-esteem and confidence and expand local social connections. At the community level it can build linking and bonding social connections and secure diverse neighbourhood participation. It offers research an effective outreach and recruitment strategy, particularly for marginalised groups, as it increases research validity.

Disadvantages of peer interviewer method

For the individual, potential disadvantages include the management of local relationships and issues of confidentiality, unsettling local perspectives and insights, and lack of familiarity with new research instruments and processes. For the community, issues of confidentiality and the potential for destabilising neighbourhood relations are important considerations. For the management of the research process, the training and ongoing support of peer interviewers is essential and has time and cost implications.

Conclusion

Local contexts of socio-economic disadvantage contribute to varied and sometimes ambivalent experiences of geographic community in neighbourhood settings. These contexts, and the strains that are generated in local social relations, are critical for grasping the opportunities and challenges of peer interviewer methods. Given the significance of local contexts, peer interviewer methods present opportunities for individuals to acquire skills and build confidence; can be used to develop connections within neighbourhoods; and can build bridging links between residents and wider communities. However, careful consideration must also be given to ethical concerns, to the ways in which peer interviewers are able to represent 'community' views and the imperative to minimise the risks of involvement for peer interviewers.

We have argued that the peer interviewer method employed in the Neighbourhood Renewal setting represents only a partial embrace of the participatory potential of community research. As such, it does reduce the possibility for transformative processes of community collaboration and community action that galvanise social change. Yet, while a partial approach does produce a partial engagement, we have demonstrated how such limited participation can be beneficial. As Peggy (peer interviewer) perceptively described, the partial participation of peer interviewing offered a stepping-stone. It is important to remember, however, that it is the wider contexts of disadvantage in which neighbourhoods are embedded that will critically shape where those steps can lead.

Discussion questions

1. What aspects of place-based contexts should be taken into account when developing and designing research involving peer interviewer methods?
2. What steps could University-based researchers take to maximise the potential advantages of peer interviewer methods?
3. What steps could University-based researchers take to minimise the potential disadvantages of peer interviewer methods?

References

Anderson, N. (1960) *The Urban Community: As World Perspective*. London, Routledge and Kegan Paul.

Atkinson, R. (2006) 'Padding the Bunker: Strategies of Middle-Class Disaffiliation and Colonisation in the City', *Urban Studies*, 43: 819-832.

Atkinson, R. and Kintrea, K. (2001) 'Disentangling Area Effects: Evidence from Deprived and Non-deprived Neighbourhoods', *Urban Studies*, 38: 2277-2298.

Atkinson, R. and Kintrea, K. (2004) 'Opportunities and Despair, It's all in There: Practitioner Experiences and Explanations of Area Effects and Life Chances', *Sociology*, 38: 437-455.

Burrows, R. and Ellison, N. (2004) 'Sorting Places Out? Towards a Social Politics of Neighbourhood Informatization', *Information, Communication and Society*, 7: 321-336.

Campbell, C. and Gillies, P. (2001) 'Conceptualising 'Social Capital' for Health Promotion in Small Local Communities: A Micro-Qualitative Study', *Journal of Community and Applied Social Psychology*, 11: 329-346.

Cameron, J. and Gibson, K. (2005) 'Participatory Action Research in a Poststructualist vein'. *Geoforum*, 36: 315–331.

Cameron, J. and Grant-Smith, D. (2005) 'Building Citizens: Participatory Planning Practice and a Transformative Politics of Difference', *Urban Policy and Research*, 23: 21–36.

Cattell, V. (2001) 'Poor People, Poor Places, and Poor Health: The Mediating Role of Social Networks and Social Capital', *Social Science and Medicine*, 52: 1501-1516.

Chui, L.F. (2008) 'Engaging Communities in Health Intervention Research/Practice', *Critical Public Health*, 18: 151–159.

Department of Human Services (DHS) (2006) '*Neighbourhood Renewal Community Survey Guide*', Retrieved 17 September 2008 from www.neighbourhoodrenewal.vic.gov.au/_data/assets/pdf_file/0010/129952/Community-Survey-guide.pdf

Department of Human Services (DHS) (2010a) 'Evaluation Framework 2009', retrieved 22 December 2011 from www.neighbourhoodrenewal.vic.gov. au/publications_and_guidelines/guidelines

Department of Human Services (DHS) (2010b) 'Neighbourhood Renewal', retrieved 22 December 2011 from www.neighbourhoodrenewal.vic.gov. au/home.

Elliot, E., Watson, A.J., and Harries, U. (2002) 'Harnessing Expertise: Involving Peer-interviewers in Qualitative Research with Hard-to-Reach Populations', Health Expectations, 5: 172-178.

Freire, P. (1993) Pedagogy of the Oppressed, New York: Continuum.

Garcia, C.M., Gilchrist, L., Campesino, C., Raymond, N., Naughton, S., and Guerra De Patino, J. (2008) 'Using Community-based Participatory Research to Develop a Bilingual Mental Health Survey for Latinos', Progress in Community Health Partnerships, 2: 105–112

Graham, S. and Marvin, S. (2001) Splintering Urbanism, London: Routledge.

Griffiths, P., Gossop, M., Powis, B. and Strang, J. (1993) 'Researching Hidden Populations of Drug Users by Privileged Access Interviewers: Methodological and Practical Issues', Addiction, 88: 1617-1626.

Guillemin, M. and Gillam, L. (2004) 'Ethics, Reflexivity, and 'Ethically Important Moments' in Research', Qualitative Inquiry, 10: 261-280.

Guillemin, M. and Gillam, L. (2006) Telling Moments: Everyday Ethics in Health Care, Melbourne: IP Communications.

Guillemin, M. and Heggen, K. (2009) 'Rapport and Respect: Negotiating Ethical Relations Between Researcher and Participant', Medicine, Health Care and Philosophy, 12: 291-299.

Klein, H. (2004) Neighbourhood Renewal: Revitalising Disadvantaged Communities in Victoria. Retrieved 12 October 2008 from www. neighbourhoodrenewal.vic.gov.au/__data/assets/pdf_file/0010/129970/ neighbourhood_renewal_revitalising_disadvantaged_communities_in_ victoria.pdf

Kuebler, D. and Hausser, D. (1997) 'The Swiss Hidden Population Study: Practical and Methodological Aspects of Data Collection by Privileged Access Interviewers', Addiction, 92: 325-334.

Lash, S. (2002) Critique of Information, London: Sage.

Liamputtong, P. and Ezzy, D. (2005) Qualitative Research Methods, South Melbourne: Oxford University Press.

Lupi, T. and Musterd, S. (2006) 'The Suburban 'Community Question'', Urban Studies, 43: 801-817.

Lupton, R. (2003) Poverty Street. The Dynamics of Neighbourhood Decline and Renewal, Bristol: The Policy Press.

Macdonald, R., Shildrick, T., Webster, C. and Simpson, D. (2005) 'Growing Up in Poor Neighbourhoods: The Significance of Class and Place in the Extended Transitions of 'Socially Excluded' Young Adults', *Sociology*, 39: 873-891.

Madanipour, A. (1998) 'Social Exclusion and Space', in Madanipour, A., Cars, G. and Allen, J. (eds) *Social Exclusion in European Cities*, London: Jessica Kingsley Publishers.

Massey, D. (1996) 'The Age of Extremes: Concentrated Affluence and Poverty in the Twenty-First Century', *Demography*, 33: 395-412.

Mcdonald, K. (1999) *Struggles for Subjectivity*, Cambridge: Cambridge University Press.

Onyx, J. and Bullen, P. (2001) 'The Different Faces of Social Capital in NSW Australia'. In: Dekker, P. and Uslaner, E. M. (eds) *Social Capital and Participation in Everyday Life*, London: Routledge.

Palmer, C., Ziersch, A., Arthurson, K. and Baum, F. (2004) 'Challenging the Stigma of Public Housing: Preliminary Findings from a Qualitative Study in South Australia', *Urban Policy and Research*, 22: 411-426.

Pyett, P. (2002) 'Working Together to Reduce Health Inequalities: Reflections on a Collaborative Participatory Approach to Health Research'. *Australian and New Zealand Journal of Public Health*, 26: 332–336.

Savage, M., Bagnall, G. and Longhurst, B. (2005) *Globalization and Belonging*, London: Sage.

Wacquant, L. (1999) 'Urban Marginality in the Coming Millennium', *Urban Studies*, 36: 1639-1647.

Wacquant, L. (2008) *Urban Outcasts. A Comparative Sociology of Advanced Marginality*, Cambridge: Polity.

Wallerstein, N. and Duran, B. (2003) 'The Conceptual, Historical, and Practice Roots of Community Based Participatory Research and Related Participatory Traditions', in Minkler, M. and Wallerstein, N. (eds) *Community-Based Participatory Research for Health*, San Francisco: Jossey-Bass.

Walters, P. and Rosenblatt, T. (2008) 'Co-operation or Co-presence? The Comforting Ideal of Community in a Master Planned Estatek', *Urban Policy and Research*, 26: 397-413.

Warr, D. (2005) 'Social Networks in a 'Discredited' Neighbourhood', *Journal of Sociology*, 41: 287-310.

Warr, D. (2006) 'Gender, Class and the Art and Craft of Social Capital', *The Sociological Quarterly*, 47: 497-520.

Warr, D. (2007) 'The Stigma that goes with Living Here: Social-Spatial Vulnerability in Poor Neighbourhoods'. In Mcleod, J. and Allard, A. C. (eds) *Learning from the Margins: Young Women, Social Exclusion and Education*, London: Routledge.

Warr, D. (2008) 'Working on the Ground to Redress Disadvantage: Lessons from a Community-based Preschool Program', *The Australian Community Psychologist*, 20: 22–34.

Warr, D., Mann, R. and Tacticos, T. (2011) 'Suits and Civilians: The Benefits and Challenges of Peer Interviewing for Exploring the Circumstances of Place-based Disadvantage', *International Journal of Social Research Methodology*, 14: 337–352.

Part Three

Managing the research process

Fifteen

Mental health service users and carers as researchers: reflections on a qualitative study of citizens' experiences of compulsory mental health laws in Northern Ireland

Damien Kavanagh, Martin Daly, Moira Harper,
Gavin Davidson and Jim Campbell

Chapter aims

- To summarise key themes from the literature on mental service user and carer involvement in research
- To provide background details of a study into service users and carers' experiences of compulsory mental health law
- To describe and analyse the reflective findings of the researchers who carried out the study
- To use these findings to explore implications for research policy and practice in this field

Introduction

There is an increasing trend in applied mental health research to build partnerships between academics, service users and carers to enhance the design and delivery of studies. This chapter describes a qualitative study in which service users and carers were centrally involved in the collection and analysis of data about the use of compulsory mental health laws in Northern Ireland. It begins with a summary of the arguments for and against service user- and carer-led research in this area. The key part of the chapter contains reflective accounts by the team who carried out the study (one service user, two carers and two academics). The accounts describe and analyse the process and ethical issues encountered during the research, as well as reflection on the personal and emotional effects of engaging with other service users and carers who, like the researchers, have had their lives profoundly affected by the decisions of professionals using statutory functions under mental health law. The chapter concludes with some recommendations on how this research approach could be embedded in other contexts.

Mental health service users and carers as researchers

Although there have been many changes in the way that mental health care has been delivered in the last few decades, concerns remain about the overuse of inpatient care and treatment and compulsory laws. It has been argued, for example that deinstitutionalisation has not necessarily led to better quality community services (Priebe and Turner, 2003; Priebe et al, 2005). Lack of appropriate community care may account for high rates of compulsory admission to psychiatric hospitals in the UK (Care Quality Commission, 2010). In addition, the introduction of new forms of community-based forms of control and coercion (Churchill et al, 2007) imply that many service users and carers are often confronted with the prospect of compulsion in widening social contexts. The views of people who have been subject to detention and their carers may provide crucial information about the use of detention and its potential impact, but these views are under-researched (Department of Health, 1999). Despite the on-going debates about mental health services a systematic review of research literature about the Mental Health Act, 1983, found that 'there is remarkably little known about the outcome of patients who have been detained' (Department of Health, 1999: 20). There is however some evidence to suggest that the process of detention may therefore have important implications for how service users and carers experience and engage with mental health services (Rusius, 1992; Leavey et al, 1997; Bindman and Reid, 1998; Lidz et al, 1995; McKenna et al, 2000).

There is a tendency, as in most of the studies identified above, to view the person who has experienced coercion as the object of study, with the academic as expert researcher. However, in mental health services, service users and carers are increasingly identifying their priorities for research and engaging in leading research themselves (Rose, 2008). Service user involvement in mental health research has been developing over the past 20 to 25 years, and there have been some recent, influential projects that have pioneered this participative approach (Mental Health Foundation 2000; Ramon 2000; Rose 2001). Hanley (2004) has highlighted the empowering nature of this type of research strategy and Faulkner (2004) has identified ways in which any potentially difficult ethical dilemmas can be dealt with appropriately. Nonetheless, it is important to acknowledge that this methodology is at a relatively early, developmental stage when compared to more traditional approaches to research in the field of mental health services (Wallcraft et al, 2009). Beresford (2005) has argued that the theoretical basis for service user involvement is that it helps reduce the distance between experience and interpretation and so may improve the quality and validity of some research. Rose (2008) has also argued that the complex issues and interventions involved in the care and treatment of vulnerable service users necessitates a range of methodological approaches, and that rigorous service user research can produce insights and data that may be crucial to identifying and understanding all of the factors involved. The other proposed benefits of involving service users include developing questions and methods that are grounded in experience; generating new knowledge and understanding; obtaining more open and honest responses from participants; producing more valid analysis and interpretation of results; and increasing opportunities participants to have a role in dissemination (Faulkner, 2004).

Davidson et al (2009) also highlight a range of benefits and have suggested this approach has the potential to improve the quality, relevance and utility of mental health research; it can ensure participants' rights are protected and can enable service users to influence research priorities. Some researchers (Hanley, 2004) have highlighted the empowering nature of this type of research strategy but emphasised the importance of providing appropriate training and support for service user researchers. This investment is important because of the risk that service user researchers may be overly subjective or become over-involved in the process (Rose, 2008). Concerns about potential bias are an issue for all designs and there are a number of features of the proposed approach, particularly the use of joint interviewing and 'blinded' analysis where researchers analyse data from other members of the research team, to help ensure that bias is minimised.

In the study described below, analysis of the researchers' accounts of the research process indicate that issues of risk and duty of care were fairly well managed. There were, however, some concerns that personal histories influenced how responses were understood and analysed. Although the service user and carers recognised the increased knowledge and skills acquired as a result of the process, the academic researchers felt more should have been invested in training and reflection, in preparation for service user and carer colleagues.

Methodology

The research project discussed in the following section used a qualitative methodology to examine the views of mental health service users and carers who had been subject to compulsory mental health laws about their experiences of in-patient detention, in particular three key aspects of the detention journey – initial contact and assessment, detention and discharge. It was influenced by the participatory imperatives described in some of the literature above. The research process involved a partnership between one service user and two carer researchers with extensive experiences of mental health service delivery, and two social work academics with interests in the field of mental health social work. The researchers were recruited through the voluntary sector organisations with whom the service user and carer researchers volunteered. Individual interviews, using mostly open questions, were used to elicit views on compulsory admissions. It was agreed that one service user should interview service users and one carer should interview carers. A third person, a carer, who had good skills in recording responses, would act as 'scribe' in all interviews. This enabled the interviewers to concentrate on the initial and follow-up questions. Interview data were hand recorded by the recorder. The data were then analysed 'blind' by one of the carer researchers and one of the academics to confirm emerging themes.

Ethical issues

The provision of clear information about the study, the absence of coercion to participate and assurance that the researchers were not involved in the person's care helped the researchers to ensure that consent was informed (Davies, 2001). An explanation of how the data was to be anonymised and used was made clear in the information sheet that was shared with participants. This should also have reduced the risk of people answering in biased ways because they thought that what they said would all be reported to the professionals involved in their care or affect their current and future care. Confidentiality was therefore assured, although with the usual restrictions that if significant risks were identified then this information would be discussed with the relevant service provider. Participants were also told they could withdraw at any stage of the interviews. The researchers made themselves available if participants required further information following the completion of the interviews and a summary of the completed work was offered to all participants. There was also support available for both service users and carers in the event that participants became upset or distressed by talking about their experiences (this also applies to the researchers, some of whom, as we describe later, were also affected emotionally by their experience of undertaking the research). Support for participants came in the form of the opportunity to 'debrief' at the conclusion of each interview, with an assurance of regular and consistent follow-up contact with the appropriate and relevant peer-led organisation to which participants ascribe. Colleagues involved in conducting the research supported one another by meeting at regular intervals to offer support and assurances at each phase of the research process; academic colleagues provided insights into the research process in addition to facilitating supportive discussion around the impact of involvement in the project. Interestingly, a core component of peer support centred on colleagues' attendance at two research seminars, facilitating further opportunity for the team to bond socially as well as professionally.

Reflections on the research experience

The following section now focuses on reflections of the researchers, which are presented using the researchers' own words, and is followed by a discussion of the main themes that emerge in these narratives.

Academic researcher 1

It has been a long time since I practised as a mental health social worker. However, I still remember the first assessment I made as an Approved Social Worker (ASW), how nervous I was about the prospect of having the power to detain someone against their will using mental health law. Becoming a university lecturer encouraged me to think, not just about how and why social workers are involved in using such laws, but also the decisions that I, personally, took, that led to the incarceration of my fellow citizens. Since then I have been involved in a number of research projects on the use of mental health law by social workers. This was the first time that I have taken seriously the prospect of a partnership with service users and carers as co-researchers and it has been rewarding as well as thought provoking.

There are three areas of learning that I have acquired during this process. On reflection, I feel I needed to be measured in the way I communicated with my co-researchers. We forget how complex and exclusive research terminology and discourse can be, so it became apparent to me to go more slowly with colleagues and explain what the terminology means – qualitative research, interviews, data, analysis of data, ethics. Once these terms are demystified, the opportunities for learning expanded; suddenly I realised that the co-researchers had such a rich understanding of citizens' experiences of the law, service delivery and professional roles. Then designing the interview schedule became that much easier. A similar process occurred when we examined the findings, the expertise brought by service users and carer colleagues was so revealing and additional to that which could be achieved by an academic-only study. For example, it seemed that they were able to elicit a great deal more of the emotional content of the interview process than I had been able to do in other studies on this topic area. I also confess that I felt perhaps too responsible for things that might go wrong; this might have been an unreasonably risk-averse assumption. In hindsight it seemed that colleagues were much more perceptive to the needs of respondents and what to do if they might become distressed. So there was no need to worry. Finally, the results of the study were predictably disappointing, and pessimistic about the capacity of mental professionals to change their behaviours, even when agency and government rhetoric dictates that they need to be more listening, more thoughtful and to try things differently.

Academic researcher 2

I was excited to be involved in this research because of the focus of the study on experiences of detention, but also because it was my first experience of service user- and carer-led research. As with my academic colleague, before moving from practice to academia in 2008, I'd worked as an ASW and so been involved in the process of people being compulsorily admitted to hospital. This was an aspect of social work that had caused me considerable thought and concern due to the complex ethical, social, political and practice issues involved. I had previously worked on this subject from the perspectives of human rights and professional practice but not from the key perspectives of the service users and carers involved.

I do think in the initial stages of designing the study we academics probably did promote a relatively conventional qualitative, semi-structured interviewing approach to the research. At the time it felt to me that it was helpful to provide views based on some knowledge of research methods and previous studies but in retrospect it would have been a more inclusive and creative process if this had developed through greater discussion and time. I suspect some of my motivation for talking about research methods was more about demonstrating that I could be a useful part of the research team. I had mixed feelings about the data collection process. On the one hand I would have been very keen to be directly involved in the interviews, as I'm very interested in this area of mental health services. On the other hand, the data collection process was a very time-consuming and demanding aspect of study so it was great that other people were doing this work. I'm unsure of the impact that having service user and carer interviewers had on how the people being interviewed responded. It seems very likely that people were more open but this is hard to establish. After feeling to some extent excluded during the interview process it was great to be involved in the analysis and reassuring that our identification of the main themes and interpretation of what the interviewees had said was consistent.

There were two further strong advantages to this approach to the research. The first was that there was a much greater emphasis on the emotional content of what the interviewees were saying than might have been the case if it was an academic-only led study. The second strength overlaps with the first as I think this approach enabled a much clearer prioritising of the issues that were important to highlight and attempt to change. The message that the purpose of asking people about their experiences was to attempt to better inform and improve services was very clearly communicated and this added clarity and direction. It is important, however, to not raise participants' and our own expectations unrealistically about the potential of this research to achieve significant changes in mental health policy, services and practice. On the other hand, this study will directly inform training for the professionals involved in using compulsory powers and may influence the ongoing debates about the proposed changes to the legislative framework in Northern Ireland.

Service user researcher

As someone who has used the mental health services for a number of years and has been detained under mental health law, I have always felt that there was not enough said about people's emotional state when being detained. So when I was asked if I would like to be part of a research group looking at detention I felt that this would be a good project. Our team was made up of two academics, two carers and myself, but when it came to the interviews we would be carrying them out as peers with the academics supporting us. First we made sure that the questions and information were set out clearly so that the interviewees would have a full understanding of what we were hoping to achieve. I personally met with the interviewees weeks and days before the interviews so that they would begin to feel comfortable with the information we would be looking for in the research. Even at that time you could see that this was going to be a very emotional but brave journey for them. We decided that we would do the interviews in pairs. Myself and my interview partner (who recorded the interview in note form) would meet with the interviewee at a time and place where they felt comfortable to speak. Most of them were happy to meet us at a local service user group office. We positioned the seats so that, as I was asking the questions, I would have the full attention of the person I was speaking with. My interview partner was positioned in view of the interviewee, but not intrusively.

I have spoken publically on a number of occasions of my own detention and know that this process had helped me. But I didn't realise how much hearing others speak about their experiences of detention would affect me and also my interview partner during the interviews. At the first interview, after making everyone comfortable with the process, we started with just a short conversation and even then people would say that this was the first time they had spoken openly about how they felt about that day or days (because most of the people we spoken to had been detained on more than one occasion). Our interviews were very open and honest. We took time to let people answer the questions but also to reflect upon them. It was like giving them permission for the first time to say that this was the wrong way to deal with that situation. Some people felt that they needed to go into hospital and others didn't, but most felt that the process was completely wrong. It made them feel frightened, angry and it made them shut down, emotionally. It took away their trust of the service and it put up barriers for their recovery.

As I sit here remembering those interviews and my own story I know exactly what they mean because even when I talk about my own story I know now that what I feel was right but what is missing when I'm speaking in public about these experiences, is that I'm not seeing the physical effect that it has on me as I did with the people interviewed. This is maybe a good thing because the people that I interviewed mirrored the pain that they carried with them. It poured from their whole mannerisms, their eyes filling with tears, the twisting of the mouth, the closing of the eyes when they spoke of certain things, the way they sat and moved on the chair was the release of a build-up of buried emotions and pain. Our mental health departments do not accept that this build-up of pain and emotion was brought on by their actions but portray it as symptoms of the illness. No-one had spoken to these people before these interviews about the traumatic effects of the detention on the day they were brought to hospital which was meant to help them, rather than contribute to an already frightening situation. At the hospital, the staff spoke about illness, diagnosis and neurosis but not one asked the most natural question of how services users felt about being brought into hospital against their will.

For my interview partner and me it was a privilege to be witness to the honesty and the thoughtfulness of the people we spoke with. We were trusted enough by them, not only to listen, but also to give us permission to record their story and use it for this research project, and that it may help others. I feel that this research has helped me also. Every day that I came away from the interviews brought me back to a dark place in my life but I also knew that I would walk out of it. Speaking with some of the people at a later date when they had reflected on their interview day they felt that someone had listened, it had helped them and that it was the right thing to have done. I hope that this research will be a good learning for all mental health professionals, for families and for friends, to know that detaining service users is not the right thing to do without the co-operation of the person they are meant to be helping. It is important that researchers listen, respect and give dignity because when they enter that room you are going into a person's life and not just a diagnosis.

Carer researcher 1

As a peer advocate working with carers and family members of people living with and recovering from serious mental health problems, I initially felt enthusiastic and hopeful at the prospect of my involvement in the conception, design, participation in, analysis, review and presentation of this research project. My initial fervour for participating in the project was associated with my enthusiasm and commitment to address the deficiencies inherent in the mental health system.

After our initial meeting with academic colleagues I became somewhat concerned by my lack of research experience and associated lack of knowledge in relation to core research terms and processes. I began to question the efficacy of the research project as a peer-led one, particularly because the design and delivery of the project was heavily informed by academic and research-led principles which governed our academic colleagues' involvement. I reflected further on this, however, and realised that these principles would facilitate us as carer and user researchers in conducting the peer-led research within a reliable and protective framework. Academic colleagues also provided support through their participation in an advisory and facilitative capacity throughout the project. Clear and concise information about the project was made available to participants a number of weeks in advance, to ensure that they could prepare themselves for contributing to the research. This assisted us in ensuring that participants were aware of the nature and extent to which they could disclose information relating to their experiences.

We had a range of concerns in advance of conducting the fieldwork with the 11 individuals, particularly in relation to the emotional impact that participation might have on those taking part. We remained cognisant throughout the process of tuning in to each interaction, mindful of the potential impact of self-disclosure of as much if not more detail and depth than the period preceding, and during each interviewee's compulsory admission to intensive mental health services. My role was to record responses, and as such my interactions with interviewees were limited. I felt somewhat uncomfortable about being in the same room and recording what each interviewee said in such an open and honest manner, as my body language was directed to my notebook, rather than looking at and listening to each individual.

My service user and carer colleagues, most probably given their heightened capacity to empathise as a result of their own personal experiences, ensured that their approach to each interview was balanced enough to protect themselves and the interviewee, while producing as much detail as possible about each interviewee's experience. We also sought to protect one another by debriefing for a period following each interview; this helped in the sense that it allowed us to make a transition from service user and carer interviewers and researchers to service users and carers. There were undoubtedly occasions when I found the content of responses difficult to cope with. I became frustrated and anxious about interviewees' experiences and also on occasions when I realised that participants found the interview experience cathartic in relation to their overall recovery journey. In this sense I found it challenging to make scientific correlations between responses which were so real in human terms. The key learning point for me, however, was that it was possible for me to incorporate my identity as a carer in a safe and appropriate manner to the role of researcher.

During the analysis phase I became more aware of the existence of a 'research language', which appeared to relate terminology to everyday experiences and processes. I suppose the beginning of the last sentence demonstrates a level of development in this regard; however, I am more acutely aware of the impact of terminology and a scientific research culture as a potential barrier to service user- and carer-led research. I have also reflected on my continued involvement in the project because I have recently become a student social worker. This made me think about my value base and sense of self as a social worker, and how this has been, and will be, affected when working with vulnerable individuals.

My involvement in this research project has also heightened my awareness of practice-based evidence, in the sense that a range of our findings alluded to sporadic pieces of innovative practice which appeared to have a positive effect on the experiences of carers and service users who participated in the project. A major strength of involvement in this study from my perspective has been the strength of our collective and diverse experiences. First, academic colleagues were able to place the findings from the project within a particular frame of reference, given their academic and social work practice experiences. Service user and carer colleagues have brought a particular perspective to our understanding of the findings. It is important we have been able to place them within the context of current professional practice and life experiences. We hope these findings will help to influence the way mental health services are delivered in this area.

Carer researcher 2

My first encounter with mental health issues occurred when my daughter took ill and, having experienced so many problems with the system, I decided to take on the job of peer advocate with a local voluntary sector organisation that advocated for the rights of carers. My hope is to make life more bearable for carers and support as many carers as possible to enable them to get help, the sort of help that, unfortunately is often missing when it comes to mental health services. My belief is that early intervention is key to helping the service user get the correct treatment which is their right. So when I was invited to get involved with the peer research project with carers it was a very interesting and humbling experience. Having worked with carers over a period of time, those who participated in the study seemed happy to be involved. It felt that there was a mutual feeling between me and the carers that there was an importance to the telling of these stories and that it was crucial that other carers would not have to suffer in the same way as others had done. The interviews were arranged to give plenty of time for carers to feel comfortable. Draft information and consent forms were issued at the start of the interview along with tea and coffee. In particular I felt it was very important that I should give my full attention during the interview, and not to take notes as this would be distracting. The questions that were asked were potentially upsetting (carers' experiences of the in-patient detention, how the carer was treated by staff). Confidentiality was ensured and participants were also told that they could withdraw at any stage of the interview.

On reflection I felt that this was the most amazing journey for me as a peer advocate, especially when listening to each carer tell their own story. The comparisons were very similar as to how they felt that staff had dismissed their presence as though they were invisible, this added to a feeling of isolation and resentment. As their only concern was for the welfare of their loved ones I felt that this was unfair. Although I had already engaged with carers at different levels as part of my job, this experience of formally interviewing them for the research project was a huge learning curve, challenging my listening skills. I also realised that, in listening to these stories I began to think about my own experiences and the realisation that there were many emotions that had got buried deep within me. Each carer had their own story and felt very happy to go into every detail, but what was surprising was that this was often the first time that they had been given this opportunity. One carer got quite upset as she had hidden a lot of these thoughts and feelings from professionals, as she put it, "No one wanted to listen." This also struck a chord for me as you are usually given a form by professionals, left and told to 'get on with it'. What was also apparent was that many of the carers also had their own physical problems to deal with. The interviews went on a lot longer than anticipated, which in many ways was good because it allowed time for interviewees to tell their own stories. At the end of each interview my thoughts were that each one of these conversations was very important and I felt a great deal of relief and gratitude. I felt that the carrying out the interviews was difficult and challenging, but they confirmed to me that all humanity has the basic right to be listened to. Being involved in the project has made me even more determined to make everyone hear the voices of users and carers. In conclusion, I am enthusiastic and optimistic that, through ongoing service user and carer involvement in research projects like this one, that the NHS, social care and public health services will acknowledge the need to change their ethos. This type of work can highlight that these important views can be valued and that professionals will understand the knowledge base that develops from such research. A summary of these reflections are captured in Table 15.1.

Table 15.1 Reflections on differing roles relating to a community research team

	Academics	Service user	Carers
Ethics and access	Took a central role in ensuring ethical approval, but less involved in access issues. Were perhaps overly anxious about ethical 'problems' that might occur during the fieldwork process	Were central to gaining access to respondents, and ensuring duty of care during the fieldwork. Were well prepared and took time to ensure ethically sound fieldwork practice	As with service users were central to gaining access to respondents, and ensuring duty of care during the fieldwork. Were well prepared and took time to ensure ethically sound fieldwork practice
Methods	Were probably too directive in deciding choice of method, and review of literature, but shared in the design of questions	Were less concerned about study design, but keen to influence the choice and type of questions	Were less concerned about study design, but keen to influence the choice and type of questions. One carer recognised the need to develop appropriate knowledge about methods to enable further user-led studies to take place
Response to interview findings	Due to past experiences of carrying out research in this area, not surprised at the rather pessimistic findings	Findings tended to confirm personal and practice experiences, but positives about how empowering the study had been for them and respondents	Findings tended to confirm personal and practice experiences, but positives about how empowering the study had been for them and respondents
Analysis	Academics more comfortable with the process of analysing the data	Less certain about involvement and expertise in engaging in the process of analysis of data	Less certain about the process of analysis of data, yet interested in contributing based on personal and practice experiences
Outcomes	Although there was pessimism about the findings there was optimism that this approach to research was valuable and could affect policy and practice	As with academics, pessimistic about findings but optimistic approach could have an impact at policy and practice levels Gained insight into the value of involvement in research and associated strengths and limitations	As with academics and service users, pessimistic about the findings but optimistic that the approach could have an impact at policy and practice levels As with service users, gained insight into the value of involvement in research and associated strengths and limitations

Discussion

A number of important themes emerge from co-researchers' reflections upon the research process. Across the research team there was a common view about the need to explore the impact of detention on the lives of service users and carers, but these were expressed in different ways. For example, both academics were keen to use the project to confirm or deny what they suspected were coercive professional practices sometimes used when mental health law was being applied in these circumstances. On the other hand, service user and carer researchers tended to view the process in terms of increased opportunities for participation and catharsis for respondents. These differing perceptions are understandable given the contrasts between service user, carer and professional identities. It was interesting to note how one of the carers had modified their views as they moved into a professional role as a student social worker.

There were also some noticeable tensions in the way that the constituent groups comprehended the research process. The academics quickly realised there was a need to pace the way they discussed and explained how they felt the project should be designed. The discourse and jargon of research methodologies had to be demystified if the project was to work. It was noticeable, however, that the academics, despite their commitment to partnership, felt 'nervous' about 'letting go' or not being directly involved in the interviews. Service users and carers appeared to be apprehensive for different reasons. Particularly in the early stages, there was an initial sense of powerlessness until they began to grasp and influence the research design and process. Despite these reservations, it is apparent in their reflective accounts that the service user and carers found the process to be empowering and illuminating, both for them and the respondents.

The academics tended to be more concerned about the formal ethical considerations in carrying out the project. For example, they took a lead in ensuring that the processes were endorsed by the university's ethics committee. Because they were not directly involved in interviews they then depended on service user and carer colleagues to ensure that ethical concerns were dealt with appropriately. It is interesting that the interviewers embraced the challenges of engaging with the emotive issues associated with detention and appeared to use their experiences to communicate with respondents. It is noticeable, in their reflections, the degree to which interviews had reawakened powerful memories and emotions in the interviewers. This is a notable, reflexive outcome that we assume would not usually occur in academic-only led research in this field.

Another important theme that emerges in the reflective pieces is the recognition of the complementary knowledge and experiences that each constituency brought to the project. Initial concerns about the complex and technical nature of the research process appeared to reduce once the fieldwork started and the researchers collected and analysed the data. Peer researchers gained confidence in carrying interviews with respondents who shared similar experiences, and the consensus about the findings tended to confirm a sense of expertise across team members.

The key findings from the project were, unfortunately, predictable. They confirmed the worries by the team that the actions of professionals before, during and after detention are very often not sensitive to the rights and needs of services users and carers. Despite this, there is a sense of optimism about the future, but only if mental health services are reconstructed to take account of the views of service users and carers. See the boxed summary of the key advantages and limitations of the approach adopted.

Key learning

In conclusion we wish to draw key learning points from these experiences by highlighting the strengths and weaknesses of this research approach. This chapter describes the processes involved in setting up a research project that examined service users' and carers' experiences of detention by mental health law. A number of important issues emerged from the reflective accounts of academics, service users and carers. Differences in perceptions about the research process were noticeable at the start, but were modified as peer researchers became involved in the fieldwork and analysis of findings. Arguably, the most interesting aspect of the project was the challenging, yet productive, emotional impact of the interviews on the researchers and respondents. This probably enabled otherwise hidden stories about detention to be told. This suggests that peer researchers can play an important role in the research process which can complement conventional, 'academic', approaches. It also reinforces the benefits highlighted in the literature of improving the quality, relevance and utility of research (Faulkner, 2004; Davidson et al, 2009). As with any qualitative small scale study, it is important to be realistic about the potential the research has to achieve significant change. In the case of this project it has had a positive impact on the researchers involved, will inform training for professionals and may affect the development of the new legal framework in Northern Ireland. In doing so it may improve the experiences of mental health service users and carers in their contact with services. It is important to recognise that the core principles of the research process, ensuring that researchers are skilled and that ethical principles are maintained, and need not be compromised when service users and carers are involved.

We accept that there were limitations to the study that need to be borne in mind when using this approach to social research. The 'closeness' of the interviewer to the respondent, in terms of identities and personal experiences implies that there is a need to be careful, if not skeptical, about issues of bias and over-identification (Faulkner, 2004). One way of at least partially dealing with this issue is to invest more in education and training for the role; in our study the academics could only offer introductory support and advice about research methods. In addition, we are conscious that the views of agency staff were either absent or only reported 'second hand' through the lenses of interviewers; ideally a triangulation of service user, carer and professional perspectives might help confirm or deny the findings. We conclude that the academic community should be more willing to engage with service users and carers and that resources need to be found to build this research capacity and thus contribute to a more rounded evidence base for interventions using mental health law.

Summary

Advantages

- The involvement of service users and carers brought a new dimension to the conventional academic approach to research in this field, particularly in terms of skills in communicating with peers.
- There appeared to be a cathartic effect created by the participatory nature of the interviews that empowered interviewers and interviewees.
- Service user and carer researchers became confident about the research process as the project developed.

Limitations

- Not enough time was spent on preparing the researchers for the task, an education and training programme would enhance such studies.
- The academics at times felt overly responsible for the processes.
- There were concerns about the potential for interviewer bias, a more triangulated approach involving interviews with professionals might help capture a more holistic picture of the detention process.

Discussion questions

- If there is a growing interest in service user and carer led research projects, how can the academic community respond to this trend?
- Should there be a balance in terms of academic and service user/carer involvement and responsibilities for these projects?
- What are the educational and training needs of service users and carers and how can these be met?
- Is it possible to develop enough capacity to enable service users and carers to carry out their own research?

References

Beresford, P. (2005) Developing the Theoretical Basis for Service User/Survivor-led Research and Equal Involvement in Research, *Epidemiologia e Psichiatria Sociale*, 14(1): 4–9.

Bindman, J. and Reid, Y. (1998) Patients' Perceptions of Coercion During Hospital Treatment and Community Follow-up, Summary of Preliminary Data, April 1998. Unpublished.

Care Quality Commission (2010) *Essential Standards of Quality and Safety, What Providers Should do to Comply with the Section 20 Regulations of the Health and Social Care Act 2008*, London: Care Quality Commission.

Churchill, R., Owen. G., Singh, S. and Hotopf, M. (2007) *International Experiences of Using Community Treatment Orders*, London: Department of Health, www.dh.gov.uk/en/Publicationsandstatistics/Publications/PublicationsPolicyAndGuidance/DH_072730.

Davidson, L., Ridgway, P., Schmutte, T. and O'Connell, M. (2009) Purposes and Goals of Service User Involvement in Mental Health Research, Chapter 7: 87-98. In Wallcraft, J., Schrank, B. and Amering, M. (eds) (2009) *Handbook of Service User Involvement in Mental Health Research*, Chichester: Wiley-Blackwell.

Davies, T. (2001) Informed Consent in Psychiatric Research, *British Journal of Psychiatry*, 178: 397-398.

Department of Health (DoH) (1999) *A Systematic Review of Research Relating to the Mental Health Act (1983)*, London: Department of Health.

Faulkner, A. (2004) *The Ethics of Survivor Research: Guidelines for the Ethical Conduct of Research Carried Out by Mental Health Service Users and Survivors*, Bristol: Policy Press.

Hanley, B. (2004) *Research as Empowerment? Report of a Series of Seminars Organised by the Toronto Group*, York: Joseph Rowntree Foundation.

Hatfield, B. and Mohamad, H. (1994) Women, Men and the Mental Health Act (1983), *Research, Policy and Planning*, 12(3): 6-10.

Hatfield, B., Huxley, P. and Mohamad, H. (1997) Social Factors and Compulsory Detention of Psychiatric Patients in the U.K. The Role of the Approved Social Worker in the 1983 Mental Health Act, *International Journal of Law and Psychiatry*, 20(3): 389-397.

Leavey, G., King, M., Cole, E., Hoar, A. and Johnson Sabine, E. (1997) First Onset Psychotic Illness: Patients' and Relatives' Satisfaction with Services, *British Journal of Psychiatry*, 170: 53-57.

Lidz, C. W., Hoge, S. K., Gardner, W., Bennett, N. S., Monahan, J., Mulvey, E. P. and Roth, L. H. (1995) Perceived Coercion in Mental Hospital Admission: Pressures and Process, *Archives of General Psychiatry*, 52: 1034-1039.

McKenna, B.G., Simpson, A.I.F. and Coverdale, J.H. (2000) What is the Role of Procedural Justice in Civil Commitment?, *Australian and New Zealand Journal of Psychiatry*, 34: 671–676

Mental Health Foundation (2000) *Strategies for Living*, London: Mental Health Foundation.

Priebe S. and Turner, T. (2003) Reinstitutionalisation in Mental Health Care, *British Medical Journal* 2003, 326: 175–6.

Priebe, S., Badesconyi. A., Fioritti. A., Hansson, L., Kilian, R., Torres-Gonzales, F., Turner, T. and Wiersma, D. (2005) Reinstitutionalisation in Mental Health Care: Comparison Data on Service Provision from Six European Countries, *British Medical Journal* 2005, 330: 123 doi: 10.1136/bmj.38296.611215.AE (published 26 November 2004).

Ramon, S. (2000) Participative Mental Health Research: Users and Professional Researchers Working Together, *Mental Health Care*, 3(7): 224-227.

Rose, D. (2001) *Users' Voices: The Perspectives of Mental Health Service Users on Community and Hospital Based Care*, London: Sainsbury Centre for Mental Health.

Rose, D. (2008) Service User Produced Knowledge, *Journal of Mental Health*, 17(5): 447-451.

Rusius, C.W. (1992) The Mental Health Act: What Does the Patient Think? *Psychiatric Bulletin*, 16(5), 268-269.

Sainsbury Centre (1998) *Acute Problems*, London: Sainsbury Centre for Mental Health.

Wallcraft, J., Schrank, B. and Amering, M. (eds) (2009) *Handbook of Service User Involvement in Mental Health Research*, Chichester: Wiley-Blackwell.

Sixteen

Community organisation and community research: women's struggle for food security in India

Janki Andharia and Neeta Hardikar

Chapter aims

- To examine how research is understood and carried out when conceived as part of a larger feminist organising process with poor and tribal women's struggle for rights and entitlements
- To explore the way research questions were formulated, the extent of power and control that the illiterate women had over the methodology and tools
- To look at the ways data was collected using indigenous methods and tools, and how findings of the research helped consciousness raising and contributed to the national campaign for food security
- To consider the complex relationship between the research process, its conception and the purpose for which it was conducted using indigenous methodologies.

Introduction

Community organisation in India is closely linked with collectivisation and mobilisation process with vulnerable groups. Activists and scholars have often collaborated to bring about a transformation in the material conditions of marginalised groups. This has resulted in community research. Action research and participatory research in India have a long history spanning several decades. They are associated with social transformation processes and human rights activism in developing countries especially in Asia. Several organisations have engaged in community research without labelling it so (see, for example, Brown and Tandon, 1983; SPARC, 1985; PRIA, 1986, 1995, 2000). Proponents of participatory research (Fals and Rahman, 1991; McTaggart, 1997; Hall et al, 1982) argue that conventional social science positivist research, despite its claim to value neutrality, is based on western epistemologies, tends to follow utilitarianism and serve the interests of the wealthy and powerful. Action research deconstructs and decolonises western epistemologies (Denzin et al, 2008) and encourages indigenous methodologies. Indigenous methodology can be defined as research by and for indigenous peoples, using techniques and methods drawn from the traditions and knowledge of those people. It may be combined with emancipatory research which endorses empowerment work, struggle for autonomy, cultural well-being and collective responsibility. Indigenous groups own the research process. It speaks the truth 'about the reality of their lives' (Collins, 1998: 198) and equips them with the tools to resist oppression and moves them to struggle for justice.

This chapter reflects on a feminist research project that was part of a process of understanding food shortages in the state of Gujarat, India. It presents community research conducted by the most vulnerable women from indigenous communities. The context, the process and outcomes of this research are discussed here. The research connects indigenous epistemologies (Rains et al, 2000) with emancipatory discourses (Freire, 1972; Lather; 1986a, 1986b; 1988). It is also located within critical theory and critical pedagogy (McLaren and Kincheloe, 2007) which embody emancipatory and empowering values.

Beginning with a brief overview of progressive community organisation in India, the chapter presents the context of collectivisation around poverty, marginalisation and women's everyday struggle for survival. This forms the backdrop and illuminates the motivation, the process and challenges of this research, conducted largely by women, with very limited literacy skills and formal education. After describing the process, the chapter concludes with the impact and key lessons learnt.

Community organisation and the work of Area Networking and Development Initiatives (ANANDI)

Progressive community organisation (CO) in India is viewed as a political process as it is concerned with power, equity and justice. As a process it encompasses all efforts that seek to redefine power relations which contribute to the experience of discrimination and marginalisation. It includes work with communities, with social structures and with democratic institutions of governance (Curno, 1978; Andharia, 2007). Much of CO practice also creates greater room for manoeuvre (Clay and Schaffer, 1984) for the voiceless, enabling the articulation of their priorities, building on their generalisable interests of livelihood security with dignity and respect. Forging linkages through commonalities of experience, developing people's confidence to negotiate with social and political institutions and practices is fundamental to CO practice.

Since the mid–1990s, progressive academic institutions have focused on critical inquiry into action and research, strategies of advocacy and collective action across sectors (Onyx, 1996). Several scholars in India believe that practice oriented disciplines must accept the complexity of a given social context and must address the lives and struggles of people with whom they work, in more encompassing ways (Andharia 2007; Bhide, 2009; Vyas, 2009). Within academia questioning basic research 'tools' and methodologies, and bringing discourse and practices closer to the daily lives and struggles of people can be a challenge. Recognising that indigenous knowledge is a rich resource for any efforts towards social transformation (Semali and Kincheloe, 1999: 15), many scholars have partnered with grassroots organisations engaged in mobilisation work (Jodhka, 2001; Andharia, 2009).

This chapter builds on one such partnership forged by the department of Urban and Rural Community Development, TISS[1] with ANANDI,[2] an activist organisation working in the rural and tribal areas of Gujarat, India. ANANDI was founded in 1995 by five women with experience in the development sector. It works with the most vulnerable and marginalised groups to enable them to move out of poverty. ANANDI believes in grass root organising and in women's rights. Although Gujarat is one of the most industrialised states in India, severe deprivation remains. ANANDI envisions women as active agents of change enmeshed in complex environmental and developmental realities that demand action. Its interventions explicitly address gender discrimination and aim to reduce other vulnerabilities such as poor access to health care, education, low wages and domestic violence. It is from this position that the emancipatory goal of critical theory in a specific historical context is practised (Smith, 1999).

ANANDI's community-based empowerment approach mobilises women from poor households in villages to analyse their everyday experiences through the lens of gender justice.[3] By 1999 ANANDI helped federate women's collectives, one of which is called Devgadh Mahila Sangathan (DMS). This federation currently has over 5000 members from about 80 villages in the Panchmahals and Dahod districts of Gujarat. Its members are primarily women from tribal societies and other marginalised groups. DMS addresses concerns related to women's basic entitlements. The mahila mandals (women's self-help groups at the village level) form the core of DMS, providing a forum where women voice their concerns and devise strategies to address them.[4]

The context and idea of community research

Global development trends have increased the gap between rich and poor, aggravating material distress and social tensions. Landlessness among rural households, the agrarian crisis and food security concerns, malnutrition and poor access to potable water, farmers' suicides and deprivation deaths – all constitute contemporary challenges to the democratic fabric of Indian society (GOI, 2011). In the eastern 'tribal belt' of Gujarat, most households undertake paid labour such as ploughing, harvesting and forest work, in addition to tilling small parcels of land for their own food. Typically, they are not paid the minimum wages stipulated by the government and there have been several instances of harassment of women by forest guards (ANANDI, 2002). The forest cover in the region has been severely depleted and the only local source of livelihood remains the collection of non-timber forest products (NTFPs) marketed as foods or processed for medicines (ANANDI, 2002). Seasonal distress migration is common and women face a number of hardships. ANANDI used feminist organising rooted in ideals of social justice, human rights and gender equality to empower the poorest and most vulnerable women and also to give voice to their struggles. Many of these struggles necessitated generating experiential knowledge and information which is not easily available in national data bases nor in research conducted by external agencies.

The year 2001 was a drought year and DMS and ANANDI started village grain banks as part of the relief programmes. During this period mapping the need for food grains per household proved to be a major challenge. Women shy away from talking about not having food at home because they feel inadequate, while communicating with so-called 'mainstream communities' or their cultural norms inhibit discussion and articulation of personal household matters. This situation needed to be explored and for women to break their silence. Many struggled to survive the consequences of disasters of drought, earthquake and communal violence.

A public interest litigation was filed by the People's Union for Civil Liberties (PUCL) in the Supreme Court about starvation deaths in many parts of the country. ANANDI and DMS had contributed to the process by collecting and sharing grassroots level data within the community as also with the national 'Right to Food' campaign.

In the years that followed activists from ANANDI felt the need to develop sharper insights about poverty and food deficits. ANANDI wanted to reach the actual and specific life experiences of tribal women. For example, they needed to understand processes and experiences surrounding causes of food shortages, how women perceived them, what kind of mechanisms they used to cope with these situations, and why it was seen as a matter of shame to talk about not having food at home.

In early 2004, during one of the monthly meetings with over 35 women leaders, when the subject of food shortages in the house and distress migration was under discussion, women were still not talking. Around the same period, several members of ANANDI and DMS had gone through participatory training workshops and began to use planning tools as part of their empowerment work. During the workshop the 'cause and effect' or 'problem tree' was used and became popular as a tool for analysing and understanding factors that created oppressive conditions for women.

Given the hesitation to discuss absence of food at home, activists of ANANDI used the 'cause effect tree' to analyse food insecurity. The trunk of the tree was the problem (food insecurity). The roots of the tree were the causes or reasons behind the problem and the branches were the effect or impact of the problem. Women leaders became very involved in the discussion using this graphic representation. The method allowed them to externalise personal and daily experiences of household food shortage. In a non-literate setting this tool became the starting point of articulating the problem which needed to be explored further.

The leaders who were present said that there was a need to chop some of the roots from the tree. They argued that unless action was taken against the root causes of their problems such as absence of land, indebtedness, or costs associated with ill health, their effects would keep re-occurring. They said that the root cause is different for each household, so in order to reach the roots, they should go and explore the situation of every member of the federation. They stressed the need to gather evidence and also to reach out. From this moment the idea of a detailed research inquiry on household level food shortages emerged.

Identifying aspects of the inquiry

The various aspects or fields of inquiry that need to be captured through the research process emerged, as the women leaders fleshed out the discussion with their own experiences, for example, the seasonal dimension of food availability. Next they identified coping strategies and detailed their nature and implications for members and their households. This work was juxtaposed with access, or rather the lack of it, to government schemes which are supposed to ensure food security to the poor. They felt that generalisations were not tenable and emphasised complex everyday realities and the diverse nature of struggles experienced by different households in different villages. The importance of developing a nuanced understanding was repeatedly emphasised by women.

In order to develop better insights, data had to be collected systematically. Recognising that indigenous ways of knowing help people cope with their political and ecological environments, the research project became a joint effort between ANANDI and DMS. While discussing how the data collection process should progress, the DMS team stated that, just as they experienced shame in talking about 'lack of food' in their homes, the mahila mandal respondents were also likely to be reticent. They stressed the importance of developing a special mechanism to broach the subject of food insecurity.

A few members of DMS suggested that they could use some more illustrations to discuss the subject of food insecurity with the respondent mahila mandal members. They expressed that the use of visual images would facilitate sharing and empathising which would help women articulate their struggles with dignity. Facilitators from ANANDI gave women coloured pens and paper to create visual images that would help capture conditions in households. The idea was to hand over power and control within the research process to design participatory methodology and the tools which women themselves could administer.

Emergence of a new instrument: towards legitimating indigenous knowledge

Women presented their depictions through a variety of pictures using boxes, trees, patterns and diagrams. For example, they showed the kind of food they ate through the different seasons of a year when food grains were exhausted. One illustration was particularly prominent; a flower with small images representing what was eaten during that month. The flower had twelve petals to represent twelve months of a year. The entire group liked this depiction and started modifying it to represent their household conditions over the months.

The key elements of seasons and the variation of food consumed were common to all the pictures. The group present in that meeting decided that the final tool would have:

- only pictures; pictures that were culturally relevant
- a way of representing twelve months to capture the distinctive agricultural or cultural activity of each month
- definitions of food insecurity ,'no food' and 'insufficient' food based on women's experiences.

This way of thinking represented a push for higher level of rigour in their own terms, capturing a variety of perspectives. ANANDI then worked on these elements and developed a slightly refined tool which became known as the 'food availability flower'.

The process was perhaps didactic at one level, sharing what the researcher and activist understands and has learnt; and at another level it was what educationists call 'discovery learning'. The activist researcher provided material through which a process of presentation of facts and experience was made possible and led women members to learn on their own those things which the ANANDI facilitator did not know in full. Knowledge is socially constructed, and since constructivists believe in their experiential and contextual accounts, the facilitator assisted women leaders in articulation and construction of knowledge. Recognising that we are not independent of the social and historical forces that surround us, ANANDI's endeavour was to unravel and understand the web of realities and experiences that women endured during periods of food shortages.

Women said that they should first use this representation of the flower with a few other mahila mandals to see if the members were able to associate with the picture and whether the research process and discussion helped them to become aware and articulate their situation with regard to the extent of food insecurity at home. This was a pilot testing of the instrument.

Startling facts began to emerge about the vast number of households that did not get two meals a day. For the first time some women were sharing their predicaments such as inability to procure work in the village. Greatly enthused by the 'voice' that the food availability flower tool gave women, tribal women in the federation put much effort into sharpening the tool and making the 'flower' as communicative as possible. The illustrations from the federation leaders of DMS and some mahila mandal members were taken to an illustrator and printer. Colour coding for three different seasons to represent (winter, summer and monsoon) was conceived, the flower was printed in two sizes – one small for each household and the other, on a large sheet, for each mahila mandal.

After finalisation of this indigenous instrument, a number of strategic decisions had to be made about how the instrument was to be administered, what information to collect and how to help any women found to be in severe distress. Choices were made and a clear conceptual structure organised around specific concerns and research questions.

Workshops were held with the ANANDI team and leaders of the federation where multiple ways of seeing and making sense of the food insecurity and seasonal dimension of food shortages were discussed. For example, the macro perspective pertaining to the state, national and global policies of food production and market forces and their impact on the poor were shared. This helped in understanding inter linkages between the individual situation and broader policies. These workshops served in part to review literature in the context of personal experiences and also helped build a platform for action.

Policy makers tended to homogenise the struggles of tribal communities and tended to blame tribal communities for their problems. ANANDI often heard them dismiss women as ignorant and illiterate, and not understanding government systems. The aim of this community research project was to understand, access and convert experiential knowledge into data that would be understood by 'outsiders'. This approach could enable them to reach policy makers and service providers who denied the existence of food shortages in tribal societies. ANANDI sought to encourage government services embedded in a colonial legacy to be sensitive to the struggles and challenges faced by the community, listen to them and re-structure services accordingly.

Process of data collection and triangulation

A strategy was developed to reach out to thousands of women as DMS leaders decided to reach out to all members by organising special meetings in each mahila mandal. Fifteen small field research teams consisting of three people – one ANANDI worker, a federation leader and a member of the local women's group were formed. Each team was provided with small flowers and a bigger 'mandal (group) flower'. They also had a spreadsheet on which to collect household information.

During the process of data collection the research team organised meetings with mahila mandals, explained the purpose of the meeting, and asked for help with the research from the mahila mandal. The team sat with groups of members and collected data. They used a socio-cultural sensitivity approach to build rapport and trust and ensured that the contextual embeddedness of data was understood.

Combining quantitative data and experiences and testimonies of struggles was not easy. Recordings were made of the data collection meetings as women explained their struggles and the gaps in government schemes for deprived families. Each research team kept a record of members who migrated out for work as this information indicated levels of deprivation. This process eventually helped enhance the movement for social justice.

The entire exercise was conducted in the local language, with researchers expressing deep respect for local culture, ways of knowing and learning. Most discussions started by asking members about what they and their families ate each day, whether the food was adequate and nutritious, and how they defined 'food security'. Definitions of food security were specific to each mahila mandal. After the small flowers were given to each member, the field research team ensured everyone understood the images. Then starting with the month in which the research was undertaken, they used coloured pencils, stones and seeds, to mark 'no food' 'insufficient food' or 'food secure' months. Each individual had enough time to discuss and then map their household situation onto the small sheet.

The processes of mapping seasonal food availability in the flower enabled each member to share their experiences of deprivation, thereby acknowledging that each had a distinctive experience. In many cases women felt supported by the fact that others were freely sharing their difficulties and their situation with the group. The stories were written up by the research team. ANANDI then transferred the data into computerised spreadsheets.

Later, women leaders extended material support and warmth to women in distress. The nature of the relationship between the leaders and researchers was one of mutual support filled with respect and dignity for the painful experiences they were trying to understand. In many ways the research acted as a process to legitimate knowledge and created solidarity across different groups while producing new forms of consciousness.

The data collection process was conducted over three months and was very intensive, with teams working an average of 10–12 hours. It assumed a campaign mode that was also intensive in terms of the grim stories women shared of not being able to feed their hungry children. A total of about 3000 households were covered through this community research.

Developing shared meaning, raising consciousness: towards analysis and action

When no one person is the expert, all participants share equally in the knowledge creation process. As the research progressed, it was clear that this dialogic process was key to meaning making (Ritchie and Rigano, 2007) and led to knowledge production not only of new findings from the empirical materials but also of the collaborative processes (Zittoun et al, 2007). Data collection was iterative and collaborative. There was interplay between the empirical materials and interpretation. The research team continued to negotiate the meaning of the participants' experiences as narrated through the conversations. The first level of analysis and understanding occurred when the members mapped their own household situation and empathised with the situation of others. After this, the next step was to reproduce the individual situation on the larger sheet so as to capture the situation for the entire mahila mandal or a group as a whole. This process helped them review, reflect and analyse the situation experienced at the mahila mandal or at small group level, representing a given set of women in a village. Through the process of discussion and analysis women in each of the mahila mandals developed better insights into the reasons for injustice, unequal distribution of resources and denial of entitlements. A lot of attention was paid to legitimating the way their knowledge was produced. Women members began to value their experiences, and their knowledge, and evaluated the credibility of the evidence.

By the end of the research period we were able to identify that food security was a cyclic seasonal phenomenon with insecurity being low over the winter months and peaking over summer and monsoon. A staggering 80 to 90 percent of households experienced food scarcity.

About 79 per cent of the families who were severely food insecure reported migrating. These findings refuted state officials' ideas about tribal communities migrating because they were looking for better pay and forced them to consider that they may have been migrating because of vulnerability.

A further aspect of the research was processual; the privileging of women's lived experiences. Most official discourse fails to recognise the struggles and hardships of the poor. Through the capturing of experiential data the team were able to describe nuances – for example, the problems of older women which had not been recognised before.

The small sheet belonged to each member – with their individual 'data' and analysis – and was left behind for them to explore ways of improving or getting out of that situation. Many women pasted the pictorial depiction of their flower on the walls or doors of their homes. It helped them discuss safety nets and also plan for possible shortages. Later it was found that they would often refer to the picture and they used this to prepare for shortages and it became a reference point to record the shifts taking place in their household level situation of food security.

The bigger sheet was brought back to a central office for analysis and to draw out future strategies for advocacy and collective action. ANANDI and DMS worked collaboratively on this. For example, in Dahod the average family size was seven to nine members which had implications for the kind of strategies the households could adopt. Similarly the decision to send children to private schools meant a huge financial drain and restricted their coping strategies during the months of shortages. Ill health of a member or inability to go to work led to starvation of the family for that day. Even when they do go to work, payments are inadequate and not as stipulated by the law. During May to September (the monsoon months), absence of food in the house was the highest as the crop is still growing, to be harvested only in October–November.

Based on the data collected, an article was written by one of the ANANDI facilitators (Chakravarty and Dand, 2006) in a reputed scholarly journal reflecting on the food insecurity in Gujarat and made policy suggestions.

The impact

This graphic representation created by women made a huge impact as they began to shed their inhibitions and share their stories about household food insecurity. The research process helped women examine the inter-linkages between the decisions they were taking. Women shared painful experiences of economic deprivation, exploitation, alcoholism, illiteracy and social discrimination and denial of rights. The research process itself led to moving beyond the experience of individual level problems to realising that this was a problem faced by the collective. There was a process of moral self reflection, a conquering of inner fears and the realisation of self worth.

As they spoke and shared, women were sad and angry. As a result of the enhanced collectivisation and solidarity women began to realise the importance of demanding that the state ensured people's right to food. The findings of this study led to the creation of momentum across the state and the establishment of Anna Suraksha Adhikar Abhiyan (the Campaign for the Right to Food Security), a state level campaign organised by a forum of like-minded organisations, unions, activists and community-based organisations. Women presented their struggles at public hearings and these were documented and presented to the district administration. The data provided substantive evidence of food insecurity which was used to develop advocacy documents pressurising the government to ensure food availability via public distribution systems. ANANDI and DMS have since held over 70 public hearings across the state in which over 100,000 people walked miles to be heard. Each of the mandals have become active in monitoring the Supreme Court's orders through community-based monitoring systems of food security schemes like the Integrated Child Development, Mid Day Meals, and national old-age pension schemes. The process enabled women to recognise that demanding their right to food was asserting their right to life. The research became a unique exercise in consciousness raising which was also later linked with campaigns on the right to healthcare (Jan Swasthya Abhiyan). The process resulted in a deepening of democracy in the predominantly feudal context of governance in tribal India.

A number of policy changes were made as women questioned the nature of development which dispossessed them of traditional rights and access to forests, thereby increasing food insecurity. Their conceptual understanding of their struggles increased and a window of interface was opened with the Food and Civil Supplies Department. They began dialogue with the officials and to negotiate with structures of a government functioning with a colonial legacy. The leaders of DMS and members of mahila mandal developed the means to contest policy makers' assumptions and systems as they collectively struggled for their rights with a new consciousness created by the research (Grande, 2004).

At one level this study could be viewed as participatory action research about women's rights, poverty and food insecurity which led to mobilising women to improve food security and raise consciousness around development and democratic governance. At another level the research process highlighted the social construction of knowledge and ways of producing it. The process of synthesising structural perspectives with individual experiences was a key feature of this community research project.

This was feminist research for women, by women and about their struggles both inside and outside the household with an effort to transform their conditions. The qualitative inquiry was dialectical, with a synthesis of women's material conditions, the way they felt and experienced these conditions in their everyday lives which then provided a strong basis for praxis and policy advocacy. The research process was reflexive and the data and its analysis helped them understand their situation individually and collectively and brought them together in solidarity. Their engagement with the issue increased and they have subsequently sustained their struggle and demands over a period of five years. The study successfully destabilised the knowledge of policy makers and exposed women's situation. The national campaign for food security has culminated in the parliament considering a National Food Security Bill in 2011. It has made a huge difference to the lives of women.

Key learning

- Community research is not simply using community members as investigators or data collectors.
- The idea of pictorially presenting seasons in the form of a flower with each petal representing a month was appealing and demonstrates the use of indigenous ways of thinking and representation.
- Being able to communicate and discover that problems are collective and systemic is reassuring and empowering.
- A communitarian ethic involving collaboration, trust and non-oppressive relationships between researchers and the researched was key to the success of the project.
- The research was based on empathy and sharing of emotionality. Such work acknowledges that different knowledge forms exist and that the cultural and power dimensions of knowledge production need to be recognised.

Summary

The chapter examined how research is understood and carried out when conceived as part of a larger feminist organising process with poor and tribal women's struggle for rights and entitlements. It explored the context of food insecurity and the process of identifying areas of inquiry, the way research questions were formulated, the extent of power and control that the illiterate women had over the methodology. It looked at the development of indigenous methods and use of the approach in over 50 villages. The complex relationship between the research process, its conception and the purpose for which it was conducted was highlighted as well as the role that the research had in consciousness raising and supporting Parliament's consideration of a National Food Security Bill in 2011.

Discussion questions

1. Explain how and why the creation of indigenous knowledge requires the adoption of indigenous approach to the development of research tools.
2. Can vulnerable and marginalised communities or communities with limited literacy skills conduct research? Justify your answer.
3. How can community research be effectively used with community organisations and consciousness-raising efforts with vulnerable communities?

Notes

[1] The Department of Urban and Rural Community Development (URCD) was established in 1955 at the Tata Institute of Social Sciences (TISS), a university based in Mumbai. The Department of URCD is now called the Centre for Community Organisation and Development Practice and offers a Masters' programme in social work. Janki Andharia is professor at TISS.

[2] Area Networking and Development Initiatives. Neeta Hardikar is a founding member and Director of ANANDI.

[3] This is done through meetings where women's struggles are given voice and issues discussed. The process leads up to forming women's collectives (mahila mandals). Systematic awareness and consciousness-raising training programmes are held and women are supported to take up issues they identify. Their concerns generally relate to women's basic entitlements, dignity and self-esteem. Asserting their rights following due process in a democracy is enormously empowering.

[4] Representatives from these self-help groups form a village level sangha (collective), which addresses issues raised by the groups. Sangha representatives form clusters of women's groups from seven to ten villages; and each cluster identifies a focal issue based on common concerns of member villages.

References

Andharia, J. (2007) Re-conceptualising Community Organisation in India: A Transdisciplinary Perspective, *Journal of Community Practice*, 15, A Special Issue on Interdisciplinary Community Development: International Perspectives.

Andharia, J. (2009) Editorial: Critical Explorations of Community Organization in India. Special Issue: Community Organisation in India, *Community Development Journal*, 44. (3): 276-290.

Area Networking and Development Initiatives (ANANDI) (2002) *Understanding Women's Experiences in Natural Resource Management*, New Delhi: Aga Khan Foundation.

Area Networking and Development Initiatives and Tata Institute of Social Sciences (ANANDI-TISS) (2005) Rights–Based Development of Women: Moving from Theory to Action. An Engagement with an Empowerment Approach to Sustainable Livelihoods and Food Security, Unpublished Research Report.

Bhide, A. (2009) Shifting Terrains of Communities and Community Organization: Reflections on Organizing for Housing Rights in Mumbai, Special Issue: Community Organisation in India, *Community Development Journal,* 44(3) July: 367–381, Oxford: Oxford University Press.

Brown, D. and Tandon, R. (1983) The Ideology and Political Economy of Inquiring: Action, Research and Participatory Research, *Journal of Applied Behavioral Science and Technology*, 19(3): 277-94

Chakravarty, S. and Dand, S. (2006) Food Insecurity in Gujarat, *Economic and Political Weekly*, XLI (22) June 3: 2248-2258.

Clay, E. and Schaffer, B. (eds) (1984) *Room for Manoeuvre: An Exploration of Public Policy Planning in Agriculture and Rural Development*, Heinemann Educational Books: London.

Collins, P. H. (1998) *Black Feminist Thought: Knowledge Consciousness and Politics of Empowerment,* Routledge: New York.

Curno, P. (ed) (1978) *Political Issues and Community Work*, London, Routledge and Kegan Paul.

Denzin, N.K., Lincoln, Y.S. and Smith L, T. (eds) (2008) *Handbook of Critical Indigenous Methodologies*, New Delhi: Sage.

Fals, B. O and Rahman, M.A. (Ed) (1991) *Action and Knowledge: Breaking the Monopoly with Participatory Action Research*, New York: Apex.

Freire, P. (1972) *Pedagogy of the Oppressed,* Victoria: Penguin.

GOI (Government of India) (2011*) India Human Development Report 2011: Towards Social Inclusion*, Planning Commission, New Delhi: Oxford University Press.

Grande, S. (2004*) Red Pedagogy: Native American Social and Political Thought*, Lanham, MD: Rowman and Littlefield.

Hall, B., Gillette A.,and Tandon, R. (eds) (1982) *Creating Knowledge: A Monopoly?* New Delhi: Society for Participatory Research in Asia.

Jodhka, S.S. (2001) *Community and Identities: Contemporary Discourses on Culture and Politics in India*, London: Sage.

Lather, P. (1986a) Research as Praxis, *Harvard Educational Review*, 56(3).

Lather, P. (1986b) Issues of Validity in Openly Ideological Research: Between a Rock and a Soft Place, *Interchange*, 17(4): 63-84.

Lather, P. (1988) Feminist Perspective on Empowering Research Methodologies, *Women's Studies International Forum*, 11(6): 569-581.

McLaren, P. and Kincheloe, J. L. (2007) *Critical Pedagogy: Where are We Now?* New York: Peter Lang.

McTaggart, R. (ed) (1997) *Participatory Action Research: International Contexts and Consequences*, Albany: State University of New York Press.

Onyx, J. (1996) Community Development in Australia: Trends and Tensions, *Community Development Journal*, 31(2): 99–103.

Society for Participatory Research in Asia (PRIA) (1986) *Learning for Health Care*, Delhi: Society for Participatory Research in Asia.

Society for Participatory Research in Asia (PRIA) (1995) *Strengthening Civil Society: Contribution of Support Organizations in South Asia*, Delhi: Society for Participatory Research in Asia.

Society for Participatory Research in Asia (PRIA) (2000) *Doing Research with People Approaches to Participatory Research: An Introduction*. Delhi: Society for Participatory Research in Asia.

Rains, F. V., Archibald J.A. and Deyhle, D. (2000) Introduction: Through Our Eyes and in Our Own Words: The Voices of Indigenous Scholars, *International Journal of Qualitative Studies in Education*, 13: 337–342.

Ritchie, S.M. and Rigano, D.L. (2007) Solidarity through Collaborative Research, *International Journal of Qualitative Studies in Education*, 20: 129–150.

Semali, L.M. and Kincheloe, J.L. (1999) Introduction: What is Indigenous Knowledge and Why Should We Study It? In Semali, L.M. and Kincheloe, J.L. (eds) *What is Indigenous Knowledge? Voices from the Academy*, New York: Falmer, 3–57.

Smith, L.T. (1999) *Decolonizing Methodologies: Research and Indigenous Peoples*, Dunedin, New Zeland: University of Otago Press.

Society for the Promotion of Area Resource Centres (SPARC) (1985) *We the Invisible: Census of Pavement Dwellers*, Mumbai: SPARC.

Vyas, V. (2009) Unionization as a Strategy in Community Organization in the Context of Privatization: The Case of Conservancy Workers in Mumbai, Special Issue: Community Organisation in India, *Community Development Journal*, 44(3) July: 320–335, Oxford: Oxford University Press.

Zittoun, T., Baucal, A., Cornish, F. and Gillespie, A. (2007) Collaborative Research, Knowledge and Emergency, *Integrative Psychology and Behavioral Science*, 41: 208–217.

Seventeen

Community researchers in an adolescent risk reduction intervention in Botswana: challenges and opportunities

Bagele Chilisa and Rapelang Chilisa

Chapter aims

- Discuss the importance and benefits of involving communities in research about their social concerns
- Demonstrate an indigenous community research approach that breaks power barriers and builds relationships between the researchers and the researched

Introduction

Against the backdrop of disillusionment from communities in developing countries and the Indigenous communities of the world (that they are over-researched and tired of research always asking the same questions and reproducing the same answer, that their world views are ignored and/or dismissed and that the outcomes of such research fail to see the world from their perspectives) there is mounting pressure to involve communities in research about their social concerns.In this chapter we describe community research informed by postcolonial indigenous research paradigms. A postcolonial indigenous paradigm articulates a relational ontology that addresses relations among people and promotes love and harmony in communities (Wilson, 2008; Chilisa, 2012). Study participants make connections with each other while the researcher is viewed as part of the circle of relations. A postcolonial indigenous paradigm is informed by a relational epistemology that values communities as knowers, and knowledge as the well established general beliefs, concepts and theories of any particular people which are stored in their language, practices, rituals, proverbs, revered traditions, myths and folktales. The research process is informed by a relational ethical framework that moves away from conceiving the researched as participants to seeing them as co-researchers (Chilisa, 2012). This chapter looks at the ways in which community research was utilised in the design and implementation of an adolescent risk reduction intervention.[1] We describe the role of community advisory boards, adolescents and their parents (or guardians) as participant- researchers in the research process. We demonstrate how indigenous methods such as the talking circle, capacity building of community researchers and building circles of relationships among participants and with the researchers were essential elements in the implementation of a school-based risk reduction intervention.

The adolescent risk reduction intervention

In Botswana, as in Sub-Saharan Africa, there is a growing concern about the risks associated with adolescent sexuality (Meekers, Ahmed Molatlhegi, 2001), and about HIV infection among youth (Gallant and Maticka-Tyndale, 2004). The Botswana HIV/AIDS Impact Survey (BAIS III) of 2008 estimated a national prevalence rate of 17.6 per cent compared to 17.1 per cent in 2004. Young people aged 15 to 19 years have a prevalence rate of 3.7 per cent. These behaviours occur within the context of social and cultural influences from the communities, the schools, the teachers and parents. In 2007, the University of Botswana in partnership with the University of Pennsylvania won a National Institute of Health (NIH) grant to identify the determinants of AIDS preventative behaviour among secondary school students aged 14 to17 years; church-based adolescents aged 11 to14 and adolescents living with HIV and AIDS aged 15 to19. The grant was also intended to fund the development of interventions aimed at sexual risk behaviour which were both age and culturally appropriate for appropriate for these population groups and to test the efficacy of the interventions in changing risky sexual behaviour.

The first phase of the research involved using a qualitative approach to identify theory-based determinants of risky sexual behaviour. The Theory of Planned Behaviour (TPB) is a theoretical framework for understanding the predictors of individual behaviour that has been frequently applied to understanding health behaviours (Ajzen, 1991). The TPB incorporates a structured data-collection approach that utilises specific, direct questions to assess behavioural, normative and control beliefs about the behaviours of interest (in this case abstinence, condom use and multiple partners). However, the use of this structured format may overlook the contextual information necessary to understand responses to these questions within specific cultural contexts. In predominantly oral societies, cultural knowledge, beliefs and values are expressed and transmitted through language, stories, songs, myths and proverbs. The collection of community language in the form of proverbs, stories, songs, myths and taboos serves as an indigenous approach that can make visible the world views of the community not included in the mainstream literature (Chilisa et al, 2011a). From this perspective, community research is not only about the involvement of communities in the research process but includes the use of indigenous research methods that makes the inclusion of communities' world views possible. The qualitative approach thus involved the use of structured qualitative interviews and the collection of communities' stories, songs and taboos on the behaviours of interest. Research participants were the adolescents and their parents. The focus of the research questions were on participants' views and concerns on the behaviours of interest, what they think should be done, how it should be done and the challenges and opportunities in implementing the intervention to change adolescents behaviour. We involved the parents as research participants to deepen our understanding of community knowledge on adolescents' sexuality as well as making the intervention inclusive of community knowledge and community input.

One of the conclusions drawn from the qualitative data was that we should design an intervention that provided opportunities for building adolescents' assertiveness and negotiation skills, and technical skills on the use of condoms. We also wanted to initiate discussions around these issues with those who influence adolescents' decision-making, namely, parents and peers (Chilisa et al, 2011b). The intervention needed to address issues of socio-cultural behavioural beliefs about abstinence, condom use and multiple partners and integrate these issues into adolescents' discussions with their peers and their parents. The qualitative data informed the design of a pilot survey.

In the second phase of the project, we designed interventions informed by the qualitative data and findings from the pilot survey. The intervention developed from the data is called 'Own the Future'. Own the Future has three curricula: 'Pulling together we will', a risk reduction curriculum for school-based adolescents (Chilisa et al, 2010); 'Arise and shine', a risk reduction curriculum for faith-based adolescents (Modie-Moroka et al, 2010); 'Living well my choice: pro health pro life', a risk reduction curriculum for adolescents living with HIV and AIDS (Phaladze et al, 2010). The goal of Own the Future curricula was to help adolescents change behaviours that increase their risk for cancer, hypertension, heart disease, unintended pregnancy and sexually transmitted diseases (STDs), especially HIV and AIDS. The school-based intervention has twelve 60-minute modules that are presented over six days. Following the intervention, there is a follow-up at three months, six months and 12 months which is carried out by the researchers; and lastly, an analysis of the follow-up data to establish the efficacy of the intervention.

The intervention integrates the Own the Future theme in the curricula to emphasise and encourage the participants to protect themselves and to behave responsibly, for the sake of themselves, their family and their community. It also encourages them to consider their goals for the future and how unhealthy behaviour might thwart the attainment of those goals. What follows is a descrption of how we involved the community advisory board (CAB) in the design of the survey questionnaire and the intervention curricula. We also illustrate the role of participant as co-researcher in an action-oriented intervention as well as describe the research techniques that optimised the sharing of power between the researchers and adolescents as co-researchers.

Community engagement in the research process

In accordance with the assumptions of a relational ontology and a relational epistemology that view research as a ceremony to build relationships, our starting point was to build strong relationships with research users and to ensure that the approaches, methods, measures, the literature and the language of the research were embedded in the culture of the researched. We engaged a community advisory board for the school-based intervention whose role was to guide researchers to the most effective ways to recruit and retain research participants and to review the survey instruments and the intervention curricula to ensure that they were age appropriate and culturally sensitive. Members of the CAB represented the diverse needs and interests of the communities served. While community involvement through the CAB members promoted ownership by the community, it also had challenges. The first challenge was with the survey instrument. The board reviewed the instrument and ruled that items on same-sex sexuality should be excluded from the questionnaire. The board argued that same-sex relationships were a foreign concept that they did not want discussed with the adolescents. Our efforts to inform the board that the concept came from our focus group interviews with the adolescents were in vain. Our failure to incorporate the data from the field implied that the adolescents' voice on what would be incoporated in the intervention was compromised. The CAB's veto had a negative impact on the adolescents' ability to represent themselves in the ways they valued and further undermined the relational ethical framework of the study that values partcipants as co-researchers with power to influence the direction of the research process. The power differentials between adolescents and their parents represented by the CAB could not be altered.

The boards also disagreed with the language used in the questionnaire. They did not like the explicit medical language approach to describing sexual intercourse. Our efforts to explain that this way of defining sexual intercourse made the questionnaire less ambiguous were again in vain. Disagreeing with CAB had the potential of rejection and sanction of the intervention by the community. Questions were phrased as recommended by the members of the boards. To address possible ambiguity of the new questions, the questions were read out and their meanings explained to participants. This compromise illustrates how in a relational ethical framework the voices of the stakeholders or service users can be accommodated as a way of building relationships and partnerships with communities.

Implementing the action-oriented intervention

We adopted the transformative participatory action research approach as a guide for implementing the intervention. The guiding principle for transformative participatory action research is purposive active enagagement and political action by both the researcher and the researched (Chilisa, 2012). Participatory action research:

> is action which is researched, changed and re-researched, within the research process by participants. Nor is it simply an exotic variant of consultation. Instead, it aims to be active co-research, by and for those to be helped. Nor can it be used by one group of people to get another group of people to do what is thought best for them – whether that is to implement a central policy or an organisational or service change. Instead it tries to be a genuinely democratic or non-coercive process whereby those to be helped, determine the purposes and outcomes of their own inquiry. (Wadsworth, 1998: 3)

We combined participatory action research with the appreciative inquiry approach to guide the implementation of the intervention. One of the criticisms made against participatory action research is that most of the approaches are problem focused aiming at discovering communities' unmet needs. Conceptions of communities as knowers and participants as researchers require researchers to move from problem focused modes of inquiry, that see communities as places full of problems and needs that can only be solved with the help of outsiders, to change-focused approaches that emphasise strength and positive images of the researched (Ludema et al, 2006; Chilisa, 2012). In the change-focused approach, the researched reflect on their qualities and move towards self-discovery. They also dream and envision the best that they could be, dialogue on strategies to implement their dream and draw a plan to take them to their destiny.

In one of the activities of the first day of the intervention adolescents were given some time (approximately five minutes) to think about the positive qualities and phrases that reflect their good qualities, that is, their strengths, character and determination. They wrote and drew on their personal shields positive images about themselves. They were encouraged to express who they were and what was special about them. They were also made aware that the shield was a symbolic personal armour that would protect them from risky sexual behaviours and health problems. Some of the adolescents thought of themselves as helpful individuals and therefore drew a hand on their heart, while others drew a heart to show that they were kind-hearted people. After thinking and reflecting on their qualities, the adolescents were also asked to share with others what they discovered about themselves. The responses were recorded in a poster some of which included being smart, friendly, responsible, kind-hearted and compassionate.

Another important activity of the first day was to get participants to think about their future and understand that their behaviour would have an impact on what they would be in the future. The adolescents then completed a goals and dreams timeline listing their goals and dreams from the time they completed it to a day five to ten years in the future. They were to discuss with their parents the goals and dreams timeline and their personal shield, and to review and finalise it on the penultimate day of the intervention. Participants were also trained to picture and regard themselves as belonging together. At the beginning of the intervention the adolescents were informed as follows:

> Today you enrolled in the teen club, 'Own the Future'. Own the Future is a club to give you the skills to take control of your life, make responsible choices, plan for a bright future and achieve your goals and dreams. Our motto in this club is 'Pulling together we will'. In this teen club, Own the Future, you promise to encourage and support each other's effort to avoid risky behaviours and achieve your goals. Your parents could also give you support. (Chilisa et al, 2011: 5)

Training adolescents as co-researchers

One of the challenges we had was recruiting the parents, hearing their voices and keeping them engaged in the intervention. We relied on the adolescents to capture the voices of their parents. Several factors can affect the validity of the data collected by adolescents. Of special consideration is their emotional and social wellbeing which can have an influence on their cognitive capacity and subsequently affect the type of responses or the quality of data they solicit from their parents. Of even greater importance is the cultural taboo on discussing sexual matters with their parents, which makes discussion very difficult and sometimes impossible. The findings from our qualitative data indicated that for the intervention to work there was need for parent–child communication about sex and sexuality. We were aware that most of the communication between parent and child involved sending children on errands and counselling, or disowning them when they are already either pregnant or in trouble (Onyewadume et al, 2011). Parents feel inadequately informed about matters concerning sex and sexuality, are embarrassed, or have difficulty finding a suitable time to talk to their children. To address the lack of parent–child communication, adolescents were introduced to seven effective ways of communication which required them to choose a time to talk to their parents; have a plan to start the conversation; be courteous; present accurate and factual information in a concise and convincing manner and always present a complete picture of the issue for discussion. They were trained on how to approach their parents and get them to discuss sensitive matters with them through role pay. This activity also got the adolescents to feel free about discussing their unique and different situations at home and how they intended to tackle them. They were probed on the specific challenges that might hinder them and were asked to suggest solutions for each of the obstacles.

Data collection

One of the concerns from a relational ethical framework is that research in communities can be exploitative if it focuses on the interests of the researcher and ignores the participants' agency to represent themselves. To facilitate adolescents and their parents' voice, each day's activity involved a process where adolescents took home an assignment that required them to find out more about their parents and the role they would play in supporting them to live healthier lives as well as find out their parents' views on the daily activities. Box 17.1 is an example of the homework assignments. It is clear from the assignment that participants were active researchers, taking action to inquire from their parents, recording their observations and interviews; critically reflecting and evaluating their action research and using the information to inform their next cycle of activity.

Box 17.1: Day one research questions assigned to adolescents

- Explain the 'Own the Future' programme and share with your parents/guardians your goals and dreams that you want to achieve in the future and your personal shield.
- Discuss with your parents/guardians the possible barriers that can prevent you from achieving your goals.
- Make a promise with your parents/guardians to always talk to them whenever you encounter problems.

During your discussion with your parents/guardians please note the following: (i) did you like interviewing your parents/guardians? (ii) What was it like to discuss your goals with them? (iii) What was the most surprising thing you learnt? (iv) Do you think talking to your parents/guardians about this has made you want to talk about other things in your life? Why or why not (v) did you learn anything about them or yourself? If yes what?

Our implementation strategy involved a systematic cyclical action of change starting with planning; taking action; observing, evaluating and critical reflection prior to planning the next cycle. Each day of the intervention started with a review of the plan for the day, then acting on the plan and ended with homework (see Figure 17.1). The adolescents reflected on their experiences to reframe the original ideas in the plan as well as amend inquiry procedures. Throughout the intervention, the adolescents reviewed the ground rules and made changes as desired.

Figure 17.1 Action-oriented intervention

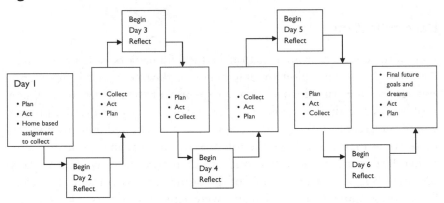

As a way of finding out what transpired at home and whether parents were indeed supportive of their children, each day started with a talking circle to discuss the homework. The facilitator found out which adolescents had completed the task with their parents; what the parents thought of the assigned task, how comfortable they were with doing the task and what made it easy for adolescents to do the task with their parents. Responses included comments such as: 'my parents saw this as an opportunity to find out about my life, they were happy that I am enrolled in Own the Future'.

Those who found it hard to do the tasks were asked what made it difficult. Their responses were listed as obstacles since they got in the way of completion. Solutions were suggested for each of the listed obstacles as a means of empowering the adolescents to overcome the obstacles and strive to complete the next activity. These talking circles informed the facilitators of the opinions/views of the parents and adolescents. The information was used as feedback to empower adolescents to get their parents involved in assisting with the activities.

Building group togetherness through talking circles

In receiving data from the adolescents on the assigned research questions, we were aware of the power dimensions within the diverse group of adolescents that had potential to silence some in the groups and that some methods such as the focus group allowed assertive individuals to dominate. We chose the talking circle as a method that could allow each voice to be heard. Talking circles are based on the ideal of participants having respect for each other and are an example of a focus group method derived from postcolonial indigenous world views. In African contexts and among Indigenous peoples, there are many occasions when people form a circle. It could be around the fire place, during celebrations or when children form circles to play games. In each of these occasions a person is given a chance to speak uninterrupted. The talking circle symbolises as well as encourages a sharing of ideas, respect of each other's ideas, togetherness and a continuous and an unending compassion and love for one another. The circle also symbolises equality of members in the circle. Wilson and Wilson (2000:11) explain that group members sit 'in a circle that represents the holism of Mother Earth and the equality of all members'. A common practice in talking circles is that a sacred object, which could be a feather, a basket or a spoon, is passed around from speaker to speaker. These sacred objects symbolize collective construction of knowledge, shared ideas and equality of participants. The holder of the object speaks uninterrupted and the group listens silently and non–judgmentally until the speaker has finished. A talking circle may consist of as few as two people (Lavelle, 2009) and as many as twelve. In most instances, a complete talking circle comprises four rounds (Wilson and Wilson, 2000). The number of talking circles may vary because of time restraints, rules and norms of each group. For the intervention, 10 to 16 adolescents sat in a circle and shared with the rest of the group what they had learned. Participants were only allowed to talk when holding a shield, a symbol for self-protection and, in the context of the intervention, protection from sexual risky behaviours. Talking circles enabled us to build group trust and cohesion and develop openness and confidence among adolescents. Each day started and ended with a talking circle.

Parental involvement

Parental interest and involvement in their children's lives was crucial to the implementation of the intervention and also for sustainable positive behaviour change. Letters were written to parents explaining the intervention and inviting them to assume responsibility to discuss their children's goals and dreams. The letters encouraged parents to envisage possible obstacles and to work with their children on the home-based assignments. Parent and child were requested to sign a pact where children promised to always discuss their assignments and to talk to their parents whenever they encountered obstacles. In addition adolescents wrote promise letters to themselves promising to practise healthy lifestyles so that they could achieve their dreams. They wrote letters to their parents informing them of the promise they had made to themselves and asking for support in their efforts. Each adolescent's pledge, promise letter and goals and dreams timeline served as documented data that adolescents collected on themselves and as individualised action-oriented outcomes. The adolescents found out more about themselves and their parents than they could read in a researcher-centric report. The individualised adolescents' reports to their parents gave voice to each adolescent and preserved each adolescent and family's uniqueness. In engaging adolescents to research on themselves and on their parents and to submit at the end of the interventions self-promise letters to their parents as well as their goals and dreams timelines, we preserved the multiple voices of adolescents that get silenced when researchers look for common patterns in their data and also disseminated the adolescents' voices to their parents. We were also able to reach a larger proportion of the community than would have been possible without engaging the adolescents, a total of 800 adolescents reached out to their parents. Involving parents was also a way of ensuring that there would be continuity of discussions on adolescent risky behaviours within families after researchers left the research sites.

Validity frameworks

Chilisa (2012: 171) notes:

> validity from a postcolonial critique framework starts with a call for recognition of conceptual frameworks, theoretical frameworks and data analysis methods derived from the researched's frames of reference and indigenous knowledge....Validity is the researcher's responsibility to go beyond banked book research methodologies to imagine other possibilities to accommodate the researched's ways of knowing and to wish for the researched as we would wish for ourselves.

Concepts of fairness, described as a quality of balance that enables all participants and stakeholders' views, perspectives, claims, concerns and voice to be visible in the research process also resonate with validity from an indigenous perspective. The validity of the pilot survey questionnaire in the intervention was enhanced by building the questionnaire items from qualitative data derived from traditional and indigenous methods to data collection. As noted, the use of songs, taboos and myths to source parents and their children's views on sex and sexuality brought into the discussion concepts rarely seen in the literature. Review of the pilot questionnaire survey by the CAB members made it possible to use language that was acceptable to the community, thus giving the community voice in the design of the intervention.

From a postcolonial indigenous perspective, research is valid if the researcher is able to move from a deficit- and damage-centered approach, in which communities are seen as sources of problems that they are unable to address without the help of the researchers, to investigations that build communities and restore hope in their capabilities to resolve the challenges which they encounter (Chilisa et al, 2011a). In the project, adolescents were trained to focus on their strengths and to use positive images to dream, imagine and begin the building of a better future. Adolescents and their parents became co-researchers with each family empowered to define their action-oriented outcomes.

Often the credibility of a research study is threatened by errors that occur when research participants resist intrusion in their lives by deliberately giving false information. Efforts to develop rapport with the community through the CABs ensured that the intervention was acceptable to the community at large. Through talking circles with adolescents, relationships were built among and between adolescents and the researchers so that they were free to communicate their thoughts. The documentation of the implementation process through completed goals and dreams timelines, promise letters and signed pacts which the participant-researchers were trained to keep safely ensured the visibility of the multiple voices of the researched from their own perspective using their own words; thus ensuring validity from a community perspective.

Key learning

- Indigenous paradigms add to the body of knowledge, other methods of conducting research and collecting data that resonate with communities.
- Capacity building of community researchers, building circles of relationships among participants and with researchers and research users in general are essential elements in community research.
- Community research should adopt change-focused approaches that emphasise positive images of the researched.
- Engaging community members as partners, community board members or as co-researchers enhances community ownership of interventions.

Summary

The chapter discusses a community research approach that draws from postcolonial indigenous paradigms with their emphasis on the importance of building relations and promoting love and harmony in communities by valuing communities as knowers and co-researchers. It highlights challenges in ensuring power balance between the researchers and communities and how these can be addressed without compromising research rigour. The chapter illustrates how a participatory action research approach that combines with appreciative inquiry to engage the researched as co-researchers, as well as transform their personal and social lives, was used in an adolescent risk reduction intervention in Botswana. In the transformative participatory approach described, community-based knowledge found in language, stories, songs and proverbs is valorised and emerging community-based data collection methods such as the talking circle are utilised in the research process. The chapter discusses conceptions of validity from a postcolonial indigenous perspective and concludes that research is valid if it accommodates community knowledge systems, builds relationships in communities and is respectful of community members as knowers.

Conclusion

The adolescent risk reduction intervention project shows stages in the process of carrying out community research that valorises community knowledge. The first stage involved collecting qualitative data to ensure that the conceptual framework for the study emanated from community culture. The methodology was indiginised through the use of talking circles, questionnaires and intervention curricula inclusive of community knowledge. The involvement of parents and their children as participant researchers began the process of a longitudinal family-based research by the families and for themselves that could continue for five to ten years to come. The letters to parents summarised adolescents' impressions of how the intervention had made an impact on their sexual behaviours. Disseminating to the parents the adolescents' impressions of how the intervention had had an impact on their lives enabled members of the community to access intervention results in a language which they could understand. This was by far the most valuable contribution to the community of parents who participated in the intervention. A quantitative analysis of the follow-up research by the authors will further shed light on the extent to which the intervention significantly changed the sexual behaviours of the adolescents.

Discussion questions

1. What are the basic principles of an indigenous paradigm ?
2. Why is it important to adopt an indigenous approach to the development of research tools in communities?
3. What kind of tools might you utilise in your research?

Note

[1] The risk reduction intervention described in this chapter is part of larger grant R24 HD 056693-05: Partnership for Capacity-Building for HIV/STD Prevention Research on Batswana Adolescents; sponsored by the National Institute for Health: USA.

References

Ajzen, I. (1991) The Theory of Planned Behaviour, *Organizational Behaviour and Human Decision Processes*, 50: 179-211.

Central Statistics Office (CSO) (2009) *Botswana AIDS Impact Survey 2008*, Gaborone: CSO.

Chilisa, B. et al (2010) *Own the Future: Pulling Together We Will, A Risk Reduction Curriculum for School-Based Adolescents*, Gaborone: University of Botswana, Unpublished manual.

Chilisa, B. (2012) *Indigenous Research Methodologies*, Los Angeles: Sage.

Chilisa, B., Nitza, A. and Makwinja-Morara, V. (2011a) Using Local Knowledge to Inform Culturally Sensitive HIV/AIDS Prevention among Adolescents in Botswana, *Pula: Botswana Journal of African Studies*, 25(1): 17-32.

Chilisa, B., Mmonadibe, P. and Malinga, T. (2011b) Indigenizing Research Methods: Language, Texts and Stories in the Construction of Adolescents Sexual Behaviours. *Pula: Botswana Journal of African Studies*, 25(1): 128-144.

Gallant, M. and Maticka-Tyndale, E. (2004) School-based HIV Prevention Programmes for African Youth, *Social Science Medicine*, 58: 1337-51.

Lavelle, L. F. (2009) Practical Application of an Indigenous Framework and Two Qualitative Indigenous Research Methods: Sharing Circles and Anishnaabe Symbol-based Reflection, *International Journal of Qualitative Methods*, 8(1): 21-36.

Ludema, D. J., Cooperrider, D. L., and Barrett, F. J. (2006) Appreciative Enquiry: The Power of the Unconditional Positive Question, in Reason, P. and Bradbury, H. (eds) *Handbook of Action Research*, Thousand Oaks, CA: Sage: 155-165.

Meekers, D., Ahmed , G. and Molatlhegi, M. T. (2001) Understanding Constraints to Adolescent Condom Procurement: The Case of Urban Botswana. *Aids Care*, 13(3): 279-302.

Modie-Moroka T. et al (2010) Own the Future Arise and Shine: A Risk Reduction Curriculum for Faith-based Adolescents, Gaborone: University of Botswana, unpublished manual.

Onyewadume, M.A and Mbongwe, B. (2011) Students and Parents Perceived HIV/AIDS Intervention Model, *Pula: Botswana Journal of African Studies*, 25(1): 94-110.

Phaladze N. et al (2010) Own the Future Living Well My Choice: Pro Health Pro Life: A Risk Reduction Curriculum for Adolescents Living With HIV/AIDS, Gaborone: University of Botswana, unpublished manual.

Tuck, E. (2009) Suspending Damage: A Letter to Communities, *Harvard Educational Review*, 79(3): 409-427.

Wadsworth, Y. (1998) What is Participatory Action Research? Action Research International, Paper 2, www.scu.edu.au/schools/gcm/ar/ari/p-ywadsworth98.html

Wilson, S. (2008) *Research is Ceremony: Indigenous Research Methods*, Manitoba, Halifax and Winnipeg: Fernwood Publishing.

Wilson, S. and Wilson, S. (2000) Circles in the Classroom: The cultural Significance of Structure, *Canadian Social Studies*, 34(2): 11-12.

Eighteen

Recruitment and capacity-building challenges in participatory research involving young people in Northern Ireland

Claire McCartan, Stephanie Burns and Dirk Schubotz

Chapter aims

- To introduce theoretical discussion about young people's participation in research
- To explain ways of involving young people in research, drawing examples from four different projects
- To highlight some difficulties of working with young people
- To give some practical examples of how to manage the community research process

Introduction

Consulting young people in social research is increasingly popular and is not confined to their recruitment as participants but extends to the design, delivery and dissemination of research. The level and depth of involvement of young researchers varies greatly (Hart, 1992; Kirby, 1999) but the move towards youth participation mirrors trends in childhood sociological theory, an imperative to seek out and listen to children's voices (Hill, 1997; Edwards and Aldred, 1999) and a changing legal and political context. The UN Convention on the Rights of the Child has influenced international policy. Great Britain and Northern Ireland have either passed (or are committed to passing) legislation[1] pledging to the principles enshrined in the Convention and have established Children's Commissioners. This changing context has helped to fuel the debate around children and young people's participation (David et al, 2001; Curtis et al, 2004), in particular in social policy-related research.

In this chapter we explore the recruitment and capacity-building challenges involved in working with young people as researchers. We will draw on our experiences from four separate participatory research projects with young people, which were undertaken in Northern Ireland over the last five years (Schubotz and Sinclair, 2006; Kilpatrick et al, 2007b; Schubotz and McCartan et al, 2008; NCB NI and ARK/YLT, 2010).

Theoretical background

Hart's 'ladder of participation' (1992) illustrates how peer researchers can meaningfully take part in research that is 'with' or empowering 'to' other children and young people (see Figure 18.1). The ladder specifies eight levels of actions, and has strong echoes of the eight rungs of Arnstein's ladder of citizen participation (1969), which showed the relationship between 'rungs' of citizen participation and levels of redistributed power in society. Similar to this and to Alderson (2000), Hart's model shows that there is a hierarchy of participation. At the top of this participatory spectrum, children and young people have the ideas about the project and set it up; they may or may not invite adults to join with them to share decision making. This gives children total control over the process of researching their needs and their increased awareness about how their world can enable them to highlight solutions to problems and lobby for positive change (Atweh, et al 1998). In reality, most participatory research projects fall short of this top level, often due to constraints at the early stages of planning when it is not always possible or practical to involve young people. What can be done, however, is to ensure the methodological approach can be reviewed regularly by the research team to enable the young researchers to become as fully involved in the research process as possible.

Figure 18.1 Hart's ladder of young people's participation

8) Young people and adults share decision making
7) Young people lead and initiate action
6) Adult-initiated, shared decisions with young people
5) Young people consulted and informed
4) Young people assigned and informed
3) Young people tokenised
2) Young people are decoration
1) Young people are manipulated

Source: Adapted from Hart, R. (1992)

Checkoway and Richards-Schuster (2003) established a number of reasons to validate youth participation in research. Seen as a legitimate way to develop knowledge for social action, involvement can enable young people to exercise their political rights, nurture active citizenship and strengthen their social development. Possible emancipatory biographical effects at the individual level are: increased confidence and sense of self-worth; new bonds and friendships; development of analytical, communication and teamwork skills; knowledge of research methodology; links to future opportunities and development of career aspirations. However, there is also a potential for exploiting young people under the guise of empowerment (Boyden and Ennew, 1997; Kirby et al, 2004). Elliott et al (2001) go as far as arguing that it is important that [young] people co-opted do benefit from their involvement in order to maintain the integrity of research.

Challenges to participatory research may, for example, arise when hierarchies exist between peer researchers due to gender, popularity and perceptions of class and identity associated with local dialects/accents, geographic location, and so on, or when children are involved in interviewing adults as well as their peers. Another challenge is to find young researchers who are close to the researched subject area, but simultaneously distanced enough to enable reflective analysis (Jones, 2004). The timescale for the project's completion, personal commitments for the peer researchers, the consent of parents, schools, youth groups, and so on may all pose further challenges and ultimately decide who can and cannot participate in a project (McCartan et al, 2004; Schubotz and Sinclair, 2006). Training and supporting the peer researchers throughout the research process can require substantial amounts of resources, and organisations or individuals must account for this if they wish to facilitate a successful peer research project (Kirby, 1999).

In summary, peer research is a process, not just a means to an end. It can not only lead to enhanced research outputs, but if managed appropriately, can present opportunities for personal development and learning and the development of social agents. In the following sections we will outline our experiences of involving young people in research projects and preparing them to become members of the respective teams.

Community research in practice

Our practical examples of working with young people as researchers are drawn from four separate research projects:

1. 'Out of the Box' (Kilpatrick et al, 2007b) was a project funded by the Department of Education in Northern Ireland and the Office of the First Minister and Deputy First Minister (OFMDFM). It lasted three years and worked with a core team of 12 peer researchers investigating

285

the outcomes of a range of different alternative education programmes for 14–16-year olds. Peer researchers were recruited primarily from voluntary organisations and had previously demonstrated some element of social action.

2. 'Being Part and Parcel of the School' (Schubotz and Sinclair, 2006) was funded by the Northern Ireland Commissioner for Children and Young People (NICCY) and explored young people's involvement in school policy-making on bullying. This project was undertaken by the National Children's Bureau (NCB) in co-operation with Access Research Knowledge (ARK, Northern Ireland). Ten 15–18-year-old peer researchers were recruited.

3. 'Cross-community Schemes' (Schubotz et al, 2008) was a mixed methods research project funded by the EU Programme for Peace and Reconciliation for Northern Ireland and the Border Regions of Ireland (PEACE II) and explored young people's attitudes to, and participation in, cross-community schemes in Northern Ireland. Eight 16-year-olds were recruited as peer researchers as a follow-up to a survey run by ARK to which they had all responded.

4. 'Attitudes to Difference' (NCB NI and ARK/YLT, 2010) was again undertaken by NCB in conjunction with ARK and explored attitudes to, and experiences of contact with, people from minority ethnic communities in Northern Ireland. This OFMDFM-funded project involved twelve 16–17-year-old peer researchers who were recruited from schools participating in the research.

Whereas Out of the Box ran over three years, all other projects were relatively short-term with an actual involvement of young researchers of approximately a period of six months. The duration of the research project has obvious implications on the pool of young people who can be recruited as peer researchers. During late adolescence a number of transitions are negotiated presenting difficulties for them to commit time and energy over extended timescales. They are facing exam pressures and possibly a move into employment or further and higher education (which may also mean leaving home and gaining independence for the first time). A challenge for the research team is thus to maintain young people's commitment and enthusiasm for a project over a number of years.

Recruitment

For both the NICCY-funded research into school bullying and the Attitudes to Difference project, young researchers were recruited through schools participating in the research project. In contrast, peer researchers for the research on Cross-community Schemes were recruited among respondents to the 2007 Young Life and Times (YLT) Survey (ARK, 2008). All respondents who had attended a cross-community project and who expressed an interest in further exploring the issues raised in the YLT survey were invited to apply to become a peer researcher.

In all our three short-term projects information sheets were sent out highlighting background information about the research, including aims and objectives as well as expectations and anticipated benefits for involved peer researchers. These information sheets were accompanied by application forms, in which candidates were requested to state why they were interested in becoming a peer researcher, what (if any) their related interests were and what other regular commitments they had that could impinge on the duties of a peer researcher. Based on this information a pre-selection of suitable candidates was possible, with the final selection taking place after the peer researcher training days (see following section).

During the Out of the Box research, the team used posters to advertise the scheme in various university and youth group common rooms, advertised on student intranets, relied on word-of-mouth to spread information of the project to youth agency workers and community groups, and looked to the organisations participating in the research to recommend local young people who might have been interested in the opportunity. Young people who had already demonstrated some aspect of social agency (that is, were already volunteers of some description or had at least a partial understanding of the social context of the research) proved to be the most reliable and suitable recruits for the research team.

In all our projects, young researchers were paid a fee and reimbursed for any expenses they had during the projects. They signed contracts which listed their responsibilities as well as the benefits of being peer researchers. On two occasions, contracts were terminated when individuals failed to meet the requirements of the post. In our experience, the money earned during the research was a welcome bonus but not a significant incentive to participate. As one of the peer researchers from the school bullying project said about the contract and the payment:

> I think it enforced the seriousness of how we needed to keep confidentiality and all the rest, it made you more aware of it. I think if it had been just a bit of fun or just a bit of experience for you, then not so much, but this time, because we were getting paid and there was a job to do, I think it made you want to do it better, anyway. (quoted from Burns and Schubotz, 2009)

Offering the potential to gain recognised accreditation or certification for peer researchers could also be considered as a recruitment strategy as, increasingly, young people are being expected to show evidence of skills outside of exam results. In our short-term projects peer researchers received certificates issued either by ARK or by NCB, highlighting the extent of research methods training they had received and what involvement they had had in the research project. The Out of the Box team developed a Queen's University accredited programme (20 UCATS points), but uptake was nil, probably as a result of it being made available towards the end of the project when some element of fatigue had crept in. Participants in the other projects did welcome the idea of accreditation at the outset, but found that the certificate and the experience they could draw on was adequate for the purposes of their CV and application forms.

Training young researchers

In our experience, the training of peer researchers has three main functions:

1. It provides basic research methods skills, but also introduces principles of research ethics and confidentiality;
2. It sensitises the young researchers for the subject area researched; and
3. It provides an important early team building opportunity.

The training programme can also provide a further possibility to select or deselect potential peer researchers, if necessary. It helps to identify roles and responsibilities based on ability range, skills and, crucially, the peer researchers' individual availability and level of commitment.

In Out of the Box, the research team drafted in a youth worker to contribute to the initial training sessions as building a strong team and group identity was seen as key to the success of this long-term project. The youth worker brought skills, experience and an entirely different approach to the training and helped generate a group collective between the academic and peer researchers.

The training for the three short-term projects we undertook also included focus group discussions among the young researchers to identify key themes we planned to explore during the fieldwork for the respective projects. Generally, the training was undertaken using interactive group work methodologies, which furthered the team building and contributed to confidence building. The small group work also helped each member to identify their strengths and weaknesses which in turn assisted the peer researchers to select roles within the team. Using role play (Out of the Box) and asking peer researchers to lead aspects of the training session (Cross-community Schemes, Attitudes to Difference, Being Part and Parcel of the School) gave the teams an insight as to how they would interact during fieldwork.

In the Cross-community Schemes project, where peer researchers were also entirely responsible for mobilising the sample for the research, the research methods training also served as a platform for the new recruits to make the relevant decisions about sampling. In this project, the senior members of the research team attended fieldwork only in an observational and supportive role, with the peer researchers managing all of the data collection. In Attitudes to Difference, peer researchers helped in the design of the research activities, piloted these during the methods training and led the group discussions during the fieldwork.

During the school bullying project (Being Part and Parcel of the School), peer researchers probably had the least remit to participate in the design of the project. To a large extent this can be explained by the fact that this research was a commissioned piece of work with quite definite expectations in terms of the methodology used and outcome. Nonetheless, the peer researchers explicitly stated that they were comfortable with this: they reported that having a more intensive involvement may have adversely affected their schoolwork: 'I mean, obviously there were points where we could have been more involved, but I didn't particularly want to be, like in the writing of the booklet. If it hadn't have been dictated to the point that it was, then I wouldn't have known what to do' (John, 18, in Burns and Schubotz, 2009: 318).

Still, the funder expected the researchers to involve young people in all aspects of the project, and here too, the training event was held in a participatory manner in which the young researchers' views on the design of the fieldwork and the particular activities was valued and taken into consideration.

Meaningful involvement

In our experience, ownership of the project is one of the conditions for an active and engaged involvement of young researchers in a study. The level of involvement of young researchers and the type of activities they are assigned to should be informed by their ambitions and by the complementary skills they bring to a project.

In Out of the Box young researchers designed a name and logo for the project. Three peer researchers were also invited to join the research steering group where they sat alongside representatives from both government departments funding the research. The other members of the steering group responded well to their inclusion and were able to field questions directly to the young people, presenting the chance to explore difficulties or issues relating to fieldwork. One of the peer researchers helped to present a paper at an international conference.

Except for Out of the Box where peer researchers were involved in the data analysis of qualitative case study interviews in partnership with the research team, dedicated data analysis days were held in all other projects we undertook. The adult researchers prepared preliminary findings of both qualitative and quantitative data which formed the basis of a much fuller discussion around the key themes which provided a framework for the final report. The draft report was then circulated to team members for comments and amendments. This proved to be a very effective way of involving young researchers at data analysis level in short-term projects. The peer researcher team had an influential role in identifying and prioritising the research findings and drew great satisfaction from this level of involvement: 'Seeing [the report], looking through, I have seen results that we found and things we did on the analysis day, so you do realise then that your involvement was like…valued' (Emma, 18, in Burns and Schubotz, 2009: 321).

Again, expectations of how much young researchers will be able to contribute at this stage must be realistic, as young people are often facing other, more pressing, priorities of exams, relationships and part-time employment which do limit the time and commitment available to the project (see Kirby et al 2001; Kilpatrick et al, 2007a; and McAlister et al, 2007).

In Out of the Box two of the young researchers contributed to the writing of one of the chapters of the final report which examined the learning and experience of being a peer researcher. They and other young researchers were also asked to present the findings of the research. For the shorter term projects, contribution to the analysis was more manageable, as was the presentation of findings. Naming peer researchers as co-authors in subsequent publications was also considered to be important.

In our experience it is beneficial to let young people take the lead during participatory research projects as their initiative can often enhance the research. For example, in Out of the Box one peer researcher arranged an introductory information session at the local cinema after securing free tickets and pizza to try and encourage good attendance. This is not an approach that the adult team would necessarily have adopted but the peer researchers felt that it was a useful way to engage potential participants by getting to know them first in an informal setting.

In Attitudes to Difference, two peer researchers conducted additional fieldwork after the team felt that the information gained so far in the participating schools was patchy. Peer researchers mobilising participants in the research on cross-community schemes used social networking sites such as Bebo and MySpace as a means of garnering support and encouraging attendance at focus group sessions.

Becoming role models

Some of our peer researchers felt an imperative to act as a confidante and, at times, a positive role model, which was missing in many of these young people's lives.

Due to the longer time period of the Out of the Box project, hierarchies within the peer researcher team emerged. Older or more experienced members progressed into a role of team mentor which also helped manage the team work in each of the four different geographic locations where the project took place. This was something that occurred naturally and could not have been easily imposed by senior researchers. However, it served well to motivate and support each local team and was a useful mechanism for the university-based researchers to monitor progress on fieldwork.

In the Being Part and Parcel of the School project, young people from special educational needs schools were recruited as peer researchers, dispelling the stereotype that only the smartest and most academically-minded young people can become involved as young researchers. A number of young researchers from this project went on to become peer mentors on school bullying in their respective schools. In one school, the peer researchers became instrumental in the establishment of a school council.

Some of the peer researchers participating in Attitudes to Difference joined Young NCB, a forum that is actively involved in decision making and policy information on matters affecting young people. Among these were people from minority ethnic backgrounds who visibly gained confidence through their work as peer researchers.

Potential difficulties

Participatory research projects pose some challenges, most of which we have already discussed, such as the role of gatekeepers, the lack of young people's research experience and the multiple pressures of time and commitment they are under. Not all of these challenges occur in all projects, and when they occur they can take different forms.

In Attitudes to Difference, the training days showed that on more than one occasion the pupils favoured and recommended as peer researchers by principals (our gatekeepers on that occasion), were not the best suited young people for the project. Some young people, for example, were already too committed to other activities, others were not able to relate to young people in the way young researchers were expected to, or they were unable to distance themselves sufficiently from their own attitudes and experiences in order to collect data impartially.

Another difficulty arose from the limited experience that young researchers had in collecting and recording data. In all research projects we conducted, young people were tasked with conducting interviews but also, in some instances, the subsequent transcription of the interview or fieldwork notes. The quality of the data at times was poor, with some of the interviews lacking in probity. Measures taken by us to remedy this problem included the provision of additional interview training which concentrated on interviewing techniques, involving video recorded role play and group feedback and adopting Elliott et al's (2001) recommendation of debriefing after each interview. This worked well because it gave the interviewer an opportunity to talk through any issues arising post-interview and helped give greater proximity to the data emerging.

Assigning roles of interviewer and transcriber to young researchers also raises issues about data security (as in any work conducted outside the confines of a research establishment). Whilst key principals of research ethics and confidentiality were discussed in the research training, the time spent on considering these issues was relatively limited.

Reflecting on the peer research process

The model of participatory research we used were developed around the practical implications and considerations of involving young people in research, with learning acquired from each experience informing the design and delivery of each subsequent project. The model developed over these different projects has helped to develop a framework which sets out to fulfil the research objectives with integrity and appropriate scientific rigour but creates real potential to empower the young researchers and the community they inhabit. Reason and Torbert (2001) have described three different pathways of action in participatory research: first-person, second-person and third person. The first-person approach requires individuals to adopt an enquiring approach to their own lives, second-person involves face-to-face enquiry in areas of mutual concern, while the third involves an impact on the community as a whole. Reason and Bradbury (2006) offer the combination of all three as a paradigm, creating an altogether more convincing and longer lasting approach. All of the projects described above do in various ways reflect all three active pathways.

Key learning

From the projects we have undertaken, some issues have emerged that we can share in order to support other researchers considering the participation of young researchers in their projects.

1. During the recruitment stage of a project we feel that it is important to provide concise and clear information to the young people (and their

gatekeepers if applicable) on the aims and objectives of the research, the peer researcher selection process, as well as the tasks for the young researchers, the anticipated time commitment, but also about the potential benefits. Application forms and contracts with the peer researchers have contributed to a positive attitude and commitment of the young people towards the research projects. We have no evidence that payment of peer researchers is necessary, but we feel that it is helpful in terms of contractual arrangements and negotiating expectations.

2. The training days have been crucial to the successful completion of the projects. We arranged our training sessions in a participatory manner, sometimes involving youth workers. Similarly, it can be beneficial to bring in ex-peer researchers as training co-facilitators as they may be best placed to respond to young people's questions on what it is like in practice to be a peer researcher. It is important to have a good balance of topic-based information, research methods skills, role play and piloting of research activities as well as organisational matters.

3. Peer researchers will need continuous support and encouragement throughout the research project. This involves, for example: debriefing after fieldwork; probing peer researchers for as much information as possible; and practical support in terms of travelling, time management, skill development and so on. It is therefore important to establish effective and reliable communication channels.

4. Young people's lives are often in transition. Realistic time frames and expectations of young people are therefore crucial. It may be a good idea to consider recruiting reserve candidates for peer researcher positions, to account for the problem of peer researcher attrition.

5. Young researchers often become positive role models for their peers. They develop transferrable personal skills, and gain expertise that may be of benefit for schools and/or organisations in which they are involved. Peer researchers may seek opportunities to develop their skills further and it is a good idea to think about progression options available for them.

6. During a research project, challenges inevitably arise around power relations between young people, but also between adults and young people. From the start, senior researchers should give long consideration to how much power they are willing to relinquish and be clear and honest with peer researchers about the extent to which they are willing and able to hand over responsibilities. It is difficult to predict what hierarchies and tensions exactly will develop during a project (for example, gender, popularity, age). It is therefore important to be sensitive towards inter-personal relationships in the project.

7. Finally, peer researchers will have a tendency to confuse their own experiences with the views of those they investigate. It is difficult for anyone to acquire and master the skill of researcher impartiality, even

for experienced academics. Peer researchers who have been employed because of their insider knowledge may be in danger of 'going native'.

Summary

Advantages and limitations

- Participatory research with young people is not better research *per se*, but the involvement of peer researchers can enhance the outcome of a research project, provided young people's involvement is meaningful and not tokenistic, expectations are realistic, and the senior/adult research team is willing to let young people have a voice.
- Appropriate research methods training, a sensitivity towards the field among peer researchers, a good level of rapport and team spirit, and the ability to develop a realistic time frame and expectations are all key for a successful project.
- Young people can benefit on a personal level from involvement in research in terms of their skills and their aspirations. They may become more active citizens, which is of general benefit for the community in which they live.
- The involvement of young people in the actual design and first steps of the research project may be limited due to funding issues.
- Young people's time is restricted: short-term projects may be advantageous.
- There is a challenge in communicating training needs to young researchers prior to the research project. Too much training may put them off – too little training may have an impact on their ability to undertake the research and consequently reduce the quality of the data collected.

Conclusion: or does peer research mean better research?

Not all research projects lend themselves to the involvement of young researchers. In our experience, having peer researchers as part of the team certainly enhanced our research projects. It can be an effective way of accessing hard to reach groups (Out of the Box, Attitudes to Difference) or it can be a quick and economical way of identifying and selecting a ready-made sample (Cross-community Schemes). Common language and dress code contributed to creating a comfortable environment allowing for sensitive and difficult subjects to be discussed.

Some of our peer researchers soon established themselves as strong role models and had a positive influence in the lives of the researched, which is a significant departure from the perceived norms of the research relationship.

It was perhaps this nature of reciprocity that enabled trust and honesty to really expose the truth of the young people's lives.

Due to the one-off character of data collection arrangements in the short-term projects which we undertook, similar relationships between peer researchers and participants in the research could not emerge. Despite this, we have evidence that young researchers can elicit information from their peers that would most likely have remained hidden had it not been for the special relationship that young researchers quickly built with their peers.

It is the very nature of the young researcher experience which is explicitly different to that of an adult. Peer research is not necessarily better per se, but essentially different and, by adding this new dimension, potentially better. Above all, 20 years after the ratification of the UN Convention of the Rights of the Child, the involvement of young researchers in participatory projects is an acknowledgement of the fact that young people have a right to be heard in matters affecting them and that they are not just the voice of the future, but have a contribution to make here and now.

Discussion questions

1. Under what circumstances can participatory research methods take full account of what young people say, without exploiting them?
2. Are there circumstances in which participatory means of researching children and young people should not be applied?
3. What are the benefits and drawbacks of recruiting young people via gatekeepers (for example, school teachers, youth project leaders, parents)?

Note
[1] England: Children Act 2004; Scotland: Children in Scotland; Wales: Getting it right 5 year action plan; Northern Ireland: A ten-year strategy for children and young people in Northern Ireland.

References
Access Research Knowledge (ARK) (2008) *Young Life and Times (YLT) Survey*, 2007 [computer file]. ARK www.ark.ac.uk/ylt [distributor], February 2008.
Alderson, P. (2000) 'Children as Researchers: The Effects of Participation Rights on Research Methodology'. In Christensen, P. and James, A. (eds) *Research With Children: Perspectives and Practices*, London: Falmer Press, 241-257.
Arnstein, S. R. (1969) A Ladder of Citizen Participation, *Journal of the American Planning Association*, 35(4), 216–224.

Atweh, B., Christensen, C. and Dornan, L. (1998) 'Students as Action Researchers: Partnerships for Social Justice'. In Atweh, B. Kemmis, S. and Weeks, P. (eds) *Action Research in Practice*, London. Routledge, 114–139.

Boyden, J. and Ennew, J. (eds) (1997) *Children in Focus: A Manual for Participatory Research with Children*, Stockholm. Rädda Barnen.

Brannen, J. and O'Brien, M. (1995) Childhood and the Sociological Gaze, *Sociology*, 29(4): 729–37.

Burns, S. and Schubotz, D. (2009) Demonstrating the Merits of the Peer-Research Process: A Northern Ireland Case Study, *Field Methods*, 21(3), 309–326.

Checkoway, B. and Richards-Schuster, K. (2003) Youth Participation in Community Evaluation Research, *The American Journal of Evaluation*, 24(1): 21–33.

Curtis, K., Roberts, H., Copperman, J., Downie, A. and Liabo, K. (2004) How Come I Don't Get Asked No Questions? Researching 'Hard to Reach' Children and Teenagers, *Child and Family Social Work*, 9, 167–175.

David, M., Edwards, R. and Alldred, P. (2001) Children and School-based Research: 'Informed Consent' or 'Educated Consent'? *British Educational Research Journal*, 27(3): 347–365.

Edwards, R. and Alldred, P. (1999) Children and Young People's Views of Social Research. The Case of Research on Home-school Relations. *Childhood*, 6(2): 261–281.

Elliott, E., Watson, A. and Harries, U. (2001) Harnessing Expertise: Involving Peer Interviewers in Qualitative Research with Hard-to-reach Populations, *Health Expectations*, 5(2): 172–178.

Hart, R. (1992) 'Ladder of Young People's Participation', in R. Hart *Children's Participation from Tokenism to Citizenship* (Innocenti Essays No. 4) (Florence, UNICEF), www.freechild.org/ladder.htm

Hill, M. (1997) Research Review. Participatory research with children, *Child and Family Social Work*, 2:171–183.

Jones, A. (2004) 'Children and Young People as Researchers' In: Fraser, S. Lewis, V. Ding, S. Kellett, M. and Robinson, C. (eds) *Doing Research With Children and Young People*. London: Sage, 113–130.

Kilpatrick, R., McCartan, C., McAlister, S. and McKeown, P. (2007a) If I am Brutally Honest, Research has Never Appealed to Me... The Problems and Successes of a Peer Research Project, *Educational Action Research*, 15(3), 351–369.

Kilpatrick, R., McCartan, C. and McKeown, P. (2007b) *Out of the Box – Alternative Education Provision in Northern Ireland*. Research Report No. 45, Bangor: Department of Education.

Kirby, P. (1999) *Involving Young Researchers. How to Enable Young People to Design and Conduct Research*, London: Joseph Rowntree Foundation.

Kirby, P., Hays, Wubner, K. and Lewis, M. (2001) 'The HAYS Project: Young People in control?' In: J. Clark, A. Dyson, N. Meagher, E. Robson and M. Wooten (eds) *Young People as Researchers: Possibilities, Problems and Politics*, Leicester: Youth Work Press.

Kirby, P., Laws, S., and Pettitt, B. (2004) *Assessing the Impact of Children's Participation: A Discussion Paper Towards a New Study*, Discussion paper for International Save the Children Alliance Child Participation Working Group.

McAlister, S., Gray, A. and Neill, G. (2007) *Still Waiting: The Stories Behind the Statistics of Young Women Growing up in Northern Ireland*, Belfast: Youth Action Northern Ireland.

McCartan, C., Kilpatrick, R., McKeown, P., Gallagher, T. and Leitch, R. (2004) *Disaffected Young People and their Experience of Alternative Education: Involving Peer Researchers in the Research Process*, Discussion Paper, European Conference on Educational Research, September 2004.

National Children's Bureau (NCB) NI and Access Research Knowledge/ Young Life and Times (ARK/YLT) (2010) *Attitudes to Difference: Young People's Attitudes to and Experiences of Contact with People from Different Minority Ethnic and Migrant Communities in Northern Ireland*, London: National Children's Bureau.

Reason, P. and Bradbury, H. (eds) (2006) *Handbook of Action Research*, London: Sage.

Reason, P. and Torbert, W.R. (2001) The Action Turn: Toward A Transformational Social Science, *Concepts and Transformation*, 6(1): 1-37.

Schubotz, D. and Sinclair, R. (2006) *'Being Part and Parcel of the School': The Views and Experiences of Children and Young People in Relation to the Development of Bullying Policies in Schools*, Belfast: Northern Ireland Commissioner for Children and Young People.

Schubotz, D. and McCartan, C., with, McDaid, A., McIntyre, B., McKee, F., McManus, M., O'Kelly, S., Roberts, A. and Whinnery, L. (2008) Cross community schemes: Participation, motivation, mandate. Final project report. Belfast: Access Research Knowledge (ARK), www.ark.ac.uk/ publications/occasional/crosscommunityschemesfinal.pdf.

Nineteen

Translating lives: cross-language community research with Polish migrants in the UK

Bogusia Temple and Katarzyna Koterba

Chapter aims

- To examine the extent to which issues of representation are addressed in cross-language research using bilingual community researchers
- To explore the epistemological assumptions made in such research about language and identity
- To discuss why it is important to consider the criteria used to choose community researchers to work across languages
- To suggest a method that can help to address issues of representation by bilingual community researchers (CRs)

Introduction

Our interest in this area stems from a recognition that the choice of community researchers (CRs) is largely framed around access to 'the community' and undetermined 'language skills'. This assumes a homogeneous community speaking a ubiquitous language with the assumption that one person can represent 'it' and communicate in an unproblematic way. Our research suggests the need to discuss the ways in which bilingual CRs are positioned within communities and to consider their language use within these communities and within the research. We suggest it is necessary to acknowledge that communities are not homogeneous and that language is used by people differently to ascribe 'insider' and 'outsider' distinctions, that is, language is used as part of a process of constructing the identities of research participants rather than just to describe identities that exist outside of language. When CRs translate what has been said from one language into another language differences across languages may be obscured. In this chapter we provide an overview of one method that we have used to begin to address some of the issues involved in representing people when writing in a language they may not speak. We use the example of an Economic and Social Research Council (ESRC)-funded research project on language and identity amongst Polish people in Greater Manchester, England. The research shows that participants recognised the effects of changing language on perceptions of self and other. It also demonstrates that the CR who carried out the interviews was included in this process of ascription of similarity and difference and that the process involved much more than simple attributions of insider and outsider status based on judgements about language proficiency.

Theoretical discussion

Researchers have argued against the notion of an undifferentiated community, that is, people who may see themselves as part of particular communities may nevertheless experience them in different ways, for example in relation to their gender, class or age (Alexander et al, 2007; Edwards and Alexander (2011).[1] In this chapter we base our discussion on Edwards and Alexander's (p 269) definition of peer/community researchers as 'people who live within, and have everyday experiences as a member of, a particular geographical or social "community", and who use their contacts and detailed lay knowledge in a mediating role, helping to gather and understand information from and about their peers for research purposes'. As Edwards and Alexander (2011) argue, any fixed definition of insider and outsider and community is problematic. They review issues in ascribing insider and outsider status to CRs, including essentialising notions of belonging and community. That is, they caution against defining belonging and community as being essentially the same for everyone. The issues in defining an 'insider' are well illustrated in our research where the Principal Investigator (PI) has previously argued that she may or may not be an 'insider' depending on what criteria are used, from whose point of view, what community is being discussed and under what circumstances (Temple, 2001). The PI could also be described as a CR if Edwards and Alexander's definition of 'living within' is applied broadly, as she has previously had extensive experience of being an active part of a Polish community, has knowledge of Polish communities, including the ones in our research, speaks Polish, has Polish friends and uses her knowledge to generate and analyse data. However, her ties to Polish communities, particularly the community that is the focus of this research, are not the same as the research assistant (RA) who was employed by the University we both worked at to undertake the interviews and to be part of the research process, including interpretation of findings and subsequent publications. We define the RA as the CR in this chapter.

There has been increasing interest in extending the critique of essentialism to examine assumptions made about bilingual/multilingual CRs and the nature of their roles as cross-language mediators (Temple and Koterba,

2009). Within social science research CRs are often seen as valuable for their language and skills as 'go-betweens', as being 'between cultures'. However, the ways in which they use their languages are rarely considered in other aspects of research, such as data interpretation and analysing findings. This is evident in research that uses CRs to interpret as well as to translate. This lack of reflexivity is surprising. Discussing the view of translators as between cultures, Baker challenges their status as 'honest and detached brokers' who operate largely in the 'spaces between' cultures (2005: 11). This point could equally well be made in relation to the current way bilingual CRs are sometimes portrayed, if not directly then indirectly, via an uncritical view of their language use and the effects of translating into a language not used by participants. At the centre of this lack of attention to the ways in which CRs use language lies a problematic epistemology and methodology that appears to assume it does not matter whom you choose to do the research, as all CRs are similarly located within communities and use language in the same way.

However, many writers from a range of disciplines have shown that people who speak and write different languages may not use words and concepts in the same way by (see Temple and Koterba, 2009 for some of these critiques). Of particular relevance here in relation to the Polish language is the work of Besemeres who argues that emotional experience is 'inflected differently in different languages' (2006: 34). She discusses the words 'anxious' and 'boję się' and bases her discussion on Eva Hoffman's account of moving from Poland to Canada to argue that 'when someone uses an emotion word to describe a feeling, the word chosen helps to shape that feeling, affecting how the person perceives and interprets it, and hence how he or she experiences it' (Besemeres). The English word 'anxious', Besemeres argues, is influenced by popular psychology in which it is good to be in control, whereas 'boję się' in Polish is associated with 'a cultural outlook in which feelings are perceived as natural' (2006: 41).

Pavlenko (2005) also suggests that there may be differences in narratives across languages, including in their structure, amount of evaluation offered and directness of emotion description (see also McCabe and Bliss, 2003). Bilingual CRs move between these possible differences and may be differently situated in relation to them. This has implications for the choice of bilingual CRs in that it indicates that whom you work with influences how words spoken in one language are likely to be understood and represented in another. Pavlenko's (2005) discussion of bi/multilingual language use suggests that interactions with others and perceptions of self and others are influenced by a variety of factors. These include: linguistic competence, perceived language prestige and authority, context of language acquisition and age of acquisition of languages. She argues that:

> Speakers who have different socialisation experiences in the first and second languages may perceive these languages as differentially embodied. Languages learned in the process of intense childhood socialisation seem connected to the body through an intricate web of personal memories, images, sensory associations, and affective reactions, while languages learned later in life, in the classroom, or through limited socialisation (for instance, the workplace) do not have the same sensual associations; they do not stir or evoke. (Pavlenko, 2005: 187)

Pavlenko suggests that in changing what people say from one language to another, bilingual speakers in effect translate lives rather than words. She writes about selves that 'change with the shift in language' (2006: 27), involving changing linguistic repertoires, autobiographical memories, levels of proficiency and emotionality. CRs may view themselves and others through different language lenses, which vary according to their different learning experiences. Changing the language used to represent people within research therefore has epistemological consequences in that it involves re-constructing the identities of others rather than just re-presenting them. Language is not a neutral medium for passing on images of people within research but is used to construct accounts of self and others in ways that can be challenged. The bilingual CR's experiences with different languages will affect how they do this.

Literature around the concept of 'hybridity', an approach that recognises that people can be influenced by more than one culture or language, provides one fruitful way to look at the boundaries between languages and cultures and the positioning of CRs within these. For example, Bhabha's (1994) work on 'culture's in-between' (Rutherford, 1990; Bhabha, 1994; Werbner, 2001), 'hybridity' and 'the third space' does not aim 'to trace two original moments from which the third emerges', but is 'the "third space" which enables other positions to emerge'. Bhabha in an interview with Rutherford (1990: 211) argues that: 'The process of cultural hybridity gives rise to something different, something new and unrecognizable, a new area of negotiation of meaning and representation' (Rutherford, 1990: 211).[2]

This negotiation of meaning is a political and ethical enterprise as it involves the representation of others (Spivak, 1992, 1993; Venuti, 1995, 1998). Examining the position of CRs in relation to their use of language, participants' use of language and the relationship between the two involves an examination of 'hybridity' or ways of being bilingual.

Within Polish communities there are divisions around gender, generation, reasons for migration as well as other factors. These factors influence who can or will be interviewed as well as what and how issues are discussed (Temple and Koterba, 2009). Language has an important role here in that it can be used as a potential marker of 'insiders' and 'outsiders' (see later in the chapter). Within our research we have aimed to be reflexive about the social position of all researchers involved in any research, including the bilingual CR (in this case the RA. We have done this by building on the concept of 'auto/biography' developed by Stanley (1990) which involves: 'an analytic (not just descriptive) concern with the specifics of how we come to understand what we do, by locating acts of understanding in an explication of the grounded contexts these are located in and arise from' (1990: 62). Extended to look at cross-language research, the concept situates all 'findings' as products of the interactions of researchers, translators, interpreters, CRs and participants. We focus in this chapter particularly on the way that the academic and language skills as well as the life experiences of the two project members influenced the findings. We are not suggesting that this is the only way to be reflexive about the use of language within cross-language research, but that it is one way to approach it (see also, for example, Blommaert, 2001, 2005). None of the approaches, including the one adopted in our research, provide definitive answers to questions about the effects of bilingual CRs on research, but they all open up the issues and aim to take seriously possible language differences in meaning construction and identification, as well as acknowledging that translating lives across languages is an ethical and political project.

Community research in practice[3]

In this section we use the experiences of an ESRC-funded project to illustrate how we examined and compared the influence of the bilingual CR and the bilingual PI. The project was based on 30 interviews with people who described themselves as Polish and lived in a city in the north west of England. This study looked at participants' views about the significance of Polish and English languages in their lives. The research was intended as an exploratory piece of work reflecting on influences on the research process of taking seriously issues of cross-language representation. It was not intended to test any particular model of community research, of which there are many (see for example, Temple and Moran, 2006), although our research approach does involve questioning just how participatory cross-language research is. Many researchers have also questioned the traditional 'academic mode of production' (Stanley, 1990) and research based on a model of taking data from communities rather than working with more participatory research paradigms. The limits of our own approach are discussed below.

Participants in our research discussed language, for example in relation to social networks within and outside their community, and in relation to integration with English society. A narrative approach was used and the researchers analysed both what people said and how they said it (see Temple, 2008). Participants were given the choice of whether to speak Polish or

English during the interview. Each interview was transcribed if in English, and translated and transcribed if in Polish by the researchers.

In this chapter we argue that the CR influenced the research in all its phases:

1. in the recruitment of research participants by finding people who described themselves as Polish for interview and getting their agreement;
2. in the conduct of in-depth interviews through the nature of the interactions;
3. in the transcription of interviews in English and translation of interviews from Polish;
4. in the preparation of reports and other research outputs.

The PI in our research is bilingual, born and brought up in England speaking Polish and sometimes describes herself as a second generation Polish woman. The RA is a recent Polish migrant. Their backgrounds, personal experiences, social networks and ways of using and understanding of Polish and English languages are different and this resulted in an extremely interesting cooperation that was used to reflect on the research. She had close contacts in the community with whom she was working and carried out the interviews. However, both the PI and RA bought their knowledge of being Polish and of Polish communities to the research and to translation and transcription.

Recruitment of participants

Purposive sampling was used to select participants. The aim was to include participants from a variety of backgrounds in terms of sex, age, place of birth, date of arrival in the UK and social networks. This stage of the project was influenced mostly by the RA (now referred to as the CR in this chapter). The fact that she is a recent migrant played a significant role in the recruitment process because the networks used were hers. Being a recent migrant was an advantage in terms of approaching 20–35 year-old recent migrants. However, in other cases it was a disadvantage, for example, when recruiting participants of second or third generation, born in the UK, as the CR didn't have many contacts with this group of Polish people. Moreover, they distanced themselves from more recent migrants in general (see below). The CR was affected by these tensions within the communities as a recent migrant herself. The PI used her knowledge of Polish communities to keep an eye on sample composition to ensure a variety of participants, including those outside of the CR's 'comfort zone'. Through the exchange of information about networks, organisations and contacts available in the recruitment process, the CR was able to interview participants from different backgrounds and to make sampling relevant to the theoretical issues under investigation. In other words, she was able to choose people to reflect a concern with the differentiated nature of Polish communities in the UK.

Conduct of interviews

As discussed above, the selection of interviews was influenced by the CR's position in the Polish communities in the area. The conduct of the interviews was also affected by her position as a migrant. An awareness and knowledge of the differences in the ways the Polish language was used in terms of lexicon and accent, for example, was important as the way participants spoke Polish was used by Polish speakers to identify someone's likely background. The CR's Polish could also be used to identify when she had come to the UK. Older people spoke a Polish that was seen as out of date by newer migrants, and sometimes with a strong accent from a particular part of Poland. Jan Kochanowski said, 'our way is still old fashioned' (transcribed by KK) referring to the kind of Polish spoken by second and third generation Polish people born in the UK. Artur Kisielewski, a second generation Polish man, described his Polish as 'ze wsi' literally: from the countryside or not educated. More recent migrants often used colloquial Polish in their interviews with slang and swear words. These differences in language use were seen as significant within the communities as they could be used to identify differences between members according to migration period and likely reason for coming to England. Jan Majczak commented on these differences in his interview saying: 'we're of the same community but we're not' (transcribed by BT). He was referring to relationships between the established Polonia and more recent migrants. Majczak and other participants mentioned that they were able, based on the way people spoke Polish, to differentiate between them and make assumptions about their backgrounds and values.

The methods used in the research were influenced by the tensions within Polish communities. For example, the project design had initially specified individual interviews. However, three participants didn't feel very comfortable talking about themselves and suggested joint interviews. Two of the joint interviews were with participants born in the UK. These joint interviews proved useful in approaching sensitive issues, such as the nature of the tensions between different sections of Polish communities. The influence of the CR's position as a recent migrant was clear in these joint interviews as the comment about recent migrants below shows. Edmund and Maryla Leśniak[4] commented in their joint interview on the present situation within the Polish community and their feeling about the post–2004 migration wave:

Edmund: 'It's … all dreams coming to an end, I think, generally. And lots of these Polish people are here temporary as well.'

Maryla: 'It's probably of the high numbers that came over that it's been such a drastic change. If it's been a trickle like it was in the 70s …. Or a slightly bigger trickle than the 70s then it might merge it better. But it's like an avalanche it just swamps everything. And that might be the end of the era because of that avalanche.'

Edmund: 'Ye, it is. And our children are one of those who are the last.'

Maryla: 'We've been fortunate but they won't be in their adult life. Ye, and it must be a lost.'

Katarzyna: 'It's sad to hear about this situation.'

Edmund: 'This is the truth. You asked us to speak frankly.'

Katarzyna: 'Of course, I did.'

Edmund: 'You might not like what you hear listening.'

Katarzyna: 'It doesn't matter if I like it or not if that's the truth. You don't need to tell me only nice if things like these happen.' (Transcribed by KK)

The research included an examination of both the influence of the PI and the CR on the research as central to the narrative approach used (Temple, 2008). The CR was interviewed by the PI to discuss her views on the research topic and her perceptions of her influence on the findings. In the interview the CR commented:

'I tried to find different respondents…some of the participants are of second and third generation and erm…those people …that's what they told me. They felt very very Polish until 2004 actually and when more and more Polish people came over they said "Oh, we don't feel that Polish any more," and they think that erm…new migrants like me and thousands of Polish people who came over…they … they actually are not proper members of the Polish community and erm…of course some Polish people…I am talking about new migrants now…they are people who are looking for trouble here and therefore the people from second and third generation don't like them. That's why when I ask some people of older generation…

not really old people but but born in the UK they treated me with distance a little bit or didn't really want to talk to me. Because erm... I am one of the new migrants.' (Transcribed by BT)

Transcription and translation of interviews

In our research both the PI and the CR were translators. The CR met regularly with the PI to analyse the translation process. The researchers discussed each interview translation in terms of content, but also for choice of words and concepts used (Temple and Koterba, 2009). The CR's knowledge of slang was useful here and points to the importance of examining what kind of language history a CR has. As Pavlenko (2005) has argued (see earlier in the chapter), there are different ways to be bilingual. Our research suggests these differences may be important within research as language experiences may affect understanding and interaction within an interview. For example, Krzysztof Biel said: 'Tylko puścił mi głuchego' (translated by KK). The phrase is used in everyday Polish, especially by young people and created some translation problems for the PI who understood all the words but could make no sense of the meaning. The phrase can be translated as 'He only let out to me a deaf.' The CR translated this as 'He pranked' or 'He beeped me' meaning that he used his mobile. However, there are no references to mobile phones in the phrase. The CR pointed out that there is no need to refer directly to a mobile phone in Polish and also that he had not used the grammatically correct version of 'głuchy'. The participant was describing how a friend had made a gesture at getting in touch by using his mobile, but had not given him enough time to respond, implying that he was not seriously intending to speak to him. The interview translations were kept with these kinds of decisions about translation choices and comments, explanations and discussions noted in the form of a translation history on each transcript rather than cleaning up the transcripts as if there were no translation choices to be made. Any problematic issues were discussed, compared with the recording and narrowed to one version.

Venuti (1995) has argued that translators generally tend to tidy up accounts because readers expect texts to be grammatically correct in their own language. By 'tidying up' we mean, for example, taking out any interruptions in flow, correcting grammatical structures and style. Venuti argues that this act of 'domestication' has the effect of introducing the source language as the baseline and Spivak (1993) asserts that this is a political act as it involves issues of representation of other language speakers. The CR in this research followed Venuti's (1995) advice that texts should be 'foreignised', that is, there should be some indication that these were not English speakers. We chose to indicate our translation choices on the texts, as well as any context relevant information. When writing about the interviews we give the Polish transcription alongside the English translation (Temple and Koterba, 2009). In other words, we tried to question the effect of using English language conventions to 'domesticate' or incorporate possible differences in meaning and styles of presentation across languages.

However, some tidying up was necessary to ensure comprehension was possible. As Eco (2003) discusses, the decisions about the balance between foreignising and domesticating texts are influenced by context. Some funders and publishers do not like texts with hedges and fillers or with descriptions of the translation process. It may, however, be important to show participants as hesitating in interviews. In our research we found that hesitations were sometimes indicative of the participant's awareness of the sensitive nature of the topic. For example, Piotr Frycz paused and changed the sentence flow: 'I think, erm ... it is definitely a difficult problem ... we need to live like ... we live like in Poland' (translated by KK). The assertion that people who come to England should continue to live as if they were in Poland was made at a time when the media were publicising the growing costs of translation and interpretation and the government were encouraging the implementation of policies of community cohesion.

Marking context on the transcript as in the example above may also be important for analysing a respondent's style and use of language in relation to the presumed nature of the research interaction: 'Always on Saturday and every Thursday we, you know, older people have lunch in our Club' (interview with Ewa Mlynarczyk, translated by KK). The way the tone of the interview was conveyed reflected the participants' presumptions about the nature of the relationship between the researcher and the CR. For example, the use of Polish 'proszę Pani' which can be translated as 'if it pleases you (female/lady)' indicates that the speaker addressed the CR formally and with respect. They were strangers, the participant was indicating the formal nature of their relationship. Other participants referred to the CR by her first name.

Preparation of research outputs

The PI led this phase of the research. The PI and RA decided to disseminate the findings in various ways, including journal articles, conference presentations, leaflets, newspaper articles and a report to the funder. The PI's research experience and knowledge of the literature was the basis for the academic outputs. The CR utilised her background, experience, language knowledge and contacts in leading the dissemination process in Polish. Leaflets in Polish and articles published in the Polish press gave Polish speakers the opportunity to read about the research findings in their own language. This division of labour was inevitable given that the research was initiated by the PI in an area in which she had already published extensively.

Not all researchers can contribute to the academic mode of production equally as there is an academic way of presenting research that takes time to learn. Training in basic research methods or the aims of the research, which is all that is usually possible in research projects, is unlikely to enable CRs to take part in debates based on vast amounts of 'great names' and argued positions. However, in the same way, the PI could not match the CR's knowledge and use of Polish of the kind needed for publishing in Polish outlets.

We did not discuss our findings directly with participants, although we produced leaflets in Polish and English about the research. This would have involved substantial resource implications and another layer of analysis. Moreover, as Silverman (1993) and others have argued, taking findings back to participants in qualitative research opens up debate about perspectives and interpretations in different contexts rather than acting as a form of validation in the sense of confirmation of original meanings. This would have been valuable but was not possible in this project.

Key learning

This overview of the issues in cross-language research with CRs suggests the need to reflect on the influence of all of the research team, including bilingual CRs and to identify the strengths and limits of the reach of the chosen method. We acknowledge that the extent of engagement and debate about interpretation was limited and that our epistemological position is by no means straightforward or easy to transfer into practice. The first of these points relates to issues of resources. Taking language differences into account in research is time and money intensive and many funding bodies baulk at the cost of doing so, while also expressing the need for community engagement. However, all researchers should be able to incorporate some language reflexivity into their work, at a minimum, by discussing translations of interviews and the CR's approach to them. The second point about our epistemological position is more complex. We realise that we have argued that there is, in essence, no essence to being Polish or any other way of experiencing social reality (Fuss, 1989). All research methods/methodologies construct versions of social reality (Law, 2004) and ours is no different. The criteria for choosing which methods/methodologies to use are themselves therefore up for debate (Rorty, 1991; Law, 2004). In our research we use reflexivity, including an awareness of the workings of power dynamics across languages and within research relationships. We have argued that the CR's translation of the words of participants into a language that they did not use involves issues of representation and an acknowledgement of the political and ontological context of research. We are not arguing that we represent Polish communities generally in our research or that our research is participatory in the standard sense of broad and meaningful inclusion of community members. As discussed above, this was not our aim as the research was exploratory. However, we do aim to make the basis of our representational claims open to review. This begins to be participatory in that it challenges the linguistic imperialism that characterises researchers who give their interviews over to be 'prepared' by unnamed translators.

Summary

We have argued that our method is one way of looking at cross-language issues of representation and that there are others, none of which provide solutions to what is essentially an unsolvable situation. We are not suggesting that the language someone uses determines their view of the social world but are arguing that it does influence it and that there are many ways to experience being a CR and being bilingual and an investigation of these ways should be part of the research process. It has been demonstrated throughout the chapter that these issues can have an impact on the research process. What is seen as an advantage and a disadvantage, therefore, depends on the context. For example, getting a fluent Polish-speaking recent migrant may be seen in positive terms by some migrants, others may prefer 'outsiders', either in terms of language, if they speak English, or position within the community. The way the translation is presented will also be influenced by audience and purpose. The researcher's role is to reflect on possibilities and to provide evidence for claims about the nature of the influence of all involved in the research, including CRs. Moreover, when researchers do not understand the languages involved, the process differs in that they are much more reliant on the CR to point out possible challenges in translation and representation.[5]

Summary: Advantages and disadvantages of building on an auto/biographical approach to investigating language use in research

Advantages	Disadvantages	Comment
Takes seriously the possibility that people who speak different languages may present themselves differently.	Danger of assuming that the language used determines someone's views of social reality.	The kind of engagement involved when the researcher does not understand the language used at all is different – there is more reliance on the CR to raise issues of representation.
Examines position of all researchers, including CRs, involved in research.	No deterministic link between social location and position of CR within community and participants' preferences.	Involves providing evidence for claims of the influence of the CR.
Introduces issues of ethics and politics into cross-language research.		This needs to include larger social context outside the research.
Involves considering training for CRs in research and ethical translation to make them active members of the team.	Time consuming and therefore can be expensive.	Training should not be limited to translation and language issues as this in effect limits the contribution CRs can make to research and is problematic it views CRs solely in terms of an essentialised ethnicity (Schick, 2002).

Conclusion

We suggest that there are no straightforward solutions to issues of representation across languages and that social science research is, as Law (2004) argues, messy. However, failure to explore these issues anchors the research firmly in the view that which language is used and how it is used is irrelevant. Moreover, ignoring the different ways in which languages portray others is not an ethical option as it uses as a baseline the unchallenged view of the CR. Bilingual CRs experience languages in different ways and these differences affect the ways they write about research participants and interpret findings. The views of CRs on the research and the people in it affect, but do not determine, findings in the same way as language may affect, but does not determine, how we present ourselves in the languages we use.

Discussion questions

We suggest that researchers working with bilingual CRs would find it useful to consider the following:

1. What are the factors that should be taken into account when choosing a bilingual CR?
2. What are the training issues for CRs around language and translation?
3. How involved does the research team need to be in discussions about translating interviews?

Notes

[1] We do not rehearse the arguments around insiders/outsiders here. Temple and Koterba (2009) and Edwards and Alexander (2011) provide a review of these issues.

[2] See Werbner (2001) for a detailed discussion of concepts of hybridity.

[3] Our thanks to the ESRC for funding this research (Language and identity in the narratives of Polish people, RES-000-22-2187). I would also like to thank the participants for their time and hospitality.

[4] We have changed all names of participants in order to protect their anonymity.

[5] See Temple et al (2006) for an example of this situation.

References

Alexander, C., Edwards, R. and Temple, B. (2007) Contesting Cultural Communities: Language, Ethnicity and Citizenship, *Journal of Ethnic and Migration Studies*, 33(5), 783–800.

Baker, M. (2005) Narratives in and of Translation, *SASE Journal of Translation and Interpretation*, 1(1):1–10 [cited 9 February 2009], www.skase.sk/Volumes/JTI01/doc_pdf/01.pdf

Besemeres, M. (2006) Language and Emotional Experience: The Voice of Translingual Memoir. In Pavlenko, A. (ed) *Bilingual Minds: Emotional Experience, Expression and Representation*, Clevedon, Buffalo, Toronto: Multilingual Matters Ltd, 34–58.

Bhabha, H. (1994) *The Location of Culture*, London: Routledge.

Blommaert, J. (2001) Investigating Narrative Inequality: African Asylum Seekers' Stories in Belgium, *Discourse and Society*, 12(4), 413–449.

Blommaert, J. (2005) *Discourse*, Cambridge: Cambridge University Press.

Eco, U. (2003) *Mouse or Rat? Translation as Negotiation*, London: Weidenfeld and Nicolson.

Edwards, R. and Alexander, C. (2011) Researching with Peer/Community Researchers – Ambivalences and Tensions. In Williams, M. and Vogt, P. (eds) *Handbook of Innovations in Social Reserach Methods*, London: Sage.

Fuss, D. (1989) *Essentially Speaking: Feminism, Nature and Difference*, London, Routledge.

Law, J. (2004) *After Method: Mess in Social Science Research*, London: Routledge.

McCabe, A. and Bliss, L. (2003) *Patterns of Narrative Discourse. A Multicultural, Life Span Approach*, Boston, MA: Allyn and Bacon.

Pavlenko, A. (2005) *Emotions and Multilingualism*, Cambridge: Cambridge University Press.

Pavlenko, A. (2006) *Bilingual Minds: Emotional Experience, Expression and Representation*, Clevedon: MultiLingual Matters Ltd.

Rorty, R. (1991) *Objectivity, Relativism and Truth*, Cambridge: Cambridge University Press.

Rutherford, J. (1990) *Identity: Community, Culture, Difference*, London: Lawrence and Wishart.

Schick, R. (2002) When the Subject is Difference: Conditions of Voice in Policy-Oriented Research, *Qualitative Inquiry*, 8: 632-651.

Silverman, D. (1993) *Interpreting Qualitative Data: Methods for Analysing Talk, Text and Interaction*, London: Sage Publications.

Spivak, G. (1992) The Politics of Translation. In Barrett M. and Philips, A. (eds) *Destabilizing Theory: Contemporary Feminist Debates*, Cambridge: Polity Press: 177-200.

Spivak, G. (1993) *Outside in the Teaching Machine*, London: Routledge.

Stanley, Liz (1990) Feminist Praxis and the Academic Mode of Production: An Editorial Introduction. In Stanley, L. (ed) *Feminist Praxis: Research, Theory and Epistemology in Feminist Sociology*, London: Routledge.

Stanley, Liz (1990) Moments of Writing: Is There a Feminist Auto/biography?, *Gender & History*, 2: 58-67.

Temple B. (2001) Polish Families: A Narrative Approach, *Journal of Family Issues*, 22: 386-399.

Temple, B. (2008) Investigating Language and Identity in Cross-language Narratives, *Migrations & Identities*, 1: 1-18.

Temple, B. and Koterba, K. (2009) The Same but Different: Researching Language and Culture in the Lives of Polish People in England, *Forum: Qualitative Social Research* [online], 10(1): Art.31, http://nbn-resolving.de/urn:nbn:de:0114-fqs0901319

Temple, B. and Moran, R. (2006) (eds) *Doing Research with Refugees: Issues and Guidelines*, Bristol, The Policy Press.

Temple, B., Edwards, R. and Alexander, C. (2006) Grasping at Context: Cross Language Qualitative Research as Secondary Data Analysis *Forum: Qualitative Social Research*, http://nbn-resolving.de/urn:nbn:de:0114-fqs0604107

Venuti, L. (1995) *The Translator's Invisibility: A History of Translation*, London: Routledge.

Venuti, L. (1998) *The Scandals of Translation: Towards an Ethics of Difference*, London: Routledge.

Werbner, P. (2001) The Limits Of Cultural Hybridity: On Ritual Monsters, Poetic Licence And Contested Postcolonial Purifications, http://p.werbner.googlepages.com/HybridityJRAI.pdf

Twenty

Mentoring refugee community researchers in the UK: an empowerment tool?

Patricia A. Jones and Ricky Joseph

Chapter aims

- To analyse the relationship between mentors and community researchers within two recent community research programmes working with migrant and refugee community organisations (MRCOs)
- To examine the use of mentoring in the process of empowering MRCOs and community researchers
- To apply a theoretical framework that takes an emancipatory approach to community empowerment
- To consider key learning and implications for future community research programmes

Introduction

This chapter focuses on the role of mentoring in the context of two projects: the HACT[1] 'Accommodate' programme 2004–7 and the Joseph Rowntree Foundation 'Making a Difference' programme 2006. Both projects included an element of training migrant and refugee community researchers to assess and evidence their communities' social and welfare needs. Commentators familiar with migrant refugee community organisations (MRCOs) generally agree that their capacity to inform service provision is often overlooked by statutory welfare providers and they are rarely involved in decision-making processes at a policy or service delivery level (Amas and Price, 2008; Hutton and Lukes, 2008; Jones and Mullins, 2009). Although not without its challenges, community research has been increasingly employed to empower refugee and migrant communities and to gain 'insider' information that can be used to influence and lobby policy makers (Clough et al, 2006; Mulhall et al, 2009). Community research programmes discussed in this chapter were supported by a mentoring system, provided by seasoned researchers, on a one-to-one basis as a device to counter different abilities, language barriers and logistical constraints of new community researchers. This chapter explores whether mentoring can also be considered a useful tool in the process of empowering MRCOs.

The process of empowerment is first discussed from a structural perspective surrounding issues of power over resources, ideology and institutional structures. By focusing on a transformative view of empowerment we regard mentoring as a driving force and, when conducted in a critical pedagogic fashion, one which encourages a participatory rather than pedantic approach to capacity building. An emancipatory interpretation to the concept of empowerment is adopted in which agency, in the shape of the mentors, played a progressive role that can be better understood using operational domain theory to examine outcomes (Laverack and Wallerstein, 2001; Laverack, 2003, 2006). Laverack and Wallerstein identify nine operational domains: 'relationships with outside agents'; 'community involvement'; 'recognition'; 'resource mobilisation'; 'problem resolution'; 'organisational structures'; 'networking'; 'critical engagement' and 'assertive participation' as spheres where community empowerment could be evidenced. Our analysis of documentation involved in the mentoring systems employed within the two projects is assessed within this framework. Documents included self-reflection and feedback notes collected during the mentoring process. The community researchers were made aware that these notes might be used to support their personal development as community researchers, to strengthen the mentoring process across the programme and to ensure that their views and experiences could be applied consistently across the programme as a whole in achieving greater accountability. Project reports were also examined to locate the wider emancipatory landscape within which mentoring activity took place. The interaction between mentor and community researcher was an important building block in achieving the outcomes of the 'Accommodate' and 'Making a Difference' community research training programmes. Our conclusions suggest the relationship between mentor and community researcher is essential to the process of empowerment in a variety of operational domains. Study of the relationship expressed in self-reflection and feedback notes increased our understanding of mentoring as a tool for empowerment in future community research programmes.

Empowerment: an emancipatory process?

Both 'community' and 'empowerment' are contested terms. Taylor (2003) located community in a globally challenging environment when she classified 'community' as those with a shared interest and shared values, both of which combine to attach agency to communities when faced with changing development in their living conditions; a definition particularly apt when applied to the MRCOs involved in these programmes. Recent policy discourse concerning 'empowerment' is a legacy from the previous government's association of empowerment with shared futures, shared values and the shouldering of social responsibility (Blunkett, 2003). The emphasis here is on communities developing capacity to take on greater responsibility for social problems albeit in collaboration with service providers (MacLeavy, 2009) and precludes the transfer of social power. Flint (2002) argues that social change brought about by 'responsibilisation' strategies such as those described in Blunkett's definition simply normalises community obligations rather than emancipates communities to have a voice in redefining welfare policy priorities and delivery methods. Jones (2007) observes that policy change via community empowerment often happens post-project, making evaluation of empowerment as outcome more difficult to assess. He argues the need to consider empowerment as outcome along the timeline of project process, enabling outcome and process to be identified simultaneously and correlated with an empowering approach towards capacity building.

Along with other formative researchers, Laverack and Wallerstein (2001) emphasise that community empowerment was originally conceptualised to describe a political activity whereby community groups redressed their powerlessness and mobilised to take control and change fundamental aspects of their lives. Batliwala (2007: 560) reinforce this view describing community empowerment as a 'centuries-old expression' originally associated with a shift in social power achieved by challenging the prevailing ideology, changing prevalent patterns of access and control over resources and by transforming existing institutions and structures.

Laverack and Wallerstein (2001) built on previous paradigms to put forward nine domains in which this process may take place. They set out to address the shortfall of linear models that tend to omit more dynamic processes where issues of organisational capital, negotiating skills and vocalising critical awareness were missing. Subsequently, they were able to provide a link between individual elements of empowerment such as personal development and networking skills with political, cultural and socio-economic contextual aspects. Building organisational leadership and structures is important to consider in models of community empowerment which relate to MRCOs and their ability to represent their communities. As Balloch and Taylor (2001) observed, empowerment is a term more likely associated with the involvement of marginalised, 'hard-to-reach' community groups: communities whose needs can only be met when they have a voice in the decision-making process. This proposes a perspective of community empowerment that sits within broader theories of social justice and policy change. Social struggle presumes collective action and an arena for negotiation that is often missing from MRCOs' wider network opportunities. Most commentators agree that the role of agency, in this case via MRCO leaders, is essential in advancing the process of empowerment.

Mentoring as an empowerment tool?

Community engagement and participation do not simply happen 'effortlessly' (Pitchford and Henderson, 2008: 94). Both training programmes started from the position of recognising the potential that MRCOs can bring to policy-making forums. Mentoring was a mechanism developed in order to facilitate the empowerment process. Furthermore, the training programmes acknowledged the need for capacity building that required the adoption of a 'critical pedagogic' approach (McLaren, 1997; Steinberg, 2001; Freire, 2006 (original 1970); Kincheloe, 2008). This perspective poses problems for traditional evaluation because it approaches capacity building in the belief of what is already there. It 'assumes that the knowledge, skill and experience to bring about change are latent within the people for whom change is needed' (Jones, 2007: 29). Critical pedagogy, based in a commitment to social justice and equality, takes an approach to teaching and learning that encourages participants to challenge dominant ideology, engage in critical dialogue and recognise the connection between local problems and their wider social context. Our study showed that the role of mentor as 'outside agency' in both programmes adopted a similar emancipatory approach, where the objective was to support and enable marginalised community groups to exploit existing potential to participate in policy-making forums.

The ideology underlying the empowerment of marginalised or excluded communities to participate has been historically problematic. Academic debate deliberates whether the empowerment process should focus on the individual or the community, although community empowerment is more consistently referred to in the literature as a process that occurs along a dynamic continuum involving: individual empowerment; small groups; community organisation; partnerships and social and political action (Laverack, 2001). Anderson (1996) added a sixth point to this continuum; the power to identify agenda priorities. She considered that this was important for ownership of both problem and solution. This transformative and incremental approach towards engaging marginalised groups embodies an asset rather than deficit analysis of capacity. It proposes a working model of community empowerment that Ledwith (1997: 118) described as one developing insight into the nature of social injustice while creating 'viable alternatives' at the same time.

In this chapter we adapted a theoretical framework that encompassed both individual and organisational dynamics in order to explore how the role of mentoring evolved over the life of the two projects. Laverack and Wallerstein's (2001) concept of operational domains provides a link between individual, contextual and organisational elements of emancipatory empowerment (Figure 20. 1). We discovered that as community researchers developed as individuals they strengthened their organisations' negotiating positions. Consequently both collective and individual empowerment could be considered simultaneously and connections made between individual and organisational social capital that has an impact on community empowerment as outcome. Doctoral research (Jones, 2010) based on empowerment of MRCOs engaged within the 'Accommodate' project as a whole suggested that community empowerment is an accumulative rather than a linear process, exposed to external dynamics and prone to uneven development. By analysing the documentation that evidenced the mentoring process in both programmes we were able to explore which operational domains dynamically connected mentors and community researchers (Figure 20.1).

Figure 20.1 Operational domains in a programme context

Operational domains of community empowerment	Programme context
Participation	Action to improve participation
Leadership	Develops local leadership
Problem assessment	Increases problem assessment capacities
Asking why	Enhances the ability to 'ask why'
Organisational structures	Builds empowering organisational structures
Resource mobilisation	Improves resource mobilisation
Links to others	Strengthens links to other organisations and people
The role of outside agents	Creates an equitable relationship with outside agents, for example, maintained by critical self-reflection (were agents empowering? facilitating? imposing?)
Programme management	Increases control over programme management, for example, increased involvement in achieving changes in policy, legislation and levels of community action

Sources: Jones (2010; adapted from Laverack and Wallerstein (2001)); Laverack, 2001, 2006

Community research in practice

The training process

The purpose of the training embedded in both of the community research programmes was to bring qualitative social research skills to a range of different communities who were experiencing language and literacy challenges. Teaching covered the purpose of interviewing, ethics, subjectivity and researcher bias, listening and inquiring, questioning, probing, question and topic guide design, body language, identifying respondents, setting up interviews and collecting data, alongside general principles of social research. Trainees were able to identify issues they felt their organisations and stakeholders needed to know in order to help understand the experiences of refugees and asylum seekers. Further group-work helped turn issues into questions and to develop interview topic guides. Through repeated, observed, mock interview and self-reflection sessions community researchers honed their interview techniques.

A second stage allocated a personal mentor to each trainee while they undertook a series of face-to-face interviews. With support from their mentor, and clear guidelines of sampling targets, researchers were required to follow a step-by-step process which took them from the point of identifying respondents, setting up, undertaking and recording interviews to completing data analysis forms, self-reflection forms and receiving detailed feedback from their mentor on each completed interview and then repeating the process incorporating the feedback received. The final qualitative module taught students how to analyse and systematically write up their data. With mentor and tutor support, researchers learned how to develop codes, theme data and create a data analysis framework, which they used to help them to prepare a report of their findings. All three modules of the training were accredited up to Level 3 by the Open College Network.

Evaluation took place in two parts, initially to assess what community researchers hoped to gain while later evaluation explored problems and achievements at the end of the programmes. First stage evaluations demonstrated that community researchers aspired to a range of learning from their involvement in the programmes, from individual outcomes such as improving their confidence levels, communication and life skills to organisational outcomes enabling critical influence based on increased knowledge of the communities they served and improved understanding of research skills and abilities to analyse and utilise the information strategically (Goodson and Phillimore, 2008a).

Programme-wide approach

The 'Accommodate' project (2004–7) was based on five multi-agency, urban partnerships at the heart of an initiative that set out to stimulate grassroots resolution to the problem of refugee housing, settlement and integration, at a time when large numbers of people were arriving in search of asylum in the UK. MRCOs were engaged by HACT to work alongside housing providers, local authority partners and others, for three years in areas where refugees were struggling to find permanent housing. The 'Accommodate' community researchers training programme was undertaken by the University of Birmingham as part of an interactive evaluation process to support the role that the MRCOs were playing within each partnership. The 'Making a Difference' community researchers training programme (2006–7) was funded by Joseph Rowntree Foundation and led by the University of Birmingham partnered with community leaders from Birmingham New Communities Network, formed out of 75 MRCOs. The purpose of this project was to build the capacity of MRCOs to use existing evidence about their communities, gather new evidence and communicate findings collaboratively to policy makers.

Both the 'Accommodate' and 'Making a Difference' community research training programmes took an emancipatory approach to empowering MRCOs that set the standard for the mentoring role within them. Phillimore and Goodson have long-established research interests into the emancipation of refugee community groups and champion their involvement in policy- and decision-making forums. They are familiar with the restrictions, lack of status and isolation that can result from MRCOs being excluded from local decision-making structures. They recognise the often overlooked potential within MRCOs for accessing and contributing to local knowledge that is fundamental to efficient and targeted service provision for new communities at neighbourhood level. There was a clear understanding that development of the community researchers as individuals was intended to have an impact on their MRCOs so that networking and capacity building together with greater representation and critical influence could build organisational capital and capacity to negotiate.

The community research training benefited the 'Accommodate' project as a whole, and increased skills and confidence were integrated into the roles that MRCOs took within the wider partnerships to influence new communities' access to housing services. Recognition of MRCO leaders' data collection skills and the position they held in their communities underpinned the radical aim of the 'Making a Difference' programme marking a move from 'policy research to action research as a developmental tool' (Phillimore et al, 2009: 12). Consequently, both community research training programmes were committed to working beyond perfunctory involvement that excluded active participation. They were set up in recognition of MRCOs' capacity to engage and with a mature understanding of the hazards involved in a token approach. This approach further legitimised and demonstrated the value that community researchers added to the overall outcomes of the programme. Figure 20.2 demonstrates some of the possible pitfalls that limit community participation. These include a failure to involve the communities beyond consultation and problem assessment, an exclusion from problem resolution, and overlooking the need for emancipator capacity building.

The wider 'Accommodate' project involving cross-sector partnerships was an innovative attempt on the part of HACT to equalise relationships between statutory and voluntary sectors and ensure early MRCOs' involvement and participatory control over research design and subsequent problem resolution. The involvement of community researchers within

Figure 20.2 Operational domains of empowerment[1]

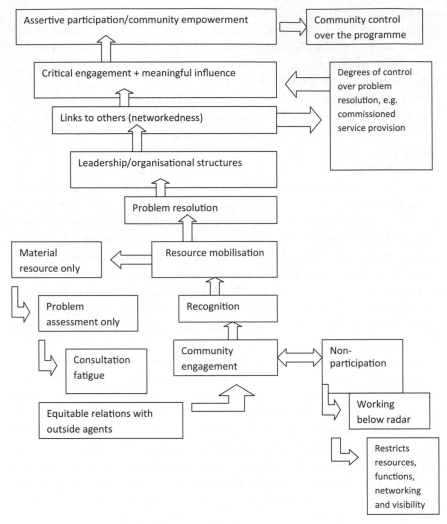

Note: An accumulative model evolved from study of the Accommodate Project 2004–07.

Source: Jones (2010: 317)

this programme meant that they were able to provide an evidence base for MRCOs' aspirations. In one partnership where a refugee forum was established, community researchers investigated what MRCOs were looking to get out of the forum; in another they explored how partnership working could be improved and in a third they examined the levels of awareness of support services for mental health provision for refugees to promote the link between mental health and housing needs (Goodson and Phillimore, 2008b). The approach to both these research projects can be theoretically located in the operational domain described as 'critical engagement' because the purpose of the community research was to enable MRCOs to exercise meaningful influence and legitimately challenge existing agendas. One MRCO leader felt that his organisation exercised equal influence in the partnership network with other service providers because they were able to 'disagree' in meetings demonstrating the force of critical engagement in the empowerment process. Research based on the 'Accommodate' project found that community leaders are vital in helping to change attitudes and have considerable symbolic status when leading the interface between newcomer and host communities. 'Part of changing ideological attitude is the ability to counter myths' (Jones, 2010: 347).

Empowerment via mentoring

One of the key factors contributing to the success of the community researchers' training programmes was the use of mentors. Our analysis showed that mentors offered support and encouraged engagement by building confidence and developing skills in such a way that community researchers eventually became critically engaged in their own learning. Community researchers were sustained and assisted to create their own solutions to problems within the research process so that they were active in achieving resolution and, over time, took control of interview procedures. Where problems were controversial or culturally sensitive, mentors and community researchers took a joint-approach to analysing and resolving them and community researchers were actively encouraged to draw on their own culturally specific knowledge and resources. Organisational capital was developed by encouraging community researchers to put their findings into wider socio-economic context enabling strategic links to be made between issues. Gradually, community researchers took ownership of the interview and analytic process to produce substantive reports that supported their community organisations' aspirations in taking a better informed and critical role in policy decision-making and service provision.

Sustaining engagement

Mentoring support was offered in a variety of forms, by email, phone and face-to-face meetings. Detailed feedback was provided on the community researchers' interview tapes, data analysis tables, self-reflection and draft reports. From the mentor feedback documents and the programme evaluation we evidenced how intently mentors took their role, adopting a longitudinal view of their relationships with the trainees, in some cases, beyond the duration of the programmes. Mentoring enabled community researchers to engage in a continual process of retrospective evaluation and self-assessment throughout. One example particularly illustrated the sense of journey from powerlessness to control that community researchers felt they had taken with the help of their mentors. In response to the question, 'What would you change' one trainee initially wrote: 'I do not think I have a choice to make so I don't think I would change anything.' Later, following discussions with his mentor this trainee was enabled to revise questions in the topic guide and modulate the pace of interviews.

One of the main purposes of engaging mentors is to sustain individual attendance and levels of participation (Phillimore et al, 2009). There were many instances of trainees growing into their role with the support from their mentor, with some surprised at the progress they were able to make after the first interview in taking control of interview logistics. We found evidence of an emancipatory approach towards confidence building throughout the interchanges documented between community researcher and mentor. A confidence-building feedback style was adopted by most mentors that included encouraging vocabulary to identify positively and acknowledge the trainees' existing capacity and accelerate emergent abilities.

Problem resolution

Mentoring began during the practical stage of the programmes and most community researchers expressed nervousness about their first 'live' interview, noted in self-reflection forms. Mentors suggested different tactics that could be used to overcome this, such as the importance of 'small talk' to relax the interviewee before the interview starts, but trainees were mostly encouraged to jointly consider solutions especially to more challenging interviews. One researcher was scheduled to interview someone for whom she had previously worked, creating some apprehension. She decided to prepare conversational questions beforehand to break the ice. In conjunction with the mentor she was able to turn her misgivings into something positive and maximise her pre-existing rapport with the interviewee to gain richer data. This was part of the learning process and an indication that the trainees were being encouraged to think about ways in which they could sharpen their interview techniques.

Organisational structures

The programmes were targeted at communities experiencing language and literacy challenges. Concerns surrounding different cultural perceptions and practices required mentors' awareness and input. There were instances where trainees identified difficulties in communicating issues which were either seen as taboo within their respective communities or were not recognised as being a 'problem'. For example, research into community access to mental health services revealed a barrier in some communities about perception of mental health issues. Sufferers were more likely to be the cause of family shame than be signposted towards professional help. Some mentors gave verbal feedback to supplement feedback and self-reflection notes to provide thoroughgoing discussion about dealing with different cultural attitudes in interview. This demonstrated a supportive and sensitive approach to joint resolution of these barriers. Strategies to deal with sensitive issues during interviewing were also tackled in detail during training sessions so that learning could be shared. Trainees and interviewees were matched where possible according to gender, cultural identity and language. Community researchers were encouraged to draw on their links and knowledge of their communities during the interview process. In this way cultural taboos were increasingly challenged and reviewed. Resolution included raising awareness through direct contact and workshops and the implementation of diversity policies by policy makers and service providers.

Links to others

Building organisational capital was central to the 'Accommodate' training programme as the community researchers related their research to strengthen the negotiating role of MRCOs collaborating with service providers across the project's five urban partnerships. Building organisational capital also featured in the 'Making a Difference' programme as training in lobbying and participation in policy-making were addressed as part of the community research course. Part of empowering organisational structures is to locate them in the wider socio-economic context. Community researchers displayed a keen awareness of the policy implications of their work and were encouraged to integrate these perspectives in the final report. Making links between social issues such as access to English language classes and mental well-being was an essential step in analysis. Associative thinking was encouraged in the self-reflection dialogue as part of the learning of techniques for presenting and utilising research findings to exert wider influence.

Critical engagement and assertive participation

Mobilising community research relies on a style of mentoring that actively encourages critical engagement and assertive participation. There were many examples of community researchers being proactive in terms of contributing their own knowledge and experiences into the way that the interviews were conducted. Mentors nurtured critical awareness in trainees and encouraged adaptation. From the outset community researchers developed the topic guide and several trainees made useful suggestions during practical application to increase its flexibility and customise some of the questions based on their understanding of their respondents. The emancipatory approach of mentors encouraged adjustments to interview materials to give community researchers more control in planning subsequent interviews. One trainee described this stage of learning development as being able to 'think on his feet' during the interview process. The practical idea of providing a separate information sheet listing existing services, so that interviewees could be signposted in order to address interim needs, was put forward by community researchers as one that would increase trust in the research programme as a whole.

At the end of each period of fieldwork community researchers were given the opportunity to prepare a report on the research findings. This element of the programme was assessed and those who chose this route could gain further accreditation. Final reports brought together all data from the interviews. Feedback from mentors at this stage was important in supporting community researchers to identify where resources could be mobilised to tackle some of the issues experienced by their communities. Certainly the potential for MRCOs to use research findings to strengthen their negotiating hands had been enhanced for future lobbying and advocacy opportunities (Figure 20.3).

Figure 20.3 Mentoring: a tool to link operational domains of community empowerment

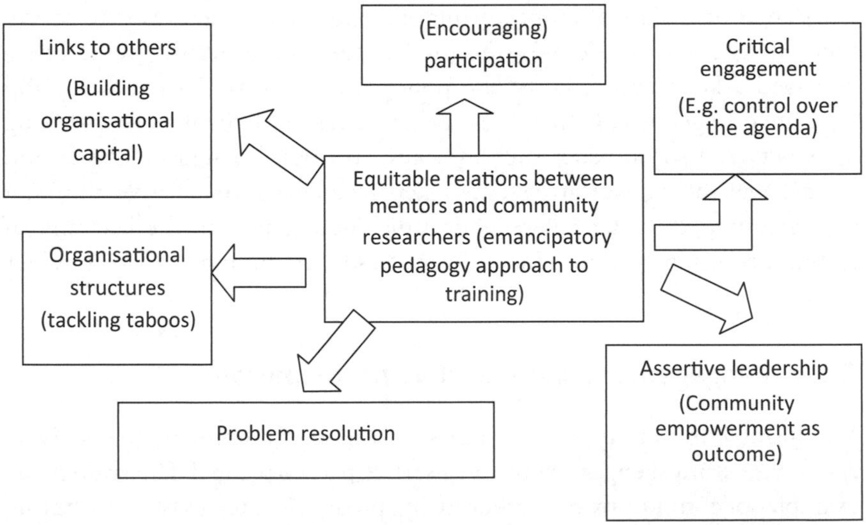

Source: Based on Laverack and Wallterstein (2001)

Key learning

It is apparent that running successful community research training programmes aimed at new communities are not without challenge. In analysing documentation recorded between trainee and mentor we have been able to identify where mentoring has succeeded in empowering researchers and, through them, their communities to participate more assertively in collaborative policy-making better to meet the needs of new community groups. Although we have demonstrated that there is scope to build on our mentoring approach, a different methodology, perhaps less equitable and more prescriptive, would have lost some of the insider perspectives that community researchers were able to contribute to the research process itself. In looking at empowerment outcomes along the timeline of training programmes, Laverack and Wallerstein's (2001) domain theory allows us to identify where future improvements and additional learning in the role of mentor could have been developed (Figure 20.1). We thought that mentors' awareness of some of the structural barriers the programmes dealt with might be enhanced, particularly where those issues related to a wider political context. For example where mental health and depression has significance for female refugee interviewees as individuals the dialogue could have been extended to discuss the underlying symptomatic circumstance. This is crucial in building organisational capital necessary for MRCOs to maximise the use of research findings.

It can be difficult for mentors to adopt a common framework when working independently and occasions offering shared learning in separate sessions for mentors may have supported this. Sharing the mentoring experience formalises the norms of encouraging critical voice and responding to community researchers taking control over the practical logistics of interviewing. Both training programmes set a standard for an emancipatory approach, and a greater partnership role in the wider programme may have heightened mentors' consciousness of this and empowered them to be more confident in embracing change and transformation. The mentors' dedication was evident from the fact that some retained relationships with participants after the programmes had been completed. This level of commitment could have been further employed to support MRCO lobbying and advocacy activities. These issues would not be unfamiliar to the community researchers as their views and experiences fed into the key learning. The mentoring programme placed a strong emphasis throughout on accountability and empowerment. Mentors sought to make the mentoring process transparent to demonstrate how it might contribute to each community researcher's personal development as well as achieve wider project aims. In fact the emphasis on an emancipatory approach enabled the community research programme to meet its wider outcomes.

Summary

Advantages

- Mentors dealt with cultural and institutional barriers in the course of the programmes
- Mentors were able to work in a bespoke one-to-one way to accommodate individual trainee community researchers
- Mentors built the continuum from individual to community empowerment

Limitations

- Mentors' awareness of the wider political context could have been enhanced
- Lone working did not offer the opportunity of sharing the mentoring experience and normalising the emancipatory approach
- Mentoring could have been further utilised post-programme to build organisational capital and critical influence in the political domain

Conclusion

Community research can be conducted with different approaches but for it to capitalise on the unsung talents of marginalised communities, an emancipatory approach is essential. This is more critical than ever for service providers who are targeting services to newcomer communities. Recognition of both MRCOs as a resource and community research as a social asset within that, is an all important step. The current climate of welfare reform and economic constraint puts a strain on all public services, yet the ingenuity and innovation within MRCOs is an untapped resource that community research can help to access. New legislation surrounding localism and community empowerment, for example, the demand for more patient involvement in healthcare services, puts mechanisms such as community research high on the consultation agenda and provides a conduit for better targeting and more appropriate service delivery.

These two programmes demonstrate that community research needs to be conducted strategically to be effective and operational domains theory serves to identify where the dynamics of empowerment really lie. For this reason mentoring is an essential element in the empowerment process and can develop individual capacity, at the same time as organisational structures, by building trust and helping to locate the social and cultural barriers to service access within its socio-economic and political contexts. Mentoring can act as an incentive to develop understanding, insider knowledge and involvement of marginalised groups into policy and decision-making where their contribution to the Big Society can be fully realised.

Discussion questions

1. Is mentoring more suited to some community researcher programmes than others?
2. How can a critical pedagogical tradition be popularised in community research programmes?
3. Can community research programmes be utilised in a climate of economic downturn?

Note

[1] HACT, originally known as the Housing Associations' Charitable Trust, has since been renamed the Housing Action Charity and works with housing providers and vulnerable communities.

References

Amas, N. and Price, J. (2008) *Strengthening the Voice of Refugee Community Organisations within London's Second-Tier Voluntary Sector: Barriers and Opportunities*, London: Information Centre about Asylum and Refugees, City University.

Anderson, J. (1996) Yes but is it Empowerment? Initiation, Implementation and Outcomes of Community Action, in Beth Humphries (1996) (ed) *Critical Perspectives on Empowerment*, Birmingham: Venture Press.

Balloch, S. and Taylor, M. (eds) (2001) *Partnership Working: Policy and practice*, Bristol: Policy Press.

Batliwala, S. (2007) Taking the Power out of Empowerment: An Experiential Account, *Development in Practice*, 17(4-5): 557–567.

Blunkett, D. (2003) *Active Citizens, Strong Communities*, London: Scarman Lecture, 11 December, Citizens' Convention.

Clough, R., Green, B., Hawkes, B., Raymond, G. and Bright, L. (2006) *Older People as Researchers: Evaluating a Participative Project*, York: Joseph Rowntree Foundation.

Flint, J. (2002) Social Housing Agencies and the Governance of Anti-Social Behaviour, *Housing Studies*, 17(4): 619–637.

Freire, P. (2006 [1970]) *Pedagogy of the Oppressed* (translated by Ramos, M. B.) New York: Continuum.

Goodson, L. and Phillimore, J. (2008a) Evaluation Report: Accredited Research Training for Community Consultants: Centre for Urban and Regional Studies.

Goodson, L. and Phillimore, J. (2008b) *Accommodate: Report of Accredited Community Research Training*, Birmingham: University of Birmingham.

Hutton, C. and Lukes, S. (2008) *Working with Refugee Community Organisations: A Guide for Local Infrastructure Organisations*, London: Charities Evaluation Services with the Refugee Council.

Jones, P.A. (2010) *Refugee Community Organisations Working in Partnership: The Quest for Recognition*, Unpublished PhD: Centre for Urban and Regional Studies, University of Birmingham.

Jones, P.A. and Mullins, D. (2009) *Refugee Community Organisations: Working in Partnership to Improve Access to Housing Services*, Race Equality Foundation Briefing Paper, Better Housing Briefing series.

Jones, V. (2007) Change from Experience: A Pedagogy for Community-based Change. Appendix 1 in S. Lukes (2009) *The Potential of Migrant and Refugee Community Organisations to Influence Policy*, York: JRF.

Kincheloe, J. (2008) *Critical Pedagogy* 2nd edn, New York: Peter Lang.

Laverack, G. (2001) An Identification and Interpretation of the Organizational Aspects of Community Empowerment, *Community Development Journal*, 38(2), 134–145.

Laverack, G. (2003) Building Capable Communities: Experiences in a Rural Fijian Context, *Health Promotion International*, 18(2): 99–106.

Laverack, G. (2006) Evaluating Community Capacity: Visual Representation and Interpretation, *Community Development Journal*, 41(3): 266–276.

Laverack, G. and Wallerstein, N. (2001) Measuring Community Empowerment: A Fresh Look at Organisational Domains, *Health Promotional International*, 16(2): 179–185.

Ledwith, M. (1997) *Participating in Transformation: Towards a Working Model of Community Empowerment*, Birmingham: Venture Press.

McLaren, P. (1997) *Revolutionary Multiculturalism: Pedagogies of Dissent for the New Millennium*, Boulder: West View.

MacLeavy, J. (2009) (Re) Analysing Community Empowerment: Rationalities and Technologies of Government in Bristol's New Deal for Communities, *Urban Studies*, 46(4): 849–875.

Mulhall, W. El-Jarad, N., Mackerras, C., Newbury, T., Li-Reeve, H., Skarzynska, K. and Wierzbicka, M. (2009) *Community Research Project: Researching the Learning Needs of People who Live in North Somerset and who have English as a Second or Additional Language*, North Somerset Council.

Phillimore, J. Goodson, L. Hennessy, D. and Ergun, E. (2009) *Empowering Birmingham's Migrant and Refugee Community Organisations*, York: Joseph Rowntree Foundation.

Pitchford, M. and Henderson, P. (2008) *Making Spaces for Community Development*, Bristol: Policy Press in conjunction with Community Development Foundation.

Steinberg, S. (2001) *Multi/Intercultural Conversations: A Reader*, New York: Peter Lang.

Taylor, M. (2003) *Public Policy in the Community*, England: Palgrave Macmillan.

Index

Note: b = box, f = figure, t = table